THE MAN WHO KILLED THE HAMSTERS

A Biography of Ian Moss

Stephen Dobson

Copyright © Stephen Dobson 2012
Book cover design by Pho Toman

Dedicated to my life partner Ian Ellard who has successfully fought cancer

The rights of Stephen Dobson to be identified as the author of this work have been asserted by him in accordance with the Copyright, Designs and Patents Act of 1988.

All rights reserved; no part of this publication may be reproduced, stored in a retrieval system, or transmitted in any form or by any means, electronic, mechanical, photocopying, recording or otherwise without the prior written consent of the publisher or a licence permitting copying in the UK issued by the Copyright Licensing Agency Ltd. www.cla.co.uk

This book is based on some true events, however, has been fictionalized and all persons appearing in this work are fictitious. Any resemblance to real people, living or dead is entirely coincidental.

Publishing partner: Paragon Publishing, Rothersthorpe

ISBN 978-1-78222-052-7

Book design, layout and production management by Into Print

www.intoprint.net

+44 (0)1604 832149

Printed and bound in UK and USA by Lightning Source

Contents

Introduction	4
Chapter One: In the Beginning	7
Chapter Two: Manchester Lesser Free Trade Hall Friday June 4 1976	32
Chapter Three: Summer is Heaven in '77	48
Chapter Four: Breaking Glass	74
Chapter Five: What twat spat?	97
Chapter Six: The weird and wonderful world of The Hamsters	127
Chapter Seven: Acklam Hall 1980	149
Chapter Eight: Ends, beginnings and middles 1981 – 1983	167
Chapter Nine: Big Moet is watching you, life after The Hamsters	202
Chapter Ten: Miseries, mithering and Moet 1987 – 1992	228
Chapter Eleven: The Stepbrothers 1992 – 2001	252
Chapter Twelve: Coming out of hibernation 2001 – 2005	268
Chapter Thirteen: Fuck the rest and do your best	291

Introduction

Hamsters Acklam Hall December 1980 – An Eye Witness Report

An attendance at a Fall gig was a pilgrimage to drink at the Holy Font of Mark E Smith's wisdom and claim this as uniquely our own. The Fall were the perfect band for those 'outsiders' who had come to celebrate their exclusion from 'Normality.'

Mark E Smith had not only been screeched at in the bar area but had been poked for good measure... He must have been in a good mood as he just went 'ha!' and left it at that.

Bands that supported The Fall were something to be envied as they must have been selected by no less than Mark E Smith himself. This meant they were to be given due reverence not normally reserved for ordinary support bands.

The name of this particular support band was 'The Hamsters', who had the same name as a Rhythm and Blues band from our native Southend on Sea, but knew that this couldn't possibly be the same band, unless Mark E Smith was playing a particularly nasty joke on us.

It is the sound of The Hamsters that crashes through the decades that have passed since that evening in 1980. The most memorable aspect was that the good looking drummer was playing his drum kit like a lead instrument which was very much at the forefront of the controlled cacophony. This particular drummer did not remain in the background and dominated much of the attention and song structures. Both the guitar and bass were tight in the way that only the self-taught can be. Clearly they were not restricted by conventionality and had learnt their own way to create songs that owed nothing to anyone. Loud slabs of raw, hypnotically repetitive, sound reverberated around the hall over and over again. There was speculation as to whether the bass player may have been wearing a kilt or a tartan skirt.

The lead vocalist was powerful in terms of build, voice and presence. He did not so much sing as roar above the loud and raucous soundtrack in a way that commanded attention. At the beginning of one song he began screaming like a demented parakeet and this elicited a mixture of amusement and bemusement from the still audience.

The sound was over far too soon and both the vocalist and drummer came into the audience to mingle after their set. On closer inspection the drummer was a curious shade of yellow and the vocalist looked like he would hit any little queer that came to congratulate him – so I didn't.

Many, many years later

Why on earth would you want to write a book on a bloke you saw supporting the Fall thirty years ago? **Colin Dobson (Authors Brother)**

Around the time I saw the Hamsters; I played one string bass in a post punk band from Southend, The Stripy Zebras and also joined another local band – The Get. Both bands make the Hamsters look famous in comparison but in 2008 these cassette recordings gained interest from Chuck Warner's American based Messthetics label which features predominantly obscure English bands from the late seventies to the early eighties.

There was a bit of a mix up and, as a form of compensation, I received a copy of Messthetics# 106, the Manchester Musicians Collective 1972-1982, the last track 'Clouds of Flies,' is by The Hamsters. Reading the accompanying CD sleeve it transpires that the singer is now involved with a band called 'Sicknurse' and there is a link to their myspace site. The Acklam Hall gig is mentioned as being one of great significance on the sleeve notes.

Early in January 2009 I sent a friend request to the myspace site with a message that I remembered the 1980 gig at The Acklam Hall. The request is accepted and an individual called 'Moet' sends a nice reply. Our messages to each other become longer and we exchange Instant Message addresses. It becomes clear that there is a shared common ground and Ian 'Moet' Moss has several great anecdotes to tell me. During one exchange I asked him if he had ever thought of writing an autobiography about himself as he was clearly a very important, if somewhat unsung, figure on the Manchester Music Scene. Ian had thought about it but that was all.

During another exchange it transpired that Ian had not been able to play the studio demos recorded by The Hamsters shortly after the Acklam Hall Gig. Quite simply, Ian did not own an old fashioned tape cassette player and I offered to transfer these tracks into MP3 format. I was extremely fortunate in that I now had very privileged access to listen to The 1980 Street Level sessions heard by very few people outside the band. As I listened to each track upon transferral I was delighted to find out that my positive memories of the Hamsters live sound had been correct and what was more exciting, the sound stood up very well to the test of time.

Ian and I met up in London, with Ian coming all the way down from Manchester by coach to return the same day. I found Ian to be a lovely, warm and friendly individual. He was extremely articulate and told me a whole wealth of really incredible stories that had happened in his life. Ian also leant me some more cassette tapes, amongst which featured his considerable output since he left The Hamsters right up to Ian's present group. The fantastic sound of 'Sicknurse' is not hobby or a rehash of previous glories but is a snarling beast in its own right pacing around and doesn't 'fit' into any conventional scene. This is the only common denominator it shares with The Hamsters.

After our meeting, I pondered on the possible fact that he would remain unheard of and that there would be no record of his fascinating life at all. During one IM exchange I asked him if I could record his life story in some format and he agreed.

My partner had been diagnosed with cancer in May 2009 and during his treatment Ian and I made a start as a form of 'distraction' for me. Ian is an intelligent individual who is more than capable of writing his autobiography. However, I had concern as to whether this would get done so my aim was to be a form of conduit for him and make sure his story was told. I had considered writing 'as Ian' but this felt false so this is a weird hybrid of Autobiography and Biography. The vast majority of this work is Ian's, I have merely chopped, changed and sprinkled 'fairy dust' to suggest some rhythm from Ian's free conscious flow of thought.

Ian was also able to arrange contributions from Craig Scanlon, Mick Hucknall and Peter Hook

I would like to thank Jon Smith for reading my efforts and for making invaluable suggestions. Steve Mardy for 'Recollections of "Moet, Denton and Destruction", Al (nee Lana) Pellay, Colin Swan, Jon Rowlinson, Simmo, Graham Ellis, Michael John Leigh, Stephen Doyle and Bob Williams along with all the other people who have contributed freely with their recollections of Moet.

In the Beginning: Birth and rebirth

Starman 06th July 1972

David Bowie's debut performance on Top Of the Pops was historical. He appeared in full Ziggy Stardust makeup in front of teenage television viewers, who like Ian, also had their parents present, much to everyone's collective embarrassment. His androgynous imagery, flagrant flouting and pouting of every convention was horrifying and yet fascinating. Male musicians simply didn't act like 'that' in those days. David Bowie made sure everyone took notice that fateful evening.

Ian was still buzzing the next morning There was just something so compelling about these strange looking, yet fascinating musicians – the like of which he had never seen before. The most thrilling element of David Bowie's performance was when he draped his arm around the guitarist (Mick Ronson) and had drawn him closer. This gesture of affection could not only be construed not only as an act of overt homosexuality but also that of defiance; a 'slap right across the face for narrow minded bigotry'.

The English Teacher, Mrs Thomason, was a young lady in her early twenties and had obviously seen the previous night's show and wanted to know what her young charges had made out of the outrageous performance;

"Did anyone see that David Bowie on the telly last night?"

This non-committal question elicited a chorus of catcalls and sheer derision.

"Quieten down now boys! Come on, now that's better. How about a vote on David Bowie? Now let's have a show of hands for all those who are against David Bowie!"

Twenty eight hands shot up.

"Now who is for David Bowie?

Only two hands went up, an overwhelming defeat for David Bowie.

One set of hands belonged to Christopher Hathaway whom Ian describes as 'a nice lad from a vaguely hippy family' whose motives for voting for David Bowie were influenced by a laid back attitude of acceptance rather than actually liking him. The second lad was Ian, who although developing in a heterosexual direction, clearly identified with Bowie's stance against convention.

"Now boys, what exactly didn't you like about David Bowie?"

"He's a great big 'puff'! Miss!"

"His music's rubbish!"

"Moss, what did you like about the performance then?"

Enquired Mrs Thomason, genuinely interested.

"It made me feel alive Miss and it excited me"
Replied Ian enthusiastically and enthused
"This lot can't appreciate originality when they see it"

His classmates began to giggle, this little tirade had transformed Ian into the official 'School Weirdo', this would be his first experience of the one against the many.

Thirsting for the Magic in the Grooves

Music has always been a life-force in Ian; right from his beginnings in Manchester, he has very early memories to the soundtrack of his story.

Ian Keith Moss (1957) and his brother Neil Edwin Moss (1960) were bought up in what Ian describes as a 'quite austere and slightly old fashioned puritanical way' by his parents, whom it was noticed were both quite a bit older than that of their school friends. Both boys were loved but did not have much in the way of what their peers would have taken for granted such as a television, telephone, car and a holiday abroad. However it was the lack of a record player that Ian and Neil felt most keenly as both brothers loved music from a very early age. The only opportunity that Ian and Neil got to hear any records was on visits to family friends or relatives;

"Aw Mum, do we have to go?"
"Yes, do as you're told, Ian!"

Sometimes a record would be put on and the ordeal was immediately made more bearable. Some of his earliest musical memories come from this period and he can remember 'The Carnival Is Over' by The Seekers and was delighted by The Beatles 'Help' and was captivated with the rather more dark and sinister music by The Rolling Stones. Ian wanted to hear more and more but....

"Aw, Mum! Do we have to go already?"
"Yes, you both had a good time, but we'll be back again"

Both parents were aware of how much their sons loved music and must have scrimped, saved and gone without to proudly present a red mono dansette in 1970. The brothers were not able to immediately buy records so kind relatives, like Aunty Jean, leant copies of Harry Secombe, Tom Jones and Cilla Black.

Ian began to start saving for records, old and new, as he 'thirsted for the magic contained in the grooves'. Amongst the early records he bought were 'Perfidia' by The Ventures, 'Telstar' by The Tornadoes (oddly enough also a favourite of Margaret Thatcher on her Desert Island Discs), 'My Sweet Lord' by George Harrison, 'Another Day' by Paul McCartney, 'Return of Django' by The Upsetter and 'Liquidator' by Harry JS Allstars. Ian also added the music of Nina Simone and also The Four Tops.

As Ian's record collection expanded the more acutely aware he became of his taste, he realised he didn't like just anything and would go for what he knew, or believed, he would enjoy. Ian had joined a youth club and found that he disagreed with his peers on their views on certain artists or music styles. In 1972 Ian's friends fell into two musical camps.

The first went for chart pop, which Ian felt was mostly garbage, but they were somewhat redeemed by the fact they also appreciated Motown, soul and reggae.

The other group, Ian considered, were 'Heavies' and liked Deep Purple, Led Zeppelin and more progressive rock bands like Yes and Pink Floyd.

Ian felt he didn't fit into either camp but had a listen to these different musical styles and none really took. He was more inclined to go back in time to find the artists he really admired and found a love for Bob Dylan, The Troggs, The Kinks and also developed a taste for Reggae music. However, for Ian, the most important band he discovered on his time travels were The Small Faces, a band he loves to this very day.

Steve Mardy, a lifelong friend of Ian's, recalls;

In 1970/71, he was the only kid in the class who went home for lunch, apart from myself, but found time to bring back a record that he'd bought during that break time which within weeks would attain the upper reaches of the music charts. I distinctly remember a Dave & Ansell Collins single he had once bought "who I asked?' but the record itself was one of those strange, and argued against outside efforts which introduced a reggae beat to day time radio.. and won the argument as a matter of fact

Ian wanted to experience the sound of live music and went along, all alone in the summer of 1970, to see Desmond Decker and The Aces at Hyde Town Hall. This was a massive disappointment as this announcement came over the tannoy system;

"We are sorry to announce that "Desmond Decker will not be performing tonight. But 'White Plains' are here to perform their recent smash hit single 'Julie, Julie, Julie, Do You Love Me' instead!"

This was a crushing blow to Ian as it had taken a lot of guts to come to this gig as a nervous thirteen year old. Not only had Desmond Decker failed to show but to add insult to injury this rubbish group had taken his place. He wandered home absolutely deflated after this non experience.

But salvation was soon to come in the form of Slade. Admittedly somewhat of a pop band but very briefly they were Ian's band of choice. Ian went along to see them, this time with his school friends Graham and Andy, with no less than Status Quo supporting. Ian can still remember the sheer excitement of this gig and the icing on the cake was provided by three girls from Salford who allowed them to kiss'n'grope during Slade's cover of 'Darling be home soon'.

Ian really felt that Slade was his band and didn't really want to share them as their success increased. Also he found that he didn't like their new material, vastly preferring the older songs. He felt as if his Slade had been taken away from him but this didn't matter too much as he had discovered that The Small Faces had a new singer and guitarist and had morphed into The Faces. This was the band with the 'couldn't give a shit 'attitude that Ian really identified with as he swaggered around town with ruffled hair. Ian had his band back again

Shock!! Ian mentions Slade. Fuck!!! I think, then it's Rod Stewart, double fuck!! It was indeed these days when I appreciated 'good pop' and have Ian's bombshells to thank that I can still tell good from bad pop **Colin Swann**

Around this time Ian began to drink and went to see The Faces play live at various venues. They were a terrific live band and Ian marvelled at their audacity as they played gigs half cut, out of tune and were quite simply, as Ian recounts 'rip roaring fun'.

However, The Faces were a form of John the Baptist for He who was to come into Ian's life in a way that was to affect the teenage dreamers of the 'seventies in a way no one could ever have predicted.

Ziggy Stardust and the Spiders from Mars

Amongst the first flush of records that Ian purchased was a copy of 'Space Oddity' by the 'one hit wonder' David Bowie and had puzzled over Bowies' strange lyrics to Peter Noone's cover of 'Oh, You Pretty Things'. Tony Blackburn's record of the week called 'Changes (1972)' had peaked his interest and momentum grew when he purchased the follow up single 'Starman' and learnt that the object of his curiosity was to appear on Top Of The Pops one week and the rest became history.

'The Hardrock' on Greatstone Road, Stretford was a new purpose built rock venue which opened that same year. This futuristic venue was able to accommodate different size audiences by means of a motorised sliding partition wall, and seating which emerged from the floor. This meant that a concert space that could hold as much as two thousand people could be transformed, within minutes, to a small intimate club. Barely a few weeks after watching David Bowie's 'Starman', Ian found himself in the audience eagerly awaiting the appearance of Ziggy Stardust and the Spiders from Mars. Accompanying Ian was his school friend Robert Middlehurst and his father Ron who had very kindly paid for the tickets. Also present in Ian's party were Steven Middlehurst (Roberts elder brother) and his friend Bob, both of whom were to play a very important part later in Ian's life.

Looking out at the audience in this impressively eerie lit and atmospheric hall, Ian remembers musing that even although 'Starman' and the album 'The

Rise and Fall of ZIggy Stardust' were both riding high in the charts the venue was not exactly filled to capacity.

In life there are few events that live up to expectation and Ian's very first Bowie concert was one of those rare experiences that actually surpassed high anticipation. In short it was 'fantastic'. Ian was very much taken with the visual theatricality of the show and yet recalls a certain vulnerability and gentleness which would be worn away over the next eighteen months of constant and pressured touring. Indeed, Ian remembers that Bowie came over as slightly awkward with his stage chatter in between songs which suggests a level of nerves owing to lack of experience in such large venues. Somehow this shyness added to the cosiness of the acoustic numbers such as 'Space Oddity' which involved audience joining in the solo refrain;

'der, der, der, der ,der CLAP, CLAP".

Ian was also lucky enough to be able to attend another show, later on during the tour, a week before the follow up single; 'John, I'm only Dancing' was released. His musical taste was obviously influencing his younger brother and Neil really proved his worth as he was able to buy Bowie's entire back catalogue with his pocket money. Both the Moss brothers listened hour after hour to albums such as 'Hunky Dory', 'The Man Who Sold The World' and although agreed upon few things, both shared a common bond in that this sound was not only sparkling it was the sound of NOW.

Dedicated Follow of Fashion – The Kinks

Ian sought to make his own individual visual statement. Before the blandness of the ubiquitous Arndale Centre there used to be a shopping area called 'New Brown Street', off Market Street, Manchester. He loved rummaging around the old boutiques when he had some spare cash and would create his very own anti-fashion statement. He was nothing if not memorable, as one of his friends, Brett recounts:

(that) He was looking the very epitome of fashion in the early seventies with his long feather cut hairdo, three-quarter length denim overcoat and his flared jeans flapping around his platform soles. Arm in arm with his girlfriend (later to be wife) he felt good when all of a sudden this 13, maybe 14 year old boy appeared in front of the happy couple. The boy had short hair dyed red, T Shirt, and a pair of bright yellow checked 'Rupert the Bear' trousers over the top of silver sprayed Dr Martin Boots. This youth caught Brett looking at him and responded with a scowl and spat in front of him

'Fucking Hippy!'

This was Brett's very first encounter with Master Moss and this impression stayed with him as he recounted this incident a good twenty five years later.

Ian would mix and match with his 'Rupert' trousers, sometimes a pair of cherry red court shoes and a jacket very similar to that of the television character 'Budgie' (played by the late, lovely Adam Faith). His appearance attracted a mixture of aggravation and admiration; he was once beaten up by four blokes for daring to wear such outrageous clobber, only to be asked around a year later where he brought his gear from by the very same assailants.

LOLA the Kinks

A troubled individual called Peter Moss (no relative thank God) joined Ian's class. Ian just sensed there was something really unpleasant about him as he had heard that Peter had 'done time' at an approved school. You know when you just don't 'take' to someone? He was that someone, or rather 'something' that was just odious. Peter kept trying to be Ian's mate and Ian didn't want to know. But he had a form of what Ian now terms 'Street Psychology'; he knew how to throw down a challenge that Ian would rise to. One day when they were in Maths, Peter leant over and asked Ian

"Do you fancy a drink in Manchester tonight?"

"What, with you?"

He was persistent and he knew full well that Ian was able to go into a bar and get served despite being four years below the legal age. Ian achieved this with a lot of front and generally got away with it. Ian was also aware that a couple of his mates maybe over hearing this conversation in the class room

Peter then decided to issue a challenge.

"You scared then?"

This cheek really got Ian's goat and he replied;

"Of course not, I just don't have that much money'

The reply was intriguing and bold;

"That doesn't matter, we don't need much, and our drinks will be bought for us"

Now this was an offer Ian couldn't really refuse. He wanted to taste the forbidden fruits of Manchester night life and didn't want to 'lose face' by chickening out.

So Ian fell right into Peter's plans and agreed to meet up later. Ian got his glad rags on and told both parents a little white lie about going to a disco at Hyde Town Hall. And this is how Ian found himself in The Long Bar in Oxford Street with a creep he really didn't like.

Now Ian may have been a bit naïve but was aware of what sort of bar Peter had persuaded him to come in to; it was no more, or less, than a hangout for rent boys and their punters. This bar was situated between a slot machine arcade and the public lavatories, which were situated outside on the street. The amusement arcade was used for procurement and the underground toilets were used for 'Business'. Some of the boys bore the scars of less than satisfactory transactions with punters. This was like a whole different world to Ian and he was fascinated by what he experienced, although did not realise that he was really being groomed and was there by means of an 'introduction' courtesy of Peter.

Peter suggested that they both decided to move on to a notorious 'Queer' bar known as 'The Union'. Ian was the centre of attraction and really enjoyed it. Sure, as Peter had promised, all the Lager and Lime Ian could knock back was bought for him by a stream of kind older men who only wanted to chat. Ian remembered thinking 'This is very exotic' as he had previously only experienced mild and bitter. To be honest Ian wasn't fazed by the surroundings or clientele but it was getting late and he wanted to go home.

"Peter, I'm off now, it's getting late and I want to go home."

"What for? Don't be such a worrier? All the drink is being paid for?"

Hmm….. Ian couldn't really claim that he had no money, which would have been a legitimate 'face saving excuse'.

Peter could sense Ian was wavering and it was time for Peter to issue another challenge, to keep Ian with him. He tapped the shoulder of a middle aged guy nearby.

"Alan meet Ian, Ian meet Alan. How about taking us to Queens then Alan?"

"Ian, nice to meet you mate! Good idea Peter! Yes, how about it then Ian?"

Again, this wasn't an offer he could refuse. Ian was going to be taken to a nightclub! If Peter had asked this in the classroom this would have scared him and to be honest Ian still felt a mixture of fear and excitement but Peter knew Ian wouldn't turn this down and his little plan was working.

The club was just around the corner, a bell was rung and the door opened, they were given a cursory once over, Alan obviously knew the doorman and everyone was in!

Once inside the club Ian was introduced to several older men and basked in yet more attention and flattery. Someone brought him a whisky sour (yet another alcoholic first) and Ian was simply not aware that he was being 'watched'. The hit song by Johnny Nash, 'I can see clearly now' came over the speakers and as Ian absolutely loved this number he got up to strut his stuff on the dance floor. A very attractive older lady came to join Ian. It was a dream comes true as she was clearly very attracted to Ian and they both enjoyed a good long snog. It took Ian around five years to realise; this sexy older lady had been either a transvestite or transsexual.

But it had just turned 2am and now Ian really, really wanted to get back home and hadn't got the bus fare.

"Peter, can you lend me 50p, I need to go home now."

"We are staying at Alan's."

"I cccan't!!"

"Course you can. Go on!"

"No I can't! Have you got 50p so that I can get the late bus?"

"No I haven't. Ask Alan if you're going."

Ian nervously decided to approach Alan, something wasn't right, Ian knew it now.

"Alan, please can you give me 50p so I can get home?"

By means of a reply he leant forward and suggestively leered;

"What do I get in return then, Ian?"

Alan decided to emphasise this point by cupping Ian's testicals through his trousers as he drew Ian towards him. To add to this disgusting liberty, some of the clientele clearly took this as some form of signal and began to surround and grope him. If Ian had displayed the fear that was mounting within him, he knew he would have been lost. Ian kept his cool and calmly repeated;

"Alan, please give me the bus fare home, my parents will be worried about me'

"Ooo! Go on then! But on one condition!

Alan took his hands away and dug out 50p. He held it in front of Ian in a clenched fist and teased;

"Promise to come back now Ian?"

"I promise Alan."

Ian lied and got the bus fare home.

As Ian waited for the bus, he realised that he had better come up with a convincing story to his parents should he be caught coming back so late at night. Ian had just been through a very distressing experience and whilst he could understand where the men had been coming from, he despised them for taking advantage of his vulnerability.

'I don't feel dirty, I don't feel ashamed, and I'd done nothing wrong..... And I'm not for sale."

Even Jesus Loved the Stooges – Sicknurse

David Bowie cited Iggy Pop as his favourite artist in Ian's musical bible - The NME It just so happened that Cream (imported from the USA) had a feature on Iggy Pop and he learned more about this 'Man/God/Holy Fool' who fronted a band called 'The Stooges'. He read about a unique sound and that live shows were wild anarchic affairs with often unpredictable displays of violence which usually resulted in bloodshed. This article was accompanied by a rather strange photo of Iggy Pop wearing both a cheesy grin and floppy hat. This image of a rather tame, impish looking man was somewhat at odds with the description of live mayhem at his shows in America. Ian was intrigued by Iggy Pop, but his records were virtually unavailable in Britain.

Another Bowie recommendation was Lou Reed, but Ian was somewhat under whelmed upon listening to the self-titled debut album, which he regarded as a crushing disappointment. However, young Neil had managed to get hold of a copy of 'The Velvet Underground and Nico'. This was much more like it and Ian's conversion was complete with 'White Light, White Heat' It seemed The Velvet Underground, in the early Seventies, were virtually unheard of in Britain, yet, unbeknown to Ian there were several other young people who were being influenced by their strange, unconventional sound.

At the same time this blank generation was also tuning in to John Peel's late night show featuring such diverse acts as the eccentric poet 'Ivor Cutler', the experimental 'Van Der Graff Generator' fronted by fellow Mancunian Peter Hamil, Pearls before Swine and David Ackles.

The music programme The Old Grey Whistle Test had a dire preponderance for bearded American Bands. The host 'Whisperin'' Bob Harris was an advocate for real, traditional musicians but despite (maybe to spite?) him some very strange bands managed to appear. For example, Ian saw an early incarnation of 'Sparks' with the keyboard player, Ron Mael, looking more Charlie Chaplin, rather than Adolf Hitler.

Yet the band that was the most influential and watched by Ian and contemporaries such as Steven Jones, Paul Cook and Morrissey was the now, infamous performance by The New York Dolls from America. Ian recalls them tottering around the studio in their platform boots and crashing into each other wearing a mix and match of ladies clothing. The fact that they were slagged off by Bob Harris on air, 'Mock Rock', made them even more appealing to Ian. There was an 'us' of the Moss Brothers and 'them' who was anyone else.

Ian became aware of the joys of 'Kraut Rock' through the discovery of a 49 pence album 'The Faust Tapes'. Besides being an absolute bargain it was totally unlike anything Ian had ever heard before. He regarded the sound as not only daring but genius and fun. It was this tape that Ian used as a form of benchmark in his relationship with his friends as all of them, without exception, really hated it. Through Faust Ian was able to access other different forms of music such as Can, The Mothers of Invention, Captain Beefheart, The Soft Machine which had included Kevin Ayres and Robert Wyatt whose solo albums Ian came to love.

David Bowie came to be very busy in the studio and produced two very important records. The first album was 'Transformer' (1972) by Lou Reed, which was vastly superior to the disappointing debut. The second, Raw Power (1973) by The Stooges meant that Ian was finally able to listen to the hypnotic ferocity of an altogether different form of 'Pop'. Besides introducing these two, relatively obscure acts to the British market, Bowie was also able to revive the career of one of his own favourite British bands called Mott the Hoople, who were on the verge of splitting up. Bowie not only gave them 'All the Young Dudes' (1972) but produced it and provided backing vocals. This was a guaranteed success and the bands tenacity managed to hold Ian's attention long after their resuscitation from David Bowie.

'He's football crazy, he's football mad.'

While playing football one day Steve and Robert told me a friend from their school was joining us in a game, I was told he was a really good player (wrong he was a crazy cunt) Ian Moss turned up with other oiks from the south side of Haughton Green. This turned out to be a regular thing and I got to know Ian and his mates really well - God bless them all. **Colin Swan**

Ian's other major passion at school was football. He was a confident player and knew how to work a football pitch. During the dark grey conformity of Comprehensive School of the early seventies Ian certainly cut a dashing figure on the field with his dyed red hair and shaved eyebrows. Ironically Ian was usually in a minority of one with his controversial views and musical tastes but football offered a form of inclusion. Ian was certainly better than many of his contemporaries but was never chosen for the school football team because of personality clashes with the games masters. This didn't particularly bother Ian as he chose to play for a local church team instead. This team was good, in fact they became very good as they easily won games and Ian was the key figure in this success as he scored goal after goal and worked well as both leader and team player.

Ian's prowess on the field was acknowledged by his school mates who started to question why Moss was not playing for the school team. Ian found himself in the rather enjoyable position of being a championed underdog and he finally played for the school team. He proved his worth and was chosen again, but this was to be somewhat of a dilemma. The church team were talent spotted by Stockport County FC and were training with this football league team.

Ian decided to approach the teacher in charge, Nick Longos to explain this new dilemma;

"Sir, I don't want to let my local team down by playing for the school that is if I'm picked again"

"Your first priority is to represent the school, Moss"

Informed Nick Longos but added

"How about you play for the School when you are really needed?

Secretly, Ian thought it wasn't perfect as what would happen when both teams required him, but agreed

"Yes, Sir. Thank You Sir."

Unfortunately, the School Headmaster somehow got to learn about this 'special deal' and Ian was called up on stage before the whole school. Ironically, a couple of years back (at the end of the first year) Ian was brought on stage and showered with praise. However this experience would prove to be the exact opposite;

"You, young man, are a DISGRACE to this school! You should be putting this school first instead of yourself!"

Shouted the headmaster, who went quite purple with fury and ordered

"Go to my office, I'll deal with you later!"

After waiting outside the office, the Head returned when assembly finished.

"Moss get inside"

Ordered the Headmaster as he breezed past Ian and sat down at his desk and informed Ian, in a calm but measured tone;

"Moss, You had better remain exclusive to the school team otherwise I will use my power with the County Football Association to ensure that you would be effectively excluded for life"

This demand instilled in Ian a huge sense of injustice and yet he knew that he had to comply with the Headmaster's command;

"Alright, Sir"

However, a chance came for Ian to get something tangible from this uneasy 'truce' with the Headmaster and the ideal opportunity manifested itself with the formation of a school magazine. Ian eagerly seized his chance by volunteering along with the laid back Chris Hathaway. Maybe Chris was just a little too laid back as Ian soon became the lead editor and called the magazine 'Never a Dull Moment' after the current Rod Stewart LP. Ian filled this with articles on his favourite music and if a teacher found himself out of favour, woe betide them, as they were often subjected to mockery by form of caricatures in this paper. Ian was able to use the magazine as a valid excuse to get out of lessons as a form of;

'School Magazine Business, Sir'

Soon his teachers came to resent his power base and the magazine was pulled after only three issues.

The Staff Versus Boys Football Match had been an annual feature since 1957 and the Staff had won every single match. Ian was determined that 1973 was going to be different and as a result the score was 3 – 1 to the boys team with Ian scoring two of the goals not without a great deal of goading the Staff Team. The crowning glory was that not only was the Headmaster's pride hurt, but owing to the hard tackling technique from Ian, literally ended up 'on his arse' on the playing fields. Of course no pupil dared to laugh at this hilarious sight – out loud.

The Teachers were to have their revenge a couple of weeks later during a Staff Versus Boys Rugby Team match. Being older, the teachers were bigger and stronger than their boy opponents and they were to use this advantage in a particularly evil way that was to affect Ian for the rest of his life.

During a scrum Ian felt a teachers hand reach and grab his scrotum and twisted violently, it was agony. Ian's testicle swelled and he was in absolute agony after this evil assault. He was sick and feverish and as a result of the attack lost a gonad. This attack resulted in constant pain in which he would often double up owing to the sheer agony of the abdominal and stomach pains. Ian felt like a freak with only one testical and his exuberant self-confidence drained from him. He no longer wanted to do the things he had once enjoyed and a lethargic depression meant that he over ate and drank too much alcohol. As a result Ian gained a lot of weight which resulted in him hating himself even more. All Ian had left was music, and even that was becoming sterile. Ian needed something new.

"A HANDBAG?" Lady Bracknell

Ian began his very first job on his Sixteenth Birthday (25 June 1973) at Seibel Brothers in Durkenfield. He was employed as a trainee handbag designer and initially believed that he would have some kind of creative outlet. He was wrong but at least he had a wage which gave him more money to spend on records, books and gigs, but most importantly this allowed him to follow Manchester United wherever they played.

About a week after Ian had started employment he happened to be flicking through the collection of his local record store in Ashton under Lyne in his dinner hour. After looking at some possible purchases he continued leafing through the second hand vinyl until he literally stopped in his tracks and could not believe what he suddenly saw! Ian had long fantasised about owning a copy of the second Stooges album 'Funhouse' which was virtually impossible to obtain in the UK. He had stumbled upon his holy grail in the 50p bargain box. Ian at first did not believe what he saw, but sure enough this was the real McCoy, the only thing was that Ian did not have all the necessary funds to secure this object of frenzied lust. Rushing to the counter, he begged the amused record shop owner;

"Please, please could you put this behind the counter and I promise that I'll be back to pay for this as soon as possible, please!"

Desperation made Ian bold. Although he didn't really know any other fellow worker at the factory and was shy and self-conscious Ian recognised a lady from his work place, window shopping in the high street, and took the plunge and begged;

"Hi, I'm Ian, I work at your factory but I've only just started so you don't know me yet, but please, please can you lend me twenty pence and I promise to pay you back tomorrow at work?!!

He must have had an honest face as the lady smiled and gave him the required balance. Ian ran back to the record shop to make sure he managed to get 'Funhouse' as soon as possible. The afternoon dragged slowly as he couldn't wait to go home and finally hear this masterpiece at last.

The rest of the family had settled down to television when Ian had finally arrived home after the longest bus journey in his life.

"Please, please can I put this record on now?"

"After we have watched the evening news, yes."

replied his mother, settling down to watch the early edition.

"AW! Mum! I want to listen now and so does Neil"

pleaded Ian, pointing to his exited younger brother who was pouring over the record cover

"Oh! Alright then, we'll never get any peace so go on!"

Conceded his long suffering mother.

Ian was able to put needle to vinyl and…….what a crushing disappointment! The sound that emitted from the speaker was too dense and the lyrics were totally indecipherable. He desperately tried to like what he heard but it was no use, true it was like nothing heard before, but he just didn't like it.

"It's not music, its noise."

Muttered Eddie, opening his newspaper. Secretly, Ian thought he had a point but no way was he going to agree with his father on this one

"Oh! No! Dad! It's really good!"

Ian insisted

"I really don't know Ian, first David Bowie…."

Tutted his mother who decided to beat a hasty retreat to the kitchen to get tea ready

"And now this rubbish!"

Ian, being Ian, didn't give up after merely one listen. He persevered and played this record obsessively and upon each play the savage bestiality of the sound began to reveal its magic to him and after half a dozen plays he finally 'got it'; it was both primitive and sophisticated at the same time. 'Funhouse', in Ian's opinion, is the best 'Rock' album every recorded and still regards this as his inspiration and friend. In short, Ian loves 'Funhouse'.

Slowly the early Seventies merged into the mid Seventies. Ian got nothing in the way of job satisfaction but it gave him money for the things he really needed in life like music, football and booze. To the casual observer, or indeed a close friend, Ian appeared to be perfectly happy with life. But the cheerful exterior hid a very unhappy young chappy….

It was a cold and wet morning and the lads from Stockport County FC had turned up to play an important game. But the club door was locked and both sides were shaking themselves and stamping their feet to keep warm. The coach went to make a phone call to see what had happened upon returning.

"Sorry, lads there's been a mix up"

"What happened?"

"Cock up over the booking"

"You're the one who's responsible"

"Just one of those things, it happens."

The coach could sense that his charges were getting restless and decided to beat a hasty retreat to his car.

"Hey! Stop!"

Shouted Ian, who was furious.

The coach's response was to switch his engine on and attempt to make a quick getaway but this was just too much for Ian who leapt on to the bonnet and daubed the windscreen with mud. Well, he had it coming to him for some time , this coach liked nothing better to do than fondle his young charges at the drop of a pair of shorts and that was only for an ankle injury…..Ian didn't play for the team ever again.

Further weight gained as Ian stopped playing football altogether and the heavier he weighed the more he despised himself. He didn't confide in anyone preferring to hide his low self-esteem from the world as he became, for all intents and purposes, a drunk and cheery clown which did not go down particularly well with the opposite sex with whom Ian felt awkward and was very low.

In order to escape the constant worry that hung around him Ian went to lots and lots of gigs, it didn't matter if they were good, bad or indifferent it was a night out for boozing. In addition to a staple diet of Bowie and the Faces , amongst the better bands Ian saw were The Rolling Stones (at which he managed to secure front row seats at The Kings Hall inside The Bell Vue showground site) Ian Hunter and Mick Ronson with the support act of Jet, Sparks, Alex Harvey and the Sensational Alex Harvey Band, Cockney Rebel, Ayres, Cale, Nico (sulky German Chanteuse who had sung with The Velvet Underground) and Eno (who was busy perusing a solo career after just leaving Roxy Music) all on the same bill. Lou Reed remains the most memorable artist that Ian had the fortune to experience around this time. Lou Reed just kept collapsing, very likely owing to the vast amount of drugs he had consumed, at one gig and had to eventually be physically supported by a roadie just to keep him standing. Ian also saw a later gig, with the 'Rock and Roll Animal' band ended in a riot which resulted in Lou Reed not returning to Manchester for ten years.

There were two bands that Ian really, really wanted to experience live. The first, 'Iggy Pop and The Stooges' were mooted to appear at the local Biker and Hippy hangout –The Stone Ground according to the music press. Ian waited and waited but nothing ever transpired.

The second, The New York Dolls, were to appear as support to the Faces (surely a dream line up) at the Buxton Music Festival. He must have looked like the sort of person who would go to see this bunch of trashy transvestites as a fellow train passenger took great delight in informing him that the drummer, Billy Dolls, had died in London earlier that week.

Ian recalls the crap bands that he endured during this period also with horror and amazement that he sat through such acts as Humble Pie and Procal Harem. The much loved and vaunted band ELP made Ian:

'Physically sick, it is possibly the worst three hours, yes, three fucking hours I have ever spent."

Led Zeppelin faired a bit better as Ian fell asleep during their performance. Selective memory loss has managed to eradicate the other overblown performances that Ian had the misfortune to attend. It was becoming increasingly obvious to Ian that music was not just becoming worse in the mid-seventies it was becoming painfully bad. Even the good bands that Ian had seen live were releasing commercial material instead of cutting edge originality. For example, Ian believes that the Rolling Stones had 'lost it' and were a former shadow of the great band they had been. The Who had become too verbose and bombastic even for Ian. The Kinks had turned into parodies of themselves and were in turn dreary and then slapstick. There was a lot of dreadful Pop Music such as the ersatz 'fifties 'Rawk and Roll' acts such as 'Mud', ''Showwaddywaddy' and 'Alvin Stardust'. The ultimate in bad glam rock was 'Gary Glitter' who too plundered the sound of classic Rock and Roll into a diluted format. The worst offenders, Ian believes, originate from America such as The Eagles, Harry Chapin, James Taylor and Joe Walsh who were immensely popular with the general record buying pubic in Britain around that time. Worse, the public, were acting and dressing if they were part of the cosy Californian life style they chose to emulate. Needless to say Ian did not wear brushed faded denim and grow long hair with matching moustache calling everyone 'Man'.

A New Band 1973/74

.....the next is we are playing snooker in Bunny's bedroom drinking homebrew and listening to Deep Purple, Ian has Velvet underground, and Bowie stuff. He curses Purple and wins the battle of the bedroom bands by contorting his face while singing vicious (cool or fucking what?) this became of my perception of Ian, he likes

what he likes and what he doesn't he slates and WILL try to sway opinion to agree, not too sure he is like that now he has mellowed with age. **Colin Swan**

In fact Ian felt so disillusioned with the state of music he decided to do something about it and formed a bedroom band with his old school friends Steve Mardy and Robert Middlehurst, who were in the process of learning how to play the guitar at evening classes. Amongst the covers they performed were 'Get Back' by The Beatles, 'Substitute' by The Who and 'One Man Band' by Leo Sayer as these were Rob's favourite songs. Their first audience consisted of Robert's brother Steven, and his mate Bob, who goaded them in to playing for them. Both thought they were the height of fashion with their wide collared shirts and flairs, Ian secretly thought they looked a right couple of tossers.
"Rubbish!"
"Sod off if you don't like it

I met Moet at Steve's house - he was in a band with Mardy and Robert. He was a sour faced cherub but as I was to find out, as sharp as pin. **Bob Williams**

Larry Gott (later of 'James') hooked up with them and it was obvious he was a very talented guitarist strongly influenced by Hendrix and Jimmy Page. Larry also recruited an older guitarist friend and the sound became much more professional.

Steve Mardy recalls that two flamboyantly dressed men, who were a great deal older than the band, turned up at Rob's house. In today's terms they would be regarded as cabaret performers and they played guitar and drums. The two men liked what they heard and a deal was put to the band to perform on the cabaret circuit. Both Steve and Rob were very excited by this proposition and wanted to go ahead, Ian had serious reservations about becoming a 'Cabaret 'Turn' and wanted them to think it over. The rest of the group decided to go for it and informed Ian of their decision. Ian's response was decisive:

'Fucking Cabaret, Fuck Off, End of Band'.

Steve Mardy wonders if Moet's input must have felt futile, as 'there were times when the band didn't quite gel'.

I first met Ian in the early 1970s through my friend, Larry Gott (long time lead guitarist with James) when we were trying to get a Rock 'n 'Roll covers band together. Larry and Ian used to sit together at Two Trees School (1968) in Denton and were good friends. **Michael John Leigh**

Ian was not keen on becoming a cabaret type performer, so Larry and I continued our search in other areas and eventually we both became members of The Velvet

Collars. I left them to join The Fall and Larry left to do other things, which eventually led to his joining "James." **Michael John Leigh (The Drummer on 'the Cabaret Circuit')**

Ian's live performance skills debuted in the summer of 1974 at the auspicious venue of The Blackpool Tower Ballroom. Ian was with his closest friend (the late) Tony Logan and another mate Derek Howarth. The lads got chatting to some girls and Ian decided to impress them by entering a talent contest that was taking place at the ballroom, a £100 prize was also at stake. Ian waited and was not impressed by the other contestants as he felt they were semi slick and semi-professional and very, very dull. Ian felt he was in with a real chance as the competition appeared totally uninspired. Finally;

'A BIG hand please for Mr Ian Bowie all the way from Manchester'

announced the greasy looking compere and Mr Bowie made his way onto the stage. The backup band consisted of a group of middle aged guys who accompanied the hopeful contestants on bass, guitar and drums. They were dressed befittingly with black suits and bow ties; clearly they were not prepared for the event that was to take place on stage before their very eyes.

Ian looked out in to the packed auditorium and felt completely confident in this setting; he knew he deserved to be on stage and what is more he felt he owned it;

'A One, a two, one two three four'

The band started and Ian leapt into action with 'Summertime Blues' by Eddie Cochrane. Ian gave it his all as he contorted and writhed around the stage, but something was badly lacking, energy. The house band was accompanying his bravura with limp and polite 'Rock and Roll'. When the first song ended he wheeled around and, his face contorted with disgust and absolute contempt hissed;

"Fucking play it harder! Fucking play it fucking faster you cunts!"

The shocked band launched it to 'Around and around' by Chuck Berry (also covered by David Bowie as the B side to 'Drive in Saturday') and whether out of fear for their lives or genuine inspiration rose to Ian's challenge. Ian felt high on the adrenalin from this performance and knew he had given this his best shot.

"Put your hands together please for Mr Ian Bowie!"

It did not matter that Ian received only polite applause from the somewhat bewildered audience and had resulted in scaring away the girls, Ian was in the process of finding what he was looking for. Ian also had captivated at least one appreciative audience member; an old Teddy Boy had him in a bear hug grip as soon as he came offstage

"Fucking marvellous that is the best thing I have seen for a long time!" raved the elderly Ted

"Eh, thanks mate."
Replied a surprised Mr Bowie.
"Come on! I'll buy you a drink!"
Offered Ian's new fan. Ian hesitated but the old rocker persisted:
"Aw! Come on."
"Ok then."
Agreed Ian.

In the bar this ancient Rock and Roller absolutely raved about Ian's performance and compared him with Gene Vincent. Ian's first fan was totally sincere; he wanted more, but did not know how he was going to make this happen.

Ian is one of those rare people that do not confirm to the rules and expectations set by friends and peers. When long hair was in fashion in the mid-seventies Ian had a short crop ala 'Lou Reed's Rock and Roll Animal' complete with insignia shaved into the sides and shades. In a uniform of browns and beiges Ian stood in black and glitter after experimenting with a one man Mod revival. Ian's look met with much displeasure from the afghan coated hippies at gigs. He simply didn't care for their 'hey man' attitude and their collective stench of patatoui oil.

Ian stalked the streets of Manchester with the soundtrack of The Stooges and The Velvet Underground going around on the Jukebox in his head. Further, earlier sounds were joining this collection and Ian continued his time machine journey in to the past to find out what was relevant for him in the present. Sixties American Garage music was discovered by Ian as sounds and attitudes he could identify with as a young outsider. The mood evoked by this particular musical genre was cool and mysterious and more importantly had an attitude of real edge that was missing from the bland sounds of the mid-seventies. Records such as 'Pushin' Too Hard' and ' Can't Make You Mine" by the Seeds, 'Shake' by The Shadows of Night, joined Ian's seven inch collection along with The Standells 'Sometimes The Good Guys Don't Wear White', The Thirteenth Floor Elevators 'Psychotic Reaction'. A particular favourite from this period was 'South End Incident' by The Beacon Street Union. This has a special place amongst Ian's collection as this was purchased on the same day as his debut in Blackpool and would be covered by Ian and Neil at a latter stage.

But Ian had not entirely given up on the present music scene and the notion of 'Pub Rock' (which originated in London) appeared to go some way towards satisfying Ian's craving for something different. Whilst such bands as 'Kilburn and The High Roads' (an earlier incarnation of Ian Dury and The Blockheads), 'Ducks Deluxe' and Graham Parker and The Rumour were interesting and different, they were not really different enough. Yet Ian describes them as;

'the start of the Yellow Brick Road that was leading me off to see the Wizard'.

Dorothy, I do beg your pardon, Ian was interested enough to give a band called 'Silverhead' a go at the Stoneground'. This Los Angeles glam metal hybrid was fronted by Michael Des Barres (husband of the infamous Pamela), who would later find commercial fame with 'The Power station' (an offshoot from Duran Duran). Nigel Harrison, later of Blondie, was on bass. What had really caught Ian's attention was that the band's visual image appeared to convey that they were very much contemporaries of The Stooges with photos' of a peroxide blond and bare chested Des Barres looking very similar to Iggy Pop.

Ian knew about Iggy's every move and it became apparent that Des Barres was clearly not wanting just to be Iggy's Dog, but was in fact wanting to be Iggy. As this 'Tribute' show progressed it was abundantly clear to Ian that this impostor was not only ripping off Iggy's moves but passing them off as his own. To add insult to injury the music was boring and turgid, Ian had heard it all before, it was just dressed up differently.

Des Barres 'Pop' had exactly what was coming to him when he decided to emulate Iggy's 'walking on a sea of audience hands'. This was the final straw for Ian and when Des Barres came out into the crowd he had the misfortune to come within mincing distance of Ian's waiting hand. Instinctively, Ian's hand became a fist and before he knew what had happened he had punched Des Barres in the solar plexus. Ian actually heard the breath come out of Des Barres as he carried on with the song and quickly retreated to the safety of the stage.

Ian was not pleased with himself for this sudden attack, but really Des Barres had bought this upon himself and Ian swore that this would never happen again. But three years later the vocalist with Generation X, Billy Idol, attempted this same feat and met with the same painful fate at the fist of Ian. Mr Ian Moss would like to apologise to both Mr Des Barres and Mr Idol unreservedly and also advises the male readers that they wear the appropriate protection if ever they decide to plagiarise this particular stage move in his presence.

Manchester

Manchester once had a thriving club scene in the 'sixties. Older Mancunians reminisce about the exciting night life at 'The Twisted Wheel', Oasis and The Magic Village. In 1975 there remained very little from the heyday of Manchester's golden age. Manchester was still very much a dirty, grimy and dangerous city clinging on to its industrial heritage as some sort of perverse 'badge of honour The head of the police force, James Anderton, cut, as Ian describes 'a vicious swathe through club land' and around two thirds of all clubs had been closed as a result of his curbing tactics. Those clubs that had somehow survived the Police purge were very much booze, bird pulling, and punch ups such as 'Kloisters' and 'Tramps'. The alternative night life dives, such as 'Jilly's' and 'Waves' consisted of

Heavy Rock Music and Speed for the discerning palette. The only club that was of any interest to Ian was 'Pips' Nightclub' (spread over five floors) in that it had an exclusive Roxy and Bowie room but it was exclusive in more than one sense of the word and Ian could not relate to the clientele of self-important posers.

On the aptly named Moss side there were different cultural experiences such as 'The Reno' and its sister venue next door called ' The Nile Club which catered for, and was run by, a virtually all Black clientele and was not only above the law; this community had its own set of rules and regulations. A lot of young Mancunians made the long journey to the legendary Wigan Casino (home of 'Northern Soul'). Ian liked a lot of the records played ('The Who, Who Song' by Jackie Wilson and 'You've Been Cheating' by The Impressions) at these all night events, but was very much put off by the prevailing fashion code and snotty attitude required to 'fit in'.

A lot of Ian's time, around this period was spent drinking heavily and attending numerous dreary gigs in a half-hearted attempt to finally find a home grown band that would inspire him. Ian had no shortage of girls but did not have a particularly significant relationship and this fact added to his ever increasing depression. Although he was outstanding at his job, and was not unpopular with his immediate work colleagues, the senior management viewed his maverick nature with suspicion and mistrust. In order to alleviate the sheer boredom at work, Ian took to smoking joints with an older Jamaican colleague called Mike or downing a quarter bottle of whisky to make the afternoon go quicker.

Blunting his emotions with alcohol was no longer enough so he took to self-harming with a razor blade to the sound of 'No Pussyfooting' by Fripp and Eno, much to his parents horrified concern. The only so called 'good times' that Ian remembers from this period is listening to tracks by Jonathon Richman and The Modern Lovers (produced by ex-Velvet Underground's John Cale) on John Peel, which to Ian's increasingly jaded ears sounded 'Incredible and full of truth'. Patti Smith and Television were names that were becoming increasingly mentioned in the music press as being luminaries on the burgeoning New York Music scene. But life in New York might have been Life on Mars, as far as Ian was concerned. He wanted 'something here, here and now, something he could touch, smell and be a part of'.

Ian found that he tended to stick with the artists that he knew best rather than buy an album by an unknown quantity, In a way he was playing it safe by remaining with Bowie, Aryes and Cale. He became an avaricious reader , Kurt Vonnegut (Slaughter House Five), John Steinbeck (Of Mice and Men), Graham Green (The Havana Affair) and Aldous Huxley (Brave New World) were much loved authors and introduced Ian to his love of words and to, a degree, replaced his love of music during this period.

The one thing that still enthralled him was football, in particular the magic of Manchester United, it was the only time he felt alive. Ian thought nothing of travelling by train every weekend to far flung fixtures and indeed, to this day he loves to travel by train. Ian was not exactly what was known as a 'football lout'. Ok, he enjoyed a few pre game (and post) pints, goading the rival side and fooling around but he was not turned on by violence or vandalism.

In 1975 Ian made his first trip abroad to Ostend to see his 'Boys in Red' in a preseason friendly match. There was a bit of trouble on the ferry from Dover, such as petty theft and throwing a couple of Germans over board, so the Belgium Police Force were taking no chances and detained, then sent back many Manchester United Supporters. Ian and his group managed to get through this first obstacle and made it into Ostend around 6.30 in the morning.

Unbeknown to them, they had stumbled right into the heart of the red light district and were able to experience strong Stella Artois for the first time and first thing in the morning. This was great and Ian felt really liberated by this experience. Unfortunately this was not to last as a crew from a Belgian ship, in a neighbouring bar, obviously heard the lively celebration and charged in to the group with knives, staves and chains. The Manchester group were larger in number, and despite the violence managed to drive them out into the street and hurled bottles to keep the invaders at bay. Assistance had been called for as the sound of screeching sirens alerted both fighting factions to the arrival of the Belgian Police Force.

As soon as Ian saw the Armed Force jump out of their cars pointing weapons and making arrests, he and his friend, John Smethurst, decided to flee this terrifying scene. They sprinted all the way to the sea front and hid underneath a parked coach to evade arrest. The combination of alcohol and sheer relief caused them to fall asleep, only the sound of the driver starting the engine, much later that morning alerted them to the fact they might just get run over. In order to steady their shaken nerves Ian and John took to calm themselves down with more Stella and get distracted by the strange hole in the ground that constituted of a 'toilet'. After feeling considerably braver both made it to the match memorable only for a song 'celebrating cult hero big Jim Holton's prowess and comparing him to Desperate Dan'. Ian and John found three more of their crowd and managed to avoid post-match trouble on the way back to the docks.

Ian thought it would be a very good idea to slide out of the packed crowd and wriggle through a barrier and actually managed to get into a comfortable cabin on a nearby ship. He decided to go up and stretch his sea legs, which is just as well he did, as the tanoy announced that the ship was just about to sail for Lisbon. The ship adjacent was full of drunken English supporters who were still singing about Jim Holton and Desperate Dan. It was a close thing but Ian managed to get back on board.

Upon arrival, the press were there to greet them and made up their minds that the violence that had happened was solely attributable to the Manchester United 'Football Yobs'. This was clearly biased reporting and Ian and his three friends attempted to redress the balance when they went en mass to The Manchester Evening News to see the editor. Although the editor did not appear the friends were given the opportunity to be interviewed and inform the public of the intimidation and unproved violence they had experienced. This featured in the paper the very same evening with a photo of Ian and his friends looking suitably moody and stern at the gross misrepresentation of them by sensationalist journalism. Ian regards this photo as the perfect souvenir of his first venture abroad.

'I Fought the law, and the Law Won'
The Bobby Fuller Four

Although Ian had briefly considered joining the Police at the age of fourteen, he soon dropped this career opportunity as he became more and more distrustful of them. This attitude was confirmed when Ian was arrested at a football match in 1974 for simply being in the wrong place at the wrong time. Oddly enough he knew what to expect before the alleged 'incident' even took place. A rare goal had just been scored by Manchester United which caused huge exuberance behind the goal posts and, as usual, the Police force came down like a ton of bricks on the perceived 'offenders' and made a big show of marching them from the ground. Ian was unlucky enough to be amongst the three or four selected for the usual display of force heavy handedness. Sure enough he had his arm wrenched up behind his back, but instead of the expected kick up the backside upon being thrown out; he was thrown into a Black Maria and was taken off, sirens blaring, to Trafford Police Station, where he was formally charged with knocking an elderly lady to the floor along with his fellow 'hooligans'. This charge clearly was a trumped up lie but the Police attempted to extract a confession from him but to no avail, Ian was innocent.

Ian was bailed to appear at the Juvenile Court inside Strangeways jail. At first his father was furious with him. But calmed down when he was eventually convinced that his son was telling the truth. This initial anger turned to confusion as Eddie pondered why the Police would lie.

It was a tense time for the Moss Family when they came into the foreboding court building. Ian felt a mixture of fear and anger as he waited to be called for his case later that morning. However, this build-up of emotions resulted in a huge anti-climax as the case was dismissed by the Magistrate, who was clearly not impressed with Her Majesties 'No Show' and ruled that Ian should be awarded costs. True, it was a victory, of sorts, but to Ian it had a hollow ring as he felt justice had not truly been done.

Several months later Ian was returning from Manchester and was seated on the upper deck of the 210 bus and was unwittingly caught up in a fracas between a young Asian and a gang of racist youths. Ian managed to stop one of the louts from physically attacking their prey but his face came into contact with a belt swung by the Asian in defence. Instinctively, Ian lunged towards his attacker, grabbed his throat and both went crashing to the floor as the bus lurched. His assailant's skull took a massive impact on the floor of the bus and as a result was knocked unconscious and a pool of blood formed around his head. Ian panicked and had to prise open the bus doors to make his escape. He charged down streets, in order to throw any would be pursuers off the scent he clambered over fences and walls and eventually made it to the safety of his home emotionally and physically battered and bruised.

Ian gets little sleep for the next three days and anxiously scours the local paper for any references to this incident. The silence was broken by a knock at the door on a cold, wet, dark evening.

"Can we have a word with Mr Ian Moss?"

on the doorstep there were two plain clothed detectives. The detectives took Ian to Gray Mare Lane station to be questioned: with no parent present as he had now turned the legal age to be considered an adult as he had recently turned 17. Ian's major concern was for the lad and asked;

"How is he?"

With hindsight and wisdom, Ian now realises this was a mistake as the Police are alerted to the fact that in front of them was a sensitive young lad whom they could intimidate into a confession. They were able to play 'Bad Cop, Good Cop' with him but he was too naïve to know at that time.

"You little shit! What do you fucking care! You are going to get exactly what is coming to you, you evil little bastard!

Screams 'Bad Cop' in Ian's face and storms out of the room in an 'absolute temper'.

In the quiet that follows 'Good Cop' is much more amenable and reasonable. Arm around Ian's shoulder he implies;

"Listen mate, I know that you didn't really mean to hurt this young lad...You plead guilty and I can state that you didn't mean to do it."

Ian knew that he wasn't guilty of assault;

"But I'm not guilty, sir, I only wanted to help him out."

Bad Cop opens the door, with a really grim expression on his face, and informs Ian;

"Your case has taken a turn for the worse; we are now going to have to charge you with attempted murder instead of assault! You are really for it now."

Ian chose to plead guilty to causing actual bodily harm. 'Good Cop' assists

Ian to write his confession which seemed reasonable and contrite, he would now be able to speak on Ian's behalf and tell the court how things took a turn for the worse. This seems like a good idea to Ian and he signs the confession.

Ian was very, very hung over at his court appearance owing to 'overdoing it' the previous evening when he had attended a celebratory dinner for winning a work related bursary award. The case is opened and Ian pleads 'Guilty' (as advised). He learns that 'Good Cop' is to present the case for the prosecution and is lulled in to a false sense of security. But 'Good Cop' transforms as his eyes narrow and he savages Ian's character so much so that Ian did not recognise the person who was being described. He began to read out Ian's statement with varying degrees of sarcastic emphasis portraying Ian as a complete monster.

The Magistrate, in summing up Ian's case, informs Ian that he is 'evil incarnate' and fines him £20. Ian had been well and truly stitched up as being 'guilty' of a racist attack and he didn't, and never has had a racist bone in his body. Initially, Ian was sick of his softness and gullibility in allowing himself to be manipulated to plead 'Guilty' to an offence of which he was completely innocent. Ian vowed never to be manipulated again and began to feel real anger and hate towards the Police Force.

The summer of 1976

I spent most of 1976 away from the north but on returning back to Manchester the very first night I met Ian who invited me to a party in Ashton -U-Lyne it was very vague but I remember us fucking off smartish because some nutter was threatening knife violence. It was at this time I discovered Ian was an 'angry young man' he wanted to go back and sort the bastard also he was rather thuggish in the Scoreboard Paddock as was Steve Mardy but that had to be admired (Robert Middi is a Blue and there is nothing to be admired there) **Colin Swan**

1976 was to be a year of huge significance for Ian; he entered this year as a less troubled young man as the crippling bouts of abdominal pain had reduced in frequency and intensity. Despite the fact that Ian was not really career minded he had progressed to the head of his department over seeing around 30 people, some of whom were considerably older than him but Ian knew how to deal with them when they stepped out of line.

Ian had begun to play football regularly again and was even persuaded to turn out in the Hyde and District League as a player for the Cock Hotel. The main instigator in persuading Ian was the Team Manager – Dennis Downworth. Dennis was quite a charismatic character; a flamboyant bisexual antique dealer, who frequently had Ian in stitches of laughter with his outrageous remarks and stories. Although Ian was not the footballer he once was, he really enjoyed playing for the team and in particular for Dennis. Even Manchester United appeared to be on a winning streak again and Ian had much pleasure seeing them thrash rival teams such as Leeds, Liverpool and Everton.

Legalise It Peter Tosh

Oh yeah and Ian shit in Dorothy's bidet after his first blast of weed **Colin Swan**

Ian's first experience of drug taking occurred with Robert Middlehurst and Colin Swan. Robert's Mother, Dorothy, lived above her shop, The Corset Parlour, in Denton Town Centre and it was here that Robert and Colin wanted to get the ambiance just right for the session. They dimmed the lights and put on Mike Oldfield's 'Tubular Bells' (of which Ian was not a fan, but never mind there were drugs after all) and sat crossed legged on the floor. In addition to the hashish Ian had also consumed the best part of a bottle of whisky and got messier and messier. So much so, that his friends decided that Ian needed some fresh air and all staggered out on to the roof via the sky light. Dorothy arrived home and guessed what was happening and managed to coax them off the sloping roof. She saw that Ian looked very ill and suggested that he needed to go to the toilet. Supporting him, in the bathroom, Dorothy waited, and waited but:

'I want to shit'

Oh dear.

It was around this time that Ian met Julie. She was beautiful and Ian was totally smitten with her. He was like a clumsy boy around her but managed to pluck up enough courage to ask her out for a date. After the date there had been a 'misunderstanding' on the part of Julie, this would set the pattern for the next 29 years. Ian knew from a very early stage that they would be together but wishes now that they had never met. But in 1976 Ian was captured by her radiance and couldn't help but fall in love with her.

Manchester Lesser Free Trade Hall Friday June 4 1976

Those of us, who are old enough, remember the summer of 1976 as a particularly hot and glorious one. But there are those of us who remember a very significant event that would shape not only Ian, but the lives of countless other young people.

Patti Smith's debut album had become a fixture on the Moss Bros record player that summer. The black and white photo of a rather boyish looking Smith, taken by Robert Mapplethorpe, was dark and moody and promised much. Although Ian believed 'it harked back to some kind of idealised Rock and Roll Nirvana' there was a lot to commend it. The lyrics were as sharp and immediate; a call to the future. Ian was a huge fan of the 'Nuggets' album (which featured many of Ian's favourite garage bands from the sixties) which had been compiled by Lenny Kaye who was the guitarist (and partner) with Patti Smith). Another bonus for Ian was that John Cale produced the album.

Bryan Ferry was enjoying hits with covers of 'The Price of Love' and 'Shame, shame, shame'. The latter hit featured the guitar of Chris Spedding (who had enjoyed solo chart success with the very proto punk 'Motorbikin'' the previous year) which enhanced the minimalist, raw sound.

Dr Feelgood, from Southend on Sea/Canvey Island, had taken 'pub rock' into the album charts. Southend on Sea, in particular, has a history of bands that perform Rhythm and Blues but previously no band had the rawness and excitement that Dr Feelgood radiated. Lee Brilleux, the gravel voiced lead singer was a perfect visual counterpoint to the psychotic guitarist Wilco Johnson who had a wild eyed amphetamine look about him as he executed his jerky, staccato stage movements.

Also from Southend on Sea came the younger Eddie and the Hot Rods who were fast, noisy and were critically acclaimed. Ian enjoyed their marvellous EP 'Live at the Marquee' but could not help but think that their sound borrowed very heavily from the past. True it was stripped down and faster but *it was American Rhythm and Blues with a Facelift.*

Manchester United was finally up for the FA Cup in early May, for the first time since 1963, and they were to play Southampton. Ian and his mates booked the weekend at a posh hotel in the heart of London's West End. Celebrations started early at the Brunswick Pub in Manchester's Piccadilly and continued after arriving in London on Friday evening. Ian decided to go into nearby Soho and managed to talk a couple of friends into coming along to continue the drinking session. Ian was hunting for 'something' and in the seedy Soho atmosphere he could almost smell this elusive quantity but the unknown answer that Ian had been searching for, although close, was not ready to reveal itself - just yet, but it would give Ian a clue.

On the way back to the hotel the gang came across some posters stuck on buildings which were advertising Patti Smith's forthcoming UK Debut performance at The Hammersmith Odeon. This was cause enough to liberate a souvenir but it was the name of the support band which caught Ian as a bit edgy, a bit menacing;

"The Stranglers."

The next morning, Patti Smith, unsmiling, looked down upon a very, very hung over Ian. Somehow he managed to get himself down to the luxurious dining room, only to be refused entry owing to just being in his jim jam bottoms.

The Cup Final was a disappointment and Manchester United lost to, Ian maintains, 'a blatantly off side goal'. Whilst the rest of the Manchester United Fans were taking their fury out on shop windows, Ian was making his own way quietly amused over a banner, that had caught his eye, which had boldly proclaimed that 'Crippen was A Red'.

There was something compellingly minimalist, almost absurdist about this statement and unbeknown to Ian, a New York Band called The Ramones were performing their own absurdist statements in The Bowery Bar, only these lyrics 'would help unshackle a generation.'

'There's no point in asking....' The Sex Pistols

The gig that the Sex Pistols played at Manchester Lesser Free Trade Hall is one of legend. The small audience present at this historic event were to be profoundly inspired and motivated by the events that took place on stage that evening. Many of the audience related to the Pistols 'get up on stage and just do it' attitude and this was to be the birthplace of the Hamsters, The Fall, Joy Division (later New Order) and The Smiths. The Sex Pistols, in a short set, reduced the distance between 'The Musicians' and 'The Audience', any one could get up and do it.

This legendary gig came about after two young students, Howard Trafford and Peter McNeish, travelled down to London in February and experienced the early days of the Sex Pistols phenomena. With the self-assured confidence of youth they managed to convince Malcolm McLaren that a gig in Manchester was not only a viable proposition but would give the band greater exposure. Peter had experience of organising and booking venues and attempted to book their college, Bolton Institute, but their Student Union didn't bite. The Lesser Free Trade Hall was a lecture venue in the historic Free Trade Hall and Peter and Howard managed to secure this.

'I swear I was There The Gig That Changed The World' by David Nolan debunks the mystery as to who really saw the first gig at The Lesser Free Trade Hall and has vital anecdotes by those who were present of what they experienced on that fateful evening. David Nolan's book is a highly readable account and is an essential part of Punk History.

Ian Moss still reads The New Musical Express religiously every Thursday. It was here that he first came across The Sex Pistols in a small article entitled 'Don't look over your shoulder, the Sex Pistols are coming'. Basically this recounted the events at a gig, in London's Legendary Marquee, at which the Pistols had not only verbally harangued their audience but has also physically attacked them. This in itself was enough to stimulate Ian's interest but the article also mentioned that the band covered a 'Stooges' song. Ian's growing curiosity was captivated by the quote by the singer – Johnny Rotten;

'Actually, We're not into music, we're into chaos.'

Ian read, and reread this over again and was much taken with the photo of the sneering Johnny Rotten (with the singers name and the caption 'it fits'). Ian wanted to know more about this group and finally, several weeks later, an advert appeared in the Manchester Evening News

"Sex Pistols
Manchester Lesser Free Trade Hall
Friday June 4
Tickets 50p"

Ian knew about the Free trade Hall, he had been to several events there, but was not aware of the Lesser Free. But no matter, he fully intended to be there.

On the actual evening he made a couple of telephone box calls to girlfriends on the way to the venue:

"Hi, how's you? I was wondering if you fancied coming to town to watch a band with me? Who? They're called The Sex Pistols, they sound great, and they play a Stooges song too. Yes....Sex Pistols... no, I'm not messing about...OK suit yourself... see you soon."

Ian ended up going to the event himself attired in a very non punk Cream Suit with suede crepe soled shoes ('Very Kevin Ayres" he thought to himself as he strolled out in the early evening sunshine. Ian proceeded to catch the bus to Piccadilly and had a short walk to Peter Street where the Free Trade Hall was situated. There was absolutely no queue, so Ian was able to walk straight in and pay for his ticket at an ad-hock cashier's desk which was manned by a rather interesting looking chap in a leather suit; Malcolm McLaren.

Ian went up the stairs and remembers thinking that there wasn't much of an audience but he wasn't that surprised. Ian has a wander around to see if there is anyone there he knew even remotely, but there wasn't, so he took a seat to the right of the stage halfway down the hall and waited. Whilst waiting Ian noticed a group of very strange looking people who were congregating around the left hand side of the stage. These were 'The London Crowd' and whilst Ian is not completely certain, this may have been the first time he clapped eyes on Jordan with her trademark beehive hairdo and geometric line face make up .

The first group on the ticket is supposed to be 'Buzzcocks'(formed by Howard and Peter, who are now much better known as Devoto and Shelley respectively) but un-be known to Ian, Buzzcocks were unable to get their act together so an emergency support act called 'Solstice' came on stage. Ian managed to work out pretty quickly that this was not the band on the ticket as they were 'scruffy, hairy, hoary old rockers playing every old cliché in the rockers handbook'. They were absolute rubbish and the 'highlight' was when they covered 'Nantucket Sleigh ride' by the despised American group 'Mountain' which had Ian squirming in his rickety seat. They did well to extract polite applause but Ian really considered walking out then and there as he feared that The Sex Pistols, judging from this dire opening act, would be no more than a case of 'The Kings Road New Clothes.'

The Sex Pistols came on stage after a short interval. They look absolutely fantastic from the very second they came on and Ian truly had seen nothing like them ever. He describes Johnny Rotten as 'a waif from a Charles Dickens Novel, but bristling with a known channelled aggression'. He wasn't smiling meekly at the audience nor posing aloof, his eyes were bulging and staring out into the audience and directed wittily sarcastic comments at the audience from the minute he stepped on stage – Ian identified with this attitude from the very second he saw him, he too had cigarette burns on his wrists. The bass player looked great in a simple tight fitting T-Shirt and drainpipe jeans and Ian immediately thought that this was a style that would suit him down to the ground. The guitarist's amp has the legend 'Guitar Nero' scrawled across it which caused Ian to muse whether this was intentional. He also looks good in his sleeveless black top and his white guitar has a transfer of a nude girl. Ian was immediately intrigued and he began to realise his true being in their image. The Sex Pistols sounded, soared and roared, they were every bit as good as they looked. They were loud, defiant in words and gesture, Ian was transfixed and stunned. Ian had found the group he had always been looking for but also realised that the searching would still continue as these four lads of Ian's generation appeared to issue a challenge;

'Think for yourself, be yourself, dare to be an individual, create something, don't cripple yourself with fear, don't accept second class rubbish, don't bow, don't kneel and don't bend'.

The songs were not long overblown affairs but were short and jagged – just what Ian had wanted and he was bouncing around in his seat grinning from ear to ear. He appeared to be the only person reacting as the rest of the audience were impassive and silent. Ian attributes this lack of reaction to either 'Manchester Cool' or quite simply that the audience were stunned. The fourth song was a cover, 'I'm not your stepping stone,' or maybe 'Substitute,' and this was enough for Ian to jump from his seat and start bopping around in front of the bass player(when viewing a documentary about this event, decades later, he saw he was in the cine footage shaking vibrantly to the music). Ian just didn't care that he might appear foolish dancing all by himself for this was music to dance to. All too soon the set came to an end with 'Watchoo Gonna Do About it?' and the Stooges 'No Fun'. When Ian looked around he found that around 70 or so audience members had in fact joined him. There then began friendly banter between Johnny Rotten about 'good' and 'bad' bands. An member of the audience, later to be known as John The Postman asked what the band thought of 'Eddie and The Hot Rods' and received the mischievous reply;

'Our imitators.'

'No Fun' was played again as an encore and as the audience departed Ian took a handbill down that had been blue tacked to the foyer window as a souvenir. Ian describes himself as 'half floating, half skipping' on the way back to the bus stop that would lead him back to boring old normality, namely dreary little Denton.

Ian recognised two other lads who had been at the show on the bus home and they all enthused about what had just taken place. When Ian got off the bus he went straight to his local pub, 'Chapel House' and handbill brandished he told anyone who would listen about the experience that was known as The Sex Pistols. Ian is no clairvoyant but he was able to confidently predict to all and sundry that this was no ordinary band and that the pub clientele would be hearing much more about them in the future.

Psycho Killer The Talking Heads

Ian, after his holy conversion to Punk, became a form of preacher and was soon extolling the virtues of the ethos of The Sex Pistols to all who would listen, and plenty didn't want to. As befitting a lay preacher Ian adopted the uniform of drain pipe jeans, pumps and although Ian's hair had been on the short side, even more was hacked off. Ian's image was of that of a new visionary and he had come up with this different look well before he saw the cover of the debut Ramones album.

This startling new image certainly turned heads in the streets of Manchester and exited calls of 'Puff' and 'Queer'. A lively, noisy pub would instantly turn silent upon the sight of Ian entering. The term 'Punk' was not in existence in the very early days of this phenomena and Ian's 'alien' image certainly caused double takes and comment.

The Sunday evening after the gig Ian called around to see his mate Robert at his father's house. Steven answered the door and informed Ian that Robert was in, but was getting ready, and offered him a drink. This was unusually social for Steven, thought Ian, as a beverage was poured out. Steven was now married with a young son and lived with his in-laws, although he tended to spend as much time away from them to everyone's mutual relief (except that of his long suffering wife).

Although Steven was making polite conversation, Ian just felt very slightly ill at ease but accepted another drink whilst waiting for Robert to appear. After finishing his drink Ian realised that he had been kept waiting under false premises, as Robert obviously wasn't in, but he wondered why Steve had woven this elaborate charade in order to keep him waiting? Steven immediately offered Ian another drink but Ian politely declined and made a move to go. Steven was not going to be thwarted and beckoned to Ian to come into the back garden with him. Ian did as he was told as he knew Steven could turn very nasty very quickly.

'Why are you Robert's friend? I am much more interesting than him!'

Steven was backing Ian against the garden wall. This really took Ian by surprise and he said the first thing that came into his head.

'I don't think you're more interesting. I think you underestimate him'

This answer elicited a violent reaction from Steven and he lurched towards Ian and pinned him against the wall.

'You don't like me, do you'?

Steven snorted gripping Ian's throat for emphasis and continued

'Well you're not going anywhere until we're friends!'

This was certainly a most unusual and original overture for friendship and Ian laughed nervously and replied

'Are you fucking kidding? We have nothing in common!'

Steven was not to be put off so easily and continued

'You don't get it do you? I want to know what you know. I want to know what it is about you that's different. I want to know why people think you're special. You're going to be my friend whether you like it or not!'

Ian laughed, not knowing whether to be frightened or flattered. It was a ludicrous situation and Ian decided to break it by giving in and held out his hand to Steven to shake on it;

'Ok! Friends!'

This answer appeared to satisfy Steven who released his grip and suggested that they both go down the pub to cement their new found friendship. Walking on the way to the 'Arden Arms', both were in animated conversation about Ian's recent experience at The Sex Pistols gig. Steven was genuinely interested in how this band made Ian feel and talked about the books he had read. Ian was amazed at how knowledgeable and witty Steven really was, it wasn't Robert who had been underestimated - it was Steven.

Both talking as if they had known each other for years, when they reached the pub, clearly stimulated by each other's company. They were joined by Mark Reeder, an acquaintance of Ian's, who had a penchant for wearing German Uniforms and for setting light to model airplanes and photographing them in flight. To his credit, he was also into music and worked at the Virgin Record Shop on Lever Street. This outlet had also sold The Sex Pistols tickets and he wanted to know exactly what it had been like. The conversation and alcohol flowed and this group of three became more and more animated, louder and louder until they were eventually asked to leave the premises.

Ian stumbled happily out on to the pavement with Steven and both wandered off home and continued their deep discussion; the best of friends.

Now that Ian had experienced The Sex Pistols any other gig would pale in to comparison besides them. In July he went to see The Who at Swansea Football Ground at the aptly named 'WHO PUT THE BOOT IN?' show. Also appearing at this festival were The Sensational Alex Harvey Band and Little Feat (one of the very few American Bands Ian appreciated, led by the prodigiously talented, but flawed, Lowell George).

If Ian had experienced this Festival before the Sex Pistols gig he would have thought this show was absolutely brilliant. But what transpired was that Ian was bored and even had to stifle a yawn. True, The Sensational Alex Harvey Band still held up well owing to the presence and charisma of the front man. But The Who, busy whipping up the surrounding crowd in to frenzy, no longer impressed Ian. He now saw this group as a form of dinosaur performing well rehearsed and staid routines. Ian felt curiously detached from all the excitement going on around him, this was no longer enough, and he did not belong. Ian had a secret that only a few people knew about, The Sex Pistols and they were the future.

Anarchy in the UK Sex Pistols Tuesday 20 July 1976

Posters that had mysteriously appeared around Manchester implied that The Sex Pistols would return to The Lesser Free Trade Hall to support a local band called Slaughter and The Dogs. Ian knew this to be misleading but was thrilled to learn that the Pistols were to return to Manchester so soon. Obviously, word had got around and the audience attendance was around 250 people. These included Ian, his mate Gordon 'Paddy' Slater with his girlfriend Jackie Blower. Also present were young brother Neil and three of his school friends. Ian would like to put the record straight regarding as Mick Hucknall (who was later to be associated with Neil and was therefore assumed that he had attended this gig) as being part of Neil's party, he didn't. According to Ian, Mick was very likely in his bedroom listening to 'Journey to the centre of the Earth', but wisely chose not to deny, nor confirm, this legend when questioned.

An extremely pleasant, rather camp, young man was on the door .Ian later realised this was Pete Shelley, the guitarist of Buzzcocks who finally made it as support to The Sex Pistols that same evening. Unfortunately, Ian's experience with the dire Solstice, lead him to make the fatal decision to have a bevvy at the Free Trade Bar. As a result Ian missed Buzzcocks that evening. This was a real shame as young Neil was very much taken with Buzzcocks, even more so that even the Sex Pistols. He experienced a form of catharsis very similar to his older brother as he excitedly described the amazing performance. Their sound was indeed a 'new form of music' that bore no relation to any conventional bands; they even had the cheek and confidence to do one note guitar solos. Neil had been playing guitar in his own band 'Osiris' and according to Ian, performed horrid rock covers. Buzzcocks 'non musicology' liberated him from playing other peoples songs and he was soon writing his own material.

When Ian eventually pulled himself away from the flow of cider the hall was absolutely packed and Slaughter and the Dogs were on stage. Ian was not at all impressed by what he saw and heard. Slaughter and the Dogs had bought their own fan base for support, but failed to get the rest of the audience on their side with preening rock star poses and cod theatrics; which involved wearing big girl's blouses and throwing flour around. There were ham-fisted covers of 'Jumping Jack Flash' and 'Rebel, Rebel' which was 'glammed up Cabaret nonsense' and their own material came over as dreary 'rock by numbers. Ian jeered out that they were 'absolute shit' and he was not alone in this informed opinion. Paul Morley (who was soon to start his trajectory to fame as an NME Journalist) reacted strongly to this display of 'inauthenticity' and decided to throw a liquorice allsort which successfully hit vocalist Wayne Barrett. This was too much for the Diva Dog and he demanded the removal of the malicious offender otherwise the show would stop ('If only' thought Ian at the time). The Wythenshawe 'rent a mob' became rather agitated and there was a distinct air of violence as a result. This was the start of when lines would be drawn in support of Punk Band factions.

At last The Pistols came on and again they lived up to Ian's expectations. They were removed from the petty squabbles that had just occurred and everyone was united in their appreciation of this classic band. This was the set when Ian first heard 'Anarchy in The UK' which was debuted at this concert.

Several likeminded members of the audiences present at the Manchester Sex Pistols gigs were inspired to immediately form bands. Curiously Ian was not amongst them. With hindsight Ian believed that he was at his happiest he had ever been in his life, happy even to the point of complacency. He was happy just to be a spectator. It was certainly true that his immediate contemporary's had not the desire nor inclination to form a band but Ian, maybe, had not tried hard enough to seek creative individuals out in an attempt to create and perform. Ian now regrets this as a missed opportunity, but fate would come to Ian later from a very unlikely source.

Ian was happy with his life; he even experienced a purpose and optimism to his life that had been sadly lacking for several years. It helped that Julie was starting to pay Ian some attention and even compliments on occasion. The evening out with Steve was far from being a one off and they enjoyed spending time together. Steve worked as a hairdresser and was very good at his job; his boss - Gareth Evans who was to find fame as manager of the Stone Roses. Steve and Ian were on the same wavelength and found out that they shared a love for football. Robert suggested that Steve and Ian played for his insurance's works team, though if truth be known, they were keener on showing off in front of each other and as a result this team languished at the bottom of the league.

Ian purchased his first car, a blue Ford Anglia, without taking a driving lesson let alone a driving test. Needless to say he was appallingly bad behind the steering wheel, but didn't care; he was out to have some fun. It was a clapped out old vehicle and Ian knew nothing about traditional car maintenance. Yet when this ancient Anglia stalled at traffic lights, which it was particularly prone to do; Ian was able to get out, open the bonnet and play around with the wires and get it to work again. The concept of stopping, as opposed to stalling, was an alien one to Ian and he would jump red lights. He once sped between two frail old ladies who had just stepped out on to the pedestrian crossing in what they thought was relative safety. Ian could see that these old dears were positively shaking with fear and anger from the safety of his rear view mirror and did not feel particularly good about what he had just done.

Ian decided to leave his car in the car park of 'The Bay Horse' pub. This car park was large and it was empty, the only other car in the vicinity was a splendid Mercedes, belonging to the pub landlord, and even this was parked in a garage. Yes, you've guessed it, somehow Ian managed to drive slap bang in to the garage containing the said pride and joy and succeeded in bringing the whole structure down on top of it.

"Whoops".

Ian got out of his own indestructible kamazi and quickly scooped up the head light and wing which had somehow become detached in the altercation and decided to beat a hasty retreat.

When Ian returned, on foot, twenty minutes later to the pub to finally get his drink, he found that the pub landlord, Eddie, was in a right old state, barely managing to pull Ian's pint for him so much was he shaking with rage. He ranted on to Ian that he was going to have his revenge on the fucking bastard that had not only demolished his garage but ruined his car and afternoon in to the bargain. Ian empathised.

The Sex Pistols were gaining more and more coverage in the music papers, particularly the NME. Ian was amazed to read that they had actually been recording studio demos with Chris 'Motorbikin' ' Spedding. The audience at the Manchester gigs had been so small, yet, there they were in the process of getting a record deal. Another band that was gaining more page space was 'The Damned' who were being compared to The Pistols. A more familiar name was Buzzcocks, the local group, who appeared to be doing rather well for themselves. A Sex Pistols headline tour was mooted in the music press, with The Damned and Chris Spedding as support acts. However, this idea was soon nixed as, allegedly, Chris Spedding believed that he should have been the headlining act.

Strange little adverts, which managed to get Ian's attention, featuring 'Nick Lowe' and 'Sean Tyler' were appearing more and more in the music press by the independent record label - 'Stiff'

And then.....

It was announced that The Pistols had managed to obtain a deal with the mega huge EMI record label and that a single would be released in the very near future! Ian had not been so very excited since he had witnessed;

'George Best doing the best run up half the length of the Old Trafford Pitch, avoiding the assault on him by Ron 'Chopper' Harris, rounding Peter Bonetti and rolling the ball before a disbelieving Stretford end'.

To add to this excitement even further was the news that the Pistols were to undertake a nationwide tour and that Manchester was on the schedule!

'A Rude Word'

The Pistols debut single for EMI, 'Anarchy in the UK', was the stuff of much speculation for the music press who were very much divided in their opinions of the forthcoming 7" single. Some believed that it would be the vital challenge that would revive the ailing music industry where as others maintained that as The Pistols couldn't really play their instruments they should be dismissed out of hand.

On 01 December The Sex Pistols and assorted hangers on appeared on the now notorious Thames Television Today evening programme. The Sex Pistols were interviewed live, after they had enjoyed a lot of 'hospitality'. The interviewer, Bill Grundy (who appeared to be as inebriated as The Pistols) more or less goaded the band in to swearing and was rewarded with a couple of 'Fucks' from the guitarist Steve Jones. Indignant tabloid 'outrage' followed this rather silly appearance and informed the great British public of the evil that had been broadcast from its television screens. One rag carried the legendary article that one labourer had been so incensed by this bad language that he kicked his television screen in rather than have his children subjected to more profanities. Besides the fact that this act would have very likely killed this chap, Ian was heard to observe:

'He must have worked on a very civilised building site then.'

Football stadiums were treated to the sight of Ian wearing second hand 'old men's' suits with white creped soles, a tatty shirt and various combinations of ties – this was Ian's latest look. Only now it had a name –'Punk' and Ian was subjected to even more insults and cat calls after the 'Today' show. Ian was not without his admirers though as at one match a band of 'Cockney Reds' sought him out for a chat comparing Manchester and London 'Scenes'. This group had their finest and most expensive fashion from 'Sex', McLaren and Vivienne Westwood's Punk boutique on London's Kings Road. Ian's style cost him considerably less, but stood up well compared to their bright mohair jumpers and leather trousers.

Despite a rather worrying review in The NME which had compared the Sex Pistols debut single to the sonic sound of Hawkwind, Ian set off to purchase 'Anarchy In The UK' on a bright Saturday morning in Ashton Under Lyne. This was the largest music store in the vicinity and was owned by a very nicely dressed, very middle class, very nice couple.

"Hello, have you got 'Anarchy In The UK', by The Sex Pistols please?"

"NO!"

The elegant proprietor looked down his nose at Ian as if to suggest that this was a 'nice' record shop and they wouldn't stock such filth!

Ian was a bit taken aback by this rather vehement answer but continued;

"Eh, You wouldn't have 'New Rose' by 'The Damned' either would you... please?"

"WE ARE NOT HAVING THAT SORT OF DISGUSTING RUBBISH IN THIS SHOP!!!'

Ian was really taken aback by the sheer venom of this reply and this shaped his revulsion men in golf attire from that moment on.

Red faced, Ian made to get out of the record shop of niceness and saw the debut album by The Ramones. He stopped to look at the cover and read the song titles which looked to Ian like 'Manifesto's of intent'. Ian wants this and returns to the record counter.

"Can I buy this record?"

"Yes'

For some reason The Ramones have successfully flown under the radar of niceness as this presents no problem for the shop owner.

"Well', says Ian

"I'D BETTER GO AND BUY IT ELSEWHERE, BECAUSE THIS IS THAT DISGUSTING RUBBISH AS WELL! GOOD BYE!!!"

Ian had made his point and looked elsewhere. Soon a black clad copy was it his hot sweaty hands.

Ian looked forward to putting a record on so much since 'Fun House'. The sound was immediate, glorious and the B side was equally as magnificent.

Ian describes this *'as more than a record, this was an instrument of dissent and subversion, bloody hell! It filled me with energy, it made me feel strong'.*

Anarchy in the UK Sex Pistols

The 'Anarchy' tour, with The Sex Pistols head lining is announced for December. Supporting the Pistols are 'The Heartbreakers' who feature Johnny Thunders and Jerry Nolan from The New York Dolls Also supporting are 'The Damned' whose cracking 'New Rose' single was the first punk single to be released. The Clash, had already courted a lot of interesting publicity and were also down as support act.

The full page adverts which appeared in the music press to announce the tour dates were totally original and owed nothing to any artwork that had gone previously. Cut out type settings, resembling a blackmail letter, over a crumpled Union Jack advertised the tour and dates and was completely different and new. Although the musical press are very much in the 'for' and 'against' camps the tabloids are having a field day with the violence and that these Punk Rock bands would surely incite corruption of youth. The gutter press demanded that this tour is banned for the sake of good old fashioned British Decency and with headlines such as 'Save Our Kids' they were attempting to appeal for law and order, with a view to raising their readership numbers. The old school fell for this 'appeal' with alarming gullibility and geriatric councils set about cancelling tour dates as the Police force and High Church applaud their decision.

Manchester was and still is a law unto itself and was not going to be influenced by this media hysteria and there was no doubt that The 'Anarchy' tour was to go ahead at The Electric Circus in Colyhurst. Ian fondly describes this venue as 'an unlovely, decaying fleapit in one of Manchester's most dangerous suburbs'. Manchester, in 1976, was a mixture of sixties high rise flats and desolate estates on huge, bleak expanses of wasteland; a result of continued neglect since The Luftwaffe blitzkrieg of the forties. Ian waxes lyrical 'The very epitome of William Blake's 'Dark, Satanic Mills' with the heritage of our industrial past silhouetting the night skyline'.

It was into this vision of poetic imagery that Ian, with his four passengers, crammed into his faithful Anglia set off in to one dank, dark Thursday evening for what Ian describes as

'A night out that will resemble the shootout at the OK Corral'

'White Riot' The Clash

That evening may have been cold, wet and miserable but Ian was warmed by his keen glow of anticipation for the forthcoming excitement he was bound to experience. When Ian and his small band of friends got out of the car they were immediately hit by the air of malevolence, as there are small groups of youths skulking about in alley ways clearly out for an evening of violence. Determined not to get involved in any fights before the gig, Ian's group ignore the taunts and cat calls and resolutely made their way into the venue as quickly as they could.

There was a large crowd inside the Circus, although it wasn't packed to the rafters. What was noticeable was how many of the natives had gone 'punk'. Admittedly it was a great deal more 'DIY' than their London fashion contemporaries but their 'look 'was equally as eye-catching. A few of the audience members appeared to have been involved in altercations with the gangs outside as they are administering basic first aid to the cuts and bruises. Even in the venue, the audience is not safe from the local populace who have taken it upon themselves to rid of the area of the evil punk rockers that have violated their patch. The beer swilling, tattooed mob manages to charge through in to the hall and viciously hit out at those unlucky enough to be within reach and kick out with steel capped work boots to inflict as much injury as they possibly could.

There were very few Punk releases at the time of this gig, so both the A and B side of 'Anarchy' were on heavy rotation along with 'Road Runner' by The Modern Lovers, 'Waiting for the man', by The Velvet Underground as well as other material that Ian was very familiar with. One record that is notably absent is 'New Rose' by The Damned, who Ian learnt had been chucked off the tour. Earlier on, another set of Local Authority Counsellors had wanted to hold 'auditions' to see if the bands were as bad as the press maintained. If the bands were deemed acceptable, then they could play. Only The Damned responded to this request and, although it is not recorded if they got the geriatric panel pogoing around, this compliance seen as an act of sheer treachery and disloyalty and were unceremoniously booted off the tour. Whilst Ian is disappointed not to see this group (He really rated 'New Rose' as a fantastic slab of adrenaline rush) he fully supported this action as this adhered to his socialist principles.

However, Ian was to finally get to see Buzzcocks with Howard Devoto on vocals. This version was the iconic one for Ian, although they would always remain brilliant, Ian describes them as a mixture of contractions: *'Hard and soft. Smart and dumb'.* Whilst it is obvious they have been inspired by The Pistols they have used them as a reference point rather than becoming 'wanna be's'. It is the growing Punk ethos of 'get up and do it' that was taking them in a direction involving arch humour and coyness which Ian thought was' fucking excellent.'

Ian over hears various conversations amongst audience members and is approached by a young chap who informs Ian that he has already seen the Sex Pistols in Torquay and that they played a cover of the Small Faces 'Itchy coo Park'. This is fascinating news to Ian and he decides to check this out and turns round and asks Steve Jones, the Sex Pistols guitarist who just happens to be standing in close proximity.

"No Mate and we ain't ever been to Torquay either.'

Our man in 'the know', who clearly wouldn't recognise a Sex Pistol if he fell over him, decides to beat a hasty retreat into the anonymity of the crowd.

Ian positions himself right in front of the stage in order to see the Clash stride on with their stage costume of overalls spattered with a 'Jackson Pollack' paint effect. Joe Strummers, the vocalist just walks straight up to the microphone and shouts

'We're the Clash! We're from London! I get violent when I'm fucked up get silent when I'm drugged up, want excitement!'

This gets Ian's attention straight away and no one, but no one, has ever managed to grab Ian like Joe Strummers introduction ever since. The Clash thrill Ian with their cheap amphetamine fuelled energy as they pirouette around the stage like broken marionettes.

'For Fucks Sake! You could hear the speed in the Fucking Sound!' This wasn't even prescription amphetamine but 'the sticking bathroom sulphate crap that was cheap and more available to ingest'. **Ian Moss**

Next, are The Heartbreakers. Beforehand, Ian didn't set his expectations too high as he knows that this group is older and suspects that they may just trade on past glories, a group that is only on this tour out of 'respect'. But No! They manage to blow Ian away as their collective experience and genuine pleasure to be 'out there' resulted in a performance that exudes confidence and a tight, tough tuneful sound. They could have rested on their laurels but their attitude of 'take it, or leave it' took any fears of 'showiness and flashiness' that Ian previously had.

Ian spots the hair of Tony Wilson, the presenter for 'So it goes' (on which the Sex Pistols had made their debut performance) in the audience. Now Ian was not keen on Tony, far too smug and smarmy for Ian's liking, but never the less he had made the effort to come.

Finally, The Sex Pistols come on stage and as soon as they appear, the local meatheads make one final, desperate dash towards the stage but were successfully ousted.

After another magnificent performance from The Pistols Ian found young brother Neil with a group small group of friends. All were absolutely petrified of the baying mob outside and Ian wished the group the best of luck and managed to cram Neil in to the back of his Anglia, who had to lie over the legs of the back seat passengers, and sped into the direction of the city centre. Well he couldn't leave his little brother behind could he?

Ian, as mentioned before, was very possibly not the best driver in Manchester and to add to this never really concerned himself with comprehending road signs. At around 1am, arriving at a junction Ian turns left into Market Street, past the building site that was eventually to become the hideous Arndale Centre. There are no other cars and as Ian nears the top of the road hidden behind the 'Lewis's' building the traffic lights change and all of a sudden, four lanes of traffic come hurtling towards him. Ian had somehow managed to come up Market Street the wrong way. In an effort to avoid the tsunami of articulated juggernaut that were aiming for him, Ian veers across the road and mounts the pavement outside 'Chelsea Girl' boutique. Ian continues his journey along the pavement crosses Oldham Street by use of a pedestrian crossing, mounts another pavement past 'Woolworths', crosses Lever Street by means of another convenient Zebra Crossing –joining a few bemused pedestrians. Finally Ian manages leave the pavement at end of Piccadilly Gardens and manages to use the road for the rest of the journey home.

The gutter press and local authorities appear to be winning their self-righteous Crusade against the 'Anarchy' tour and more and more dates are pulled. As a result the tour returns to the Electric Circus a mere ten days later. Ian has trouble finding travelling companions this time, maybe the thrill of the drive may have been a bit too much for them or maybe these gigs were too close together? Ian decides to take the bus to Collyhurst all by himself and when he arrived found that barely a quarter of the audience that had been present over a week ago. Ian wondered if the violence that was so prevalent at the last gig had scared people away, or it could have been a simple case of merely ticking a box called 'See The Sex Pistols' and once was enough?

Buzzcocks were not on this time, but Ian enjoys The Clash and Heartbreakers even more as he can pick out more of the musical hooks and decipher the lyrics, the songs are beginning to lodge in Ian's mind. The Sex Pistols appear more relaxed and possess great poise and authority. They were absolutely awesome and this gig, Ian remembers as being their best.

'I see we've got rid of all the tourists'

Mocks Johnny Rotten looking out in to the depleted audience
Ian smiled at that remark and thought 'Fuck 'em' and The Sex Pistols really did make him feel good to be alive again.

Summer is Heaven in '77 Marc Bolan

1977 was for Ian 'a year of the highest highs and lowest lows'. The New Year's Evening Celebrations were a portent of things to come. Ian was out with his mates at 'The Red Lion' in Denton. Midnight was fast approaching and Ian went to the bar to get the drinks to toast the New Year in. As he waited patiently he is viewed with hostile distain by a group of middle aged men.

"You one of them Punk Rockers?"

Demands a particularly large and unpleasant looking beer gut.

Ian decides to ignore him, but this doesn't deter the fat blob, who grabs Ian's lapels and shouts:

"I'm fucking talking to you! You Cunt! You're a Fucking disgrace!"

Ian does not want to inflame the situation, so refuses to rise to the bait and attempts to reason;

"I just want a drink mate, no mither, leave me alone".

This response appears to infuriate this great ape even further and he pushes Ian backwards against the wall so forcefully that his head went back and hit it. This situation is going to turn very nasty, very quickly but the pub landlord jumps in and separates the two.

"You get out! And don't come back!"

He yells at Ian, yes Ian, and continues

"We don't want your sort in here!"

Ian decides not to protest his innocence, it would be pointless so instead he shakes his head and decides to leave without a word to anyone, not even his friends who are oblivious to what has just taken place. On the way out, Ian grabs an empty bottle, just in case. As it happened he wasn't followed out in to the winter chill. Cold it may have been, but Ian's blood was boiling with rage in the early hours of 1977.

What do I get? Buzzcocks

Despite this decidedly unpromising start to the New Year Ian is lulled into a false sense of security as the first few months of 1977 are rather good; new bands to see and classic records to buy. In addition to this Manchester United are on a winning streak, playing with gusto and bravado. Most importantly Julie and Ian appeared to be getting closer and closer. It was a very innocent relationship with no touching or kissing, but they became intimate in terms of sharing confidences and spending a lot of time together. Ian likens their relationship to *a cauldron of emotions waiting to simmer over.*

Julie used to joke that they could never really be together as they were The

'Hippy' and the 'Punk'. But both knew that as sure as they were oddly matched they were meant to be together. Each attempted to get to know each other better through their contrasting taste in music. Julie listened to The Pistols, The Damned, Patti Smith and 'Low' by Bowie which was Ian's favourite; she hated them. Ian suffered Ritchie Havens, Al Stewart, Ralph McTell and the nauseous James Taylor, all for love.

One wet night, Julie appeared to be really troubled and Ian wanted to know what was wrong and eventually she confided in him. Ian believed her reasoning to be muddled but this played on his mind and upset him. However, he had agreed to meet up with his old friends, Colin Swan and Steve, later that evening and didn't want to let them down. Maybe this was what he needed anyway so all three found themselves at 'The Phoenix' where there was a DJ who spun a smattering of Punk along with the more traditional Rock and Roll records.

As soon as The Stranglers 'Go Buddy, Go' came on all three hit the dance floor. Ian has always loved to dance and lose himself in the music. All three lads have a huge laugh, gooning and mugging about. Colin decided to go that little bit further and grabs hold of Ian's shirt at the front and, with one mighty tug, tears it from his back. Ian thought this was a huge joke, hugged Colin and had some more to drink.

Warm Leatherette – The Normal

It would be fair to say Ian wasn't exactly sober when he was travelling back home to Denton;

'I'll walk round to Julie's Parents and wait a few hours until she gets up and say my piece to her"

This seemed like a really good idea to Ian as he walked in the torrential rain. Shirtless Ian had to pull his coat around him, believing that this act of selfless devotion would impress upon her the sincerity of his devotion. It was worth getting soaked to let her know that he really cared.

After Ian had walked a mile, thinking beautiful thoughts about this romantic act of self-sacrifice he was woken from this reverie by a loud

"BANG'!!!!

From the corner of his eye he saw a figure being catapulted from a Mini that was wrapped around the lamppost. Ian ran into the garden and found a young lad, around his own age, covered in blood. He had come through the window screen but was still conscious, as Ian managed to help him to his feet draping the young guy's arm around him. Mercifully, Ian managed to flag down a passing motorist to help and the Police arrived, very soon after, at the scene of the accident.

"Thank Fuck'

Ian thought as an ambulance was called to take the young lad, who had now lapsed into unconsciousness along with another lad, who had been in the car, off for treatment.

Ian looked a real fright. He was not only soaked but was literally covered in blood. Ian was then taken to the Police Station, as he assumed he was to give a statement. But instead of the warm welcome he was expecting he was forcibly thrown into a police cell. Bloody Hell! He thought he would be given a nice, hot drink and a towel but instead he found himself thrown in to a cell with just a bed.

About five minutes after Ian tried to make himself comfortable as there was no mattress, a policeman comes in.

"You ready to give a statement, you thieving little bastard?!"

Ian tries to explain what has just taken place and he is ordered to;

"Stand Up!"

As Ian does what he is ordered the Policeman thumps Ian in the stomach. Ian keels over in pain and makes his way back on to the bed as the Policeman leaves the cell.

Ian wants to sleep but the door is opened again by two Policemen very shortly after.

The Police continue to interrogate Ian by punching and screaming at him;

"Where have you been then, Sunny Jim?"

"I've just come back from an evening in Manchester, I live in Denton"

"Then what the Fuck are you doing in Audenshaw? "

Ian had to admit he looked all wrong, covered in blood and shirtless but was not going to have these bastards extract a false confession from him again. Ian was tired, shivering with cold, frightened and helpless but he stuck to the truth.

"Your two mates, who you nicked this car with, might not make it."

The Policemen continued with their intimidating interrogation technique in an effort to break Ian's spirit;

"You are in BIG trouble and you had better start talking if you know what's good for you!"

Ian was absolutely determined not to confess to a crime he had not committed, they could hit him all they wanted, which they continued to do until they left him alone for an hour.

An older Senior Ranking Officer comes with a blanket which Ian wraps around him. Ian is then taken into a room with desks and chairs; a nice cup of tea finally arrives;

"I am really pleased to inform you that your story corroborates with what I have just learned from one of the lads who has now regained consciousness. This lad has just made a statement and his vindicated any involvement concerning you."

Ian is not impressed, but the Officer continues;

'I apologise for what has happened, but you do appreciate that we do need to catch criminals and sometimes innocent bystanders, such as yourself, can get caught up in this through no fault of their own."

Ian is nonplussed by this explanation and the Station Superintendents comes in to the room and offers Ian a lift home.

"Sorry about what you experienced in the Police Cell, son. There will be no official record kept, but I do want to put things right for you and if ever you need a 'favour' just call for me?"

Ian is just relieved his ordeal has finally come to an end and he just wants to go home, now.

"Thank You"

Ian knew that he would never need that 'favour' and the words of a song by Bob Dylan came to mind;

'To live outside the law, you must be honest'

Both of his parents were very suspicious of Ian's account of events, surely it couldn't happen twice....could it? Anyway it was too late to go for work so Ian caught up on some much needed sleep. When he explained his day's absence at work, he failed to convince his doubting bosses.

Even Julie failed to be impressed by the act of dramatic devotion to her and informed Ian

"You're fucking stupid. My problem was only a storm in a teacup anyway'.

Ian realised he should have taken legal advice concerning his bully boy interrogation by the Police. But instead he retreated to the safety of his bedroom with the soundtrack of 'No Pussy Footing' and the self-harming began again.

'Turn Blue' Iggy Pop

It was Ian's mother, of all people who spotted the article in the Manchester Evening News and as soon as Ian arrived home she passed him the paper

"Here you go, love. There's something to interest you!"

Ian took the paper and she was absolutely right. The headline indicated that David Bowie was to be playing keyboards at The Apollo for no less than Iggy Pop. For once, Ian is stunned into silence at the thought of this dream combination. This was a very low key gig and tickets were to go on sale tomorrow and.....

"Oh, No"

"What is it pet?"

Asked his mother

"I won't be able to queue for the tickets tomorrow and they are going to all sell out"

"Don't worry son, I can easily cycle there on my lunch break'

His father kindly offered.
"Dad if you could that would save my life, but the queue will be massive"
"Don't worry, son"
Eddie smiled at Ian.

Ian still has this lovely mental picture of his elderly father, with his bike, chatting cheerfully in the queue with all the Bowie Clones and Proto Punks

Ian's expectations were high, so high he genuinely wondered if Iggy Pop could live up to them, he was the fantasy soundtrack to Ian's life. On the night Ian was virtually beside himself with anticipation and excitement.

Hunt and Tony Sales came on stage to herald the imminent arrival of Iggy Pop and David Bowie. Ian was aware of the pedigree of these two musicians as they had both played with Todd Rundgren. Ricky Gardiner came on stage closely followed by Bowie who was the very personification of effortless cool in a casual shirt and corduroy trousers. Iggy Pop, appeared to a huge cheer, and looks very different from The Stooge album covers with black, slick, short hair matching his stage attire.

The band launches into 'Raw Power' and Ian is tingling with sheer joy. Ian's breath is sucked out of him when '1969' is experienced live, at last! The sound was stripped down and stark with no frills, almost punk-like in its minimalism. Although the sound and Iggy Pop are just great, Ian experiences a form of mild irritation with the large Bowie faction who are making it abundantly clear who they are there for. Ian just shakes this irritation off – this is Iggy's night and Ian knows it.

New songs are debuted, such as 'The Dum, Dum Boys' introduced by Iggy as a eulogy for anyone who knew The Stooges, other fallen souls and those barely standing. Ian nearly wiped away a tear after Iggy finished this announcement.

The highlight, for Ian, was a new number called 'Turn Blue' which was a dramatic number about an overdose. Ian can still feel the shiver down his spine when Iggy turned his face into the full spot light and declared

"Jesus, this is Iggy."

Ian was later stunned when he later bought 'The Idiot' and this brilliant track was not on the album.

More Stooges songs followed, 'TV Eye', 'No Fun' and 'I Wanna Be Your Dog.'

Ian reflected on the show on the way home. There was none of the wildness and savagery he had expected. If anything the show had been disciplined, tight and there was no excess of any kind. Ian believed it was a glorious triumph for Iggy. With hindsight Ian speculates that there were plenty of future Manchester Band members who were present that night who would plagiarise that raw and striped down sound and claim it as their own.

Go ahead Punk, Make my day Clint Eastwood

Ian has fond, vivid memories of the records, he purchased in the early months of 1977. He can still recall exactly where he got each record and even snippets of the conversation he had with the record store assistants. He was able to track down the rare debut EP by Buzzcocks but even this valuable find was overshadowed by a copy of The Stooges debut LP. Amongst the other significant purchases were ' This Perfect Day' single by The Saints, 'Less than Zero' by Elvis Costello, 'Marquee Moon' by Television, the 'Damned, Damned, Damned' LP, 'White Riot/1977' by The Clash, and 'Trans Europe Express' by Kraftwerk.

Ian was regularly consulted by his peers on what were good records to buy as he knew what 'the real deal' was and which bands were merely jumping on the Punk bandwagon.

This respect pleased and flattered him -superficially. But below the surface, the self-destructive aspect of his personality was beginning to manifest itself again. One night in Cox's Bar, after drinking alone, an inner demon compelled him to rage against the world and that it needed to pay him some attention. He lowered his trousers and stood at the bar facing the room and started to scream abuse at the clientele. Ian was immediately ejected from the bar and got no more than about twenty yards before he collapsed in a heap, in the middle of the road and curled up into a ball.

'There's a body in the road!'

Ian was vaguely aware this was a female voice and footsteps came towards him;

'Are you OK, Mate?'

A male voice asked and reassuring hands were laid on Ian's back;

'Bloody Hell! It's Moet!'

It was none other than Ian's guardian angel Robert!

Robert had finally managed to secure a date with a girl he had been chasing after for ages, but this came to an abrupt end when they found Ian lying in the road. Although it is true to say that Robert wasn't exactly pleased, he managed to get Ian out of danger and half carried Ian home.

Ian thought LSD was good as he believed it gave him great spiritual and inner truth and the more he took the better this introspection became. The truth of this is debatable but the major side effect was that it caused him to be increasingly analytical of even the most mundane chore… It was becoming increasingly harder for him to function and cope in everyday life.

The drug intake was not helping his volatile relationship with Julie, there had been a dreadful emotional trauma and Ian was tipped over the edge as she called it a day. So on the evening of the cup final Ian found himself travelling to London in John Smethhursts car, with Eric Cox and Ritchie Bewick, continuing to self-medicate with a bottle of whisky after a session at the pub. Ian was absolutely paralytic when he arrived in London and thought it would be a good idea to take on a Canadian backpacker resulting in a massive fight in which Ian came off far the worst. John took Ian, who was bleeding profusely to the local hospital. At 2am, after a long wait, the Casualty Nurse decided to administer an injection and Ian's trousers were lowered, catching sight of the huge needle and jumped of the trolley and screamed:

"No needles, NO NEEDLES!"

Ian wanted to escape, trousers still half mast, and hotly pursued by Doctors and Nurses he ran through the wards delirious with drugs, drink and fear before being ejected by security.

When Ian regained consciousness, he experienced a curious sensation of moving up and down. Was this the result of a lethal combination of drugs and booze? No the resourceful Ian had managed to locate lift and fall asleep in it. The lift stopped and the door opened to reveal a smart, middle aged lady carrying a briefcase. The sight of a blood splattered would be attacker caused her to scream and she fled in terror. Ian hightailed his way to Euston Station where he met up with some fellow Manchester United Supporters who took him for a dip in the local swimming baths and after a good breakfast Ian felt almost human again. After finishing in the café Ian saw a copy of 'Raw Power, even though he and Neil owned a copy, he purchased it anyway, feeling like it was some form of talisman.

More booze followed before the cup final in which Manchester beat Liverpool 2-1. Not that Ian saw much of it as he kept falling over, ironically only seeing the goal scored by Liverpool. Things did not improve as Ian managed to get in to another punch up with a Dutchman after the match and was thrown out of the bar at Dorchester for being disruptive. The crowning glory was being sick over The Statue of Eros in the presence of several disgusted tourists before managing to spend the rest of Saturday night in a chair next to a lift. Still clutching his precious copy of 'Raw Power' Ian began the long weary hike back to Manchester

Play that funky music white boy! Wild Cherry

Ian was a tastemaker for us. He turned me on to the Who and the Pistols and Syd Barrett among others. He is a passionate man who is unafraid to express his opinion. And he LOVES his music, which is never a bad thing **Mick Hucknall**

Everything was not complete carnage and utter chaos in Ian's life as he began to spend more and more time with Steven, who had moved to nearby Droylesden, with his young family. Steve delighted Ian with a gift of 20 Kinks singles which he managed to 'liberate' from his father in law.

It was around this time that Steven set about trying to convince Ian that they really should form a band. It seemed like a good idea, but Ian was not so sure as they would have difficulty attracting like-minded individuals who could play. Robert was originally mooted as a member but Ian knew that wouldn't work. Steven suggested other potential band members known to both of them. Ian knew they would not fit in…they thought Rory Gallagher was cool! The name Bob Williams, Steven's long term friend came up time and time again. Ian would have approached Bob, but he was currently working in the South of France. Admittedly, it was this Bob's free spirited attitude that met with Ian's approval but both he and Steven would have to wait until Bob's return.

During a conversation Steven confided to Ian that he has had enough of family life and he just wants to escape. He has planned to go to Newquay for the summer and was going to leave imminently. This was a shock to Ian and he felt as if Steven was really deserting him and not Trish (the long suffering wife).

Ian was bereft and wanted to make the most of their remaining time together and they went into Manchester the day before Steven's departure. Both made the best of their talent for getting drinks off people, as they had no money and did rather well out of using their considerable charm and nerve. They somehow managed to end up in a predominantly Black Club which was situated in Fenel Street (behind the Cathedral). The funk music appealed to both lads but both good will and money had run out. But Bacchus was not going to let them down as the dance floor was cleared and ten chairs were placed in readiness for…..a drinking competition! Needless to say, Steven and Ian were first in the line of entrants and there was a good humoured atmosphere as the rest of the competitors took off their shirts, waved them around and flexed their muscles in a parody of machismo.

10 pints of fresh, foamy beer were given to each contestant and then a fanfare to prepare and then shouts of

"Down in one, go, go, go!"

Steven and Ian took gentle sips, little fingers aloft, clinked their pint glasses together in a toast and exited the stage to roars of laughter and applause from the crowd

The night ended up with Ian crashing out on Steven's sofa, but he was able to get up in the morning and wave Steven 'Farewell' for now.

Glad to be Gay Tom Robinson Band 1977

Whilst Ian could not fault young Neil's impeccable taste in music (he liked what Ian liked) his sartorial style was highly suspect in Ian's opinion. With hindsight, Ian wonders if the choice of the flared jean 'scruff' look was a statement of individuality. During a conversation that eventually took place between the brothers, many years later, it transpired that Neil did feel that Ian had cast an enormous shadow over him.

Neil chose to hang out with his smelly 'hippy' friends in such dives as 'The Spread Eagle' in Ashton and 'Jilly's' in Manchester where Ian once found himself standing next to Howard Devoto at a neighbouring urinal and asked;

"Howard, what's this about you forming a band with Glen Matlock?""

"Not on the same wavelength"

Was the suitably enigmatic reply from the man of mystery. Howard was going to take his own time and direction.

When Ian got up for work he often found he had to step around the Afghan coated bodies of Neil's new friends, who had crashed out in this parent's living room. Both parents were very considerate and tiptoed around them for fear of disturbing the huddled forms.

"Oh! Ian! Don't wake them!"

Pleaded Ian's Mum in a loud stage whisper as Ian went towards the record player;

"Don't worry Mummy."

Came Ian's reply in a rather precocious tone;

"They're so fast asleep I bet you don't hear a peep out of them.'

Ian knew full well that these youngsters were merely 'pretending' to be asleep and if they were who cared because he was going to put his music on. After a good blast of both A and B sides of The Sex Pistols Ian headed out to work. Well, it had served them right really, that group had very likely been listening to some crap like Lynyrd Skynyrd. Why, Ian had more than likely done them a favour and had provided some form of decontamination service to get rid of all that rubbish they had listened to the night before.

Mick Hucknall was about the only one of Neil's friends that Ian hung out with too. His first memory of is of a young Mick, aged no more than 5 or 6, singing during school dinners at St Lawrence Primary School.

Mick Hucknall had sung in a variety of 'cover's Rock Bands singing numbers by The Rolling Stones and Ted Nugent. But both he and Neil had taken to writing their own material and were busy rehearsing for the cult band later to become 'The Frantic Elevators'. One day they proudly came to Ian and announced;

"Hey Ian, We've decided to call ourselves 'Elevation'!

"Why?"

"It's a track on the 'Marquee Moon' album, you know by 'Television'

"I know that! It's an awful name! It sounds too old and reminds me of velvet loon pants and love beads!"

Both lads looked absolutely crestfallen by Ian's rejection. Sensing that Mick and Neil obviously valued his opinion Ian decided to help out;

"Aw! Give yourself a chance lads! How about 'The Elevators', you know, just like Rocky Eriksson, you know the "Thirteenth Floor Elevators?"

So it came to pass Ian had helped to create the name that would launch Mick Hucknall's first notable band.

Ian would occasionally bump into Mick in a pub during lunch times. Mick was there with his college friends exuding confidence and charisma, all qualities that would propel him towards stardom. Once in a while, Mick would accompany Ian to gigs. They both went to the first 'Stiff' Artists Tour and a freebie at The Electric Circus with the Jam, Buzzcocks and Penetration on the list. Later, both attended a gig with The Tom Robinson Band (TRB). Mick Hucknall was self-assured enough in his own sexual orientation to bellow out the lyrics to 'Glad to be Gay'. The young Mick Hucknall was good company; furthermore he was a positive influence on young Neil, who also shared Ian's tendency to be somewhat insular and withdrawn at times.

(If you don't wanna) Fuck (Me) Off Wayne (Now Jayne) County and the Electric Chairs

Kim Scott was a lad who had started work on the same day of work as Ian and bonded over a shared love of Stevie Wonder. However they were spending less and less time at Technical College, owing to work pressures, and Ian voiced his concern over this. Kim agreed and Ian suggested;

"Ok, let's sort it out.'

"Ok."

"Let me do the talking, just back me up."

Both lads went marching straight up to the office to see Phil Leech, the manager,

"What's up Lads?"

Ian states their case concisely and Phil Leech listens intently and replied;

"Oh, I see, and just how big an issue is this to you?"

Ian feels very confident, as if he holds all the aces and stated;

"It's simple. Sort it out and or we give our notice in as from now"

Phil Leech is visibly stunned by this reply but also picks up from Kim's reaction that this is news and turns to Kim, looks him straight in the eye and asked;

"This is your position as well, Kim?"

"Ww well.... I wouldn't go quite that far."

Ian was furious at this treacherous turn coat who had backed down out of fear. Ha! Ian could practically smell the poo in his pants. So much for 'Unity in Strength'. Ian never forgave him for this betrayal.

Ian was viewed with a curious mixture of suspicion and admiration by his bosses at work. There was no doubt that he was a talented young designer who had proved his worth by winning several awards 'Indeed, one of the awards led Ian to be invited for an interview on the local Red Rose Radio station (Blackburn). Coincidently, Ian found himself sharing the waiting area with no less than Ian Dury and The Kilburn's whom he had the pleasure of seeing the previous evening.

Ian wasn't too bothered by the fact that Senior Management had 'their eye' on him; he actually quite liked this as it kept him on his toes. Although he only had eyes and heart for Julie, he was still very much the object of admiration from the opposite sex. Two girls at Ian's work place decided to 'compete' for Ian's attention and began to make up stories in order to wind each other up. These stories escalated and began to compromise and implicate Ian. Ian felt his trust and friendly nature had been betrayed. As a result, he just wanted this unpleasantness to end, went straight to the top, and handed in his resignation to the podgy hands of Mr Clive Eyre, the new millionaire owner of the company. Mr Eyre was taken aback but knew of Ian's prowess and asked;

"Ian, I want you to reconsider. You are the future of this company and if you are unhappy I am sure we can work things out. Please give me some time to see if we can come to some form of arrangement."

Ian had nothing to lose and decided to see what happened out of interest's sake. Mr Eyre was as good as his word and, after a series of internal meetings, gave Ian a hefty pay rise and gave the two girls a severe reprimand that would result in them being sacked if ever they tried to bad mouth anyone ever again. This was fair enough and Ian decided to stay with the company, he was virtually 'untouchable'.

Ian had actually become rather good friends with the previous manager, Phil Leech, who had been made redundant as a result of the takeover. Phil was a really nice bloke who had smiled with recognition when he espied Ian's Edgar Broughton Badge pin at the original interview in 1973. Furthermore Phil was certainly no stranger to performing and played in 'The 'Biggles Wartime Band' that had echoes of 'The Bonzo Dog Doo Da Band'. This band had quite a following on the Northern Folk Circuit and meant that Phil was no dullard.

Phil asked Ian to help in his quest to set up a new company as he needed a top drawer designer. Ian was only too happy to help Phil out and got a delicious sense of pleasure 'moon lighting' away from his workplace, maybe this would result in a form of 'Industrial Espionage' that would bring Ian's employers down? Ian enjoyed their twice weekly work sessions and learnt a lot from Phil's chats. Phil also opened Ian's eyes up in a few matters and Ian leaned, even more, the importance of not taking things on face value.

Ian had yet another admirer at work called Carol; who had since become engaged to his old nemesis Kim Scott. She worked very closely with Ian as he was her departmental head. Ian was aware that she 'liked' him but certainly did not encourage anything beyond a good working relationship.

It was the day of Carol's birthday and Ian had given her a nice card. It so happened that Carol had celebrated a bit too much during her lunch hour. This was no real problem and Ian decided to take her off machinery for the afternoon. Carol saw Ian's Birthday card as more than a kind gesture and wanted to let Ian know that she knew what this really meant. She decided to amplify this knowledge by coming up, repeatedly to thank him for the card and draped her arm around Ian each time. As the factory is open plan, Kim can see exactly what Carol and Ian are 'up to' and Ian does not want to exasperate the situation

"Come on now, Carol, cut it out now and get back to some work!"

Carol will not be put off so easily and declares loudly;

"You are the love that I never wanted! But I love you more than anyone else"

Everyone in the factory can hear this declaration of unrequited love and she continues;

"I'll give you everything.....Love, money..... Food and Sex!"

This is too much for Kim and he totters over to Ian in his high platform boots with flairs flapping furiously. Actually, Kim was a dead ringer for Peter Wyngarde with a moustache, the usual medallion swinging between his unbuttoned flower motif shirt and using dialogue that would not be out of place in a 'thirties film warned Ian;

"If I catch you ever talking to my girlfriend again.... I'll punch you on the nose!"

It was the final straw and Ian slowly rose from his stool and said;

"Fuck Off."

Then he head butted Kim. Kim reeled in pain and ran, not unlike a drunken whore, in his high heels screaming;

"Sack him! Sack him!"

Ian shook his head, he actually felt sorry for him.

God Save The Queen The Sex Pistols June 1977

The frenzy whipped up by the media resulted in 'God Save The Queen' being banned from any radio play which increased sales. Banned, number two in some spurious record chart, Ian didn't care it was their best record yet. But Ian found it difficult to even walk down the streets such was the campaign of media hatred against Punk Rock. The lyrics could be construed as a direct attack on her Majesty and Ian found the constant experience of being verbally and physically assaulted very wearing. However, to counteract this, his relationship with

Julie had blossomed and for a brief period both are blissfully happy. Ian has even taken to drinking sensibly and is genuinely sunny in a way he hadn't been since he was a very young boy.

However, all was not completely clean in Ian's life. He had hooked up with an old friend called Jim Davis who was into high quality prescription amphetamine and frequently broke in to dispensing chemists to steal this drug. Jim was a veteran of both' Wigan Casino' and The Blackpool Mecca' as well as host of lesser known Northern Soul venues. Jim found it hard to score acid but Ian was able to locate this drug with ease a mutual arrangement came to pass. Julie, when she found Ian's stash, flushed it down the toilet. He was only mildly pissed off and rather pleased that she thought enough to protect him against himself.

All was contentment between Ian and Julie, but it was to be their differing attitudes and taste that would cause a very serious ruction. She had very middle class values and Ian was rooted in working class socialist politics and his tastes were more eclectic and unconventional.

This difference in musical taste and attitude finally surfaced when Ian took Julie to see 'Joy Division' at the Factory Club in Hulme. Headlining were the highly controversial band, Suicide, from New York and Ian absolutely loved their minimal, stripped down electro synthesiser form of Rock and Roll. Suicide were subjected to a stage invasion by some members of the disgruntled audience who proceeded to kick and punch the duo. Ian really admired Suicide's sheer nerve as they proceeded to finish their set.

On the way home a discussion concerning the merits of the 'Suicide' sound was instigated by Ian as Julie was very, very quiet. After listening to Ian extolling the originality and sheer guts exhibited by 'Suicide' that evening Julie could take no more.

"Ian, I thought they were really stupid and I didn't enjoy listening to that shit! Why can't you check out some real music like Cat Steven's?"

"Fuck that! I would rather put my own eyes out with hot needles!"

Very soon after this 'musical difference' Julie dumped Ian. Now he wasn't to know that this would be a familiar pattern in their relationship and was absolutely devastated, he was sure that they would never get back together again. All the cheerfulness and sunshine was replaced by a dark depression which would last, in varying degrees, for the next ten years until he learned how to control this beast. Ian made himself ill by speculating about 'what might have been' and turned to self-harming himself in the sanctuary of his bedroom. In addition to the self-mutilation with razor blades Ian also tried to numb his pain with neat whisky and barbiturates.

One night, Ian was on the bus back from Manchester after wandering the streets like a soulless zombie. The alcohol had failed to numb the pain and he found himself sobbing, uncontrollably, to the embarrassment of his fellow passengers. The only person who asked Ian if he was 'OK' was the bus conductor who wouldn't take Ian's fare. Ian felt touched by this genuine and human concern, but by the time Ian had got home he had icily resolved to kill himself. He wrote a note for his parents and hunted for some tablets that his mother took for a heart condition, Ian reasoned that if he took enough of them they would induce a heart attack. Ian found them and swallowed them down with a glass of water. But they wouldn't stay down and he kept bringing them up. Persisting, Ian swallowed them again and again until they all stayed down. Ian cleared up the vomit around the kitchen sink, turned the lights out and lay down to die.

It's true that saying 'Things look better in the morning'

Ian woke up with the sun streaming through a crack in the curtains, he didn't know whether to laugh or cry, but he felt no compulsion to finish the job off. As he was the first to have awakened he rushed downstairs to destroy the letter to his parents – after having a little cry when he read it. Ian went to bed and he knew full well what would happen next and he was absolutely correct.

About an hour later the bedroom door flew open and there stood one furious and upset Mother.

You selfish so and so! You've taken ALL my tablets! After your cheap thrills how on earth am I going to manage to go on until my next prescriptions due! My ARTHRITIS will be AGONY"

Ian could have laughed at the absurdity of the situation. Ian had managed to take the wrong tablets, bloody 'eck he couldn't even do that right.

Later on that morning, Ian went to Ashton to get some paints, brushes and pads. Ian wanted to do something creative but, yet again this was to prove to be a mere and temporary diversion but little did he know it; help was on the horizon in the form of a homeward bound Bobby Williams.

Ding Dong! The Frantic Elevators

Mick Hucknall and Neil identified with 'Lennon and McCartney' and their inspiration was more Mersey Beat than Punk Rock. But what they lacked in modern day inspiration they more than made up for in sheer hard graft. Both lads were constantly writing and rehearsing new songs, and whilst Ian lauded the hard work he also wished that they would just 'lighten up' once in a while.

All their perseverance finally paid off when they unveiled 'The Frantic Elevators' in the late summer supporting Bethnal at the Rafters venue. Mick certainly looked the part, Ian had to admit, but the rest of the band, Mark Reeder, wearing a German uniform, on bass and young Neil did not exactly look terribly 'New Wave'. The drummer, Steve Tansley, took the prize for naffness in his split loon pants and Afghan Coat. Despite this totally uncool look, they won the audience over and received warm applause. Word soon got around and 'The Frantic Elevators' became regular fixtures on the local circuit and as well as appearing at Rafters, they also managed to appear at the prestigious Factory venue and even the legendary Band on the Wall.

Ian rather liked their short, quirky songs which were fresh and tuneful and he was quick to offer genuine encouragement. The band evolved into a much more competent outfit over a long period, but Ian remembers their 'baby step' days with much fondness. Mick was a brilliant vocalist but rather unfortunately he chose to coil himself in the microphone stand as he had seen Howard Devoto do. This earned him the nickname of 'Squid' which resulted in Mike dropping the mannerisms and developing his own style.

If truth be known Ian was closer to Mick during this time than he was to his younger brother. This was a shame as Ian knew that Neil had his own troubles but there was coldness and a distance between the two brothers which meant that Ian couldn't really help. For example, Mick and Neil had wanted the band to go in a more rootsier, Rhythm and Blues sound, but Mark wanted a much more experimental sound. Again Ian's opinion was sought and instead of supporting his brother, Ian sided with the direction that Mark wanted to pursue. Not that his opinion was taken any heed of as this was Mick and Neil's band; and anyway Mark was soon to immigrate to his spiritual home of Berlin where his ideas would come to fruition.

Another Green World Eno

Bobby Williams was no drinker, I saw him once demand that we all go for Chinese food, after ordering his food he had one sip of a lager and when his meal turned up his head collapsed into his food but to be fair, he had been drinking for several hours beforehand Colin Swan

Bobby Williams, as photos taken at that time testify, was strikingly handsome. Young girls would compare his features to that of David Essex, David Cassidy or Paul McCartney and he would use his good looks to full advantage on the unsuspecting teenage fan club. Ian would later name him 'Cute Bobby' which sort of backfired as Bobby hardly rose to this bait.

Bob Williams was also deemed to be very cute by females and when I heard a bimbo say "Bobby, where have you been Bobby". I thought I was going to choke Colin Swan

At last Bobby had come back to Manchester at the very beginning of autumn. He was tanned from working on the French Riviera, which added to his good looks. The concept of 'Punk Rock' crossed over the English Channel and the French were absolutely intrigued by this, word had reached Bobby and he wanted to find out what all 'the malarkey' was about.

As fate would have it both Ian's and Bobby's fathers, Eddie and Stan, were close friends and played snooker together. Eddie proudly bought home a painting that had been given to him by Stan and made the mistake of asking Ian what he thought.

"It's absolute rubbish"

The painting depicted a very cutesy wutsey country scene, complete with running stream next to a cottage complete with smoking chimney. The painting, despite Ian's critique, took pride of place on the wall. It transpired that the painting was by none other than Bobby and it was the subject of much gentle teasing from Ian. It was Bobby's 'Green Period' and Bobby would laugh along with Ian. His self-deprecating sense of humour really appealed to Ian, who acknowledges that Bobby is a talented artist who just had a penchant for some really dodgy compositions.

Besides Eddie and Stan's friendship, both had a lot in common. They came from very similar backgrounds where luxuries were not taken for granted and Bobby too, had a job he disliked. But like Ian, he was imbued with a new puritanical work ethic and worked hard at his job in a local photographic studio. Both knew they had to earn their keep and were good workers.

Bobby and Ian's parents lived close together and Bobby would frequently crash out on his parent's sofa. After Bobby came back from France, he and Ian began to see a great deal of each other. Bobby was a huge reggae fan and kept Ian in constant stitches with his constant use of Rastafarian colloquialisms such as 'I and I' and shrieks of 'Jah Rastafari! Like many a good white Rastafarian Bobby loved his 'pot' and one could say that he smoked this religiously.

Bobby could also play guitar and he and Ian did a very loose version of '"Woolly Bully' by the sixties group Sam Sham and The Pharoes. Anyone who has ever 'heard' this classic would agree that the vocals are virtually indecipherable, this was part of the appeal for Ian as he could make his own words up whilst Bobby strummed along to the increasingly bizarre script.

Ian asked Mick and Neil if he and Bobby might play at a "Frantic Elevators" gig as some form of support at a working men's club at which Mick collected the glasses. Both Mick and Neil eagerly agreed.

I can't believe they allowed any of us on that stage! Thanks to their kindness they did. I have wonderful memories of that place, which I see now is a curry house!
Mick Hucknall

The evening comes and the audience has to stand through a dire Punk parody band that was recruited by Mark or Neil. The nepotism continued as Craig Paulo, a friend of Neil's, plays acoustic guitar complete with a really contrived American accent, this at least merited some sniggering from Ian and Bobby.

Then they were on! Bobby and Ian were fortunate enough to be backed by the 'Frantics' rhythm section and this gave them an extra edge. They chose to debut a song entitled 'You', in fact this was the title and the single word lyric. Ian intoned 'You' in a variety of fashions, whilst Bobby chugged along with the riff. Both Bobby and Ian really enjoyed themselves and the 'Frantics' (Steve and Mark) are having a blast too, the audience even gamely try to pogo to this surreal thing

After a loud blast of applause they all launch into 'Woolly Bully'. Oh dear, it was out of tune, out of time with the wrong chords and wrong words but it crackles with absolute energy. This experience is exactly the same as Blackpool, three years earlier and again Ian knew that he owned the stage.

As soon as the set had begun it was all over and both are showered with compliments, Neil even hugs Ian – which meant one hell of a lot to Ian at that time. Mick Hucknall is genuinely impressed even though he believed that 'You' was a wicked parody of a 'Frantic Elevator's' number of the same title. Ian laughs.

"Ian'

Mick began quite seriously;

"You were great just then, miles better than I thought you'd be. You have to carry on now. You're great on stage a tiger!"

It is then time for The Frantic Elevators go on stage and continue to do a very professional set. Ian knows that Bobby and he have made a start but the previous mantra of 'When Bobby comes back' had now turned into 'Where's Steven"?

The Part Time Punks by The Television Personalities

Ian was in pretty much of a mess around this time and couldn't get his act together. This was mainly due to Julie's rejection of him and he needed to be far, far away. A typical weekend began with tea with his parents. He would go into town and spend his wages on drugs and alcohol. The midnight bus to London Victoria left from Chorlton Street Bus Station, and there was always a long queue. If the bus was full, Ian would invest in a bottle of spirits and with a handful of speed and wait to catch the 07.00 bus to London. Sometimes he would march in to smart hotel reception foyers and wish the staff a hearty;

'Good Night!'

Those staff who were alert enough realised that this dishevelled creature could not possibly be a guest and shouted for Ian to stop. Now the chase was on! Sometimes Ian ran and managed to find a hiding place and the staff just went back to reception. There was no fun in this so Ian managed to creep downstairs and say;

"Boo!"

And all the fun would begin again. Usually this game ended with Ian being booted by security with a warning never to darken their revolving doors ever again. He played this entertaining game of 'hide and seek' at The Grand, The Midland and The Thistle. When Ian decided to pay The Portland another visit, the staff had no sense of fun and the Police got involved. Ian was thrown into a Black Maria and taken to Bootle Street station. Unfortunately, it was the Police's chance to have some unpleasant fun at Ian's expense. This incident was enough to put a stop to Ian's Hotel and from now on, if he missed the bus, he would seek the comparative safety of doorways.

If Ian was lucky, he managed to get a seat on the crowded midnight bus. Once he remembers falling asleep and woke up with a damp patch on his leg and it smelt of piss. The drunk, snoring next to him, had urinated over his Ian's leg. To add insult to injury, the piss had soaked into Ian's stash of speed for the weekend. But as Ian was so strung out on he acted as if nothing had happened, so intense was his drug induced paranoia.

After arriving in London, Ian would make straight for Soho and walk around singing 'No Fun' to himself. Dreaming was so much preferable to real life and Ian would imagine that he was a lost prince returning to his kingdom. It should be said that Ian was rather tasty at this stage in his life as he had lost a lot of weight and his hair was blonde and curly. He was approached by some louche men who wanted to do 'some businesses' with him. Ian found it rather fun to have some attention paid to him. But this 'cherub with a poisoned heart' enjoyed being something of a 'prick tease' but had absolutely no intention to bring this to a climax.

During one of these jaunts Ian was approached by a chap, in his mid-twenties, who asked Ian if he would be interested in appearing nude in a Gay magazine called 'Vulcan'. Ian was intrigued enough to go outside the office in Camden later on that day, but lacked the confidence to go in. This is a shame as the photo insert section in this book would be even more interesting.

During the daylight hours Ian would go up and down Kings Road as this was where all the phoney 'Punks' would choose to parade their part time wears. When Ian got bored of sneering at these 'Punk Mockers' he would go to visit a museum or art gallery. On one occasion Ian went to Stamford Bridge to watch Nottingham Forrest (then managed by Brian Clough) beat Chelsea. Ian's supply of speed was constantly washed down by a stream of alcohol.

Once evening had broken Ian would make it back to Soho, which he loved. If it was wet and chilly, so much the better as Ian felt this added to the atmosphere of excitement and best of all, no one knew Ian. If he had wanted to seize the moment he could have done, but was in no fit shape.

Ian got talking to a group of 'Punk's' in The Ship in Wardour Street. It was obvious, to Ian, that they had just purchased their smart and overpriced outfits in Carnaby Street and were out to impress. Ian listened politely to all their nonsense but his interest perked up when they revealed that they had some drugs to consume. Ian challenged;

"Show them, then!"

Reluctantly, a hand full of pills were pulled out of a pair of bondage trousers and displayed for Ian's closer inspection. This was a bad judgement as Ian snatched them and swallowed them in a heartbeat. The group was mortified and began to threaten Ian, but he knew they wouldn't follow through and giggled as they stormed out of the pub.

Ian had always wanted to go to the Marquee and finally made it through the hallowed doors later that same evening. Many of Ian's favourite groups and artists had played there, such as David Bowie, and Ian wanted to experience this venue and belong. But he was disappointed to find that this famous venue was full of 'Punk's', including the gaggle who had so generously donated their drug intake....

"Cunts! Fucking Fakes! Impostors"

Ian jeered and a fight looked as if it might erupt. Bouncers were called over and

"Calm yourself down, or you're out, mate"

Ian agreed and went to the bar and had another drink which did nothing to calm him down. The DJ was spinning the worst form of 'Punk' music such as 'The Vibrators' and 'Generation X', bands which had jumped on the bandwagon and had been signed up to major labels. It was fake and the fakes present at The Marquee were lapping it up. Ian was becoming increasingly hypersensitive and thinking really, really unpleasant thoughts.

The main band, The Depressions, come on stage to play their set. They look very pretty in white and matching blonde spiky hairdo's and the music they played was just as false sounding. The bunch of posers that passed for a 'punk audience' just loved their big chorus' and patronising rubbish, but there was one voice of dissent and it was becoming louder and louder

"FUCKING CUNTS! YOU ARE ALL FUCKING CUNTS"

Ian was grabbed, still screaming, by the bouncers who threw him out on the streets, push him to the ground and then proceeded to kick his head in. This was a complete contrast to all the fakery in the club; at last this was much more like it! This was real and Ian grins up at the lights and his assailants.

Ian's head is over the side of the pavement in the gutter, he can see blood

running towards the drain in the rain water. Ian remembers thinking:
"Work tomorrow, I must be getting off"

Beat on the Brat The Ramones

The Manchester Music Scene consisted of a lot of petty rivalry and bitching between local bands. The 'Frantic Elevators' were gaining a big following but their intensity was often construed as a form of arrogance and they simply didn't dress the part. The fact that they were gaining a very good reputation very quickly had not gone unnoticed by local groups. One such group was a dodgy, nearly forgotten bunch of glam tarts known as 'V2'. Now it would appear that 'V2' had no gripe with 'The Frantic Elevators' but some of their friends decided to beat up both Mick Hucknall and Neil quite badly up.

Shortly after this unprovoked assault Ian took some LSD and went out with Mick to watch Wayne County and the Electric chairs at Rafters. Ian was in a pleasantly dopey mood watching the antics onstage, when suddenly his arm was grabbed

"Gotta go, it's that bunch of bastards that beat Neil and me up!"

Mick was really scared and wanted to escape before he was assaulted again

Ian was in a really mellow state of mind but he knew that Mick couldn't run away. He might escape this time but the enemy would sense fear and would get him sooner or later

"I'll deal with it, Mick"

He goes over to the group and interrogates each terrified individual. The entire group denied being involved but, Ian decides to pour his pint over a gang member's head before leaving them, there was no further trouble.

Lust for Life Iggy Pop

'The Idiot' was the first solo album to be produced by Bowie. Iggy's vocals were suppler than in 'The Stooges' and the lyrics were funny and thought provoking combined with the perfect icy, visionary soundtrack created by Bowie. For Ian and Neil, this record stood out as being a classic.

The second, 'Lust for Life', was also produced by Bowie and was recorded under virtually the same circumstances as the debut. Yet, for Ian, this album was less reflective and more upbeat with a few notable expectations such as 'Turn Blue' which was the live number Ian adored. But it was the title track, 'Lust for Life' that issued a direct challenge to Ian's lifestyle. Ian was comforted by the thought that someone else, Iggy, empathised with what he was going through and the intriguing thought;

"If I can do it, so can you, you pussy"

Echoed around Ian's head and he really did try but this was to take time.

In October, Iggy was scheduled to play at the Apollo and Ian knew that he would be able to get tickets on the door as Bowie would not be appearing.

On the day of the gig Ian managed to turn up for his usual Sunday game with his football team. He was still suffering the effects from excessive alcohol and drugs from yet another joyless evening in Manchester but he didn't like to let his mates down so wobbled around the football pitch much to everyone's embarrassment. The Manager, Dennis, was rarely lost for words, but he was on this occasion and could only shake his head and look at Ian with a pained expression.

After the post-match pint at the local, Ian found himself being ignored by the rest of the lads for his cringe worthy ineptness on the football pitch. Ian felt like a 'naughty school boy' in disgrace and fumbled around in his pocket and found some magic mushrooms that had been given to him the previous evening.

"Oh well, down the hatch then!"

Thought Ian, as he emptied the contents of the silver foil into his mouth.

Twenty minutes later, Ian was in a right old state and was laughing hysterically at nothing in particular. He realised he possibly couldn't go home in this state so made his way to a friend from work, John Kenyon, who was visibly alarmed but gave him numerous cups of tea and sat though 'Jug Band Blues' by Syd Barrett again, and again and again. Ian really related to that particular track on that afternoon as it was the sound of a man falling apart. At last,

"I'm off."

"Goodbye."

Responded John who had done his best to make Ian feel safe and secure that afternoon and was still worried about young Ian, but knew better than to stop him

Ian decided to see if he could catch Iggy's sound check at Ardwick. He arrived to see Iggy surrounded by a small group and he was busy signing autographs. Ian observed this scene with dead eyes and drool running from the side of his mouth. In his drugged and confused state he believed he detected some sort of irony in that Iggy and he had now changed positions concerning drug abuse. The band launched in to a cover of 'Louie, Louie' which was one of Ian's favourite songs and they did it well.

Ian then proceeded to the pub; well it was opening time and was lucky enough to bump into Mark Jones, who was one of Neil's friends. Mark was good company and his presence managed to sooth Ian's inner turmoil. All Ian can remember about the gig was that Iggy had a large horse's tail swishing around from the seat of his pants as he cavorted around. Ian has since been told that it was a really good show, he was there, but not there.

Ian's social circle increased with some notable additions. Brian Leah, a veteran of the Northern Soul scene was indeed 'the oldest Punk in town' at over thirty and he really looked more like 'The Fonz', from the popular TV show 'Happy Days', rather than Sid Vicious. He had a deadpan humour which Ian really appreciated and was drawn to the energy of the punk sound. He was also about the most hard-core drug user Ian had ever met and consumed copious amounts of Amphetamine.

Brian was once spotted by a mutual acquaintance Roger; squatted against the outside walls of the Wigan Casino, head in hands, as the dawn broke.

'Where are you going later Brian?'

Asked Roger

"Hospital"

Came the deadpan reply.

Bobby knew a married couple called Anne and John Daniels who also became very good friends of Ian. They were a few years older and could remember the days of 'The 'Twisted Wheel', the birthplace of Northern Soul with great fondness. They also had a fantastic huge and varied record collection and Ian and Bobby were frequent guests at their remote stone cottage in Glossop. They were a friendly, hospitable couple and only too happy to share their supply of dope and homemade wine to the sounds of Bob Dylan, Neil Young and dub reggae.

Once in a while everyone would pile into John's car and head into Manchester to catch a band or two. John generally stayed sober and impassive but Anne would get merrily drunk and after a few more would emulate Britt Elkland's weird dance scene from the film 'The Wickerman'.

At the end of the evening, Ian would feel snug and safe, curled up under a blanket on their sofa or floor, and watch the dying embers of their open fire. He was safe from himself, as these kind people brought out the best in him and he would sleep soundly as a result.

Alas, these spells of contentment were only transitory as Ian began, more and more, endlessly tormenting himself over what had happened between Julie and himself. He went over and over what could have been and should have been in his head, over and over again.

Ian buys a pack of razorblades and waits at the bus stop he knows she will catch her bus. Julie appears and upon spotting Ian looks very uncomfortable and doesn't want to talk. Ian takes out a blade, holds out his arm and in a macabre Pete Townsend like guitar chop brought down the blade and slices through his wrist, once, twice three times.

The other people who are congregated at the bus stop gasp in horror.

"You Stupid Bastard."

Said Julie and Ian turned and walked away into the night.

As a result of his injuries Ian had to go on sick leave. The 'official' explanation was 'a gardening accident', this version also kept Ian from a psychiatric assessment and very likely from being sectioned under the Mental Health Act. Despite the fact Ian was off sick, his work mates from the shop floor insisted that he attend the Annual Christmas Lunch that had been booked. Despite Ian's excuses, he was persuaded to come along and was really touched by the warmth and kindness shown to him by his fellow workers.

Ian had no spark and no vitality, Christmas Day was dismal but Bobby popped over to see him and asked him if he would like to go to Torquay. He had friends there and they would put the pair of them up. Whilst Ian didn't know Bobby that well, as yet, he was touched by the idea of being invited and maybe this would be a good chance to get to know each other better, so Ian agreed to go.

On Boxing Day both Bobby and Ian decided to hitchhike down to Torquay, in order to save what little money they both had. There is nothing like hitch-hiking in the sleet and snow to bond people together, unfortunately there is also nothing like trying to hitch a lift as a duo, as drivers are much less likely to stop. Somehow Bobby and Ian managed to get as far as West Bromwich Albion's Football Ground, another three hours freezing and teeth chattering, the lads decided to catch a bus into Birmingham City Centre. They actually managed to find a café that was open and ordered two orange juices. The ever resourceful Bobby literally had something up his sleeve and slipped some contraband vodka into each glass. The glasses were topped up and two hours later, when the vodka ran out, both Bobby and Ian staggered to get a bus to Exeter and then, blowing the limited budget, to Torquay.

Uptown Top Rankin by Althea and Donna

It was late in the evening when the lads made it to Torquay, but just as Bobby had promised, they had a roof over their heads by two of his friends Wendy and Claire.

In the morning Bob helps Ian change his bandages and both girls noticed
"What's up with him, then?"
Bobby assured the girls
"He got a bit upset and hurt himself but he's going to be ok"
Bobby was obviously too busy changing Ian's bandages to notice the exchange of sour looks between the pair; but Ian did.

Both lads decided to go out and have a couple of drinks in Torquay. It turned out that they could only afford a couple of beers as most of the money had gone on the bus journey.
"Not much is it?"
Worried Ian after they have both counted up their pennies;
"Don't worry"

Was the optimistic reply and then Bobby went into a nearby restaurant and soon returns.

"Problem solved, I'm working tomorrow and the day after."

Ian could not help be impressed by how resourceful Bobby was and celebrated their good fortune by going out that evening. Bobby certainly knew a lot of people in Torquay and this helped to solve the immediate drink problem as he chatted away whilst Ian fed the jukebox to play 'Uptown, Top Rankin' by Althea and Donna.

It had been a good night and proof was to be found in the severity of their respective hangovers the following morning. Still, Bob bravely gets up and manages to go to work.

The two housemates come down stairs make tea and toast, making a huge point of ignoring Ian. This created a really unpleasant atmosphere and Ian just wished he could fade away. The girls were purposely making small talk and Ian decided that his bandages needed changing and had a go; it was too much to do one handed;

"Would one of you just help me with this?"

This request merits a look of faint disgust at Ian, a joint shrug, and they resumed their chat. Ian struggles with the bandages and gets his shoes on to go out for a walk.

The indifference displayed by the girls had really upset a very vulnerable Ian. Any self confidence that had been gained over the last couple of days had been crushed. Ian reaches a cliff top and finds himself standing at the very edge and looking down below.

It would have been just so easy to jump.... He thinks of Bobby having to tell his parents about his death. No, that just wasn't fair on Bobby to have to sort Ian's mess out. Suddenly the lyrics to 'Lust for Life' come into his head and Ian decides 'Life it is then'. Ian turns away from the cliff edge and walks back to the house. A friend of Wendy and Claire turns up and is offered food and drink. Ian sits in the corner looking at the floor.

At last Bobby cheerfully breezes in after his day washing pots. Ian is really pleased to see him and Bobby comes over to inspect the bad job of Ian's bandaging. Bobby decides to redo the bandages and said;

"Look at what I have got for you!"

and produces a cooked steak from his pocket wrapped in a paper bag;

"Compliments of the Chef!"

As Ian wolves this down, it suddenly dawns on Bobby that his unfriendly girlfriends have been less than hospitable to Ian in his absence.

"Didn't anyone help you with your bandages?"

Ian shook his head

"Have you had *anything* to eat today?"

Again Ian shook his head.

There is nothing scarier when a really nice person gets angry and Ian was to learn that Bobby's wrath, when provoked, was immense. Turning around to face Wendy and Claire, he keeps his cool but is very, very angry

"I've fetched a friend here, to be among friends. I've been a good friend to you both haven't I? He's one of the best people you'll ever meet and you couldn't even make him a cup of tea and a slice of toast! You have both let me down very badly!"

This unexpected burst of controlled temper has shocked the pair and immediately they become contrite. Ian accepts their apologies in a kind of blur as he was overwhelmed by Bobby's opinion of him. Bobby could have chosen to pass this incident over, but he didn't and Ian was forever in his debt. Bobby had offered kindness and friendship at a time when Ian desperately needed it.

The boys decide to go out for an evening and Ian espies a 'Bikers Only' Bar

"No."

Bobby was firm

"Please, please, please?"

Bobby relents, reluctantly and both go in the bar which is small and full of large tattooed, leather and denim hairy men wearing an attractive fragrance of motor oil.

Ian decides to camp it up and minces over to the huge mean beast of a Biker resting his belly on the bar.

"Two halves of Lager and Lime Please"

Why Ian never added 'Ducky" is very likely why he is alive today but the beer monster looks unconvinced;

"Have you read the sign on the door?"

Rattles a very heavy baritone

"Yes."

Was the rather matter of fact reply

"And what machine have you got?"

Ian swells his chest with pride and after a dramatic pause,

"Honda 50"

The bar monster looks even more unconvinced as to the authenticity of the two bikers, especially the camp one, but serves them anyway.

Ian has a look at the juke box and it is full of absolute rubbish, but miraculously manages to find "20th Century Boy" by T Rex.

As Bolan's howl emits from the juke box Ian does a pirouette worthy of Nureyev and preens about like a regular Nancy in front of the horrified bikers. Bobby shows great presence of mind and grabs Ian's arm and gestures towards the bar tender who is looking absolute daggers at Ian as he reaches down under the bar and slowly reveals a

FUCKING BIG AXE!!!!!!

"We'd best be off then! Be seeing you"

Screeches Ian 'Mincing' Moss, as they run out the door.

When both had got to safety they burst out laughing. Who would have thought it Ian was laughing at the end of the day?

Breaking Glass Nick Lowe

Robert and Ian had discussed flying the nest and getting a pad together. In January 1978 both moved into a property on Taunton Road in Ashton under Lyne. To call the facilities 'basic' would indeed be somewhat of an understatement. The communal bathroom was shared by eight flats and even Quentin Crisp might have balked at the condition of the flat, for every surface was covered in grease and the floor had acted as a litter tray to a colony of feral cats. Robert and Ian had to spend several hours scraping up the cat shit, in between having to rush outside to vomit owing to the sheer stench. Ian only has to hear 'Do anything you wanna do', by Eddie and The Hot Rods and 'I think we're alone know' by the Rubinoos to bring him right back to this odorous deep clean. Another record from this period that recalls those pungent odours is 'Take me back home' by Slade as Ian recalls walking into Ashton with Robert singing this song and the line;

"I had enough to fill up Hills left shoe."

Came out as

"I've had enough of bachios lab chute."

"What the Fucks a Lab Choo??!!"

Managed Ian in-between laughing uncontrollably and Robert saw the funny side and joined in too. Despite the stench, hard work those four days fumigating the flat was very cheerful.

The regular haunt on a Thursday night was 'Rafters'. Sometimes really classic bands played there; Pere Ubu, The Fall, Magazine, The Heartbreakers and Throbbing Gristle. On a bad night Ian would have to suffer the likes of 'Slaughter and The Dog's' and Ian was not a huge fan of 'Joy Division', who appeared as support most weeks, owing to their champion the DJ John Gretton. A typical evening was spent taking a shed load of barbiturates, a barrel of cider and inventing even more outrageous wild dances.

After one such evening, Robert decided to go to his parent's house but had lost his key. He then tried to break in and got into such a violent argument with his father he decided to go back to the flat where Ian was fast asleep. Despite all attempts, Robert could not rouse Ian, so instead of sleeping in the communal bathroom, he decides to wrap his coat around him for protection and proceeded to hurl himself through the bedroom window. This massive crash must have alerted the neighbours as both landlord and the Police are called, but Ian is still fast asleep, oblivious to the traipsing around him.

Eventually, Ian is woken by the cold winter air blowing around his face and finds himself covered in a mixture of snow, glass and blood. He turns over to face

Robert who is still awake, their eyes meet
"You Cunt."
Ian added;
"You had better fix that fucking Window"
Then proceeded to shake the debris off the quilt and get ready for work.

Party, party Elvis Costello and the Attractions

That window never got fixed and the winter evenings continued to be perishing. There were compensations to be had living in a meat freezer though, Ian was away from his parents and was relishing his new found freedom. He cunningly covered over the cracks and holes on the bedroom wall with posters such as "Dance to the goodtime music of The Sex Pistols' and 'If it ain't Stiff it ain't worth a fuck'. Lenny Bruce had pride of place over the fireplace and on the living room wall, instead of ducks, were three toilet seats, flying in formation of course.

The kitchen cooker wasn't actually connected to the gas supply and the only way of 'cooking' was to mix hot water from a small hot water geyser with some instant mash and beans. This was the 'Chef's Special' and was the only item on the menu for every single day.

The electric meter ate the 50p pieces that worked the small heater and both lads figured it was cheaper to go to the local cinema around three to four times a week. They smuggled a bottle of wine concealed in their overcoats, no matter that the films were not that good; they were warm and saving money.

Ian and Robert had established one house rule at the very beginning of their tenure –"No Parties". They knew that there would be a lot of cleaning up and didn't want to be doing this on a regular basis.

Ian decided to have a 'quiet evening in' one Friday as he had to get up early to go to London to watch Manchester United play and had just gone to bed. Not long after the door was flung open and there was a lot of general merriment, his 'twat mate' had decided to break the 'no party' rule. Robert crashed drunkenly into the bedroom and thought it would be a great idea to get Ian involved. Ian got up as he knew that if he attempted to tell him off Robert's drunken 'happy' mood could turn at the slightest, perceived provocation. Robert was the toughest man Ian had ever known and the threat of inflicting physical damage was greatly increased when he was pissed. No, Ian would have a 'quiet word' at a later date so he got dressed to join the party.

The loud party group consisted of Steve Mardy, Steven Middlehurst, Mark Henshall, and Don all were drunk and intent upon having a good time. No sooner had Ian vacated the bedroom, Robert and his girlfriend Karen decide to leave the group and go to bed. Again, sober Ian decided not to say anything about this liberty but Steven does and flings open the bedroom door.

"Robert! Don't be so fucking rude! Get up and join your guests!"

Robert's mood quickly switched from 'buffoon' to 'Psycho' and growled back; "Fucking get out Steven!... I'm warning you..."

Before Ian could resolve the situation, Steven threw his beer over Robert and Karen. Robert jumped out of bed and with two martial arts type blows felled Steven. As Steven writhed around the floor in absolute agony, Ian attempts to reason with Robert and receives a kick in the groin for his efforts and joins Steven curled up in pain on the bedroom floor. Robert gestures 'blowing smoke' from his gun and joins Karen back in the bed. Steve looked at Ian, shook his head and gets up. As he does so he picks up the empty beer bottle, smashes it and sticks it right into Roberts back; Karen screams.

Ian had enough, put his coat on and left the flat to the sound of people shouting and running around.

A frustrated, hurt and angry Ian sat in the 'Open 24 hours' Launderette waiting for night to turn into day so he could go to London. After all that Manchester United get trounced by Arsenal, yet again.

Never Mind The Bollocks Here Really Is The Sex Pistols!

It took three weeks for Robert to apologise after giving Ian the silent treatment. Finally, when Ian came home to a candle lit supper of mashed potato and the finest Australian white wine money could buy Ian had to admit, Robert might be a violent psycho, but he knew how to dress a table with a borrowed lace table cloth and candelabra.

It helped that they were not constantly in each other's company as Robert was usually out with Karen. This meant that Ian could bounce around to a constant supply of Iggy, Otis, James Brown and Ralf and Florian. In addition to buying a constant supply of 7" records Ian continued to listen to the excellent radio sessions by such artists as 'The Slits' and 'Souixsie and The Banshees' on John Peel's evening show. Bobby was a frequent visitor and Steve would turn up most weekends. If Robert was in on a Saturday, he was usually up and about watching 'Tiswas 'and when it was time to play his Bruce Springsteen and Jackson Browne records Ian would often go for a long, long walk.

Bobby and Ian would spend a lot of time in Manchester together. If there was a film starring their favourite actors such as Robert De Niro, Jack Nicholson or Al Pacino, they would generally check this out. Otherwise they would go out with the intention of just having a few drinks, which often turned into a mammoth session lasting into the early hours of Sunday. During one such spree Ian vaguely remembers meeting the classic comic – Marty Feldman, but he was so pissed at the time, he can hardly recall anything.

'The Only One's' were Ian's very favourite band from this time ever since he had been hooked upon their debut single 'Lovers of Today'; he also got to know the band very well. This band had a fascinating pedigree. For instance Alan Mair, the bass player, had been in an obscure 'sixties group called 'The Beatstalkers' ('Scotland's answer to The Beatles' ran the advertisements of the time) which was of special interest to Ian as their debut single, 'Over the wall', was penned by none other than David Bowie well before he was famous. These guys were very approachable and Ian had several interesting conversations with the lead singer, songwriter and guitarist, Peter Peret. Ian guessed that Peret was influenced by Syd Barett, but it turned out that it was Bob Dylan. The drummer, Mike Kelly, was the oldest member of the group and had previously been in the cult progressive rock band - 'Spooky Tooth'. Ian was especially fond of the quiet guitarist, John, who's 'Modern Lover's' T-shirt he coveted. Another bonus was that the 'Only One's' were not above sharing their soft drugs when chatting with their friends and acquaintances from outside the band. It wasn't an 'us' and 'them' situation, it was people of equal status meeting and chatting.

One Thursday night both Bobby, Ian and Steve went to see 'The Only One's' at Rafters and amongst the sparse audience, are Steve Jones and Paul Cook at the bar. Ian got chatting to them and found out that they were doing a store promotion for the 'Never Mind the Bollocks' album in Manchester.

"Where are the others?"

"John and Malcolm are at Nottingham Crown Court" (Regarding the obscenity case regarding the use of the word 'Bollocks' in the album title)"

Replied Steve Jones

"And fuck knows where Sid is!"

Interjects Paul Cook, with his eyebrows raised, both Sex Pistols laugh.

"Paul, I like that T-Shirt. You don't fancy swapping do you?"

Enquires Ian. Paul has a good look at Ian's brand new Fred Perry Polo T-Shirt in royal blue and replies

"Fucking right I do! You sure?"

Ian does not need to be asked twice and takes his top and receives a battered, Vivienne Westwood original. At the time it seemed Paul had got the better of the bargain as he preened and smiles in a brand new, straight from the wrapper number.

'The Only One's' set is subjected to friendly banter from Steve Jones and Pete casts knowing looks in Steve's general direction as an acknowledgment.

Pete and the rest of the group join the two Pistols after completing their set. The Only Ones were a classic band but just didn't pull the audience in great numbers. They often gave a blistering powerhouse of a set but it appeared that they were swimming against the tide.

Ian goes off to find Bobby and Steve to have a drink and a chat. As they were just about to leave Ian turns to say good bye to the two Pistols who are just behind them on the stairs

"You need to get off?"

Asks Steve Jones and continues

"We could get a drink back at our hotel if you fancy?"

"All the drinks are on Richard Branson!"

Chuckles Paul Cook.

With an offer like that, what right minded person would refuse?

It transpires that the two Pistols are very likeable and down to earth back at the bar at The Midland Hotel and the drink flows as promised. No subject is off limits and both give the distinct impression that all was not well within the Pistols camp. Both are pissed off at the escalating violence that seemed to follow them everywhere but acknowledged that this had really made Johnny Rotten especially worried and paranoid. The group is joined by the cast of a group of actors, including Dinsdale Langdon, who were appearing at The Royal Exchange. A bit of good natured teasing is exchanged on each side and more drinks consumed. The party begins to disperse when Steven Middlehurst decides to use a velvet draped curtain as a urinal, much to the horror of the hotel staff who hastily close the bar.

Ian decides to join both Steve Jones and Paul Cook to reconvene to another room to continue drinking; but both Bobby and Steve decide to pass on this golden opportunity. Room service was called but the evening has peaked and not much more drink is consumed.

Ian woke up hours later, stiff from sleeping in a chair. Both Pistols are fast asleep in separate twin beds in a hotel bedroom.

"Oh Fuck! What time is it?"

Paul Cook stirs and looks at his wrist watch;

"Quarter past eleven mate!"

"FUCK!"

"You supposed to be in work?"

"Yeah, I'd better dash, see you mate, cheers"

"Yeah, see ya.......don't work too hard"

As Ian walks up to Piccadilly, he realises that he has to be at work in some format or other because it is payday. As he waits for the bus he reflects on the enormity of the event that has just taken place; Fucking Hell! A night on the town with the scourge of society and tabloid newspapers!

Ian is in a sorry state when he gets to work, stinking of stale beer, Paul Cook's 'Anarchy' T-shirt and very, very hung over. He decides to act as if nothing has happened but later that afternoon, he is called into the office by senior management.

"Where were you this morning?!"
"I was at the Midland Hotel"
"And what were you doing at the Midland Hotel?"
"I was on the piss with The Sex Pistols"

A resounding gasp of horror resounds around the Board Room from the three Senior Management and look at each other in disgust. Oh dear, Ian is in trouble now, but he didn't care that magical evening had been enough and the look on their faces was priceless. Two magical words "Sex" and 'Pistols' have given Ian so much joy.

Subway Train The New York Dolls

Ian was eagerly consulting his watch on the train back from Ipswich, after an afternoon at the football. All the lads wanted a last orders drink at Stockport as they would miss the beer boat if they waited until Manchester Piccadilly.

It looks as if they are gonna make it as the train approaches Edgley Station....
"It's not stopping!!!!"

The emergency cord is pulled and the train comes to a jarring halt sending the lads crashing onto the floor.

Ian *really* wants a drink now and jumps down onto the tracks to the sound of dogs barking and loud whistles being blown. Torch lights are being shone in Ian's direction by the Police welcoming committee. But, suddenly, the Police turn back and Ian is not slow to realise why, the vibration from the oncoming Manchester to London Express train is shaking the railway line.

"Oh Fuck!"

Ian sprints across the track and in his panic, vaults onto the relative safety of a wall. Somehow the wall is thicker than Ian anticipated and there is a bloody good reason why. As Ian pulls himself on to the top he realised that this is part of the viaduct structure that dominates the Stockport skyline, there is a certain death drop to the streets 100 yards below. The ferocious jet stream that came from the London bound train knocks him sideways but Ian grabs on for grim death until the express passes by. Heart in mouth, Ian jumps down from the wall and has to really work to clamber up the steps that are half way up the side of the train. His mates are open mouthed as they pull a very bloodied and soot covered Ian back into the carriage after his near death experience.

Eventually the train moves and arrives in Manchester, too late for that last drink.

Smelly Tongues The Residents

There was a strange taste in Ian's mouth as he rushed to meet Julie, the taste of forbidden fruit. His mouth had just been expertly explored by another's tongue, every filling had been caressed and passionate saliva had been exchanged. Still in his work clothes Ian knew he was on the late side and didn't want to keep Julie waiting any longer than necessary. Julie had agreed to meet for reconciliation and Ian didn't want to spoil his chances.

Julie was not best pleased to be kept waiting and snapped;
"Where have you been?"
She could tell that Ian had been drinking and scowled even more
"I've been in 'The Happy Shepherd with Steven"
"HIM!!"
There was mutual dislike on both Julie and Steve's part.
"We've just been barred from there!"
Ian could barely suppress a giggle and Julie's expression demanded an answer.
"We were kissing each other"
Beamed Ian. Julie looked as if Ian had hit her with a wet fish and replied
"Goodbye"
Julie turned on her heel and headed off home.

Oh dear ducky, that didn't go too well did it? Never mind, I'm sure there will be lots of other chances to get back with Julie.....

It would be true to say that Bobby, Ian and Steven were public serial snoggers. Not for them the namby pamby quick dry smack on the lips, or peck on the cheeks exchanged by all heterosexual young men when they are pissed but the full blow deep throat job. What fun was to be had by simulating sexual passion on a pool table in a crowded pub!

This form of 'male bonding' took a more bizarre turn when all three were present, in a crowd of friends, at a Buzzcocks gig at 'The Mayflower' club one evening. A lot of drink had been consumed and a bottle had been broken. For some inexplicable reason the troublesome trio decided to start lacerating each other with the broken glass... It was almost a form of ritualistic trust as each took it in turn to mark each other's chest, face and arm. The peer group and other bystanders were equally repulsed by this display of mutual maiming, this added to the enjoyment of cutting each other up.

Ian espies Pete Shelley in a roped off enclosure and decides to talk to him. Pete having a quiet drink with friends and family turned to greet the bloodied casualty in front of him. Pete was very concerned at what he saw and invited Ian to take a seat to have a drink and called for someone to bring hot waters and towels. Ian was gabbling away to Pete quite happily and didn't really notice that it was Pete who proceeded to clean him up when the water arrived. Buzzcocks songs had really struck a chord with Ian and told Pete about the lyrics to 'Love You More' and how he related to the finishing line of...

"Until the razor cuts"

Pete stopped mid dab, looking absolutely horrified and spluttered out

"You cut your wrists because of MY song??!!!"

"No, no!"

Replies a rather embarrassed Ian and manages to reassure Pete before leaving him to the peace of his family.

"What a kind, lovely man' thought Ian as he made his way back into the throng, an opinion he still holds to this very day.

Albertos Y Los Trios Paranoia, were, for want for a better description 'a comedy group' that had somehow become associated with the 'New Wave' of entertainment. Their 'Snuff Rock' EP featured mildly amusing 'Punk' titles such as 'Gob on life', somehow they deserved that fate that was to befall them at the Free trade Hall one eventful evening....

Now Steve and the lads actually quite liked Jon Mcgeoch, the guitarist from Magazine (later with Siouxsie and the Banshees, Public Image before his untimely death) but he had managed to wind everyone up by being seen chatting with the spud boys of Devo who were the support act for the evening.

"You fuckin' shameless arse licker!!"

Was one of the friendly insults hurled at John, who had the sense to take this in the spirit it was meant and Steven could only turn to Ian and wink;

"Just keeping him on his toes!"

The Albertos took to the stage and it was all very 'clever, clever' and 'funny, funny'. In other words just too middle class and safe for Ian's liking;

"This is tedious"

Complained Ian and continued,

"I'll liven it up"

Ian bolted down his drink and broke the neck of the bottle and went to the front of stage where the band was playing. Tearing his shirt off, he began to run the jagged glass edges over his torso and blood ran everywhere. The audience weren't sure whether this display of self-mutilation was part of the 'joyous ode' to New Wave entertainment but the tousle haired guitarist, Jimmy Hibbert, stared in horror and disbelief at what was taking place in front of him. Jimmy sidled over to the vocalist, C.P Lee, to draw his attention to mad man stage front. Ian laughed out loud went back to Steven;

"Mission accomplished"

Steven nodded his head in agreement.

A young audience member was much taken by with Ian's 'performance' and insisted that he come and spend the night with her. Ian thought her request most peculiar but only too willingly obliged her desire. But he could not help but reflect that it was ironic that anyone could find him remotely attractive when he was so full of self-loathing and felt so ugly.

Violence Grows The Fatal Microbes

Most Sunday mornings were spent playing football, Ian played more for the fun of it and as the team was still managed by the flamboyant Denis Downworth there was much gaiety to be had. Denis's girlfriend had a team of seamstresses at her disposal and the lad's skimpy kit was in need of constant repair. After one mammoth repair session, the girls decided to have a bit of fun and the repaired kit now sported ribbons and bows in pink silk. This frivolity was a bit too much for some of the lads who tore the offending items but some of the team, including – needless to say, Ian, kept them on to howls of derision. Maybe it was the laughter, perhaps the taunts but the lads in pink silk played a blinding grudge game and as Ian said;

"...the opposition became more concerned with the ferocity of our tackles, rather than the frills that covered our tackle"

At that time Ian was a walking Clairol chart and turned up for one Sunday match with his hair home dyed a garish shade of green. As the team kit was green, Ian felt as pretty as a picture as he charged around the not so green football pitch. But, alas, as Ian perspired and the sweat began to run – so did the dye, thus transforming into the Incredible Green Hulk.

Ian usually spent Saturday night at his parents for convenience sake as he needed to be in nearby Denton the following morning to play football. After the game he would have lunch at his parents. One Sunday lunch was interrupted by the sound of knocking at door and Ian answers it to find Bobby on the doorstep. He told Ian that Robert decided to throw a party in Ian's absence the previous evening and that Steven had turned up. The inevitable happened and Steven had attempted to attack Robert with a club, but had come off worse as he was no match for his much stronger younger brother who then proceeded to throw him out. Steven returned and launched a frenzied attack on Robert with a broken bottle. Robert made no effort to fight back and when Steven had finished simply asked;

"Are you done now?"

Robert's injuries had resulted in muscle and nerve damage to his arm and had been rushed in for major surgery during the evening.

A couple of evenings Robert returned to the flat with his arm in a plaster cast, but was remarkably good humoured and even philosophical about the incident. He was sick nursed by Matron Moss who scurried around looking after him and was even treated to having the record player pump out his awful Peter Frampton records, our lad of the beer lamp even listened with him, such was his nursing dedication.

One might think that the two brothers would never speak to each other again, or maybe stay out of each other's sight for some considerable time period.

But, no, within a mere fortnight they had called a truce and Steven was allowed visiting hours, it was as if nothing had happened, or was it……..?

A couple of months later, Ian was present at a Rich Kids gig at Rafters. He spotted Steven who came over and hugged him. Ian could feel a wet patch against his T shirt and as they parted saw that Steven had a gaping wound pouring blood from his chest.

Steven had just invited Robert in turn to maim him with a broken bottle, payback Middlehurst style. He had even put the bottle in Roberts's hand, now they were even. Steven persuaded Ian to come to the hospital and this provided an unexpected bonus for the pair of them. The pair, rather foolishly, were left alone in a treatment room and they proceeded to rifle drawers, cabinets for medication which they stashed in their pockets until they were rudely interrupted by an annoyed looking doctor who furiously proceeded to suture Steven's wound up. This resulted in an angry, red scar for the rest of his life.

Trish was absolutely furious with Steven when he came home and collapsed on baby Arron's bed, with little Arron asleep inside the cover's

"You stupid, selfish get! I can't stop you hurting yourself but I won't let you hurt Arran as well"

Ian just kept very quiet during this tirade, Trish was absolutely right. Somehow Ian felt as if he had somehow conspired in Steven's behaviour and he just wished he could disappear.

It seems appropriate to mention the loaf on the loaf incident.
After we discovered a Field with magic mushes in it, I was sick to the back teeth of them couldn't face it but Moet hadn't had any so after downing a hand full of maggot ridden mushrooms he was in his element, sporting a cravat and tweed suite, we toured the boozas and by then I was also sick of Moet's antics. I got the bus and Moet followed all red faced and gibbering. on the top deck we sat separate I could hear him giggling and snorting laughter but tried to ignore him only for it to get bizarre I couldn't resist and took a glance back. What a site Moet was sat near the back and in hysterics with a brown loaf hollowed out and plonked on his head, a nice couple were sat opposite in terror one side of them pebble dashed with the innards of the loaf, I got off. **Bob Williams**

Some new lads had entered Ian's growing social circle – 'The Droylesden Set' consisting of Steve Molloy, Mez, Alex, John Crutchly and Tim. They became friends of Ian as they were friends of Steve Middlehurst and, strictly speaking, it was 'two groups' within larger group;

'The Birch' was a cellar bar in Ashton with a DJ, who thought he had great taste in contemporary music by playing the likes of 'The Doors', 'The Stones,

'Pink Floyd and other outdated dinosaurs. Bobby, Ian and Steve, were not shy in coming forward in letting the DJ know that his taste was outdated and this pertinent observation frequently resulted in a stand up row in which they were asked to leave. Along with Steve Mardy, they were then driven back to Anne and John's to listen to some proper music. Very often, the group stayed over as it was impossible to get back to civilisation.

In the early hours of one such morning Steven's expression suddenly became pained.

"Shit! I forgot Trish"

He exclaimed;

"I left her in The Birch"

He then shrugged his shoulders and carried on; she would have had to make her own way back.

During an evening session of magic mushroom picking in a school playing field the group of 7 or 8 blokes was rudely interrupted by the Police. The hallucinogenics were kicking in and Ian found the situation ludicrously humorous and couldn't stop giggling during his interrogation, unlike some of the other lads who had become very jittery and paranoid. However, as technically no real offence had been committed the group was given a verbal warning and escorted off the premises. It seemed like a good idea to go back to Steve Molloy's flat in an effort to calm down. Whilst at the flat, Ian had a good long, hard stare and informing Steve Mardy that his skin had now taken on a greenish hue and was now translucent. Fortunately, there was a logical explanation to this phenomena, the group decided, this was due to his Irish heritage and no more was said.

Like a rolling stone Bob Dylan

Ian was a huge Bob Dylan fan and the recent 'Planet Waves', 'Blood on the tracks' and 'Desire' were played along with 'Pretty Vacant' and 'Another Girl, another planet'. Therefore when he heard that Dylan was to play Earls Court in London; he was very keen to go. The group of friends knew that in order to obtain tickets they would need to queue up all night long. A clever 'relay' system was implemented as Anne, John, Bobby, Ian, Steven and Geoff Wickham took it in turns to hold their places in the long queue and then getting much needed alcohol from a nearby Gay Night club," The Stuffed Olives", as well as having a fling around the dance floor. Fortunately, Hyme and Addison's record shop took pity on the growing queue of patient fans and opened their doors at 02.30.

On the evening of the concert there was a real sense of 'Theatre' in the concourse of Earls Court which was populated by jugglers, clowns and stilt walkers. Anyone who has ever been to Earls Court will know it to be a vast aircraft hangar of a venue. It really does take an artist of considerable merit to get the audience to totally forget the less than favourable surroundings; Dylan was such an artist and didn't disappoint with his 'Wild Mercury Sound'. Along with the old numbers such as 'All along the watchtower' and 'Masters of War', Ian was equally as captivated with the newer numbers 'Changing of the guard' and 'Baby stop crying'.

More post show drinks followed the terrific concert and it was time to, very quietly, sneak into the guest house. When the group arose the next morning and again tried to navigate the stairs with minimal disturbance, Geoff's pair of wooden clogs clattered loudly along and they quickly decided to run out the door, laughing at the insults that were hurled after them: they had manage to evade paying for their accommodation.

Squeezing out Sparks Graham Parker and the Rumour

On Thursday, in late summer, Graham Parker and the Rumour play a cracking set at Manchester's Alexander Park situated on Moss side. It's a free gig with a wonderful atmosphere, lots of booze and Ian has managed to score some 'bush. Ian and Bobby meet up with a couple of good looking girls. An over-exuberant Anne needed to be dragged, kicking and screaming, from Graham Parker and the Rumours as the van needed to head off south.

The next evening is spent in Glossop. After meeting up with Anne and John they go to the local 'Northern Soul Club' which was wall to wall baggy trousers and bowling shirts. The small group did not feel very comfortable with the clientele and someone suggests that they move on to a reggae club, Ian burst out laughing at the irony of a 'Reggae Club' being held in this very white British, middle class area.

'Glossop Fucking Reggae Club!!'

As they enter the sparsely populated Church Hall where this illustrious event is being held, Ian's worst suspicions are confirmed. The music being played is drivel such as 'The Police', even Bob Marley is represented by his pop hits. This is just too good an opportunity to miss sending up and the group hit the dance floor and take the piss. Their actions have been noticed by a group of tough looking chaps who come over and ask them to leave.

Ian answers back as the group are being shown the way out

"We have no intention of staying mate! This is not real Reggae Music! Who are you going to put on next? Liberace? Tom 'Fucking' Jones? Engleburt Humpledink?"

This response results in them being forcibly ejected out of the door. Ian wasn't that bothered, ok, just a little peeved but Steven has different ideas. Before anyone knows what is going on, Steven has managed to get hold of a fire extinguisher and has aimed it at the group of 'bouncers' and fired. The jet of foam hits the 'would-be assailants' who go crashing back into the hall. Steven pursues them around the hall, chairs are overturned and glasses smash as the people try to escape the carnage that is going on.

"Bye! Have a good night!"

Cries Steven, tossing the fire extinguisher on to the dance floor and joins the rest of the group to a hasty retreat to the waiting hire van. Off the group speed, being chased by the 'Reggae Rebel Rousers', bottles and bricks.

Never Trust a Hippy

The next morning the group van reaches The Blackbush Festival where Dylan is headlining. It was a vast festival with around 200,000 in attendance. Ian tries a little experimental combination; Speed and Space Dust which produced an exciting 'tingle on the tongue. The group splits up into two; Bobby and the two Steve's go off in search of alcohol and drugs, whilst Anne, John and Ian forgo the pleasure of alcohol to get a position near to the stage and also to avoid the long trip to the stinking latrines.

"Misty in Root's" Reggae was relaxing but not exactly exiting. Despite doing their best, Graham Parker and The Rumour, came across as being somewhat lost at an event of that magnitude. Ian can't really recall that much of Joan Armatrading and Eric Clapton's sets either.

As evening fell it was finally time for Bob Dylan. Although the set was a virtual duplicate of Earls Court it was still absolute magic and Ian could not help but reflect that the aura that Dylan projected really came alive in front of such a gigantic crowd. As Dylan played live Ian knew he was watching a legend who had influenced and provided a soundtrack for a generation with his articulate songs. Some artists may have sold more records, but Dylan's influence was the largest of them all.

The show reaches its climax with 'Forever Young' and flickering lighters are held aloft and swayed in time as a tribute to this 'scruffy little man onstage'. Of course this sort of event is common place at stadium rock venues today, but this was the first time Ian had experienced this and his bemusement quickly turned to amusement when John pulled a raised arm down to light his spliff for his own convenience!

The three managed to locate their van and eventually Bobby turned up with a large earthenware jug and offered;

"Do you want some cider?"

"Where did you get that from?"

Asked Steven

Bobby looked very pleased with himself and replied

"From some hippies. I swapped it for half a bottle of vodka"
And then took a massive swig from the jug and offered it to Steven.
Steven puts the brim to his mouth but sniffs the liquid inside and....
"It's Piss!"

His face contorts in disgust and holds the offending article well away from him.

"Is it Fuck!"

Bobby grabs the jug back and takes a large gulp in defiance. And then he realises and drops the jug on the floor, the colour has quite gone from his cheeks and he attempts to vomit. Bobby has swapped his vodka for the contents of a hippy piss pot. Oh dear, much merriment was had at Bobby's expense that night, until this event became the substance of legend and I am not taking the piss.

Night Nurse by Gregory Isaacs

A trip to Sheffield, one Saturday morning, seemed like a jolly good idea, so off set Bobby, Ian and Steven to catch the opening hours and stayed until closing time which was 02.30. There was no such thing as Pubs being open all hours back in our day and the lads had to make their own amusement until the Pubs re-opened in the afternoon at 5.30. There wasn't a speed tablet between them so they decided to imbibe a bottle of 'Night Nurse' each. This in itself was a long, drawn out procedure as each chemist had a limit of one bottle per purchase. The lads were veterans of pharmaceutical products such as 'Do Do's' and 'Benzdrex' and were fully aware of these unpleasant 'legal' self-medications as a substitute for the real thing, but they were desperate and each downed a bottle of the sickly substance.

Bobby and Steven decided to go to a cinema, to pass away the hours until opening time watching a 'Laurel and Hardy' double bill. Ian, however, preferred to go to see Sheffield Wednesday and Bury FC at Hillsborough.

Ian found it really difficult to keep his increasingly heavy eyelids open during the match and could feel his legs about to give way. With astonishing presence of mind, he informed a crowd control Policeman that he was really a Bury supporter, who had wondered over into the Kop by mistake and that he had received nasty threats from opposition supporters. This did the trick as the nice Policeman escorted him to a safe seat in the stand. But, as hard as he tried, Ian couldn't keep his eyes open......

When Ian wakes up, he feels motion and realises that he is face down in a van with a man and a woman in front. He must have wandered out of the stadium and taken advantage of a vehicle with an open door! Presumably this was a husband and wife going out for the night who were unaware of their uninvited passenger. God knows where they were heading out to, rather than wait to see if he can make an unnoticed exit....

"Hello"
Says Ian leaning forward
"AAAAAAAGGGGHHH!!!!"
Screams the lady causing the male driver to momentarily lose control, careering wildly over the road, before coming to an emergency stop.

The driver flings open his door and marches out. Meanwhile, his lady wife jumps out of her seat and runs up the middle of the road, succeeding in stopping traffic, screaming

"IT'S THE RIPPER!"

Both the back van doors are flung open and the driver grabs hold of Ian by his lapel with one hand and punches him around the head with the other. In-between blows, Ian manages to speak,

"Err....Sorry Mister... You don't know if there's a bus back to Sheffield... Do You???"

All of a sudden the driver stops punching Ian much to the bemusement of the crowd who have gathered around to watch.

"It's the RIPPER!"

The wife informs the spectators.

"He's not the ripper, Love"

Informs her husband, letting go of Ian's lapels, causing him to stagger against the van for support

"He's a bloody nutter, but he's not the Ripper"

Decides the driver shaking his head and consoles his tearful wife.

One of the spectators decides to get involved and pushes Ian

"You bloody Nut!

He shouts

"You deserve a thrashing!"

"Is there a bus stop nearby?"

Was Ian's response.

This response causes much more shaking of heads and wringing of hands but the drama is over, leaving Ian to admire the countryside and how to get back to his mates.

Meanwhile, back at the cinema, Bobby has passed out. Steven flings him over his shoulder and carries the unconscious form to 'The Penny Black Pub' for their opening hour rendezvous with Ian. Dumping Sleeping Cutie in a seat, he gets himself a drink and waits for Ian. He waits and waits until he wonders if he has got the wrong pub? He doubts himself and picking Bobby up again decides to go and look from pub to pub, having a drink and dumping Bobby in a chair to the amazement of each pub's clientele.

Eventually, even Steven feels himself succumbing to the slumber induced by the Night Nurse cocktail and decides to catch the train home, carrying

Bobby to the station and plonked him on. Now the train ran between Manchester and Sheffield, eventually Ian joins the train and finds a still slumbering Bobby.

Now had they had enough?

Had they Heck! The lads decided to go to the Mayflower Club where they proceed to insult both a dreadful London Punk band and the lousy DJ.

The tough looking owner is impressed.

"I like your style, how would you like to DJ next week?"

"Go on then, mate"

Replies Ian.

Bodies by the Sex Pistols

I remember Lemmy having the horn for Anne until she came across as a mass murderer **Steve Mardy**

So the next Friday Ian is spinning records that he likes at the Mayflower. It's a decent sized audience of around 400. But he is being subjected to a censorship policy by the owner who wants him to plug some forthcoming gigs by playing records by the artist

"Here's a great record from Ian Gillan, who used to be with Deep Purple who will be appearing here very soon"

The words stick in Ian's throat and his tone betrayed his lack of enthusiasm. Still Anne, John and Bobby turn up and Wilco Johnson takes to the stage. At least Ian can have a well-deserved rest from the crap he has to play; he takes the decision to ensure this evening is going to be a one off.

Wilco's 'Solid Senders' have a really good go but, to Ian, it's not the same since he broke away from Dr Feelgood. There isn't the same magic and what was once brilliant now meanders around somewhat. Wilco knows this and jokes;

"Motorhead have nicked our audience!!"

They were playing at the Apollo Ardwick Green same evening

Wilco continues

"...They've finished now and here to join us is... Lemmy!!!"

On comes Lemmy on to the stage and things improve dramatically for the band and everyone is happy.

Ian gets his £20 fee and when asked if he would like to come back for a return session replies

"Thanks, but I have got a lot on at the moment"

John and Anne invite Ian and Bobby to come back and Lemmy comes over for a chat. Anne asks Lemmy

"Do you fancy coming to our house, we've got 'Boddies' there?"

Somewhat surprisingly, Lemmy appears not to know the colloquialism for 'Boddingtons' Beer and recoils in disgust (and not a little fear)

"Bodies? You've got fucking bodies in your house!....Fuck that! I'm off"

Never mind, Ian drinks Lemmy's share and finally gets to play the records that he wants to play.

Flat Mate by The Stripy Zebras

It had to be said that Robert was not the best flatmate in the world.

Ian had found out that various people had sent him money through the post for his 21st Birthday, Ian had not received these envelopes. Although Ian could not prove anything it seemed highly suspicious.....

Ian was attempting yet another reconciliation with Julie and it was agreed that they would have the flat to themselves. After a drink both Ian and Julie came back to the sound of Dylan's 'Blood on the tracks' playing. Ian knew that this was not a good sign and his instinct was proved correct. When Ian unlocked the door to let Julie in, they were both greeted by the large scrawl of 'Karen – Love' in blue gloss paint on the walls.

Ian walked into the bedroom and confronted Robert;

"You fucking prick"

"I've taken an overdose"

Was the pathetic wail

"Fucking die then, you cunt"

Was Ian's unsympathetic reply as he knew Robert was being a drama queen and wanted attention?

Ian had to take a rather dumbfounded Julie home; again any attempt at patching things up had been ruined, and was still fuming when he got back to the flat. He was so annoyed that he made himself a bed on the lounge floor rather than sleep in the same room as Robert.

Ian awoke the next morning to find a note lying next to him. It was from Robert and it was an apology for his behaviour the previous night and that he had borrowed £10 from Ian's pocket. This really was the final straw; the selfish twat had left him skint and was Swanning around town.

It so happened that two friends of Ian, Tony Logan and his girlfriend Lynne, were in desperate need of a lodger at their house in Hyde. Tony had accumulated large gambling debts and Ian managed to strike up a mutually beneficial deal.

When Robert came back the following day, Ian informed him of his decision to move out. Robert wasn't best pleased as he couldn't really afford the joint rent by himself and was furious. When Robert had calmed down he resorted to giving Ian the usual silent treatment for the rest of their tenure together.

Happy House Souixsie and the Banshees

It was a case of 'out of the frying pan into the fire', as not long after Ian moved into Tony and Lynne's abode they both decided to spilt and left Ian alone in a house that even an Estate Agent would hesitate to describe as 'with potential'.

The house was owned by 'Smiths Boneyard' factory which was at the end of the road. The stench that came from the smell of animal fats was known as the 'Kingston Stench'. Ian carried this heady aroma around in his hair, clothes and pores, you would smell him before you saw him and you would certainly be aware if you had just missed him. Tony had started 'DIY home improvements' and as a result the stone floor was bare and as the outside toilet was broken, Ian could only use the facilities at the nearby 'White Gates' pub during open hours. In addition, Ian had to turn up, towel in hand, to beg to use a friend's bath as the bathroom was 'under construction'. To add insult to injury, Ian had no bed and had to sleep on top of a blanket on the cold floor. It was just as well there was nothing to steal as both front and back doors could have been kicked in quite easily, worse this meant that Robert could come and pay him a visit.

It was no surprise that, after just one month, Ian's health began to suffer and he developed the most atrocious earache. As there was no medicine, Ian choose to self-medicate with a bottle of whiskey. He woke up with a hangover from hell and went to a nearby phone box to ring in sick, unfortunately a 'friend' saw Ian and reported that he was 'as drunk as a skunk' to the work place, as a result one day's pay was docked.

Patti Smith was on at The Apollo Theatre and Bobby and Ian wanted to go to see her, but they are without tickets and funds. No matter, they took a microdot of LSD and check out the venue for possible ways to gain admission. Irony of ironies, Patti Smith and her band arrive and are greeted by a small crowd of fans wanting autographs. Bobby's good looks catch her eye and she drawls;

"You're cute"

And gives him a customised 'Rock 'n' Roll Nigger' plectrum, whilst Ian laughs hysterically, before disappearing into the building.

One hour later both lads manage to prise open a fire door and they're in!

It was a good gig and Bobby decided to join the band onstage and sat cross legged on the floor, Patti and the band didn't mind that 'Cutie' was there. But, Bobby pushed his luck a bit too far and decided to take a picture and was thrown out by the bouncers. Ian stays and really gets into the rebellious and 'Fuck You' attitude of Patti Smith and in his chemically altered state reflects on the unfair way his work place had just treated him.

When Ian gets back to his hovel, he is convinced he must write his resignation letter and does so straight away. He woke up the next morning and still feels that this is the right decision and promptly hands in his notice. This time, his resignation is accepted with

"That was a very interesting letter......."

Ian is alone, in a hell hole, with no income.

Sex and Drugs and Rock and Roll Ian Dury and the Blockheads

Ian had experimented with drugs but around this time he finally got the chance to sample some hard core substance abuse courtesy of Brian Leah. Bobby, Ian and Steven were at a pub, 'The Concert', and Brian invited them to try opium, this was an opportunity too good to miss so off the group went to shoot up in Steven's kitchen, ensuring a rather concerned Trish was not allowed in.

The substance was cooked and each arm was tourniqued and a vein found. It was Bobby's turn to go first and he collapsed on the floor as soon as Brian withdrew the syringe. This was a worrying turn of events but neither Ian nor Steven wanted to lose face and each received a fix from the same syringe. Fortunately, Bobby was revived and it was time to go back to 'The Concert'.

Within a few minutes of returning, Ian projectile vomited his evening meal over the flock wall paper and the group decided to go to 'Rafters.

Ian was in a warm, stupefying chemical bliss as he realised what hard drugs were like. He was happy to just sit and take in Chris Spedding who was backed by the musicians from Marc Bolan's band on his final tour. His mind wandered and he thought of the Damned, who had been the splendid support act on the Bolan tour....Why he had been happy just drinking cider... and taking 'Do Do's.... Wow! Look at him now!

Ian really enjoyed his opium experiences but only shot up a couple more times owing to an incident with morphine. Brian owed Bobby some money and offered to shoot him up, it got so far as the needle was in Bobby's arm and....

"Take it out. I've changed my mind"

"I'll have it"

Offered Ian and was shot up with a mixture of Bobby's blood and Morphine.

Ian did not feel very well the next morning and resolved there and there to stop it. The hard drugs were seductive and needed to be resisted,

Bobby still continued to be an occasional user but Steven did not have the necessary self-control to quit or limit usage, he was to pay dearly for this.

Brian had turned from 'liberating' medication from his local workplace to breaking into Chemists in the evening. He finally went too far when he held up a sub post office at gunpoint and was sent to jail. However, he left something there to always remind them, a gun in a shoe box on top of Steven's wardrobe.

Soldier, soldier Spizz Energy

As Ian couldn't afford a television he read, and read, and read. The other source of entertainment was playing his music. He was aware that there was nothing in the way of sound insulation and was considerate as to the volume and time at which he played his records. Ian was also aware that there was a small child next door and did his best to keep as quiet as he could.

One night both Bobby and Steven came over for a pre gig session to partake in some cannabis oil and listen to a few records before going to see X-Ray Spex. The next morning Ian is interrupted from his reading by a knock on the door, he comes to open it and…

CRACK! He is knocked to the floor by a fist and is subjected to a frenzied attack. The assailant is none other than his next door neighbour, who is on home leave from the Army. Ian is stunned, he has done absolutely nothing to provoke this attack, he barely recognised him, and after the assault the neighbour launches in to a verbal diatribe;

"I FUCKING HATE YOU!! Any more of that Fucking Racket and I WILL Fucking Kill You!!"

Ian didn't retaliate or attempt to defend himself in any way; such was the state of his black depression. He merely closed the door and tried to continue reading, but he couldn't concentrate and tried to reason why he had been subjected to such a vicious, unprovoked attack? The only thing he could think of was that the wife and mother of the Soldiers child was always very nice to Ian. Maybe he suspected them of having an affair when he was away on duty?

Ian had turned vegetarian around six months ago and managed to resist eating any form of obvious meat. However, the winter was becoming increasingly freezing and, one day; Ian had no money and was absolutely famished. The only food in the house was a pack of ancient sausages that had been left behind by Lynne and Tony. Ian took them out of the fridge and after slight hesitation decided to cook and eat them as he was just so hungry, principles would have to be abandoned.

One day, after cashing his giro, Ian hid some of the money in the water tank and took the bare minimum out with him. A couple of days later, when Ian went to retrieve it, he found that it had vanished. After a frantic search, the truth dawned on him that a 'friend' had stolen it, this realisation made him hurt and sick. He knew who had stolen his money but couldn't prove anything, not even a sausage.

The Sex Pistols were in the last throes of their ill-fated tour of America, which would result in the eventual split. Ian noticed that Johnny Rotten looked old, tired and in pain, not unlike Ian.

All I want for Christmas is me two front teeth

How come Bobby, Ian and Steven are listening to a selection of Classical Music being played by The Halle Orchestra in the illustrious surroundings of The Free Trade Hall? No, they didn't bunk in but are there courtesy of Ronnie Middlehurst who is a man of cultured tastes and is not stingy about sharing experiences (remember it was he who treated Ian to his first Bowie concert). It is the second half and all the lads are beginning to shuffle around in their seats and are itching to make some noise and have some fun. Although the boys have somewhat eclectic tastes, this is going on too long. But they appreciate Ronnie's kindness and after having one last drink with him, making sure he was thanked it was time to dash off and for the evening to really begin!

"That looks like an interesting Party in that Posh Restaurant?!"

"Let's crash it and see if we can get in, we are dressed for the part!"

So Ian puts on his best 'refined' voice and informs the doorman

"Excuse me we are with the party, we don't appear to have our invitations on us, but we are expected"

Amazingly this bluff worked and they manage to join the party and are soon helping themselves to complimentary glasses of wine.

"Ay, isn't that that lad we saw earlier on?"

Steven spots the young violin soloist they had enjoyed listening to, now he had been impressive and was about the only highlight. The young soloist was surrounded by sycophants and other members of the orchestra. Anyone else would have kept quiet for fear of blowing their cover but I think we all know what is going to happen...

"Fuckin' Sound that Mate! You can't half play! What's this party all about then?"

"Err, Thank you. It's my Birthday actually"

"Nice One! You fancy coming out with us? You must be dying to let your hair down. You know get away from these oldies?"

"No Thank You. I have to stay here with my guests."

"Oh well, your loss mate! We'll just have a couple more drinks to toast your birthday and we'll be off!"

The look of relief that swept across the young Birthday Boy's face was palpable and after a final toast of;

"Up yer Bum!"

The uninvited guests departed.

'Pip's' once laid claim to the unproven fact that it was 'The best Night Club in Europe'. Admittedly, it was impressive in that it had a different theme for each room in its split levelled building but, in truth, its best days were behind it. Ian wanted to check out the 'Bowie' room; they'd all had a few and discovered that the place was full of pathetic poseurs taking themselves very seriously. This was too good to miss and the lads took to the dance floor and really took the piss with camp mugging and over the top posing.

Bobby went over to get some drinks and Ian could hear shouts above 'The Jean Genie', Bobby was being threatened, clearly someone has taken real offence at the boys piss taking. Ian goes over to smooth things down and as soon as he reaches the bar a bottle is smashed in his mouth. Ian staggers back and feels broken teeth in his mouth and can taste blood. Immediately, he feels himself in headlock, arm up against his back and a pair of bouncers bundle him up the stairs. He is then pushed into a room and has his photograph taken. Ian knows that this will mean he will be barred for life and thinks

"Thank Fuck for that"

"Mick, I'm only dancing"

Ronnie Middlehurst had a senior position at 'Ashworths International'. He was aware of Ian's reputation and offered him the position of Head Designer of Handbags. Ian gladly accepted, it would solve his financial problems and keep him occupied, and was due to start in the next month.

Christmas Day night was spent with Mick Hucknall drinking Ian's Christmas present from his dad, a bottle of scotch and a bottle of rum. They had always got on well together and stayed up to the early hours of Boxing Day morning talking about their similar musical tastes, James Brown and the sheer physicality of The Pretty Things.

A few days later Ian and Mick went out for a long drink together and were pretty much 'Three sheets to the wind' when they decided to go into a Rockers/Bikers bar in Ashton. Now there must be something about Bikers bars, maybe the inherent machismo that brings out the flaming creature about our Mr Moss because both he and Mick Hucknall decided to start camping about to 'Honky Tonk Woman'. Such a display of sheer fairy behaviour has never been witnessed since in Ashton as the future superstar and Ian dancing with each other, hips gyrating, pouting their lips and touching each other. This display of blatant poofery got the desired reaction

"Fucking Queers!"

"Backward Cousin Fucker!"

Both were ushered out of the bar and were pissing themselves with laughter.

This incident prompted a set of lyrics from Mick Hucknall,
we went to the spread eagle about 10 o clock
and man we pissed
man we pissed them

man we pissed them yeah
and we wanted some rock and fucking roll
and wether we got some rock n roll
lo yoyo
rock and fucking roll you cunts
hooooooooopoola
Alas this never made it onto 'Stars'. As Ian himself postulates; "Shame really."

"What Twat Spat?"

It was a good start to 1979. Ian's reputation as an exceptional handbag designer was the main reason why he had so readily been employed by 'Ashworth International'. The work was well paid; easy and only three minutes' walk from home.

Ian learned of the death of Sid Vicious one night at The Factory in between the sets from The Scars and The Human League. Alan Wise (who was a promotion agent) made the sad announcement with the interesting observation;

"...the poor young man would probably have been happier and healthier stacking shelves in Tesco..."

Ian related more to that part of Alan's speech which reflected upon the cult of celebrity; Sid had become a form of visual 'ideology' that was supposed to represent 'Punk' but instead represented 'Product'. Ian mused it really was time to 'get up on stage and do it anyway', but the idea of forming a band only existed in late night, drunken conversations with Steve and Bobby.

Ian's father had never been to either of Ian's properties but went to call on him in February. Ian was out, but Eddie looked in through the windows and saw the shameful conditions. Eddie was very, very upset at what he saw, so much so he had tears in his eyes when he asked Ian to return to the family home. Ian hated to see his normally cheerful father so upset and walked his meagre possessions back to Denton over the next few days.

Public Image PiL

We became band mates and went to loads of fantastic gigs, I'm so glad he remembers **Bob Williams**

Bobby, Ian and Steven met in the 'Unicorn Pub' the night that John Lydon (nee Rotten) presented his new band, Public Image Limited (PIL) at the Kings Hall, Belle Vue. They were planning to bunk in and Ian, in particular, really wanted to see this band as they were just as non-conformist as the Pistols. They were eager to experience a new sound that encompassed both dub reggae and the avant garde.

Inevitably the conversation turned to the notion of forming a band together and Steven asked his two companions;

"Isn't it about time we got this group together? You know the one we keep talking about forming, but haven't?"

Bobby and Ian readily agreed and as there were just the three of them, somewhat unusually, they were able to discuss this idea fully.

"What shall we call ourselves?"

Asked Bobby, a very good question indeed and one that prompted an immediate response from Ian

"The Hamsters"

He did not want any macho sounding nonsense name for a band and went for something sweet and cuddly, a name that would provide a direct contrast to the music and ethos of the band. He was getting ready to fight his corner...

"Yeah! Sounds good to me!"

"Nice one! Mate!"

Now that the matter of the name was settled, next came the decision of who should play what in the band?

"Bobby, you're the only one who can play the guitar"

Bobby had to own up to being the ideal choice.

"Tell you what; I've always liked the idea of being a drummer. It'll be dead easy to play"

Volunteered Steven and continued

"Moet, that leaves you with singing, and, yeah, you had better play the bass as well"

The idea of being a lead vocalist was no problem as Ian had proved to himself that he could do this bloody well and surely he could pick up how to play the bass, it only had four strings and went 'boom, boom'.

Once The Hamsters were formed it was time to go and get in to see PIL. Both Bobby and Steven managed to scale the 20 foot high gates with relative ease, but Ian got a spike stuck up his trouser leg and had to hang upside down until the seam gave way and toppled down onto Bobby and Steven. They circle the building and eventually spy an open sash window. Ian and Steven hoist Bobby up and he scrambles head first in to what turns out to be an occupied toilet cubicle. The startled inhabitant literally pulls his trousers up and flees. Bobby rushes to push out the nearest fire exit door and hearing the calls of the security opens a fire door and urges;

"Run like Fuck"

So they do and find themselves on the right hand side of the stage as the band members of Pil are coming on from the opposite side. All the audience are out of their seats so the lads jump into the exited crowd and successfully thwart the security guards.

PIL were well worth the split trouser and Ian was very much taken with 'the lack of rockisim'. Jah Wobble seated throughout the performance, provided dominant heavy, reggae like bass and the Spartan sound of Keith Levine's waspish guitar complimented each other perfectly. Most noticeable was John Lyndon's demeanour, he appeared to be much happier and seemed confident in his decision to throw down a challenge to create new music. This was a challenge that could have been directly issued to the newly formed Hamsters.

After leaving the concert, they were really fired up and decided to bunk into the Mayflower to catch another live band. After yet another fire door was breached they found the very epitome of "Punk Rock" on stage playing for them, for it was none other than "'The UK Subs!". This particular band was much older than their contemporaries and played every cliché in the 'Punk A to Z' book. They deserved their reception from The Hamsters;

"Fuck off back to London, you talentless twats!"

"The UK Subs" just continued as if nothing unpleasant was happening and ignored the insults hurled at them from their audience of three Hamsters. When the band had finished, The Hamsters decided to mount the stage to tell 'The Subs' what they thought of them;

"Useless Cunts!"

Even then the professional 'Subs' didn't respond, why should they? They had played their gig and would get paid. This non reaction infuriated Ian even further; all the joy and spontaneity had been taken out of the music as this band appeared to be only in it for the money. The 'Subs' were the polar opposite of PIL, and represented the very worst of 'cashing in'.

After deciding that they weren't going to get any rise from 'The Subs' The Hamsters went to get some drink at the bar and they were immediately approached by the manageress and she chuckled;

"I'm Pam. Don't think I didn't see you three sneak in but as you're here I might as well take your money over the bar!"

The lads thought this was a reasonable proposition and Pam continued

"You didn't like the band either?"

"They were fucking rubbish"

Agreed Ian.

"They cost enough and no one has paid to see them. These agents who send us these groups are useless"

"You should put our band on, The Hamsters"

Replied Ian.

"You think you can do better than these? Get us some people in?"

"No problem"

"Ok then, you want to play next Friday?"

All The Hamsters eagerly agreed. They were a couple of hours old and already they had a name and their first gig.

I Ain't Been To No Music School by Edbanger and the Nosebleeds

The very next day the first Hamster rehearsal and song composition took place around Steven's flat. Bobby brings his guitar, Ian some ideas and Steven beat the rhythm on a biscuit tin and also provided lyrics. Two hours later there are seven songs, including 'Ordinary' (an early Hamsters staple number that would be revived decades later as 'Cute Bobby') and the oddly prescient 'Computer Dating' which included such seminal lyrics as:

'Computer Dating
Lots of waiting
Computer Dating
So Frustrating'

Alas, there is no recording of these numbers as these were dropped as more evolved songs were created.

Ian was aware that a local band, 'Abdominal Pain' was about to play a gig at Haughton Green Youth Club that very night and declared that The Hamsters should play and it was agreed this would be the ideal live debut with Neil guesting on bass.

There was some degree of nepotism as regarding the appearance of 'Abdominal Pain' at this Club as the drummer's father was the local Conservative Counsellor. Now Counsellor Terry Cain was not the biggest fan of Ian or Steve and was absolutely flabbergasted when The Hamsters turned up at the club. His first reaction was to deny them entry, let alone the opportunity to play but Ian made 'Abdominal Pain' an offer they couldn't refuse,

"If you let us play tonight, you can play with us at the Mayflower Club"

Even the good Counsellor realised that his son's band would get the opportunity to play at a prestigious venue but was still not convinced that The Hamsters could even play their instruments and offered them an audition. Admittedly both Bobby and Ian had performed live but Steve had yet to sit at a drum kit, let alone play it, as for Ian and his bass playing......But, nothing gained nothing ventured and The Hamsters had to prove they had the 'X' Factor.

What Steven lacked in experience, he more than made up for in bravado and attacked the drum kit like an explosive combination of Palmolive and Mo Tucker. Ian's bass playing consisted of the odd 'boom' but he was a confident vocalist. All this chaos was held together by Bobby. It was more than a good attempt as they knew they had got the gig and the 'judges' agreed.

An hour later the audience, consisting of school children, witnessed The Hamsters' auspicious debut. This was really Punk Rock and the teeny punkies were not slow in coming forward and did what was expected at a Punk Gig, they began to gob, shout, and pogo, pogo, pogo. Four songs were played and Steven decided he had had enough of the teenage thunder of phlegm and got up from his drum kit and came round to the front and like some sinister pantomime villain demanded of the youngsters;

"WHAT TWAT SPAT?"

This was an irresistible invitation to which the audience replied as one:

"WHAT TWAT SPAT? WHAT TWAT SPAT? WHAT TWAT SPAT?"

This captivating chant went back and forth between the stage and band. Eventually, Steven saw the funny side and went back to his drums and played a beat to the chant as Bobby improvised an accompanying riff.

The adults who are present at the gig are absolutely furious, and demand that The Hamsters 'Leave The Building' but they are ignored; the chanting continued for FIFTEEN minutes.

Eventually, it took the arrival of the police to remove The Hamsters off the stage and escort them from the premises, much to the disappointment of their young fan base. Adrenaline was running, and all the band were on a natural high (for a change). But they had one question ...

"Why didn't we do this sooner??!!"

"Are you ready Bob?"

"Ok"

Are you ready Steve?

"Uh, huh"

"Well, alright fellas, Hamsters are GO!

Hamsters Introduction to The Mayflower gig

I was just a bit young to be part of the first wave of punk which I am glad about because I think we sampled some great moments without being too despondent. We discovered the Mayflower club June 1979 being impressionable 16 year olds **Simmo**

The line-up for the Mayflower gig was pretty impressive and Ian worked like a Trojan to ensure that there would be a decent sized audience as he had promised Pam. In addition to the opening act, 'Abdominal Pain', Ian had managed to persuade 'The Frantic Elevators' to top the bill. The 'Frantics' now had two well received singles under their belt and were managed by the renowned Roger Eagle who had DJ'd at 'The Twisted Wheel' in the 'sixties and now owned the legendary 'Eric's' band venue in Liverpool. Roger was able to add a couple of regular 'Eric's' band, one of which was 'The Ozone's', to appear before The Hamsters in the running order.

Steven purchased a drum kit with a loan from his father. Ian brought a microphone and bass guitar from Mick Hucknall. But the most significant purchases, from Mick, proved to be a PA system and a pair of homemade speaker cabinets, as this meant they could turn up and play anywhere. Bobby managed to locate a rehearsal room in the very centre of Manchester (next to 'Mother Macs' pub in Piccadilly) and the group began work on more new songs that very same week. It quickly became apparent that it was Steven who was to write the vast majority of lyrics for Bobby to put music to and for Ian to sing.

Ian was finally putting his dreams into reality and virtually overnight, he had transformed from the sad, negative dreamer into a vibrant positive personality with the newly realised ability and confidence to make things happen. The day job had become a mere vehicle for financing the band and became somewhat of an inconvenience as it prevented Ian from spending more time on the band. Each of the three Hamsters brought 'something' into the group and sparked off each other in a way that no other member could ever hope to do.

"**Mayflower Club, Hyde Road, Gorton**
Tonight on stage
Frantic Elevators + The Hamsters
Admission 50p"

Announced the advert in the Manchester Evening News, barely seven days old and there it was, in black and white, the Hamsters second gig.

The Mayflower, whilst being far from full, had a respectable turn out. As Ian sipped his pre gig drink he felt strangely nerveless, almost detached. It was almost a feeling of anti-climax as all the work and excitement had gone into setting up the gig. Bobby was his usual unflappable self but Steven was screwing himself up into a ball of nervous tension. Ian was used to watching and enjoying a band, but from that evening on he would find himself comparing and contrasting The Hamsters to any group he saw, especially when they were on the same bill.

Finally it was Hamster time and off they launched into the theme from 'Thunderbirds' to begin their set. The Hamster classic,' Friday night at the chip shop' was debuted amongst the 'older' songs and this would prove to be a staple of their live set. Although The Hamsters were well received Ian was acutely aware that they needed to develop to the standard of the 'Frantic Elevators' and fast. Right from the outset, The Hamsters took themselves seriously and wanted to be proficient and worthy of respect. Not for them the camp novelty of 'So bad, it's good' they set out to be a real band.

Mick Hucknall was asked what he thought of the Hamsters;
Never as good as the Frantics! The absurdism made it AARTT

Social Drinking The Hamsters

Social drinking habits will make you a man,

School leaving age no time to understand

Pam was so pleased with the turn out that she offered Ian further bookings at The Mayflower; this was a reciprocal arrangement as The Hamsters would become a 'resident' band and Pam would not have to go through cheating agents.

Eventually, the plectrum tumbled that Ian could not sing and play rudimentary bass at the same time. So it was decided that Robert should take up bass duties with the strict proviso that he should do as he was told and no more. Everyone was aware that Robert would want to bring his own songs but he was rather good at 'rock god' stage posing.

A typical band rehearsal would begin in 'Mother Macs' with good solid two or three hours of drinking. The band would arm themselves with a bottle of 'Aussie White' each and a bottle of spirits to share during the rehearsal. When the rehearsal was over the evening would finish off at 'Cyprus Tavern'. However, this was small beer compared to when the band played a gig. Steve was often a bag of nerves and depended on alcohol to function and Ian and Bobby would never say 'no' to a drink. Ian muses on why such a terrific amount of excess alcohol was consumed and, with hindsight, believes that this was to blot out the collective concern that 'the whole thing would fall apart at any time'. Drinking temporarily drowned fear and elevated confidence, and very probably gave inspiration for lyrics and tunes that may have been restricted by sobriety.

However, the drinking could either really make or ruin live performances. During one show at The Mayflower Bobby was in such a drunken state that he cut his hand to ribbons on the guitar strings and splattered the stage in blood. He gamely tried to carry on, but his playing became worse and worse as the set 'progressed'. In addition to this, Robert was in such a state of inebriation he couldn't even plug his bass into the amp properly and kept going back to lean over to attempt to make sure the lead was in the correct socket. This was too much for Ian, also slightly worse for wear, who kicked Roberts behind each time he bent over to sort the amplifier sound out. Ian also screamed abuse at Robert, who just sulked.

The audience thought this unprofessional behaviour was part of the act and loved it, although in fairness Steve and Ian did hold the show together and stopped it from deteriorating into complete farce. Dennis Downworth thought that show was a huge scream and insisted that he pay for all the drinks for the rest of the evening.

I'm a Cunt the Hamsters

I'm a cunt, I'm a cunt
I do everything I shouldunt

With (out a) doubt (my favourite song is) 'I'm a cunt" I like its bare bones honesty.....punk attitude was and should always leave you remembering **Steve Mardy**

Pam introduced Andy Zero and Rob Crane (who unfortunately died during the time this book was written and Ian attended his funeral) to the band. Andy was the editor of the pre-eminent 'City Fun' which featured bands from Manchester and Rob was the manager of 'Armed Force'. Both recognised that The Hamsters were unique to the local scene and were early supporters. The band soon found themselves being compared favourably to The Rolling Stones in a feature which appeared after only four gigs and were given support to 'Armed Force' and 'Foreign Press' (managed by Peter Hook, bassist from 'Joy Division'). Again, The Hamsters were received enthusiastically and as a result were invited to perform at 'Stuff The Superstars' which intended to showcase the very best of Mancunian bands. Admittedly, the initial reaction was to refuse as they would be appearing with 'Real' bands and it was still early days, but this was too good an opportunity to miss out on.

Before this daylong event, The Hamsters played at a 'Right to Work' event in Hulme and arrived to find that the gig was being picketed by feminist protesters. Even more surprisingly, The Hamsters soon found out that it was <u>THEM</u> who were the reason for this protest owing to a new song –'I'm a Cunt' that had debuted during the previous show. The protesters claimed that The Hamsters demeaned female bodies and obviously took offence to the title, rather than listening to what the song was really about (quite simply, a Man, who is a Cunt). Not that this bothered The Hamsters one bit and they had a great gig with Steven, who was playing furiously, in constant danger of falling down the back of the stage as his drum stool slipped further and further back.

The band was received even more enthusiastically than usual and the audience were shouting out for songs that they had heard before. This meant that they were already building up a fan base in a very short time.

"The first time we saw the Hamsters was at the Stuff the Superstar gig but it wasn't the gig that did it for us as the following months the Hamsters were always on hand to perform whether they were wanted or not whether they had equipment or not. They were totally off it and we loved them. The Hamsters were a punk band!" **Simmo**

The Hamsters were so nervous on the big day that they choose to forgo their usual sound check for fear of appearing incompetent in front of the 'proper' bands. Instead, they chose to go to 'The Unicorn' for some 'Dutch Courage'. Robert and Bobby settled for beer, but Ian and Steve felt in need of several large brandies. After knocking back a substantial amount of alcohol it was time to venture out in to the sunlight. When coming back to 'The Mayflower' the lads were greeted by the terrifying site of several hundred punters queuing around the block. This was too much for Steven. He looked absolutely horrified and looked to Ian for reassurance, but the terror was mirrored right back at him and he jacknifed and vomited there and then. Ian managed to hold it together but the realisation that they may well be very badly out of their depth became confirmed by the sheer number of people who were going to attend.

When the lads entered the hall, it was already busy and the 'alternative' stalls were doing a brisk trade in T-Shirts and Fanzines. The band was approached by two lads who appeared to recognise them;

"Hi Mate! We've come up from London to see you!"

There was a shaking of hands.

"Eh, Sound Mate"

"Yeah, we can't wait to hear you! You're the 'Northern Sham 69' aren't you?"

Ian thought this was rather funny and chortled

"We are nothing like those mugs! They are fucking useless, fucking idiots!"

His mood was further lightened by the expression of sheer horror from their London 'Fans'. God! Ian might have just as well sodomised their mother such was the revulsion on their faces. "Good" thought Ian, "Just what I need, some friction to rev me up".

"Shovel Robinson" were the opening act and, despite the fact they were on the same bill, Ian rather liked the sound created by the guitarist. All too soon it was the Hamsters turn and it was time to report to Bernard (AKA 'Gordon the Moron' from 'Jilted John') who was the compere for the show.

"What sort of band are you then?"

Enquired Gordon.

"I've no idea...You tell me afterwards"

Replied Ian.

Ian certainly looked the business in his pink T shirt with silk screened 'Hamsters' logo as they strode onto the stage in front of a packed audience. He wasn't at all nervous and felt in complete control. The energy that came from The Hamsters crackled right from the very first note; aware they had won the hall over. The audience knew they weren't experiencing the usual, meaningless 'Punk Thrash' and instinctively sensed something original. The Hamsters songs were little stories and Ian knew that the dynamic lay in the power of his narrative. Bobby and Steven provided a thrilling soundtrack and what Robert lacked in musical expertise he more than made up for in visuals as he gurned??? and snarled throughout all the numbers. Ian was not to be outdone by Robert and managed a funny little tap dance and grinned from ear to ear.

After four songs Ian announced;

"I would like you to all join together with us for an artistic happening"

The collective groan of the audience was clearly audible as Ian produced a violin case and made a show of slowly opening it. The disappointment turned into bewilderment when Ian revealed that the case contained a picnic that had been lovingly prepared for Ian by his doting mother.

"OK! We are now going to re-enact 'The Feeding of the Five Thousand!"

Explained Ian, as he handed out cheese sandwiches and fairy cakes to the outstretched hands of the audience members. The disappointment had suddenly turned into a warm wave of approval.

"Friday Night at the Chip Shop" was played during the feast and the applause that followed it reinforced the fact this was fast becoming a very popular number. The Band finished off with their great sing-along number – "I'm a Cunt" and the cheers were absolutely deafening and moved Ian to announce;

"The Hamsters. Not a joke anymore"

Steven would henceforth remind Ian of this statement and take the piss out of him mercilessly, but Ian genuinely believed that this gig was a pivotal moment in the history of the band.

Gordon the Moron came back on stage and turned to face the audience as he grabbed the microphone.

"I asked these lads what sort of a band The Hamsters were"

He turned to face Ian and continued

"The answer is a GREAT Band!"

He then held out his arm to encompass the whole of The Hamsters and shouted;

"Let's have some more applause for THE HAMSTERS!!!!!!!"

Gordon was not finished, as in between each set, he continually asked for more applause for The Hamsters and was constantly reminding the audience what a great band they were.

Ian was on cloud nine and drunk more and more to celebrate the undoubted success that had taken place. He managed to irritate Paul Morley and his arty friends who accused him of formulating 'Kitchen Sink Vignettes'. Ian didn't care and informed them that they were;

"A bunch of stuck up cunts".

Ian soon became rather sozzled. So sozzled it seemed like a good idea to join 'The Frantic Elevators' in an impromptu cover of The Clash's 'White Riot'. Ian remembers dueting with Mick Hucknall with his black football mate Greg Clarke in tow. Next came The Fall; Mark E Smith continued to fascinate Ian with his sinister malevolence. 'The Distractions' were poppy and sounded rather good with a haze of alcohol. But it was Joy Division who were the show stealers, their album 'Unknown Pleasures' was released that same week. Even Ian, who normally wasn't that keen on this particular band, realised the significance of that event and remembers that show as a classic performance. The artist known as 'John the Postman' (he really was a postman) finished off the evening in his own inimitable way, the perfect end to a perfect day.

During the gig, Ian was befriended by a group of youngsters who had formed their own 'Hamster' tribute band called 'The Rodents'. A week later Ian was in Gracie Field's home town of Rochdale (She was otherwise engaged in Capri unfortunately) and joined 'The Rodents' in a stirring rendition of 'Telivisionitus'.

I first saw Ian perform in The Hamsters at the "Stuff The Superstars" gig at The Mayflower in Belle Vue; Manchester and was blown away by their excellent performance and in particular by his charismatic stage presence. **Michael John Leigh**

Where have all the bootboys gone? Slaughter and the Dogs

The Mayflower debuted the 'Funhouse' evening and The Hamsters played in the inaugural week. This fledgling night was immediately supported by local bands in order to be promoted as a viable alternative to 'The Factory' (owned by Tony Wilson). One of these bands, 'Glass Animals,' was all female. Ian knew Rob Crane's Girlfriend, Cilla Glass, and they got on well, although he admired the two other band members; he was met with cool disdain from them. The very fact that he was associated with Steven, whom they both despised, meant that he was suspect and they may have misread his natural friendliness.

The week after The Hamsters performed at 'The Funhouse', Ian went to watch both 'Glass Animals' and 'The Liggers' (another female band). 'Glass Animals' opened and their heavy feminist and lesbian agenda really alienated most of the audience, some of whom went to the DJ booth to put a record on. Ian was aware of what was happening and protested loudly and single handedly managed to prevent records from being played. The band members must have been aware that Ian had managed to prevent them from being an early exit, but it was just as well Ian expected no thanks as none was given. 'The Liggers' followed on stage and were better received, Ian has always liked this particular group in terms of music and these were one of the few bands that The Hamsters related to as people.

One evening, just before "The Fall" were to play their set at 'Funhouse', Ian was approached by a big wild lad known as 'Ozzie'. 'Ozzie 'was the leader of a self-styled band of hooligans who were huge 'Slaughter and the Dogs' fans'. Mark E Smith had made some less than favourable comments about Slaughter and The Dogs in the music press and Ozzie informed Ian that 'The lads' were going to trash both the band and their van. Owing to his status in the Hamsters, Ian commanded a huge amount of respect and attempted to reason with Ozzie that it would be 'The Funhouse' that would suffer because if word got out that it was unsafe for bands to perform there it would result in closure. By beating The Fall up they would only be beating themselves up?

It so happened that Ian had drunk a bit and thought it would be wise to warn The Fall to go sooner on rather than later. He managed to get back stage and went straight up to Kay Carrol, The Fall's genuinely scary manager (and partner of Mark E Smith), and explained the situation to her in the presence of the band. She gave him one hard, cool look and spits out;

"Who the fuck do you think you are? We can sort things out ourselves!!"

"I don't think you could, Sweetie"

This reply really gets Kay's back up and she snapped back;

"Fuck off out of here, you!"

"Not without a kiss"

Ian puckered his lips up.

"FUCK OFF!"

Kay was getting rattled and the band members are enjoying her discomfort. Ian turns to go, but decides to have the last word

"You're not very good now....without Martin (Brammah)"

The set went off without incident.

"Stupid songs, stupid songs

Stupid songs keep going on"

Stupid Songs The Hamsters

The Hamsters! Ah! the memories! I'm 50 now but when I was 18/19 back in 79/80 one of the groups that made a massive impact on me was Moet's Mob. I saw them live about 6 times supporting the Fall or on the bill with other Manchester music legends & I loved them. Songs like Friday Night at the Chinese Chip Shop (as I called it then) & I'm a Cunt stuck in the memory bank for decades. They were aggressive & surreal & working class & rough & ready but there was something very intelligent going on **Stephen Doyle**

As you may have guessed, The Hamsters were essentially Bobby, Ian and Steven, and which ever bass player they had to put up with. However, Ian thought it would be a nice gesture to invite 'Muppet' (Paul Smart) from 'Armed Force' to join him onstage for a song. This turned out to be a bad mistake as mid-way through the duet, the drums suddenly stopped and Ian, sensing danger, moved sideways and narrowly avoided the cymbal stand that Steven was wielding from crashing down on his head. Ian reacted quickly, grabbed a Newcastle Brown Bottle, hit Steven around the head a few times with one hand, whilst gripping him with the other. When Ian released Steven, the pair glowered at each other and Steven returned to his drum stool. There was a stunned silence and 'Muppet' had wisely retreated stage right. However, the band started playing, as if nothing untoward had occurred. This incident was never discussed, or alluded to, but Ian would never issue any further 'guest' invitations again.

Steven wrote the vast majority of the lyrics, which were very good and often funny in a barbed kind of way. Ian also wrote lyrics, but accepted that Steven's ideas were often much superior and although he had no trouble singing Steven's words, it did tilt the power axis of the band and created 'Ego Issue' between the pair. Whilst there was an uneasy alliance between Ian and Steven as regarding song composition, Robert persistently wanted the band to attempt his ideas but the band simply didn't like what he had written. It was around this time that Bobby and Ian gave various characters they knew, nicknames from 'Gormenghast' (the fantasy trilogy written by Melvyn Peak) and Robert was dubbed 'Swelter' after the brooding, malevolent chef. Robert sensed that 'Swelter' was no compliment and ironically, the more he brooded the more he became more like his fictional counterpart.

The situation had to come to an end and one evening, "Swelter", came to the rehearsal room waving a sheet of papers and demanded;

"Either we start work on this......."

He handed each member of the band a sheet, and then dramatically declared "Or I LEAVE!"

Oh dear, talk about shooting yourself in the foot and burning all your bridges at once.....

The band each looked at the lyrics for Roberts song, the enticingly titled 'Blackpool Holiday' and didn't even bother to look at each other and, as one, replied

"Good bye Robert!"

Actually, they did very well to stifle their laughter, as Robert solemnly picked up case, containing his bass guitar, and marched out of the rehearsal room. They had the common decency to wait until his footsteps were out of earshot before they roared with laughter. Thank Fuck he had finally gone!

However, there was the problem of a replacement. If The Hamsters could have done without a bass player, they would have but they realised that it was a necessary component in their sound. Steve Molloy made repeated overtures to Steven that he was the perfect bass player for The Hamsters, but was rejected. Ian approached Steve Mardy, who was the bass player with 'The Hoax' to improve his status. Steve decided to remain with this band, which is notable only for the fact that they had a young drummer, Mike Joyce..........

If truth be known, Ian was bit miffed that Steve chose to remain with this sad little band. They were unbelievably bad, with matching lyrics:

"We are locked out of Society,

Because we want to be...
and we don't care!"

Ian once asked Steve, after having to suffer listening to this.

"What is that SHIT??!! Have you NO shame??!!"

And merely received a shrug, and an enigmatic smile, by means of a reply.

Steve Mardy, in response to my question as to what did he like about Hamsters answered;

'getting away from them at the end of the night without Moet badgering me to join them

However, Steve acknowledges that

.... *there was never any let-up with Steve Middlehurst even in the pre-band days and you had to be as out of it as he was in order to be in his company......and I am not and never was a chemical repository for the pharmaceutical industry. Steve was the drummer but was completely 'off the wall' and so for sanity's sake I kept a wide berth of them all for a while. When we (The Hoax) were in the presence of the Hamsters, at a gig either in the audience or as a support act??(Not too sure here?) Steve frightened the rest of the band even to this day. But he always stayed tied to his actions in whatever circumstances. Moet must have had the patience of a saint with him in order to progress the band at that time.*

To Prove I Am A Man by The Hamsters

"Tattoos tattooed on my arm
Love and hate across my face"

Steve Russell literally sailed in to the position of bass player; he had been working as a hairdresser on a cruise liner. The Russell family were parental friends and Steven had been a close school contemporary of Bobby and Steve Hamster. He couldn't actually play bass but went out and purchased an expensive guitar and amplifier with speaker cabinet which demonstrated admirable commitment, plus the fact he had a car was another point in his favour. To Steve Russell's credit, he somehow managed to pick up the bass lines very quickly and the band was performing within two weeks of Robert having his bluff called. Speaking of which, Robert was not speaking to Ian; again.

My own experience of The Hamsters, at Acklam Hall, bears testament to the fact that they would often mingle and chat with the audience. They were not in the least aloof and struck me as being approachable. Ian has a friendly disposition and people tend to confide in him. This lead to Ian being a form of 'Big Brother' to many of the young audience members, who asked his opinion and looked to him for advice.

Ian was keenly aware of his influence and would use this to genuinely try and help people. One such girl was Kathy who was hanging around with a bunch of really obnoxious right wing skinheads who regularly attended Hamster gigs. None of the band consorted with this mob whose very presence conveyed an atmosphere of violence at every concert they came to. Ian warned Kathy of his fears but Kathy insisted that they were much maligned and that Ian should come and watch the band that some of them had formed. Ian agreed to check them out and what he heard and saw troubled him deeply. They turned out to be rather good in a brutish way, and he saw how they could potentially influence a young, gullible audience with their diatribe of hate and intolerance.

The presence of this unwanted fascist element at concerts gave The Hamsters a bad reputation by 'association', either out of repulsion, or fear, the audience numbers dwindled. One night, at The Mayflower, the audience numbered just four but The Hamsters still gave their all, and more. In fact, so energetic was Ian, that he managed to break his microphone early on The set had to stop, audience were brought a drink and off Ian raced, with Steve Russell driving, to borrow another microphone from Mick Hucknall. A mad dash back and Ian only managed to break Mick's mike in the first song. They couldn't get another one so Ian had to bellow at the top of his lungs in an attempt to make himself heard for the remainder of the set. It was a good night but something needed to be done about the 'Gorilla's in the midst'......

On a Saturday evening at The Mayflower, around 50 or so skinheads turned up to find Ian attired in a girly, pink blouse and matching amber wig. The 'Real' men were not impressed with Ian and shouted abuse. The more they jeered, the more Ian fluttered his eyelashes and bitched right back at them. Eventually, a few skinheads made for the stage to give Ian a good kicking but instead received some well-aimed cracks with his microphone stand and Steven finally managed to make a well-deserved use of his cymbal stand to repel the would be boarders. These bullies, like all bullies, turned out to be cowards and pushed people out of their way to make good their escape; never to darken a Hamster gig ever again.

Unfortunately, Ian later learned that Kathy had been gang raped by the Skinhead group, at a party; Ian is still angry and sickened by the evil actions of this gang in whom Kathy had mistakenly trusted and even defended.

Bobby and Ian decide to go and see the 'The Hoax' for a laugh and they didn't disappoint. They had the nerve to hand out lyric sheets to the audience and their set was full of the usual pretentious nonsense. They spotted Craig Scanlon, guitarist from The Fall, at the bar with another lad (who turned out to be his cousin Wayne Edwards) and decide to go and have a friendly chat. Maybe Craig remembered Ian's warning to Kay and feels secure enough to confide that he has some 'dope'.

"Give it here and I'll go and skin up?"
Offers Bobby

The goods are handed over and Bobby goes off to the privacy of the toilets to roll a joint. He returns with a communal spliff which is passed around.
"Where's the rest of my dope, mate"
Enquires Craig.
"The REST? It all went in that joint....and there wasn't much"
"Not MUCH!"
Splutters Craig
"That was to last me a week!"
Both Hamsters burst out laughing
"Lightweight!"

Love and Romance The Slits

There was a lot of interest shown in The Hamsters from the opposite sex. Steven was, of course, married and though he had his numerous faults – infidelity was not one of them. Both Bobby and Ian were single and good looking, but did not take that much advantage of the numerous offers as the band was their top priority. This left all the rich pickings for the bass player (no matter who that bass player happened to be) and Ian, to this day, muses about the level of commitment displayed by the various bass players that passed through the band as they appeared to have much more time for 'love and romance'.

It so happened that Steve Russell formed an attachment to a young girl who came to see The Hamsters at Burnley Football Club. Some days later, the girl confided in Ian that the sex had been much rougher than she had expected and she was genuinely upset and frightened. Ian saw that Steve Russell had taken advantage of the situation and had abused the trust a young person had put in him. Ian went to have a quiet word with him and Steve Russell did not appear to be overly contrite; from that moment on Steve's days as the bassist were numbered.

A couple of weeks later, Bobby, Ian and Steve Russell were out for an evening. Steve Russell had informed Ian that whilst the songs The Hamsters played were 'alright' they really should attempt to improve their set by playing covers by Todd Rundgren. This observation sealed his fate. Later on he got out of his car and left the engine running and left Bobby and Ian waiting:
"Go on Ian, drive"
After the Todd Rungren suggestion, Ian really needed no further encouragement and sped off to Steve's driveway, leaving the car running and lights on. No one displayed him any sympathy when he turned up for the next rehearsal in a sulk. Steve Middlehurst curtly replied
"It's only a fucking car"

Steve Russell was to meet his nemesis at his final gig that very same weekend. The gig, owing to the atmosphere between Steve Russell and The Hamsters, was lacking in spirit and Steve Middlehurst decided to do something about it. He got up from his drum kit and went over to his old school friend, tore his bass off him and flung it off the stage. He then pushed Steve in to the audience and kicked his amplifier off stage for good measure too. Steve Russell didn't attempt to defend himself in anyway and ran away from the broken heap that had been his equipment. The Hamsters finished as a three piece and felt much better for it.

Steve Russell saw Bobby and Ian coming out of the 'Gardener's Arm's' a few months later, took one look and ran. It would be a full twenty years before Ian saw Steve Russell again.

Al Capone by The Specials

The music charts of that year were very much dominated by the updated Ska Sounds of 'Two Tone' records. Bands such as 'Madness', 'The Beat' and 'The Selector' enjoyed huge commercial success. The most successful band, 'The Specials', originated from Coventry and it was at Lanchester Polytechnic that The Hamsters were to play with 'Armed Forces' one Saturday evening.

The band allowed Robert to play bass one last time. After a good drink at 'Grants' (opposite 'The Factory in Hulme) two coach loads of bands and fans set off for Coventry. Fuelled by more alcohol at a local pub upon arrival, everyone was in the mood for a good time.

The dance floor was packed and The Hamsters were on first and managed to go down a storm with the audience. Two new songs, 'Putting in the match' (a Steve catalogue of horror's number') and the celebratory 'La di da di da' (penned by Ian) were debuted and went down very well. Ian was pleased to catch Robert really enjoying himself and determined to go out on a high. Robert pulled poses and high kicks before finally smashing his bass through the speaker cabinet and demolishing his equipment announcing;

"I won't need these again"

This last performance, Ian suspects, must have been very cathartic for Robert as it gave him closure and earned back respect from The Hamsters.

"Armed Forces" followed did not go down so well. This band had nice melodies but lacked both rhythm and charisma. What passed muster in Manchester, didn't cut it in Coventry.

The Hamsters were not exactly security conscious and a large part of their equipment was 'liberated' for souvenirs when the band was relaxing. The band was pissed off, to say the least, when they came to pack away only to find there wasn't that much to pack away. Ian was seeing what could be salvaged when he was called to a private room by the Social Secretary who said;

"Ian, that was a great set and I'd lack to bring you back with one proviso?"
"Sound, yeah what?"
"Just fetch another band with you."
Exclaimed the Secretary rolling his eyes and shrugging his shoulders
"I never want to hear Armed Force again."
"Ok then, Mate. We'll sort something out"
Replied Ian as he shook hands on the deal.

Ian said nothing about the invitation on the coach as it headed back North; he wasn't the gloating kind and liked the band members who had been very supportive. However, one could say that 'Armed Forces' had been 'sent to Coventry', in a manner of speaking, by the Social Secretary.

Slow Death by Flaming Groovies

Martin 'Lettuce' Whittle was Rob Crane's flatmate. He believed he could get the band gigs and, in the grand tradition of Hamsters bassists couldn't actually play, which meant he was recruited as Steve Russell's successor. Martin had been a fan for some time and soon proved his worth as he was quite happy to be told what to play and melted into the background.

In order to ease Martin in, a gig was played at a Derbyshire pub for a 21st Birthday party for an employee of Vidal Sassoon. It was a scream from the very beginning as Steven espied the huge, inviting buttocks of the landlady and began to practice on her ample behind. It should be noted that she didn't exactly dissuade him so much fun was had all around. The fee of £100 was the largest they had received to date and Ian truly believed that the world had gone mad.

Ian turned up for rehearsal the following Tuesday to find the rest of his band mates with shaven heads clearly worse the wear for booze. The Vidal Sassoon hairdresser had shorn them but it transpired that they had spent the Birthday gig fee on drunken revelry. They were all clearly pissed out of their heads when Ian arrived and Steven did not exactly ease the situation with his offer;

"Come on Mo, let's have a drink'
"Fuck off! You're a bunch of cunts!"

Was Ian's furious response, as he stormed out of the door. Ian was angry and disappointed; this was also the first time that a rehearsal didn't take place.

'The Frantic Elevators' had been invited to play at the forthcoming gig at The Lanchester Polytechnic (at Coventry) but, first, played a great gig with The Hamsters at Nelson with 'The Not Sensibles'. Both Frantics and Hamsters shared a van to get to this gig courtesy of an individual known as 'Mez'. Now it so happened that Mez got on very well with a rather attractive female member of the audience. She liked him and invited him back home (her parents were away). To be honest, the bands were wanted to go straight home but as 'Mez' was the driver (for no pay) there was no argument.

Her brother was also present and made the bands tea as they settled down into the comfy chintz chairs and homely surroundings to wait for Mez and his sister to finish off what they had started upstairs. Time dragged on and Ian and Bobby decided to see if they could bring back some food and went out to see what they could find. After about forty five minutes they returned to find a scene of sheer fear and chaos. Steve was standing, with a knife in his hand, pinning Brian Turner (bass player) against the kitchen wall. Brian's face was a picture of terror, eye's wide open and dripping sweat as Steven fixed him with a manic stare as he held a knife to his throat. Brian must have been trapped for the best part of half an hour but Bobby quickly persuaded Steven to stop this immediately.

With hindsight, Ian wonders if a form of denial concerning Steven's erratic behaviour was occurring, instead of remonstrating with Steven, the band simply went home as if nothing untoward had happened. Brian Turner was a most inoffensive chap, small, rather timid and good natured, and Ian wonders what on earth could have provoked such a violent reaction from Steven?

The next day, Neil had something to say to Ian;

"We are not going to Coventry with you and we are NEVER playing with The Hamsters again".

Will You? By Hazel O'Connor

"You bloody Twat! You didn't bring a fucking corkscrew did you?"

Steven was not happy; he had just taken the edging of a bottle of white wine to find out that it wasn't the usual screw cap. Bobby, Ian and Steve were on the train to Bristol, to visit Geoff Wickham and his girlfriend, and were about to have a social drinkie.

"Ey, don't mither! I'll get it open....somehow"

Replied Ian. He was nothing if not inventive and persistent as he attempted to push the cork down into the bottle with nothing more than a biro. Eventually he managed to push the cork down, but the wine had coloured with the ink from the knackered biro. Not to worry, Ian had got it open and it was blue lips all around.

The Hamsters were watched with much amusement by a studious looking fellow, who was sharing the same compartment. Ian, being the perfect gentleman in any situation, offered their travel companion a swig which he accepted with good grace.

Now the ice was broken, conversation flowed and the young gent revealed that he was working hard to fund a film about the modern music scene. He had just made a documentary about hearing aid for the BBC in an effort to raise collateral. His amusement turned into interest when he learned he was sharing a carriage with no less than The Hamsters. He became quite animated and told the band;

"You have charisma and you look good"

He was a personable, interesting guy and managed to get some facts about the band

"We rehearse in the City Centre"

Informed Ian.

"Oh, that's great! Would you let me come and see you?"

"Yeah, no problem"

This would be film maker, was getting more and more animated, almost feverish in his enthusiasm to come and see The Hamsters at rehearsal.

As the train pulled into Birmingham New Station, it was time for their new friend to get out but not before handing them his business card and said;

"I'll come to your rehearsal, bring some drink and we can go out for a few pints after?"

"Sounds good"

"I may be able to turn things around to your advantage, now make sure you ring me?"

"Yeah, no problem, matey, sees you next week"

He got off the train and looked really, really pleased with himself

"What's his name, Ian?"

Asked Steven, as soon as the train door was closed and they waved him off.

"Brian Gibson"

Replied Ian and thought for a second or two and asked

'Shall I ring him then?"

"Fuck That"

Was Steven's reply

"Exactly"

Agreed Bobby and reasoned

"We don't want some big shot at our rehearsal, we'll get nowt done"

Ian's attitude was very much the same and crumpled Brian's card up and dropped it on the carriage floor and the lads carried on drinking Blue None.

Later the band learned that Brian Gibson not only made his dream a reality, he made it into a feature film called 'Breaking Glass'.

I had too much to dream last night The Electric Prunes

Eventually the train arrived in Bristol at 9pm and the lads were greeted by Geoff and his two mates and introduced them:

"This is Rick and this is Mike"

"Mike, mike...... testing one two, testing one two"

Laughed Steven, as he gleefully slapped Mike around the head, and blew into his ear. Geoff, Mike and Rick looked slightly bemused at Steven's antics. This unease continued when everyone went to the local bars and ended when the three lads ended up at Geoff's pad where they met his girlfriend.

Ian had bought 'something' for the weekend and had a good stash of homemade amphetamines known as 'Backstreet Blues'. When the lads had settled in the front room, Ian took a couple and wandered the streets of Bristol for an evening tour; it still remains one of his favourite cities.

When Bobby and Steven awoke, they enjoyed a good breakfast of 'Blues'. The main reason for their trip to Bristol was to gate crash the Glastonbury Festival and Geoff, very kindly drove them there at around midday. It was easy, in those days, to get in for nothing, as security was much more lax than it is today. The site was still big but there were only around 2,000 in attendance. Ian was really only there to see 'The Only Ones' but as soon as he had settled down on the grass, he became afflicted with the most agonising stomach cramps. Bobby and Steven, too, were curled up in absolute agony. Ian managed to scurry to some nearby bushes in an attempt to evacuate his bowls, but could only retch up green bile. Geoff was bewildered by his three friends rolling around in agony and running off in to the bushes, but he kept his patience and was more concerned rather than cross and wondered:

"Is it summat you've eaten? I'm Ok?"

"In a way....I think some bastard has laced my Blues with strychnine...scuse me..."

Ian had to go off rushing into the bushes again as another wave of poison hit his gut.

To add to Ian's pain, he literally had to sit and suffer the grimness of Carol Grimes, and to add insult to injury, the wretched 'Leyton Buzzard's'. Enough was enough and Ian came to a decision;

"Listen, I am gonna go and find out what time The Only Ones are playing and we can go after that?"

There were no disagreements with Ian's suggestion and he staggered out into the stage area and fortunately managed to bump into John Perry, the guitarist from The Only Ones. It was just as well as the effort of walking the 30 or so yards had resulted in Ian becoming very wobbly and sweaty.

"Hi John!"

"Hey! Hello, good to see you"

"What time are you playing?"

John looked a bit taken aback and replied

"LAST NIGHT!!"

If it wasn't so funny in a perverse way, Ian could have cried.

Geoff decided to take his friends back to Bristol and took them to a Bikers Bar. Not surprisingly, the clientele viewed them with much suspicion as The Hamsters kept hanging around the Gents making strange groaning noises. They kept going back to the Gents, in one's and two's and were informed;

"You had better leave"

No one was in the mood for an argument and did as they were ordered.

The rest of the night was spent fighting over one washing up bowl to throw up into and Geoff's bedroom was regularly traipsed through to crash into the toilet. Geoff and his girlfriend did not have much sleep either, owing to the loud retching and constant Hamster traffic.

The next day, the worst was over and they quietly trudged back to Temple Mead Station. Like a ghastly hangover, they vowed never to do it again, but of course they would.

I've just been listening to a rehearsal of early Hamsters on audio tape. I can even date it approximately because audio tape being audio tape there's a recording of a radio news item at the end. It is sometime after August 1979 and on it from my own p-o-v, the quality of such classic tracks like 'Televisionitus' are very heavy. I'm not a music know-all so can't make an exact band comparison with the Hamsters but Moet sounds like he is exorcising his darkest demons and of course getting over shyness & possibly potential stage fright...nervousness?? But since the 'bedroom band', in 5 years he has still got the bug for cover versions. There's quite an original cover version The Hamsters do of 'You really got me' by the Kinks. **Steve Mardy**

Sound system Hamsters

Both Bobby and Ian were huge reggae fans, a fact had not gone unnoticed by Rudi Clemmens – who besides being a club owner was a form of unofficial 'enforcer' as he was trusted by the Police to 'keep a lid' on the various illegal activities that took place on Moss Side. After Pam had finished cashing up she would take the boys to The Reno and The Nile where they enjoyed a couple of 'after hours' drinks with the local black clientele. The mere fact they were there as Rudi's guests, meant there was no trouble.

Rudi knew that both lads were intrigued by the concept of the 'Sound System' and invited them to such an event one Saturday Night. A 'Sound System' event was very much underground event and relied upon word of mouth. When the two lads came along, they were the only white faces in a crowd of around a thousand clubbers. The extreme fascist National Front Movement (the precursor of the British Movement) had gained a presence in large urban areas which were heavily populated by ethnic inhabitants. There was a shit load of racial tension in Manchester at that time but although the boys were initially viewed with mild curiosity by the crowd, they soon got into conversation and beer was flowing. Ian makes the pertinent observation that two black boys would not have been made so welcomed if the situation had been reversed.

At one end of the hall were the local sound system crew – 'President Sounds' and at the other end were the rival system from Handsworth, Birmingham; both blasting their music through homemade systems consisting of speakers housed in wardrobes . It wasn't so much the sheer volume of the competing sound systems that won the audience over to the winning side, Ian remembers; it was the bass system that shook up the body and made it irresistible to dance.

The lads enjoyed this experience, not to mention the copious amount of 'ganga' consumed, that they welcomed the opportunity to go back two weeks later when it was the turn of Brixton London Crew to challenge President Sounds to a match, fantastic! It was put to Bobby and Ian that The Hamsters play a set at a forthcoming sound system. Now this was an offer that deserved to be considered; a real 'Punky Reggae Party'! Now whilst Ian liked the idea he had some initial reservations but agreed when both Rob Crane and Andy Zero maintained that;

"This could be so symbolic! It will really break down the barriers….It is important you do it as it will send out such a positive message that we are one"

Ian nodded his head and said;

"Yeah, I agree I know all that stuff, but listen to me; I am not going on that stage playing through our tiny PA system after everyone has been blasted by a massive wall of sound. We'll just look like fools and die on our arses!"

"No problem"

Replied Andy and continued;

"If you agree to do it, we'll get Oz Sound Systems to put up a proper rig"

This sounded like the ideal solution and Ian agreed for The Hamsters to appear at the next sound system event.

Greatest Cockney Rip Off The Cockney Rejects Friday 28 September 1979

"REJECTS, REJECTS, REJECTS"

The 800 strong audience was baying for current chart act, 'The Cockney Rejects' who were booked to play at The Mayflower that evening. Whilst Ian was not their biggest fan, he very much believed in supporting The Mayflower which was very much his playground. He was a well-known figure and knew the staff very well.

Ian is approached by Rob and Andy who look very worried.

"Ian, mate, the Fuckers aren't gonna show, it clashes with their schedule and we have only found out NOW! Bastards!...Fucking Hell! There's gonna be a riot! Moet, mate, can you make the announcement?"

Ian shakes his head in disbelief and replies;

"You're throwing ME to the lions?"

"Suppose so"

Was the grim faced reply

"Ok, no problem"

Ian chortles and makes his way up on to the stage to the microphone stand.

"I've got something to tell you boys and girls. Did you see The Cockney rejects on Top of the Pops Last Night?"

Huge cheers greet Ian's announcement. Surely he must be on stage to introduce them?

"Well just as well, 'cos you won't be seeing them tonight!"

The cheers quickly turn in to boo's and Ian continues;

"Because they now think they're too big for lot, too good for you. They're stopping in London because; frankly they don't give a shit about you. They don't give a shit about our club; all they care about is being Fucking Pop Stars. I'm sure you'll agree that they are just a bunch of cunts and they don't deserve you? I hope you understand. This isn't the club's fault; they have been chasing them up and only now got a 'no show'. This is the fault of the Cockney Rejects, so I say FUCK 'EM!!"

There are murmurs of agreement and head nods from the disappointed audience.

"If you're patient and queue, you'll all get your money back. In the meanwhile, would you like me to sing for you?"

The audience applauds their approval as Ian has sung before when acts had failed and was always good value.

"Ok, here's a couple you may know...."

Ian sings 'Chip Shop' and 'I'm a Cunt' to the percussive backing of the audience clapping and stamping their feet in time.

Ian felt as if he had electricity flowing through his veins and at the end of his 'turn' announced;

"I'm off to see Joy Division; anyone who feels like coming along is welcome to join me"

Ian leaves the stage to loud cheers and has his hand shaken and back slapped by the appreciative audience.

'Beat on the Brat with a Bass'

"...that chicken again eh?" Peter Hook

So Ian sets off for The Factory with around 30 fans and a chicken in tow (yeah, ok, he'd brought that earlier for the family Sunday lunch). Upon getting to the bar he gets talking to Peter Hook. Both were vaguely aware of each other but struck up a very interesting conversation consisting of their mutual reasons for joining bands and their taste in music. Upon hearing the new Joy Division single, 'Transmission', being played over the PA system Ian remarks
"I hope this sells well"
"That's not the important thing."
Peter Hook replied and continued after a sup of his beer;
"We have made a record of which we are really proud and that is what counts the most."
Ian is really impressed by the honesty and conviction of 'Hooky's' reply. As both he and Hooky are getting on well, he thinks of all the fans that have come along from The Mayflower and tells him of the disappointing evening so far. He asked Hooky, point blank;
"Would it be ok if I go on stage before you to sing a couple of numbers for the Mayflower Club crowd? There's quite a few who have come down?"
Hooky nods and replies
"Yeah, sure, why not?"
and heads off to the dressing room.
Ian climbs on to the stage and approaches a microphone, the Mayflower set see him and start chanting
"HAMSTERS, HAMSTERS"
However, the road crew are unaware that Ian has permission to 'open up' for Joy Division and view him as an uninvited intruder and attempt to get him off stage. Despite Ian's protestations, he and his chicken are manhandled offstage with the chants from the Mayflower lads still going on.
Joy Division come on stage and play their opening song but the Mayflower section are still chanting 'Hamsters, Hamsters' right through the number and continue into the second song. To be honest, Ian is rather relishing this but, tactfully, decides to treat a hasty retreat to the upstairs bar in order not to stoke things up and is, therefore largely unaware of what was taking place for the rest of the evening. The chanting continued and Hooky sort of 'lost it' and came wading into the audience, swinging his bass guitar to sort out the Mayflower crowd. The whole atmosphere became really violent and unpleasant.

"...seems quite surreal all that? I take it this night was the night of the riot when I hit that kid with my bass?" **Peter Hook**

After Joy Division finish their set, a very angry, red faced Hooky comes up the stairs, bass in hand. Ian spots him and innocently enquires

"Go ok?"

"FUCK OFF"

Came the red faced response.

Ian is perplexed and manages to sit down with Hooky and the evening finishes off amicably enough over a few beers.

Years later Ian had, what he describes as a 'Woody Allen Zelig Moment', when he was being pestered by an obsessive Joy Division fan, who wanted to know if Hooky really beat up Ian with a bass guitar and won't believe Ian's recollection. Exasperated, Ian actually realises that Hooky is actually sitting next to him at the bar and taps him on the shoulder, deciding to put lie to this urban myth, once and for all, and asks;

"Hooky, have you ever hit me with a bass?"

"Have I heck?"

Was the concise reply. Occurring to Ian, the obsessive didn't know whether to laugh, or to cry.

Two Sevens Clash by Culture Saturday 29 September 1979

Upon arriving at the Mayflower on the night of "President Sounds V The Hamsters", Ian can see that whilst the sound system is being set up, surprise, surprise there is no PA system.

"Fucking Wankers!"

Shouted Ian.

Ian now found himself in a very tricky situation as he knew that The Hamsters would not be able to play. The situation was complicated by the fact the 'The President' (aka Tony) had come to see The Hamsters the previous week and after leaving The Mayflower club was followed out and beaten up by some thugs. Ian overheard some remarks about 'giving that coon a slap' and made sure they had a taste of their own medicine. But, by pulling out, they could leave themselves open to the erroneous accusation that they didn't really want to be involved in a black event after all.

Ian decided the best thing to do was to come clean and had the humiliating duty of explaining that The Hamsters could not play without a PA system. Ian was absolutely seething, he had really wanted to play this gig and felt he had let his friends down, despite the fact it was he who had been let down very badly.

Steve Mardy drove the equipment van (sans Martin) to The Russell Club which was closing that very same night. The Original Mirrors were to be the closing act and Ian caught site of the promoters, Alan Wise and Nigel Bagley, in the cafeteria of the venue, all of a sudden, a rather good idea came to Ian and he greeted them with;

"Hey fellas! We were due to play at The Mayflower tonight, but we've been fucked about so I've got the band and equipment outside all ready to come and play for you. Free! How about that?!!"

Alan and Nigel were not at all keen on this offer and explained

"The stage is all set up, the band has sound checked, you can't possibly go on there now"

Unbeknownst to them, they had just shot themselves in the foot and Ian immediately grasped the opportunity;

"No problem..."

Explained Ian

"We'll set up on the dance floor, play through our amps, we just need a microphone!"

Steve Mardy was told to play bass and the band was on as soon as the doors were opened. The adrenaline was high that evening, and all the pent up aggression and frustration was very apparent in The Hamsters performance. They soar, they roar and let rip. Steven's drums are sliding around the dance floor (there was no mat to hold them); Bob and Steve Mardy have to keep kicking them back into place.

I can't remember what we played or who saw the gig that night. I was probably looking over my shoulder all the time waiting for Steve Middlehurst to throw a wobbler and destroy everything within ten feet of him......... but hey that's rock n roll. **Steve Mardy**

Ian remembers wishing that he was in the audience so he could see this great gig upfront. The early arrivals are clearly enjoying themselves at the spectacle in front of them and are clapping and cheering The Hamsters on and then.....The power was switched off.

Groans and jeers are rebounding around the dance floor, but Ian is far from feeling defeated. He is acutely aware that the crowd who has being enjoying them is furious at having this treat stopped sharply and they voice their disappointment. The Hamsters managed to blow off the cob webs of conformity in this historic, but unloved venue.

Barry Adamson, the bass player from Magazine, rushes over to congratulate them as they pack up their equipment;

"You guys are the best thing I have ever seen!"
He enthuses and offers;
"You MUST play with Magazine!"

Despite Barry's obvious enthusiasm this didn't actually transpire as Record Company contracts insisted that support acts 'buy' this privilege. Barry was very apologetic, but Ian understood and appreciated his support.

Ian Broudie, from the Original Mirrors (later of the phenomenally successful band –'The Lighting Seeds'), also came over to congratulate them. It was a good way to finish off the final night of The Russell Club and Ian stayed until the bitter end, drinking and thinking.

An interesting postscript comes from Steve Mardy;

.....the feature film '24hr party people' which reconstructed the last night at the Russell Club..., the Hamsters contribution was resigned to the cutting room floor & didn't even make the DVD extras

Ole Spain The Hamsters.

The peasants are revolting
The foods revolting too'

The lads were hard at it writing new material and had their own unique musical language;

"Play this one as if you're a chicken."

Sometimes, it was, Ian reflects 'like trying to chisel a huge piece of granite into shape with forks and Spoons'.

"This one should be like sweaty blue cheese."

The band had taken the decision to concentrate on new songs, and were not going to perform live until they had a set they were satisfied with.

"Make me feel like I've been running really hard"

It was a risky decision as it could mean that the momentum they had built up could be lost. But the band knew they were capable of doing much, much better and exiled themselves to the rehearsal rooms three times each week.

"Oh Fucking Hell Moet! I don't know what you sodding mean!"

Tempers got frayed and unkind words shouted but slowly but surely this hard work resulted in classic Hamster material such as 'Ole Spain', 'Stupid Songs', 'The Operation', 'Social Drinking' and 'Maggots'.

The band chose not go to other gigs, during their self-imposed 'sabbatical from live performing', instead preferring to hang out in 'Old Men's Pubs' for a quiet drink. Once in a while they would go to 'Cobwebs' situated on Whitworth Street, and have a boogie to Disco and Soul music.

"Spurtz" were one of the local bands that Ian really rated and liked. They were young, high spirited and had a cheeky attitude. Andy, the dress wearing guitarist, was a good looking chap, Rat, the drummer, often raised a smile and the young female singer, Corky was mature beyond her years.

Corky approached Ian one night;

"Moet, howzabout The Hamsters playing on Boxing Day at The Cyprus?"

The Hamsters were waiting for the right event to showcase the new material. They were certainly not short of offers but it had to be right. The Boxing Day Event was a Musicians Collective and the 'Muso's' were not The Hamsters greatest fans. Ian knew this and replied;

"We're not in the collective Corky, you know that."

Corky grinned and replied;

"Of course! That's why it's such a good idea! It will really shake them up; make them open their minds and ears? Yeah, I'll get a lot of stick for it, but I really want you to play

"OK!! You're on!"

I wanna be your dog Iggy Pop and the Stooges

The Hamsters are going down a storm at the packed Cyprus Tavern and Ian's football mate, 'big' Pete Whitefield is having to act as impromptu security as the crowd surge forward and are in danger of engulfing the band.

"I wanna be your Hamster."

Sings Moet Pop to the vast throng of bodies, who are only kept at bay by Pete, with his muscles and tartan tam o shanta. The new material is going down well, much to the band's delight. A few old numbers are played but this is an excellent first act to set the scene for the main band, 'The Not Sensibles'. The Hamsters needed to be the first band on, you see; otherwise the amount of alcohol consumed could adversely affect their performance.

Only around half the numbers were performed, before Pete finally lost the battle and the audience completely overwhelmed the band. This didn't really matter, the new songs had gone down even better than hoped for and the lads were positively buzzing in the van afterwards. All was well, The Hamsters had new belief and optimism as a new decade loomed around the corner.

Gigs Cyprus Tavern Boxing Day 1979

Hamsters

Their first gig for a while with Not Sensibles. The place is packed and not the atmosphere most conducive to listening to them. From what I remember they have changed radically from the old band and have a new bassist. I have never heard anything like this before a solid thumping rhythm from the drummer, sparse minimalist bass and guitar. The effect is like jazz (I bet you never thought the hamsters were a jazz band did you?). Like Captain Beefheart, Siouxsie and the Banshees and Ludus. According to all the rules what they do is impossible but still they do it. Singer Moet gives image and direction. He's an instantly identifiable figure, identify with him, he's large and he's probably on your side. The words I caught were intelligent and incisive. About image, the scene, about allsorts. I didn't enjoy this gig because I couldn't see or hear properly I am looking forward to a gig where I can get into it. The first time the Hamsters got on stage they hadn't a clue how to play any instruments and didn't realise they were going to play to people. Thought you might like to know that. **Uncredited**

Dead Rodents Scare

The Hamsters played the Boxing Day Party at The Cyprus Tavern to a packed house of enthusiastic fans who leapt all over the place regardless of any concerns like 'dancability'.

Vocalist Moet informs us that of the fifteen songs they played not one was finished due to the over active crowds. 'We enjoyed the atmosphere, but it killed us'. As by the sound of it they have an awful lot to offer music wise as being a good laugh it's to be hoped their not nipped in the bud by fans who's main concern and a good one at that is having a good time. **Both articles from City Fun Number 15, Volume One.**

The Weird and Wonderful World of The Hamsters

Ian was now working in Ron Middlehurst's Greengrocery along with Steven and Robert. He was held in such high regard that he managed to get every sacred Saturday off.

This meant that Ian could go out on a Friday evening and company would always find him, as everyone either knew Ian, or wanted to get to know him. One such individual was Andy Zero and they would often spend the early hours of Saturday morning at Andy's flat in Mossley listening to records and debating what was 'good' or 'bad' about various bands. It should be mentioned that Andy was no syphocant and heated debates would follow, but it was all mostly amicable.

Ian met the extraordinary Al (then Alana) Pellay, through Andy, well before she enjoyed a very successful career. Al describes her younger self as 'a bit 'draggy' and gender ambiguous'. She would go out in full Gloria Swanson glam to the local pubs and was perfectly capable of looking after herself and stepped in when Ian received a head butt for simply wearing a smoking jacket over his combat fatigues.

"Fuck off home, your dads waiting for his blow job!"

Ian's tormenters stopped in horror when confronted by this fantastic hybrid vision somewhere between Liz Taylor and Dame Shirley Bassey screaming like a demented fishwife.

"Straight Boys? More like straight up each other!!"

Then, out of the blue, she decked the bully who butted Ian with one well aimed fist. As Al recounts

'If any twat started back on anyone with me they may as well have signed their own death certificate because I was one Black Bender that weren't going to tolerate shit from any one.

Al recounts that she was introduced to Ian by Mark E Smith (whom she had supported at The Russell Club) and

"...Ian was small, slim, very unassuming...an academic number one (hair) crop and quite shy...wearing a navy blue V-neck sleeveless jumper with white T-shirt underneath and jeans....so he had all of that I had had my Max Factor and a nice Fuck Off black feather boa, ha! (ala Miss Swanson merges with Dorothy Squires; I loved a reb!)

Andy Zero would sometimes stay at Ian's parents' house. One could smell when he had been a guest as he owned a pair of the most rancid feet that could easily stink a whole house out. One day at Ian's home – with both parents present, he suddenly decided to come out to Ian with the unexpected announcement

"I feel like I'm a Woman trapped in a Man's body. I could castrate myself."

Ian's Dad merely decided to continue reading his paper and his mother busied herself, loudly, with preparing the lunch. Ian simply changed the subject as he knew that Andy would come out with the most inappropriate declarations. For example, Andy had decided to audition as a drummer for The Fall and before he started, he confessed to all and sundry

"I've been so exited; I've had a wank over this before I came here."

Surprisingly he didn't get hired.

There was a party in Mossley and this was attended by Ian and Andy, along with Bobby and Steven. During a conversation, in the back yard, their hostess came out and after removing her underwear, squatted in between Andy and Ian, urinated and informed them;

"I'd like you two to fuck me. Do you fancy a threesome?"

It isn't very often that Ian is lost for words, but he was on this particular occasion.

Bobby and Ian, unusually, ran out of steam and were tucked into bed.

Sometime the next day they arose to find Steven seating, reading a book, amongst a sea of naked, entwined bodies on the living room floor. He was the only one who was fully clothed in his usual black outfit with his hat on and collar up. Upon hearing Bobby and Ian he raised his eyes, looked at them, nodded and scanned the naked mass and said, somewhat disinterestedly;

"Orgy"

"What did you do? Steven?"

Chorused Bobby and Ian in unison.

"I just ignored them......the best I could."

The lads continued to spend a lot of time with Anne and John and whilst, getting ready to go out, Ian and Steven espied two large tablets on their friend's side board.

"One each? Go on then."

The tablets were certainly on the large side and it was rather difficult trying to swallow them, but with a bit of perseverance they managed to get them down. An hour or so later, both were in a Zombie like trance. Anne sensed something was up and asked;

"What have you boys taken now?"

"Those pills that were on the side board"

On hearing this, the normally placid Anne hit the roof and wailed;

"Oh My God! Ned's ill, you've only taken the horse's tranquilisers!!!"

John took both Ian and Steven to sleep the sleep of the unjust back to Glossop.

At another occasion, after some drinking and magic mushrooms at Anne and John's, a lad called Eric turned up. Ian thought he was a bit over friendly and he got fed up when Eric commandeered the record player to listen to The Beatles over and over again. Eventually, Ian lost his sense of humour and groaned;

"I'll take those Mop Tops off! It's been done to death"

And proceeded to put his choice of records on. But as soon as Eric got his chance, on went the Fabulous Four again. Somewhat unusually, Ian was feeling edgy and aggressive and began to abuse Eric verbally.

It was suggested that the group go outside, maybe to clear the atmosphere, and everybody trouped to the nearby cemetery. Ian decided to dance on the limestone chips on the top of the gravestones to make them spark. When he saw that this action was freaking Eric out he did it even more. Our normally, kind and considerate Ian was becoming nastier and nastier to Eric. Maybe Eric decided that a game might break the tension and suggested;

"Let's play hide and seek?"

"Yes! You hide and we won't find you!"

Cackled Ian evilly and continued;

"Why don't you just Fuck Off?"

Upon returning to the house, Ian urinated into Eric's crash helmet. Of course the inevitable happened and Eric, upon leaving, put the helmet on and the contents spilt out on to his head.

"Someone's put cider in it"

He announced much to the merriment of those present.

When Ian awoke in the morning he remembered how badly he had treated Eric and felt real shame.

Less than a month later, Eric spotted a complete stranger in a phone box, opened the booth door and stabbed her repeatedly until some passers-by managed to overpower him. He is still being held at a secure psychiatric unit to this very day. Ian heard about this and the cold hand of horror gripped at his heart. Yes, Eric had issues, but Ian genuinely worries if his bullying had tipped this vulnerable being over the edge. Ian immediately made a conscious decision to never behave like that to another human being ever again, no matter what the provocation.

Art Fuck – Virgin Prunes

Finally, Ian managed to persuade Manchester Polytechnic that The Hamsters should play a suitable showcase. At first, a support slot to 'Splodgenousabounds' was originally offered, but Ian had the credibility to decline this novelty. Elliot, the Social Secretary, was then able to offer a gig with 'Performance' on Thursday followed by the prestigious 'John Peel Road show' on the Saturday, the prospect of which really exited Ian as he knew the Hamsters would be the best band on the evening. He was not so excited to be on the same billing as 'Performance' who were a band of dismal art rockers. Normally, Ian would have declined this appearance, but it was strongly rumoured that Joy Division would also be playing on the same bill. Something told Ian that there was something 'not quite right' with this rumour, as it emitted from the Polytechnic, and it was strange that the vocalist from Joy Division, Ian Curtis, who knew nothing about this gig when asked

Ian's worst suspicions were confirmed on the night of the gig as there was handmade poster

The Hamsters
Performance

The name, Joy Division, was at the top of the bill, but it had been crossed out, the audience had been lured there under totally false pretences and Ian was furious. .

Because of the blatant deception to get The Hamsters to play, it was hard to take this event seriously and the band just fooled around. Half-baked songs were attempted and the band was loose and sloppy. Here is what City Fun made of the event.....

THE HAMSTERS, THE POLY AND THE BAN

Certain parties have made it known that they do not want us to write about the following, not writing about these incidents would amount to censorship and needless to say we don't believe in censorship. What follows is an account of human folly read on.....

On Thursday 21st February, 1980, the Hamsters and Performance played at Manchester Polytechnic. The Hamsters played a set that though containing elements of their unique magic had its effectiveness greatly reduced by the band refusing to take themselves or their music seriously. I enjoyed it, but I'm a friend of theirs. I left after the Hamsters and what follows is based on the words of one person only.

When Performance were on, one of the Hamsters got on stage in a manner not acceptable to the band or the Polytechnic. At some point after this one of the gig's organisers 'lost his temper' and attacked one (all?) of the Hamsters. A fight followed and in the aftermath, everyone and their dog got barred.

There are two sides to every story, if all parties concerned had spent a bit of time considering that the other side had a point of view that could be equally as valid all the above could have been avoided. Think about it. **Andy Zero**

Performance followed and were pretentious rubbish but unintentional humour was to be found at the expense of a lithe, male mime artist clad in a tight fitting body stocking prancing around the stage. There were howls of laughter at this unfortunate individual who gamely kept going until he was joined on stage. Yes, you've guessed it, this was too much for Steven to resist and he joined in the mime, by simulating sodomy with the mime artist. Ian felt uneasy at Steven's stage invasion but there was nothing he could do. Suddenly the Security Staff rushed on to the stage and proceeded to exercise more force on Steve than was strictly necessary, but another faction of Security immediately waded into the audience to attack the rest of The Hamsters, who had nothing to do with Steven's on stage shenanigans; it was almost as if they were primed and ready for this violent confrontation. The rest of the audience moved away as Security really laid into the Hamsters. Chairs went flying, girls were screaming in terror at the bloody carnage that had unexpectedly unfolded in front of them. The Hamsters fought back valiantly and gave as good as they got and more. Robert was in the audience and joined in. Eventually Security realised the Hamsters were not going to be an easy push over. Instead, they had to content themselves with merely watching The Hamsters load their van.

The next day Ian got a call from Elliot;

"You are off the bill on Saturday. We consider you to be a jeopardy to the whole event. We have to consider safety. Furthermore, The Hamsters are banned from The Polytechnic"

"Cheers mate! Thanks a Fucking lot"

was the dead pan reply.

Ian later heard that three of the acts, as a result appearing on 'The Road Show' were offered sessions on the John Peel Show.

"Bastards"

was Ian's immediate reaction, as he knew that The Hamsters would have blown any of those bands out of the water on that evening.

Ian just happened to bump into Ian Curtis, later that same week, at a Slits show at Belle Vue and told him of the deception and got the acknowledgment

"I don't care much for those bastards at the Poly either"

Friday Night at the Chip Shop The Hamsters

It's Friday Night at the Chip Shop
And I may be here awhile

Ian was invited to attend the 'Weird Tales' tour when it came to the Mayflower in May of 1980 (which was to prove to be a very busy month for the band). Both the Fall and ATV had loose links with this project, and despite reservations, reluctantly Ian agreed to come along and support this venture.

When he arrived, he found that the audience was radically different from the usual crowd; they were younger, hairier and less rowdy. Ian also found it much easier to strike up a conversation with the bands. Ian was very much taken with local band 'Danny and the Dressmakers' who impressed him with their enthusiasm and total lack of ego.

Ian was introduced to the main organiser, Grant Showbiz (who was also the sound engineer) and found that they both had a common love of Kevin Ayres – who Grant knew personally and had even gone to stay with him in Spain. Grant was a genuinely nice guy, smiling and talkative, although neither knew it at the time, Grant was to play a significant part in Hamster world.

Ian was invited to kick the proceedings off and was happy to perform accapella versions of 'Chip Shop' and 'I'm a Cunt' to a huge round of applause. After 'Danny and the Dressmakers, came 'Zounds' and 'The Mob'. The show closed with a very talented, all female act, 'The Androids of Mu', whom Steve Mardy recalls:

(who) the hamsters had supported I think more than once during 1980. I played their record & the hamsters rehearsal tapes back to back once & found them to be a classical combination, a bit like champagne & oysters.... and a primeval force to be reckoned with **Steve Mardy**

Grant asked Ian if The Hamsters would like to play some gigs on the tour and Ian thought that was a really good idea and readily agreed.

In which the status certainly ain't Status Quo

The 'Weird Tales' tour, on which the Hamsters played on as occasional guests, turned out to be rather good in terms of exposure to large audiences. However it was the close friendships that were formed which meant a lot to the Hamsters at that time, hell; even Steven behaved himself. The tour took place on an old school bus driven by a friendly biker called Tim, who was the boyfriend of 'Cosmic' – a member of "Androids of Mu'.

Also on the tour coach were The Mob who also turned out to be a great deal of fun and contained two fellow Mancunians – Mark the 'pin up' of the band and Curtis. Kif Kif Le Baton is somewhat of a legend in the 'indie scene' and Ian remembers him as a man full of original ideas. One time, a fellow traveller, Jonathon took along a very expensive movie camera to capture the Nottinghill Carnival. He was somewhat laid back and trusting, he never saw the camera again.

However, it is Grant Showbiz, who was the mainstay of the tour and Ian is still in contact with him. Grant was a huge supporter of The Hamsters. Continually offering encouragement in his warm and enthusiastic way he helped the band believe in themselves.

The tour happened to take on a lot of venues in London, which was where the 'Androids of Mu' had a squat. Ian spent a lot of time here, and was enlivened by the politically aware atmosphere and feels that a lot of self-development took place in this nurturing environment. It also helped that Ian was unknown in London and could go around freely.

The Hamsters just finished their sound check at The Spread Eagle (maybe Ian's camp routine with Mick Hucknall had been forgotten rather than forgiven) and Ian went to the bar to get a drink;

"That were alright"

Nodded the ruddy faced landlord as he pulled the pint and in a tone that conveyed a mixture of question and demand continued

"BUT, You're not going to play that tonight when a crowds in are you? You're gonna play some Zepp and Quo aren't you?"

Ian looked the barman straight in the eye and calmly stated;

"They'll hear what you've just heard. We won't be pandering to the Neanderthal cunts that come in here"

End of conversation.

It is a mystery as to who booked 'Weird Tales' tour at The Spread Eagle. Some of the bands' children were bought along in tow which did not please the regulars. But this was nothing in comparison when they saw that 'their place' had been invaded by 'alternative types', there was a very, very unpleasant atmosphere.

The Hamsters, as usual, opened and played to a much divided audience. Their performance crackled with tension and aggression and part of this can be heard on a cassette release by 'Chaos' Tapes (which also features an interview with Mark E Smith). The few fans that were present were scared into silent submission by the tough biker boys and a young Hamsters fan was badly beaten up in the toilets afterwards.

The bands that followed were not exactly warmly received mainly owing to the air of latent aggression; The Hamsters saw the bus off to ensure it left safely. However, Ian later learnt, that the bus was stopped shortly afterwards by the police, who proceeded to search for four hours for any 'illicit' substances. Amazingly, nothing was found and the bus was allowed to go. Ian strongly suspects that the Police were 'tipped off' by someone present at The Spread Eagle.

Why Kittens should really let Hamsters go before them....

The Lemon Kittens are playing on stage at London's Centro Iberico. At first Ian was rather keen to see this opening band as he was an admirer of both the vocalist Karl Blake and Mark Perry, who was on drums.

"Hmm, they are dragging on a bit"

He thought to himself after he purchased yet another drink and put out the umpteenth joint of the evening. His mind wandered during the set, it had been a top day so far. The Hamsters had a good time at the 'Legalise Cannabis' campaign rally, earlier on, at Hyde Park and they had also eagerly been following the results of the Cup Final which had taken place earlier on that day.

In addition, he had also spoken to Nick Turner, the saxophonist in Inner City Unit, who was due to go on after The Hamsters. Nick was a natural raconteur and had entertained his bar audience with Hawkwind (his previous band) smuggling drugs through customs in instrument cases. Ian had the nerve to ask him about Lemmy (ex-bass player) and Nick confessed that he felt that some of the spirit of the band went with him. Ian got the distinct impression that Nick felt he should have stood up for Lemmy, but the fact that Lemmy was enjoying huge current success with 'Motorhead' appeared to appease any residual guilt.

"And now for our last number"

Announced Karl Blake

A mixture of 'Thanks' and 'Fuck's' could be heard, mainly from the Hamsters who began to line up by the stage to go on next.

The last number just went on and on. The Lemon Kittens had played a lengthy set that was boring and improvisational; they were to pay dearly for this self-indulgence.

Just when they thought the song was over, and the Hamsters were visibly straining at the leash, the song started up again.....before Ian could react, Steven strode up onto the stage and went straight up to Mark Perry and punched him. The legendary editor of the seminal 'Sniffin' Glue' fanzine and founder of ATV was then unceremoniously pulled off his drum seat and hurled to the floor. After a good ten seconds, the band realised that the drum beat had radically altered and turned around to find a grinning maniac hammering the kit. They simply stopped dead and left the stage.

"We're the Hamsters"

Announced, Ian as the rest of the band strode on to plug in their instruments, and drunkenly slurred;

"..The BEST band in Manchester!! Better than Joy Division, better than The Fall and better than The Buzzcocks!"

The band proceeded to play the messiest and sloppiest set to date but it was very well received by the audience. But Ian felt that the band had made complete twats of themselves the next morning as he awoke with a hangover that felt like; he too, had been clouted round the head by Steve.

In which we learn why Martin was called 'Lettuce'

In the grand tradition of Hamster's bassists, Martin was an outsider from the start. He had a rather taciturn and phlegmatic nature which meant he was the butt of the band's jokes, he didn't exactly help himself with his inability to laugh things off and was often on the verge of tears, so cruel and incessant was the bad natured teasing. The flat, in Hulme that he and Rob Crane shared was infested with cockroaches and thus earnt the name 'Cockroach Corner', another thing to wind Martin up with.

The Hamsters had been offered a slot at Stonehenge but chose to appear at 'The Squat' instead. Ian later learned that this had been a wise move as many of the 'Punky' bands were beaten up, raped and pillaged by the biking contingent.

There is a healthy crowd at 'The Squat' and The Hamsters are on top form and are appearing in front of an enthusiastic audience, which include members of The Fall.

Martin decides to kick a microphone stand into the crowd and this uncalled for action immediately infuriates Ian who kicks Martin up the bum and barks at him

"Who the Fuck do you think you are?"

Ian doesn't need to wait for an answer and continues;

"Some kind of Fucking big Rockstar!"

Ian decides to publicly humiliate Martin and demands;

"Apologise to these people who've come to see us"

Martin hesitates and Ian goads him with;

"Go on! Tell them you're sorry for being such a prick!"

Martin looks like a naughty schoolboy and goes to the microphone Ian is holding in his direction and says;

"Sorry."

Everyone bursts out laughing at Martin and the set is then resumed.

The first person to congratulate Ian when he comes off stage is Mike Joyce, who is present with his girlfriend:

"That was so good, Moet!"

He beams and offers his hand out for Ian to shake.

By means of a reply, Ian sprays him with a mouthful of cider and now accepts this was inexcusably bad behaviour on his part, he was just so wired at the time.

The three Hamsters hit the bar with a sulky bassist in tow. Ian is getting really fed up with all this sulking and demands

"Oh for God's sake! What's wrong now, Lettuce?!!"

"You fucking now and don't call me Lettuce."

Martin whined.

"I can't help it Martin. You are so very wet and green. But fucking cheer up now."

"I suppose so."

Sighs Martin resignedly.

The Fall come and congratulate The Hamsters.
"You are Fucking Wonderful"
"We know."
Mark E Smith comes over to Steven and asks;
"Would you like to play some gigs with us?
"We'll see if we can fit you in I suppose. You'd better ask Mo."
Was the nonchalant reply before Steve turned away from The Fall front man to get another drink at the bar.
This was the perfect response and Ian, despite turning summersaults in his stomach, followed in a tone that conveyed casual disinterest;
"Yeah, we'd be up for playing with you at some point'
The dye was cast and Ian could have floated away.

Big Man, Little Man Crass

It is impossible to state how important and influential Crass were to the disaffected youth of the late seventies and early eighties. This Punk Anarchist band played music that was original and intelligent. Therefore it was a real coup for The Mayflower to have them play, despite The Factory's best attempts to poach them.

Bob and Ian were present at this gig when a very drunk Steven showed up. He hadn't got any money and ordered Bob and Ian to pay for his drinks; he wasn't exactly grateful when his demands were met either.

The Poison Girls played a magnificent set and then the surprise of the evening came on, none other than the unannounced Pop Group. They had been involved in some media spat with Crass and came to perform to illustrate that both groups had made up. They proceeded to play a short, but fantastic set.

Steven came back to Bob and Ian and demanded
"You gonna buy me another drink, then?!!"
Bob believed he had brought Steven enough; it wasn't as if he was being thanked and replied;
"No"
Upon hearing this refusal, Steven's eyes narrowed and then he brought his head forward to Bob's. Bob's head jerked backwards and broken teeth flew from his mouth. He spat blood out on to the floor, looked Steven in the eye, shook his head and said;
"You're pathetic"
Before walking away.
Ian was stunned; Steven had just attacked Bob, his band mate and oldest friend.
"What HAVE you done??"

Tears welled up in Steven's eyes and he murmured;

"I don't know……. I'm so sorry"

Ian shook his head at Steven and hissed;

"Well, you've really, really fucked things up now. Why don't you just fuck off now?"

And then went off to see if Bob was ok but he had gone. Ian wanted to get away and went to the pub across the road to be alone. Unfortunately, word of Steven's violence had got around and Ian's notion of a quiet drink had to be abandoned as person, after person came to ask him exactly what had happened.

Steven slunk in to the pub and sat down and an acquaintance noticed how forlorn he looked and said to Ian

"I feel so sorry for him"

This really was the last straw for Ian; he got up and roared in Steven's direction;

"SPARE YOUR FUCKING PITY! HE DOESN'T DESERVE IT!!!"

Ian then stormed out of the pub in an absolute fury.

Steven came along to the rehearsal room the next day, with Steve Molloy as support. He wasn't contrite enough for Ian's liking and he really laid into Steven with a scathing verbal assault. Steve's reply was, to say the least, bizarre.

"I'll buy Bobby a telly to make up for it"

Ian was flabbergasted and managed to stammer out:

"You Fuckin' What?!! A Fucking Telly?.....To say sorry for smashing your fucking teeth in, Mate?!!!

Steve Molloy genuinely believed that he was being diplomatic when he added

"Bobby will be really grateful, you know?"

Ian just couldn't believe his ears and sighed.

"See you on Tuesday; we can discuss a new guitarist then"

Steven just looked at the floor

Imagine Ian's surprise when an eager Bob appeared at Tuesday's rehearsal. Ian didn't say anything during the rehearsal but afterwards asked Bob

"I thought you had left mate?"

Bob nodded and replied;

"I was really angry and upset, but I realised it would be even worse if I lost the band as well"

Bob never got his television and to all intents and purposes it looked like this unpleasant incident was water under the bridge. But both Bob and Robert informed Ian;

"You know you'll be next don't you?"

'I never really communicated with him (Steven) and I'd probably detected that it was all a veneer and he probably behaved like it for good reason' **Al Pellay**

First Recording Session

The Hamsters' very first professional recordings were performed live in front of an invited audience, which included Mark E Smith and Kay Carol. Two songs were to be taken from the set as part of the 'Manchester Evening Noise' compilation for City Fun Magazine. This album would lead to a nationwide tour, the Hamsters were right to be sceptical (it never transpired) but agreed to participate.

A rig was set up at a church hall in Stalybridge by Oz P.A. Company, who were Manchester's premier sound system. The Hamsters did the very best they could, under very trying circumstances, and came up with a compelling primitive sound. It was the first time they had been recorded and as instructions were issued from the sound system, Steven actually spoke back into the monitors as if they were giant telephones. This caused much amusement from the audience but they managed to get a total of nine recordings, which included the brand new track 'Animals", which denoted a development in their song writing ability and creativity.

At the end of the set Mark E Smith and Kay Carroll came over to Ian and they were positively beaming and offered;

"Would you like to support The Fall at Rafters, two weeks from now?"

Ian wasn't going to play the hard to get card twice and answered

"Yes"

This was real progress, The Fall were amongst the most influential and respected bands in the UK and there was no way that 'Rafters' would have offered the Hamsters a gig under any other circumstance.

As Ian was socialising with Mark E Smith and Kay Carol, he realised he had forgotten something very important in all this excitement:

"Shit, I'm supposed to be at a Wedding Reception!"

Originally, Ian was to have been best man at Derek and Christine's Wedding, but had to pull out owing to this evenings recording commitment. Ian managed to get to the reception, very late and was very apologetic. Fortunately, his friends understood and forgave a very shame faced Ian. A brawl on the dance floor, with Ian observing from the side lines, was a perfect end to a perfect day.

Thy Legend Goes Before Thee

Ian believes The Hamsters notoriety was both a blessing and a curse. They were an explosive commodity and were both envied and reviled by many of their peers. This resulted in a form of exclusion actually worked to their advantage as they were able to retain their integrity and creativity. However, certain urban myths regarding their outrageous behaviour began to spring up. One such rumour was spread by City Fun Magazine, which claimed they trashed Tony

Davidson's rehearsal studio, they never actually set foot in there. Despite Ian's best efforts, these rumours were instrumental in them not getting gigs at the local Polytechnic. This was ironic, as The Hamsters could have attracted even larger audiences than 'Armed Force' or even 'The Frantic Elevators'.

This is why Mark E Smith's offer of a support gig at the prestigious 'Rafters' venue was so important, by supporting The Fall they managed to get into several venues (including the Polytechnic) that would have refused entry under any other circumstance. The Hamsters were always treated with kindness and respect; they always received a 'rider' and were well paid.

In a way I suppose we were a little envious of their ramshackle approach, The Fall was getting more successful, touring constantly and, as a result, things were getting a little more regimented so we looked on The Hamsters with slightly dewy-eyed nostalgia. In those days I remember Moet, despite being the singer, as something of a secondary figure. The obvious booming presence was Steve Middlehurst, partly because of his simple but cool drumming, the fact he mainly wrote the songs, surreal lyrics and all. He was also a huge pain in the a**e, sometimes funny with it, sometimes boring with a holier-than-thou chip on his shoulder. I think part of that was about us being in a 'successful' band. The guitarist, Bob, was kind of a Mini-Me Steve. I think Moet was frustrated by being over-shadowed by these larger-than-life characters and tried to over compensate but it was an ill-fitting suit at times.
Craig Scanlon

Both bands became friends and Ian's opinion on other bands' performances, including The Fall, was much valued. The other band members of The Fall, Marc Riley, Craig Scanlon, Steve Hanley and Mike Leigh (soon to be replaced by Paul Hanley) would watch The Hamsters set and became keen fans. The Hamsters didn't rest on their laurels being in such challenging company and always played their best, not wanting to fuck this great opportunity up.

Ian became known as 'the builder' by the some of the audience, as he looked as if he had walked straight from work on to the stage. However, it became apparent they believed this was a 'look' Ian had conspired to create

Upon hearing how he got his nick name, Ian roared with laughter and explained;

"I look like this because I really have come straight from work, it's not an image!"

The Fall also became part of the trusted circle that were invited back to Anne and Johns to sample magic mushrooms for the first time. Maybe Ian's decision to play 'Dragnet' (The Fall's previous album) over and over again was not a wise one, as this resulted in one Fall member wetting their trousers.

"..I remember lying, mashed in a cottage in Glossop during the mushroom season and Moet's face inches from mine. "I want to be your friend, Craig. Let me be your friend" he bellowed. "F*ck off", I said......" **Craig Scanlon**

Moss V Middlehurst

See this band if you want any idea of what they're like......
They wanted to be 'the worst band in the world'
You might think they're crap
I'm a cunt; I don't think that we are
Everyone was shouting 'Hamsters
When the Hamsters did come on the stage
Everyone was dancing and shouting 'Chip Shop'
I can only remember three of the names
'Cunt', 'Chipshop' and "TVitus" I think is their best song
The other two are just joke songs
and very often people ignore them as songs which are serious
I said serious
While they're busy shouting 'I'm an Cunt' and 'Chipshop'
Never mind I just think 'TVitus' is really good.

Steven Middlehurst Tape Transcript

Deep down Steven was very insecure and Ian knew this. However Ian's confrontational nature meant that he wasn't afraid to challenge Steve over his own self-importance. For example, Steve would be at a post gig bar referring to the Hamsters collective work as
"My Songs....."
This was too much for Ian and he had to butt in...
"Excuse me Mr Middlehurst, these are OUR songs. You don't bloody write the tunes do you now?"
"Yeah, but I come up with the lyrics"
"In that case mate, why don't you just get up on stage and read them all by yourself as poetry then?!"
Upon reflection, Ian knew that he should have allowed for Steven's lack of confidence, but if something needed to be pointed out......
This uneasy song writing alliance added to the mounting tensions within the band and it was usually Martin who ended up as being the verbal punch bag; the poor chap was looking even more morose than his natural self. On one occasion he had been ordered to hire a van to get the band and equipment to drive to a fundraising gig for 'Legalise Cannabis' campaign at The University of Sussex in

Brighton. The band were waiting at 'The Nelson' on that Friday evening and Martin returned......with a Ford Escort car. The Hamsters, upon seeing this totally unsuitable mode of transport went ballistic;

"It's fucking tiny!"

"Well, it's the...

"SHUT UP! YOU IDIOT."

"...best I could.."

"SHUT THE FUCK UP LETTUCE!!"

"The only one they had."

"You bloody hired it; you can bloody drive it and no drink for you!"

Martin really got it the neck and was made to cram their equipment into this most compact of transport whilst the rest of the band got roaring drunk. Eventually, the band was ready for the off and Ian got down to consuming the bottle of brandy he had brought along for the journey.

The trusty Ford was speeding down the motorway when Steven felt queasy, decidedly ill and wound down the window to vomit. He managed to shove his head out of the front passenger window and

"WHOOOSHHH"

the contents of his stomach flew out and slapped straight into Bobby's face. It was just like a scene out of a John Waters Movie as Bobby sat in the back of the car with his face caked in vomit.

"PULL OVER! LETTUCE! PULL OVER!"

Martin managed to pull over on to a hard shoulder and Steven was very apologetic

"I'll clean you up Bob!"

and went out to grab handfuls of grass to wipe Bob's face, unfortunately cutting him up with the sharper shard edges.

Later on in the journey, Ian had finished the brandy and was dying for a break and made Martin pull over in a London suburb just as dawn was breaking. He managed to find a convenient graveyard and espies a cheerful, whistling postman winding his merry way as he makes his deliveries; but even better, there is also an empty milk float.....

"Whoopee!!"

Yells Ian as he pilots the milk float, but his journey is short as he collides with a nearby garden gate and is grabbed by the irate milkman who attempts to hold Ian captive and swears;

"Bastard! I'm going to get the police on to you!"

"Yeah, yeah! Ha!"

Ian pushes the milkman off and runs back to the car, whooping and hollering; what fun!

Oh, They Do Like To Be Beside The Seaside

Ian was shattered by the time the ford eventually arrived in Brighton at around 08.00 am and decided to have a kip. The rest wandered off to get some breakfast and have a look around. Ian vaguely remembers that he was awoken around midday to go out for a drink, but refused as he still felt pretty rough. He was finally made to wake up later by a very drunk Bobby and Steven, Martin then drove them to the venue.

The University Campus was a great deal of fun as it had lakes and streams, of course everyone ended up in the water, but Martin was the one who got more of his fair share of being pushed about and he really lost his rag;

"I've had enough, you treat me like shit!"

If Martin was expecting some sort of sympathy he was to be disappointed, for all he got was a chorus of wicked cackles.

"You bastards are evil to me!"

He reached into the pocket of his sodden trousers and flung the car keys at his tormenters and limped away. This dramatic action was met with a chorus of further laughter and Martin turned around with a really hurt and pained expression

"Come on Martin"

Ordered Ian, dangling the keys at him

"You know you're not going anywhere"

Martin could see the logic in this and came back, defeated, resignedly taking the car keys back from Ian.

The venue was massive with a large high stage. The Hamsters decided to have forty, dry, winks and after draping their muddy and sodden clothes on the radiators. The audience came in to find the lead act fast asleep in their pants. Steven realised what was going on and woke the other band members up and changed to the sound of throbbing disco music. The preparation consisted of a few more drinks and a dance.

As The Hamsters waited in the wings, ready to play, the organiser of the benefit made what he obviously considered to make a passionate plea about Police brutality and criminalisation of those to smoke pot. To illustrate his point he lit a huge spliff

Ian cringed in embarrassment and muttered

"Fucking winging hippy"

Bobby giggled and shook his head, agreeing

"What a wanker"

Steven just stared....and then bolted across the stage knocking the speaker off stage with a perfectly executed ruby tackle. Ian just hoped that Steven hadn't killed the speaker but the rest of the band stride on stage and Ian announces

"We're The Hamsters, we're from Manchester 123...."

Now Ian speculates that there is a school of thought that bands play better when they are drunk, now any one subscribing to that particular philosophy really should have seen the Hamsters set that particular night. Ian maintains they were sluggish, out of tune, out of synch and there was no spark. But despite all this outstanding drunken incompetence the set went down extremely well, the songs obviously still managed to speak to people, and The Hamsters were virtually mobbed by an adoring audience after their set from hell. Ian wasn't pleased, the band had let themselves down badly, he believed........

About 5 years later Ian took it upon himself to cheer up a coach load of Brighton and Hove supporters who had just lost the FA Cup to Manchester 4 -0. Ian was, as he put it, 'well refreshed' and came on to the coach and announced;

"Hello, I've not come to gloat but to wish you a safe journey home and hope that when the disappointment wears off, you'll remember the fun you've had here and being here. And to cheer you up I'm going to sing you some songs"

Ian launches in to 'Chip Shop' and 'I'm a Cunt', the mood on the coach changes and soon everyone is stamping and clapping in time. Drinks are passed up the bus for Ian and a voice pipes up

"I saw you at The University of Sussex! The Hamsters! Great Stuff!"

Whilst it is nice to be remembered, Ian still feels shame regarding the terrible performance The Hamsters gave on that muddy, wet and drunken day.

Love will tear us apart Joy Division

Ian Curtis's suicide on 18 May stunned not only his family and friends but the whole of the music industry. Joy Division had such a lot going for them, but Ian Curtis chose to end his young life and he hung himself.

About two or three weeks after Ian Curtis's death, Ian went to see 'Crispy Ambulance' in 'The Millstone's' upper room. This concert was sparsely attended, but amongst the audience were Hooky, Bernard Sumner, Steve Morris and their manager Rob Gretton. Ian decided to go and say 'Hello' and was asked to pull up a chair. The mood was sombre but the band responded to Ian's questions about Ian Curtis and their own future. They were definite about continuing in some shape or format and Alan Hempstall (vocalist with Crispy Ambulance) was considered as a lead vocalist as he had stood in for Ian Curtis when he had been ill.

Ian and Rob Gretton got on very well, both talked about football and both agreed to differ over the merits of Manchester United and Manchester City. Ian liked Rob's candour and honesty; there was no bullshit with Rob.

Ian debated the numerous merits of The Fall with Hooky who admitted:

"I can't get past Mark Smiths horrible voice"

It was decided to go and see 'Psychedelic Furs' at Rafters when the Millstone had closed Ian and Rob got there first and managed to get in, but unbelievably Hooky, Bernard and Steve were asked to pay the full asking price; which they couldn't afford. They were regarded as 'just some lads out of a band' rather than the legends they later became. Ian managed to hold back his disgust at the door as both he and Rob managed to negotiate a reduced entry fee for the band.

Martin limps out, Jon strides in Summer 1980

The fury of the Hamsters was at its zenith at the Tuesday rehearsal and it was Martin, as usual, who got the full frontal assault. Ian was especially vicious as he savaged Martin's continual incompetence so much so that Martin tore off his instrument and stuttered;

"Gggoo Ffuck your sselves!"

Yet again, another bass player made the walk of shame from the rehearsal room and was spared the sound of laughter echoing around him. Actually, that came later as the band experienced the sheer relief of having Martin finally leave after four months.

"Bring on the new"

voiced Ian's attitude upon Martin's departure.

"...The Hamsters were quite a big name at the time and Steve was a local celebrity for being a psycho nut job. I had just left school and was practicing with some mates at local Conservative club – Steve came in to watch us and laughed at how shite we was.
I think they had just ditched Martin the Lettuce and Steve approached me to join the Hamsters. Obviously, being shite was the first part of the Hamsters entrance exam
As scary as Steve was, he was connected with the Manchester music scene in a big way. Playing gigs was everything to me at the time – Steve provided the ideal opportunity to do this" **Jon Rowlinson**

"This is Jon; he's our new bass player"

Stated an emphatic Steven, introducing a tall, gawky lad, dressed in denim.

"Oh aye, where did you find him then?"

Mused a curious Bobby, regarding the nervy, smiling figure who was shuffling around.

"At a bus stop carrying a bass guitar,"

It had been a week since Martin limped out of the previous rehearsal and Steve had literally grabbed their replacement bass player off the street, or so he led the rest of the band to believe.

"How old are you then, Mate?"

enquired Ian who thought this lad looked rather young and his suspicions were confirmed when the teenager smiled;

"Eighteen"

"Any objections then?"

asked Steven, who was eager to get on with the rehearsal, knowing full well that there wouldn't be. Personally, Ian's first impressions of Jon were that of a simpleton as he nervously kept smiling but any port.....

"What sort of music do you like?"

Enquired Ian.

"Thin Lizzy and The Stranglers."

Ian just about held his tongue and feared the worst. This was not only a nit wit, who was already beginning to irritate Ian with his persistent cheeriness, but also one with no musical taste. Ian knew it; it was going to be an uphill slog with this one and wearily went up to the rehearsal room with the new boy in eager tow.

But Ian was wrong, very wrong as it transpired.

Not only did Jon manage to pick up every bass line with only the cursory of run throughs but he was able to expand and improve upon each and every line; Jon recalls:

"The songs were good and I loved playing them

The Hamsters were no longer a three piece with a twat on the bass, Jon was able to add a melodic fullness, that had previously been missing and the band sounded tighter as a result. For the first time, ever, Ian found he was able to use the bass as a vocal guide and he could have kissed Jon but said;

"Yeah, that's ok, heard better, but that will have to do for now"

After all he didn't want to admit to Jon that he had mysteriously become a vital force and, heck, he may not even want to turn up again as he was a really good bass player. But Jon picked up the fact that Ian was rather impressed but, on the other hand

"Steve felt as if the Music had lost something. I just played to what Bob was playing and had not heard any of the material before anyway, so could make no comparison.

Jon recalled that Bobby's guitar was wildly out of tune and got no thanks for rectifying this anomaly as Bobby is tone deaf (it was from this moment on that Jon had his suspicions about Bobby).

All Along The Watch Tower Jimi Hendrix

"I had seen loads of bands there anyway but never played the venue (or any venue to be honest) To be actually on stage with a huge PA was mind blowing" **Jon Rowlinson**

Ian and Bobby waiting to go on stage in the low ceiling cellar known as 'Hippy John's Cave' to appear as guests on the 'Weird Tales' Tour. Bobby had rolled up a spliff as both were settling down to watch 'Zounds', when as if from nowhere, two bouncers appeared and shoved Ian against the wall and his hashish is taken out, examined, and then put back without a word.

"What the Fuck...."

Exclaims Ian and then the penny drops, he is being set up for a police raid and decides to swallow a quarter of black hashish. At first Ian is ok, and even manages to nod civilly to Martin, who is much happier to go back to being a fan instead of a victim but twenty minutes later this drug is really kicking in and he describes himself as having transformed into a 'Frothing wreck', twenty minutes after that he was feeling even worse and had to get up and face an audience consisting of hippies.

In his drug induced state of paranoia Ian is acutely aware that the crowd were visibly shifting away from the stage as soon as The Hamsters stepped on and experienced radiant waves of alienation. Ian now feels a real mixture of hate and fear towards these wretched hippies and he is not alone as the rest of the band expresses their contempt for the audience with a blistering sonic boom wave of sound devised to punish their detractors. Jon, in his debut gig, was indeed the calm in the eye of the storm and pulsated with rhythm, Bobby slashes away and Steve is a blistering whirlwind. If the audience were hoping for 'peace and love' they got a shrieking 'Attila and The Banshees'.

The boo's and slow hand claps got louder and louder, only Grant Showbizz in the DJ booth appears to be the only person relishing this power house of a set. He manically announces over the system;

"The Hamsters! The Hamsters! They are the next band who will be appearing on 'Fuck Off Records'! The Hamsters are the best band in the north!"

This doesn't impress the audience who want no more of these wretched rodents but they are to get a treat denied to the most stalwart fans until now, an encore!

"This one's for all you hippies!"

Ian jeers

"Bobby Dylan, Jimi Hendrix, eat your heart out! This is 'All Along The Watch Tower'!"

This is as much of a surprise to the rest of the band, as it is to the audience, because they haven't played this one but attempt a rough approximation of this classic. This impromptu cover finishes to deafening boo's, but Ian doesn't care, like Jimmy Cagney in 'White Light' he feels 'top of the world'.

Grant comes over to join the laughter and hugging that is taking place amongst the triumphant Hamsters and declares:

"We've got to get you in the studio to capture this!"

Ian can't sleep that night owing to all the muddle and strangeness that permeates his consciousness.

OWWW WOW WOW GRRRRR!!!!!!!

Animals by The Hamsters

I can't remember what the bass was
He did 'Fuck all'
Steven Middlehurst Tape Transcript

Despite being a great deal more proficient, and creative, than his predecessors, being a bassist was not an easy life for Jon. He knew what to expect from the raucous, alcohol fuelled rehearsals and managed to create order from chaos. The group sensed, that with Jon's ability, they were able to translate ideas into song structures, one such idea 'Clouds of Flies' was finally brought to realisation by Jon's sinuous bass line. The band was constantly working on new material as well as updating older numbers.

However, Ian had a couple of real problems with Jon.....

Firstly, Jon preferred to play bass with his fingers, in homage to his Jazz hero –Jacko Pastoris. Ian hated this as he believed the use of a plectrum made towards a much harder sound. Jon would often be playing bass lines, using his fingers, catch Ian's look of sheer malevolence, and shamefacedly pick up the plectrum to appease Ian. But every now and then he would forget. One such occasion was after a run through of a new number called 'Social Drinking', it didn't sound right to Ian's ears and when he looked around he found out that this was due to Jon's jazzy fingering of the bass frets. Ian saw red and flung his bottle of Guinness straight at Jon's head, fortunately, Jon managed to duck and only caught a glancing blow, but the bottle exploded into fragments on the wall behind him. Jon looked absolutely shocked and Ian realised that if he had hit him at such close range, there could have been real injury.

"Pick that Fucking plectrum up!"

Barked Ian. This was as close as Jon would get to an apology and the band carried on.

"I didn't give a fuck to be honest. I am never bothered about physical confrontation and don't hold grudges –I was still playing in the band, so unperturbed"

Secondly, the band made 'animal noises' during the genuinely terrifying anti vivisectionist number called 'Animals'. I can recall this number being done live and it was simple, but very effective. However, Jon would often feel very self-conscious making these 'banshee like' noises and would often 'forget' to join in. One night, when the Hamsters were supporting The Fall at the F Club, Ian noticed that Jon was not exactly going for full 'Animal Magic' in front of the packed audience, yet again, during this number. Ian calmly strode over to Jon and;

"He also attacked me on stage at the F Club in Leeds for not making animal noises...we laughed about it afterwards."

Afterwards, Ian reflected upon his monstrous behaviour towards the gentle Jon. Maybe it was because he cared so much about the band he had sought to 'cure' Jon with violence? Or was that an excuse to justify his disgraceful behaviour and maybe he really was a monster? It genuinely disturbed Ian when he behaved this way towards others, but he appeared to be unable to stop himself.

Don't look at my hair style – it might fall over

Hamsters Review City Fun (Vol 2., number 5)1980

THE HAMSTERS, a band. A strange band with a strange reputation. Some people don't like them; think they're uncouth, yobboes, rude, fools, not nice. Some people think they're the best band in Manchester. Tonight they're in Leeds.

Sometimes the Hamsters give out a magnetic cohesion that makes this r'n'r shit more than worthwhile, tonight wasn't one of those nights. It was hard to know how much it was the acoustics of the club and how much the band. Some songs came across ok and some never seemed to leave the confines of the stage, everything sounded muffled. Musically the closest reference point is a cross between The Fall and DAF - but that is misleading. Both the drummer and guitarist have an original style, the Hamsters are unique. All the band look totally normal, but do things that are totally unconventional. One song is about walking dogs or something and features all the band making dog-type noises that I find hard to believe come from a human...

Of their songs I don't like; 'I'm a cunt' and the one about 'Got to Prove That I'm A Man' – I don't know if these are tongue in cheek and I'm missing the joke, or what. Whichever, they're cutting it a bit fine for my liking. That's what's good about the Hamsters though; most of what they do leaves me slightly stunned. They're on a different wavelength to anything else. They're always laughing. They make me want to work out what they're on about. If you see the Hamsters, open your mind and ignore your prejudices. They might make you laugh

Acklam Hall 1980

The Hamsters
Seen them loads of times
Mostly at The Fun House
Really Good Laugh
Really Good Laugh
Tony Wilson asks
Moet the lead singer
'What kind of music do you play?"
"Stupid Music" his reply
Which about really kind of sums it up
Steven Middlehurst Tape Transcript

A couple of weeks later Ian is relaxing in the bar enjoying a post-show drink, it is a good evening as both Spurtz and Glass Animals are playing too and Ian really wants to catch both acts.

"Ian, I've someone who wants to meet you."

Greets Andy Zero who has sidled up to the bar besides him.

"Eh, What?"

Exclaims Ian, and upon turning around sees Tony Wilson attired in a rather silly long white mackintosh. Tony invited him to come and talk at the back of the DJ booth with Andy Zero present. What could this be about?

"My Good friend John Dowie"

Began Tony Wilson who was referring to the 'punk poet' who had released a record on Wilson's Factory Record label.

"Saw you on the floor of The Factory a few weeks ago and he has been raving about you, insisting that I come to see you, says we should release a record by you, what time are you on?"

Ian grinned and replied;

"Too late, mate!"

This reply throws Tony Wilson somewhat and, perplexed, asks;

"You're not headlining tonight?"

"We don't worry about being seen to be on top of the bill, mate."

Explains Ian and continues;

"We're not that insecure and anyway we'd be too pissed to play later!"

Tony isn't sure whether Ian is having a joke or not and persists;

"What sort of music do you play?"

Well, a stupid question deserves a stupid reply;

"Stupid music."

Tony Wilson really looks puzzled and seeks clarification;

"Why do you describe it like that?"

"It's ours, I can describe it anyway I like"

The conversation is getting stranger and stranger, and not a little strained. Ian catches Andy Zero's face incredulous with disbelief; he is shaking his head slightly.

Tony Wilson gives up and says;

"I'll try to catch you sometime"

"Come early."

Grinned Ian.

Tony holds his hand out to shake Ian's, but Ian has a drink in each hand and manages to slosh some over the white raincoat.

"Whoops"

Apologies Ian.

"Sorry."

Ian's smile conveys otherwise.

Tony Wilson shook his head and made his escape. Andy Zero stands and looks with Ian with an expression of absolute incredulity.

Ian chuckles and has a good long slurp of his drink; he didn't want to join The Factory gang.

The Hamsters; Available for Children's' Parties and other functions

The Hamsters played at Dukinfield Community Club. Now I was from Dukinfield which was dull. The town at the time has a swimming baths and a cemetery, so you either went there for a swim or to get buried. The Hamsters and all fans assembled in the Top Astley pub. Needless to say the locals weren't impressed. The gig as usual descended into chaos and the police were called. Somehow the personnel of the band had something which always descended into wonderful anarchy. **Simmo**

The best fun the Hamsters ever had was well away from the cynical Manchester 'Music Scene'. Much more fun was to be had playing to an audience of under Sixteen's at the local Dunkinfield Youth Club.

Even Steven was to be found to be having a great time and had a genuine rapport with the young audience who simply adored the 'smiling madman' on drums. The youngsters were out to have fun and were much more appreciative of The Hamsters vibe, running around and going wild.

Ian collected a vast array of tambourines, maracas and vibrio slaps and the group would invite the youngsters to come on stage during the last song to come and bash away and yell into the microphones. This was a huge hoot for the kids and was as loud as it was fun. The Hamsters saw no need to bring the wildness to a close, and actively encouraged the youngsters to go for it, but the youth workers were shifting around uneasily as the 10 pm curfew was in danger of being breached. Eventually, the workers attempted to halt the noisy basing and screaming, but were ignored by everyone. The police were called and broke up the proceedings and ordered the band to load up the van, making sure that they do. But the kids have not had enough and stand across the road and chant in defiant salute;

"HAMSTERS, HAMSTERS"

Unfortunately, this harmless fun resulted in The Hamsters being banned from playing at the youth club; in fact all bands were now banned from playing ever again. Ian felt sick about that.

"..We started the Can Club at the Cypress Tavern as an altruistic, almost hippy-like project, where we would put on bands we would like to see. But mainly so we could Swan around all puffed-up and important, smiling benevolently on the awe-struck crowd. Another perk was refusing free entry to people like snap-jockey, Kevin Cummings, who had the deluded belief Manchester was his oyster because he owned a camera and a trench coat. We'd charge a minimal amount and split the takings with the bands, just retaining enough money to re-hire the place and P.A. We booked Orange Juice, the notsensibles and, of course, The Hamsters. The place was a great success. I remember the notsensibles' manager insensible with joy when we handed over their £300 takings from the door. That was a lot of money in Burnley. I think he bought a street with it.." Excerpt from 'My Struggle' **Craig Scanlon**

Ian became resident DJ at the Saturday Evening 'Can Club, run by The Fall' in the basement of The Cyprus Tavern (located in Princess Street). Ian was intrigued by the name and knowing that the band were huge 'Can' fans asked:

"Is it named after the Krautrock band then?"

"No"

Was the enigmatic reply.

"It's can rather than can't"

Mark E Smith decided to put Ian to a challenge one evening and requested;

"Can you play something by King Crimson then, Ian?"

Ian was not phased one single bit and was able to reply confidently

"No problems Mark"

pulling out 'Cat food/Groon' from his record box. Unfortunately, Ian rather spoilt the moment by playing it at the wrong speed, but decided to brazen it out and no one appeared to notice.

On another Saturday evening both Jon and Bob were having a drink at 'The Garrett', just across the road from The Cyprus Tavern before coming over to join Ian. It was a real old fashioned pub populated by middle aged couples and even had a tap room where the men played cards and darts.

Jon had a secret and he felt he could confide in Bob, he leant across the table, and in hushed tones informed Bob;

"Bob please don't say a word to anyone...."

Bob's ears pricked up, but he replied;

"Of course not, mate"

Jon hesitated and then decided to let Bob in to his secret:

"Whenever I get the chance when I'm alone at home, I like to dress up in my sisters clothes, I'm a transvestite."

Oh dear, he'd chosen the most inappropriate individual to confide in as beer sprayed from Bob's mouth as he struggled to contain himself. He failed, valiantly and at the top of his voice announced;

"You like to wear WOMEN'S clothes! You're a TRANNY! BRILLIANT! Ha! I've just got to tell Moet!!"

Bob rushed out of a deadly silent pub with all faces turned to a red faced; open mouthed Jon, who had no choice but to follow Bob.

"Bob was a wanker for doing that!! I was still unsure about cross dressing and wanted an opinion from a friend. He shouted it out, not out of surprise, but to embarrass me.
My suspicions about Bob had been confirmed – cunt." **Jon Rowlinson**

Bob blabbed Jon's secret out to Ian, who was standing at the DJ booth with a microphone in his hand. When Jon came in to the basement, Ian announced;

"Ladies and Gentlemen, I'd like you to put your hands together for Jon, our cross dressing bass player"

An unwanted round of applause greeted Jon as he knew he had been 'outted'.

I was mildly annoyed, but rather pissed!! It was the morning after that I groaned to myself. But like I say, it was soon water under the bridge and soon forgot about the incident.

He also made another confession to Ian and revealed that he also had somewhat of a masochistic streak (which as Ian thought again was no bad thing for a Hamsters bass player). But even Ian had to wince as Jon recounted the time he had nailed his scrotum to the stair banister at home. If this wasn't enough, Jon felt the pain was not sufficient and ripped himself off the nail. Ian looked upon this geeky boy quite differently now.....

Kind payment 'in kind'

Pam, Jon's girlfriend, was not exactly into the concept of monogamy, much to poor Jon's dismay. Mind you, her reputation did sort of precede her as everyone knew about the backstage encounter with Rat Scabies which resulted in an abortion. She also had a photograph with Bob Geldof (singer of Boomtown Rats) fondling her ample assets.

If Jon had any ideas that he was going to be her one man woman, he was sadly mistaken as firstly Ian, then Bobby enjoyed her considerable charms.

It should be said that young Mr Moss was riding on the crest of the wave and was rather guilty of overconfidence. Although he had no interest in promoting, not to mention experience, it seemed like a jolly good idea to invite Nick Turners 'City Unit' to play at the Mayflower '.

On the Tuesday before the gig, Ian eventually realised;

"Fuck, I'd better do something...."

The promotion vehicle was now in full flow and Ian got out a hard pen, wrote out a poster and stuck in up in the Virgin records window. Ian would have to concede it wasn't exactly 'hard sell' but better than nothing.

On the momentous Wednesday evening, a massive PA system has been erected and the Hamsters open the proceedings to a vast, throbbing thong of......12 people.

Ian is terribly embarrassed about the disgraceful turn out, but Nick and the band are true professionals and instead of getting mad, go out and do a terrific set to the privileged few, giving as much effort as when they supported Hawkwind at Alexander Palace to an audience of around 4,000 people.

What happened next, still has the capacity to embarrass Ian and he wasn't very proud of himself at the time but he approaches Pam (Jon's girlfriend, not the manageress of The Mayflower Club, otherwise a different turn of events may have taken place) and explains;

"Pam, love, these guys have come all the way from London. You can see how few people have turned up and this means there isn't any money for their trouble. I can't face them so I'm going to go home. Would you go back stage and...."

"Look after them??"

Pam's face lit up at this suggestion and she nodded enthusiastically and reassured Ian;

"Don't you worry Moet! I'll make sure they leave happy"

Ian knew he could depend on Pam and beat a shame faced retreat as the band were coming to the end of the set. On the way back home he rationalised his actions, the band were going to get some form of reward and Pam clearly was going to get what was coming to her ..... and tomorrow was another day.

Now Jon may have had masochistic tendencies, but even this 'Kindness to Strangers' was the last straw in his strained relationship with Pam and they broke up soon after.

White Mice The Modettes

The Modettes were an all-girl group who never quite lived up to their classic debut single – "White Mice". Their name was very slightly misleading as I, like many others, thought they were part of the 'Mod Rival' groups such as 'Merton Parkers' and 'Secret Affair'. But in subsequent interviews the girls were keen to emphasise that they weren't part of any revival and claimed the name was pronounced 'Mow Dettes'......hmmmmm.

Anyway, both Bobby and Ian liked the debut single and decided to check out the girls set at The Mayflower one evening after having a few beers. When they arrived, there was a curiously large amount of skinheads in the audience and Ian wondered what an earth they were all doing there. He was told that that the skinheads were looking for trouble as they were going to beat up the mod bands that were going to appear.

It must have been a bit of a surprise when four females strode on to the stage and played a vaguely feminist set, this really confused the Skinheads but they decided to take action as they were all there in force. One by one they clambered onto the stage until the Modettes just surrendered and walked off, leaving a heaving mass of racist idiots chanting

"Hitler was Right"

"There's no black in the Union Jack"

This diatribe of hatred just kept on and on until Ian saw red and decided to do something about it. He began to fling plastic glasses at them with unnerving accuracy. The fact Ian was in the audience meant he was at somewhat of an advantage, as the louts couldn't see exactly who was flinging drinks at them as they were blinded by the spotlights.

But one of them, Barney, had the unusual intelligence, to actually shield his eyes and peer in the direction of the missiles. This ugly bull dog of a thug jumped off stage and charged straight at Ian, but Ian was ready for him and managed to get Barney in a head lock with his left arm and proceeded to thump him viciously with his right fist, again and again.

The Skinheads realised what was happening and surrounded Ian, who was still thumping the living day lights out of Barney. One of the Skinheads, Woody, knew Ian (and Robert) and decided to use reason rather than force;

"Listen mate, let him go!"

Ian ignored this plea for clemency and just thumped Barney even harder

"Moet.....just leave it.....please."

Begged Woody who was tugging at Ian's sleeve (though not at his heart strings)

"Moet....just let him go...We'll leave, I promise, no trouble."

Upon hearing this last offer, Ian shoved Barney on to the floor (well, his fist was beginning to hurt a bit), dusted his hands together and looked Woody right in the face as if to imply that now was a good time to go. Woody was as good as his word and the gang left the building.

Ian was aware that he was being looked at and when he turned around he saw 'The Distractions' who were gawping at him, absolutely horrified at the violence that had just taken place. Now The Distractions happened to be one of Ian's favourite bands but this cut no ice with Ian turned upon these wimps;

"What the Fuck are you all staring at, judging me?"

This demand was met with an awkward silence, obviously it was wise to keep quiet but Ian continued;

"You stand there with your Rock against Racism badges and you feel 'right on'. Well let me tell you something! Badges mean SHIT! You have to stand up against these cunts"

The band looked away in sheer embarrassment, fortunately for them; Bobby took Ian's arm and gently led him away.

"Mr Skinhead, I don't like you
Mr Skinhead, I'll kick you in the head"

Mr Skinhead Enola Death

This skinhead gang were gaining a certain, unpleasant notoriety around Oldham and Rochdale. So much so, that their taunting of the large Asian Community and the dabbing of swastikas on their houses was reported in the Manchester Evening News.

Ian fucking hated them.

One evening, Ian ends up in 'The Cyprus Tavern' and finds Woody and around fifteen skinheads in the lounge. There are a few murmurs when Ian came through the door and went to the bar to order a drink, but nothing happens and Ian decides to ignore them.

Eventually, nature calls and Ian goes off to relieve himself. As he stands at the urinal, Woody comes in and starts to put up BM propaganda stickers up. After finishing, Ian reads one, spits on it and pulls it off the wall. As Woody stickers 'em up, Ian pulls each one down and destroys it. Woody looks at Ian and attempts to reason;

"Moet, we each have our views, you respect mine and I'll respect yours. Just leave those stickers alone, ok?""

"Fuck off."

Woody puts another sticker up and again Ian rips it off the tiles.
"Ok, just leave it."
Says Woody and offers his hand as a truce.
Ian spits in the open hand and snarls;
"FUCK OFF Woody, you're a stupid cunt"
Ian glares at Woody with absolute hate and if truth be known, Woody looks rather crushed, almost pathetic.

Both stand, staring at each other and the skinhead gang enter the toilet, one by one until the gents is wall to wall bone head and Ian. It is clear that they are waiting for some signal from Woody to lay into Ian and rip him apart like a pack of wolves. Ian is too full of anger and hatred to be scared, he is focusing on when the attack commences because he will bring a couple down with him.

Ian is well aware that he could well up in hospital but he is determined that Woody will join him. Hate is pumping around Ian's blood and Woody is aware that Ian, in this adrenalin fuelled condition, is a dangerous weapon. Woody is confused and frightened, he knows that if one finger is laid on Ian, he will be the one to suffer the dangerous consequences. Woody begins to back down and pleads;
"Just shake hands and leave it"
Again he proffers his hand and again Ian spits on it
Ian feels the collective sharp intake of breath from the pack and he is ready. Woody's temples pulse, but he turns on his heel and orders;
"Let's go"
The rest of the gang file out behind him, out of the club and into the street.

Ian begins to shake and his breathing becomes laboured, the 'flight' is kicking in after the 'Fright'. A lad, who Ian knows, comes in to the toilet and asks,
"Are you alright there?"
Ian is too shocked to reply, so the lad leads him out into the bar and orders a large brandy; hands it to Ian and advices;
"Get that down you and get out of here before they realise what you've done to them"
This is good advice; Ian downs the brandy in one and, still somewhat shell shocked, wanders out on to the street. There he is greeted by one of the most ludicrous sights he has ever seen in his life; the skin heads are goose stepping, in formation in the direction of Piccadilly.

A couple of weeks later, Ian is in 'Rafters' with Marc Riley and Craig Scanlon to see TV Smiths Explorers. Woody and his wife, Wendy, come in and sit at a nearby table, Ian decides to ignore them but after twenty minutes, Wendy comes over and takes a seat right next to him and asks;

"Ian, will you please come and talk to Woody."
"You must be fucking joking."
Was Ian's incredulous reply.
"He's packed all that BM stuff because of what happened after that incident with you. Ian, Woody really likes and respects you. It is because of you he has packed that BM shit in! No one has ever wanted to fight him over it, he's really sorry...."

Ian draws a breath and calmly replies;
"Tell him it's too late now, Wendy. You can tell him I'm glad he's seen sense, but it's too late for him and me."

Wendy nods and goes back to their table and they left shortly afterwards.

Ian has never seen either of them since that evening.

Hamsters on a wheel

Andy Zero invited The Hamsters to play support to the increasingly popular Joy Division at the newly opened Osborne Club (located just outside the city centre) as part of a benefit raiser for Fun City Magazine. Ian was excited by this proposition as this would help to readdress the popular perception that The Hamsters were no more than a bunch of crude yobs.

But, fate intervened in the unpleasant form of Factory Records who insisted that 'A Certain Ratio' must be the sole support act. Andy Zero was caught between a rock and a hard place; Joy Division (the main Factory Record band) would only 'be allowed' to appear if the support act were fellow label mates. In his favour, Andy whilst agreeing that 'A Certain Ratio' should appear on the bill, tried to negotiate room for The Hamsters too. The answer was a very clear 'No' and although Andy was really fed up that the benefit had been 'hijacked' he felt he had no choice but to give in to Factory Records demands.

In one sense, Ian wasn't that surprised, yet another golden opportunity had been snatched away and instead the band had to settle for a gig at The Can Club instead. The gig, as such was ok, but Ian felt that the band was just going around and round in circles, they really had become Hamsters going round and round on a wheel...To add insult to injury, the band loaded up their equipment in to Robert's car, and went for a few drinks, upon returning found the car had been broken into and they were now a band with no instruments.

The downfall of the club was, of course, The Hamsters. They claimed, and I still don't know to this day if it was true, that their equipment had been stolen from their van parked outside The Old Garrett. Like fools, we emptied the Can Club coffers for them to 'buy' new equipment. We knew they were lying vagabonds but, unfortunately, we loved their music. **Craig Scanlon**

It so happened that, on occasion, 'hot goods' found their way back to second hand music shops and The Hamsters decided to check out if 'A1 Music' had been offered any of their equipment. It was somewhat of a long shot, but the lads traipsed into Manchester the very next day. It so happened that another local band, 'The Undercover Men' were loitering outside the music shop and a snide comment greeted Ian:

"Look at you lot! Now you're getting famous you're off buying new instruments."

and was followed by the bitchy;

"Amazing what a ride on The Fall's coat tails can do"

The band members were lucky not to get a good slapping from Ian, he was anxious to get into the store, so retorted;

"I'll sort you out when we've finished here."

To no one's huge surprise, the Undercover Men, really had gone under cover and were nowhere to be seen. Which was just as well, as they would, undoubtedly, have got a good kicking when The Hamsters came out empty handed and very pissed off.

John Peel

"Saturday, first of November, Fun City Benefit at the Poly. Can you do it?"
Asks Andy Zero.
"Love to, Andy, but we're banned"
replies Ian.
"I can't see it being a problem, it was months ago and I am sure it's all forgotten"
Assures Andy
"Ok, pencil us in!"
Smiles a relieved Ian, after all Andy knows best.

It's an impressive bill boasting not only The Hamsters but The Fall, Orange Juice, the Au Pairs and Joseph K compared by Alana Pellay; but the real draw is that none other than John Peel will be the DJ at this event.

The Scottish group, Orange Juice are invited to play at 'The Can Club' on the evening of 30th October by Craig, Marc and Steve. In order to keep Orange Juice's expenses down to a minimum, Ian supplies the PA that Mick Hucknall sold him and is the DJ for the event. The Fall also supply accommodation to ensure that the band don't incur any more expense than is necessary.

Ian meets Orange Juice in 'The Garrett' and was charmed by these Scottish lads with sparkling eyes, they looked fantastic in their tweeds and complimentary floppy fringe haircuts. This band also has the rare distinction that Ian enjoyed them stone cold sober, although not out of choice, the naughty rascal had managed to catch a sexually transmitted disease (My money is on Jon's Pam) and was on a strict course of anti-biotics .He really enjoyed Orange Juices performance and went home really looking forward to the benefit gig the next day.

Ian is still in a good mood when the band goes to set up the next day; however he is met by a very worried looking Andy Zero, and two tough looking bouncers, who inform Ian;

"The Student Unions went absolutely nuts when they heard you were playing! They ordered me to take you off the bill but I have told them that if The Hamsters don't play then the whole show is off. It's in the balance and Elliot wants to see you now."

Ian hugged Andy, he had fought their corner and was obviously determined not to be dictated to as to who should appear on the bill a second time. The bouncers ushered Ian up to an upstairs office, where a very serious faced Elliot was seated behind a desk, flanked by two more well-built bouncers. This was a scene calculated to impress; Elliot stared at Ian and Ian stared right back at Elliot.

It was Elliot who broke the silence;

"I don't really want The Hamsters to play here today, but it seems I have no choice."

Elliot then leant back in his chair and continued;

"But let me tell you this, the slightest hint of trouble..."

Elliot paused for dramatic effect;

"I'll have your legs broken."

Ian merely nods and asks;

"Is that it?"

Elliot doesn't answer and Ian goes back to re-join his band.

Ian has a good time, despite having to remain sober and is introduced to John Peel, who informs him;

"Ah yes, The Hamsters. I have heard a lot about you and am looking forward to finally catching your set."

Orange Juice requested to open the Benefit as they have to make the long journey back to Glasgow that very same day. So The Hamsters will appear before The Fall.

Ian has decided to go for a 'Lounge Lizard' (sort of) look in a suit and silky pink seersucker shirt. The Hamsters play well, in fact the Hamsters play very well. The chemistry is there and the lads know that they are on top form by the mere fact that they burst out laughing upon catching each other eye. They are just as well received as any of the more established acts by the capacity crowd. This is a triumph and a vindication of their presence on the bill. The band finish and, as usual, mingle with the audience and are congratulated by fans, both old and new.

Alana Pellay remembers turning around to Kay Carol, during their set, and remarking;

"Do you know what? I find them quite camp! Not Gay but camp"

Alana Pellay is verbally abused by an audience member as she takes to the stage in a glamorous confection to introduce The Fall, but Alana is not the sort of girl to put up with this nonsense and bashes her 'tormentor' with the microphone stand to loud cheers.

Unfortunately, the abuse continues when The Fall come to the stage and a projectile is hurled at them. However, Kay Carol spots the culprit and marches over to thump him, hard. Like Alana, she is a well-built lady and not to be messed around with.

Mark Smith is in full caustic mode and announces:

"Two Tone bands are Ska Idiots! I want to Thank The Hamsters for injecting some reality into tonight's proceedings."

It transpires that the Au Pairs have broken down on route and are unable to make their set in time. Necessity is the mother of invention and a 'Super Group' is hastily assembled to 'top' the bill. This newly formed headliner consists of Tony Wilson on guitar and Ian bluffing it on bass. As they band is tuning up, Tony leans over to Ian and requests;

"Give me an 'E', Ian."

"I haven't a fucking clue what an 'E' is!"

Tony Wilson smiles back and with Kay Carol, on inspired Yoko Ono wailing vocals, a right royal din is made for twenty minutes.

What a result a great show and no fractured limbs, surely a result?

Ian listens to The John Peel Show on the following Monday evening to see if 'Peely' has anything to recount about the Polytechnic gig, he does;

"I saw The Hamsters on Saturday; I'd heard great things about them. Without doubt they're unique and very interesting. But, something about them disturbs me; there's a darkness about them......Anyway, they're playing with the Mothmen, at the squat on Bonfire Night, so go and make your own minds up"

Whilst Ian is flattered that The Hamsters mention a special mention, it isn't exactly a ringing endorsement.

Yellow Man

Steven had become very unwell and had to be hospitalised in the isolation ward, in Monsel Hospital, owing to contracting hepatitis. He looked dreadful as his skin and eyes had turned yellow from jaundice and became tired very, very easily. The Doctor informed him that recuperation to full health would take several weeks.

The band had been offered a two night support slot at Acklam Hall, in London's Nottinghill with The Fall. It was apparent, to Ian, that Steven was very weak and needed to recuperate. However, it would be a real shame to miss a gig at this prestigious venue and decided to have a word with Kay Carrol;

"Kay, I'm really concerned about Steven, I really don't think he would be up to playing two gigs, one after the other, in his condition"

"I'm sorry; do you want to pull out then?"
sympathised Kay.

"Well, I was thinking we could just do the one?"
suggested Ian.

"Yeah, fine. "Furious Pig" can do the other evening."
decided Kay.

Although Ian was very worried about Steven's health, a day's recording session with Grant Showbizz, was to follow straight after the gig at Street Level studios. Ian was still concerned if the band had made the right decision when Steven had difficulty climbing up the stairs to the rehearsal room in an effort to join in for one evening. Two new exiting new songs had been created: 'Rumps' depicted the rise of the proletariat and the subsequent over throw of their puppet masters. 'Pot Horse Street' was a keen observation on middle class aspirations and social climbing. But Steven, owing to the exertion of merely climbing the stairs was too exhausted to set up his drum kit, let alone play it. The two songs had to be put on the back burner for the time being instead of making it to the recording session.

Steven's health was a real concern and if he was too unwell to play, Paul Hanley from The Fall was prepared to sit in. The debilitating illness was taken its toll on Steven, he had become quiet and withdrawn, very disconcerting indeed.

The movers and shakers of the independent London musical scene were not aware that Ena Sharples (Jon had come 'en femme') and Dick Tracy (Steven attempting to hide his yellow pallor in the shade of a trench coat and trilby hat) were riding off into the sunset to play for them.

Acklam Hall 11 December 1980

"I CANNOT EVEN REMEMBER THE LOCATION OF THIS PLACE? But then I have done a play on Broadway and some top tens in between! Ha-Ha!" **Al Pellay**

"Darlings! How are you? How was your journey?"
greeted Alana upon the band arriving at the venue

Alana was now living full time as a woman in London (although did not commence hormone treatment until 1983 ably assisted by Jayne County) and was working on material with The Pop Group.

"I look forward to hearing 'More of a man (than you'll ever be), more of a woman (than you'll ever have) on the radio" replied Ian.

"Darling!"

exclaimed Alana whose face lit up at this prospect;

"You're just SO sweet!"

Alana gave Ian a huge hug, she was really happy and this mood set the tone for the weekend.

The Fall had already arrived and Mark E Smith came up to Ian and said

"Come and have a drink with me and the journalist from Sounds. You will need to see how this works"

The band kept silent during the interview, which was held in a pub in Portobello, but were taking lessons from the master at work playing with the press. However Jon is not paying full attention and has caught the eye of a rather attractive girl and in Jon's words;

"I remember missing the sound check because I had found a tranny friendly girl who would drop them for half a lager."

Up went both sets of skirts and the affair was consummated in a bus shelter. Both Ian and Bobby were amazed and exchanged glances which conveyed;

"Why HIM???"

The Hamsters had a lot of friends in the audience and the band is completely sober when they come on stage. Upon reflection Ian had complete confidence in the material but was concerned that Steven may have been pushing himself too hard. As an audience member I was unaware of this and was impressed with his drumming ability, which was quite unlike any drumming I had heard before. Ian also felt that whilst the band played steadily enough there was a certain pizzazz lacking. I tend to disagree as the audience was rather unresponsive in only the way a London audience can be. However, Ian felt that people were reached and enjoyed hearing the Hamsters. The set consists of the material that is to be recorded at the Street Level recording studio along with 'I'm a Cunt' and 'The Chicken Song'.

All too soon the set is over and the band were congratulated backstage and who should come over to greet them but no other than Mark Perry;

"I enjoyed you much more than last time!"

He offers, with a knowing twinkle in his eye.

Ian is really pleased that Mark didn't hold any grudges; this acknowledgement of The Hamsters meant a lot to Ian, as Mark Perry is a person who Ian greatly admires.

The Hamsters are also introduced to a member of Wire, who are still one of Ian's favourite bands;

"I liked your performance."

Steven was increasingly becoming more uneasy with all the praise, so Ian takes him out to mingle with the audience and to watch The Falls set.

The evening is finished off nicely in a haze of marijuana smoke listening to King Tubby around The Androids of Mu's squat.

Street Level Studio Session

Grant Showbiz had proposed that The Hamsters would record an album worth full of songs to be released on 'Fuck Off' records. Initial studio sessions would commence the very next day after the Acklam Hall debut.

It was unusual, The Hamsters were up early and they were sober. They decided to head off to the Imperial War Museum to kill time and a girl was outside the doors begging for money;

"Here you go, love."

said Steven as he extended a handful of change.

"No!"

refused the young girl, who recoiled in horror at the scary sight of her yellow benefactor.

The band traipsed around the museum until Bobby and Ian decided to creep away, leaving Steven absorbed in the military paraphernalia, to have a quiet drink or two.

In the afternoon, Andy dropped the band at the studio and headed off as he had an important meeting with Rough Trade records regarding nationwide distribution of 'City Fun'.

To call the studio basic, would be an understatement, but in some ways this worked in the bands favour as they immediately felt quite at home and it had everything they needed. For the film buffs reading this book, the actual studio toilets later became the infamous location shot for 'Trainspotting.'

Grant explained that he wanted the band to play live in the studio and this material would be the basis for further overdubbing and production to be done in the next few weeks. The main purpose of this first session was to get them acclimatised to a studio environment.

After setting up, the band went through each song and the best take of each was captured. The Fall popped in to the studio to see how the band was getting on, a lot of tracks were being completed very quickly and often in one take. Necessity, regarding Steven's frailness, instigated that the vast majority of The Hamsters set was recorded that afternoon. The band listened to the rough mixes of the songs and went to the pub. Andy Zero came to collect them and the van headed back up North.

The band were not to know it, but Ian reflects that what should have been the beginning of something really big would be the last time that the band would do anything significant together for a very long time.

Neil had to sit and suffer listening to the Hamster recordings when Ian and

Andy got home. Even though 'The Frantic Elevators' had released a few singles, he was aware that his big brothers band had recorded an albums worth of material. Ian was a little hurt by his younger brothers pained expression and lack of enthusiasm for the recordings but knew that The Hamsters were now in a position to overtake 'The Frantics'.

Ian was proud and excited at what had been created.

The Beginning of The End

The Hamsters, the band that tried to eat the whole of the Manchester music scene..... and burped before the start menu! Like the Frantic Elevators they were the nearly band, or the band who were too frightened to go ahead and do it or real. When you hesitate in the indie sector that's it...the moment has passed like the end of an orgasm or finishing a good pint. Then you have to stand in line and wait for the moment again....and as Rotten once said 'only stupid fools stand in line'... **Steve Mardy**

Life can be so unfair at times. To all intents and purposes it really did feel like The Hamsters star was in the ascendant, but in reality disintegration was just around the corner......

The band had been offered headlining gigs in Preston and Blackburn, but owing to Steven's fragile health, these had to be put on hold in order to give him time to recover. However a gig at The Cyprus Tavern, on Christmas Day, was booked as it was agreed that this shouldn't be too taxing and Robert was invited to join the band on twelve string guitar (on a strictly 'one off basis').

On the evening of the event, the band gathered at 'The Old Garrett', all except for Steve who was late. When he eventually arrived it was clear that he was extremely unwell and suffering in great pain.

"What an earth is the matter?"

asked Bobby.

"Sorry....My nerves got the better of me"

Began Steven as he eased himself in to a chair;

"I took some sulphate... I thought I could handle it but I ended up in the hospital"

"Steven..."

began Ian, who was more concerned than annoyed;

"There is no way you will be able to play tonight"

"It's my fault, I don't want to let you down... who else can you find?"

replied Steven, who was wincing in pain.

It so happened that Paul Hanley was sitting at a nearby table and was aware of The Hamsters predicament and came to the rescue:

"Hey! I know your material pretty well. I can drum for you... that's if you'll have me!"

This was a very kind offer and made absolute sense.

"You sure?"

checked Ian

"Yep, looking forward to it!"

was the positive reply

There was another person who needed to be asked:

"Steven, you came from your hospital bed to be here"

"Ah, well, I've always wanted to see The Hamsters."

was the laconic reply.

The Hamsters may have had different bass players, which made no difference but when one on the unholy trio wasn't present the magic wasn't there. Paul Hanley's drumming was much more proficient than Steven's in a technical sense but it made the band sound like any other band. It was Steven's unconventional lead in speeding up and slowing down that gave the songs that 'something extra'. Ian tried really hard to inject some life, but although the audience appeared happy enough, Ian knew there was something very important missing and that important something hugged him as soon as he came off stage:

"That was fucking terrible, the band was useless"

informed Steven who had Ian in a bear hug, released his grip and looked at Ian;

"But YOU were fantastic! I didn't know how good you was until tonight when I was able to watch you! I'm proud of you!"

"Ta Mate, I tried hard"

replied Ian who was trying very hard not to show how deeply touched he was. Steven genuinely meant this as he wasn't the sort of person to acknowledge other peoples contributions easily. Ian remembers thinking that this could be some sort of beginning and that maybe, just maybe. they could both work more harmoniously together in the future.

After going to the bar to buy Steven a soft drink and himself a drop of something harder he was approached by Cath Carrol and Liz Naylor of the Glass Animals. They had never, ever came over to speak to him ("this is a first" Ian remembers thinking):

"We loved you"

they both positively cooed;

"We never thought we'd say that"

both girls looked at each other and continued:

"We'd still like to cut that drummers balls off though"

Ian laughed and agreed;

"Yes! I often feel the same!"

The drinks had arrived and it was time to return to Steve;

"Goodbye!"

Ian and The Glass Animals smiled at each other. Surely this was a good sign, even Cath and Liz had been won over by tonight's performance and Ian knew that, with Steven, they could do even better. Ian felt a mixture of happiness and optimism.

Crystal Gazing Hopes for 81 (taken from City Fun Vol 2 Number Six)

New Order: Awarded National Honours
Alana Pellay: Will rival Pontin's for Camp Popularity
Vic Goddard: Triumphant Entry into Chartsville
Linder: Becomes 'the younger man's Joan Bakewell
The Hamsters: Fall Protégés make big in a small way

Ends, beginning's and middles 1981 – 1983

Steve didn't chuck me out of the Hamsters –his bullying and menacing behaviour became too much for me. Nothing was actually said, we just went our separate ways. **Jon Rowlinson**

Jon would usually bring a gift or two to rehearsals. Sometimes it was a hat; maybe a pair of gloves and the band didn't ask too many questions as to where he got them from. But when a whole pallet of goods 'liberated' from his workplace turned up at the rehearsal studio Jon had gone too far. The rest of the band were not happy and insisted that he remove this booty;
"I can't shift this right now!"
protested Jon.
"Get rid of it"
ordered Ian, who was very annoyed.
"I'll get it out of the way tomorrow."
promised Jon.
The band had no choice but to go ahead with the rehearsal whilst the 'received goods' had to remain just inside the entrance.
Bobby got a phone call from the manager of the printing firm (who let the band use the space as rehearsal);
"I want the lot of you out and don't come back again!"
"Why?"
asked a bewildered Bob.
"You are storing stolen goods in my warehouse! Take your equipment and go!"
barked back the manager.
Bob had no riposte to this, as Jon's goods had been caught red handed. The manager's good will and trust had been betrayed and he had every right to insist that The Hamsters never darken his warehouse door again.
Jon really got it in the neck from the rest of the band. He was solely responsible for losing a prime rehearsal space and Bob, Ian and Steven were furious with him. Matters didn't improve much when a replacement rehearsal space was found. This new space was dank, dark and depressing and was situated in a cellar underneath a driving school office. This repressive atmosphere reflected Ian's doubts about the new material.
At the next rehearsal history had repeated itself:
"I've sacked Jon."
informed Steven.

Ian was seriously pissed off about Steven's decision. Not only had Jon easily been the best bass player in The Hamsters, this decision really made Ian feel uncomfortable; did Steven now consider himself to be the leader of the band of brothers?

I Will Survive Gloria Gaynor

Wayne Edwards, besides being Craig Scanlon's cousin, was also a huge fan of The Hamsters and knew the band very well. It felt like a natural choice for Ian to ask him to be Jon's replacement and he readily accepted.

When Ian and Wayne arrived at the Denton rehearsal 'Dungeon' both Bob and Steven were waiting and were eager to demonstrate some new material that they had been working on that very afternoon; Ian felt left out. If the material had been really good, that would have been fine but they were nasty little put downs regarding Steve Molloy.

"There is no joy in these songs and they strike me as petty and a bit pathetic"

Both Bob and Steven looked surprised and to drive the point home, Ian continued;

"I've written better songs compared to what you have just played me."

"I've written much better songs than you!"

was Steven's defensive response and after a bit more bitching the band got down to rehearse with their new bassist.

Wayne struggled manfully to step in to Jon's high heels but it was hard work. The rehearsal had started off badly and was not improving in the repressive, dank basement. Ian also was trying really hard, but his heart was no longer in it. Somehow the small dark room was a mirror image of the sound being half heatedly recreated by the band. For the first time in their history, the band was merely going through the motions and this concerned Ian.

After the equipment was packed away and the band headed off to 'The Kings Head', Ian came to a decision. Maybe it was coming into the fresh air after the dankness of the cellar but Ian suddenly found clarity of vision and the courage to say what had been bothering him;

"Lads, I might as well tell you. I've decided to leave the band."

This announcement was met with silence as the band walked to the pub. Ian had expected an argument, or at least questions about why he wanted to leave, but nothing was forthcoming. Ian decided to try a different tack and asked Wayne;

"Do you want to come with me, or stay with Bob and Steven?"

"I'll stay with Bob and Steve, Moet."

replied Wayne decisively.

Ian was a bit hurt by this reply but decided that he now had a clean slate to start from; fair enough it was Wayne's loss.

Both Steven and Bob, Ian found out much, much later, believed that Ian was being a bit of a 'Drama Queen' and didn't take this announcement as seriously as it deserved. Maybe if they could have talked things through, a further attempt could have been made to work together. But, unfortunately, owing to the fact that they were all strong personalities, no one backed down and an invaluable 'what if' was never realised.

Ian genuinely believes that all three band members lost 'something' when Ian left The Hamsters and that Steven, in particular, never fully forgave him for leaving the band that fateful evening.

The Hamsters carried on without Ian and many good songs were written, the 'Steve Molloy' songs were never played again but Ian had a point to prove and he needed to prove it quickly.

The Mo Mo and the Do Do's

"One of them stuck out in my mind was Momo and the Dodo's (I think they were called)

He nicked a guitarist from the Eltifits called Graham. He was a weird kind of musician and played like Robert Fripp" **Jon Rowlinson**

He was big, honest, sincere, serious, committed - and funny. I played in quite a few bands late seventies/early eighties, and Moet's lyrics were far and away the best - simple, true art, not the pretentious word-play that obfuscates the lyrics of other bands. His dark humour on the songs we recorded together still makes me laugh and his sometimes brutally honest depictions of ordinary life were uncompromising. As a person he was gentle, warm and friendly, and I am proud to have known him. One of the good guys. **Graham Ellis**

Ian had been impressed by Graham Ellis's guitar playing and stage presence. It just so happened that Ian spied Graham in Rafters and decided to take the bull by the horns;

"Hi, I'm Moet."

Ian introduced himself, shook hands, and came straight to the point;

"I'm looking to put a band together and you are my number one choice for a guitarist, interested?"

Graham was taken aback by the directness of this approach, momentarily, but laughed and replied;

"Go on then"

Graham smiled and shook his head and continued;

"Everyone's trying to be so cool, nobody but NOBODY lets that mask slip."

Both Ian and Graham decided to get a drink and retreat to a corner to have a quiet word. Soon both were enthusing and making plans about the band.

"What are we going to be called?"

asked Graham.

Ian already knew the answer;

"Mo Mo and the Do Do's, in fact just the Do Do's would do"

"That's an original name; don't know what it's about?"

replied Graham with a furrowed brow.

"Mo Mo is me, Moet. Do Do's are an amphetamine you can buy over the counter"

"Ok then, Mo Mo and the Do Do's it is then"

decided Graham and a thought suddenly struck him;

"Hey, do you know what; I can get us into the cellar underneath the 'War on Want' Shop to rehearse in!"

"The one on Oxford Road, you mean?"

asked Ian, hopefully

"Yes, that's the one! How about next Tuesday say six thirty?"

Ian was really excited and gleefully agreed

"Yes! Yes! Yes!

"That'll give me time to sort out a drummer by then"

mused Graham.

This new band was already a huge boost to Ian's fragile confidence and he had got his mojo back again. Ian was so excited that when he got home he couldn't sleep and immediately began to scribble lyrics for his new band.

Bob and Steve did not share Ian's newfound joy, when he told them about his new musical venture the next day. Maybe it was then they finally realised Ian was not going to come back.

It Will End Mo Mo and the Do Do's

The grand Georgian façade of the 'War on Want' office building was also the venue for 'The White Noise Club' which was located in the cellar opening after band rehearsals. Graham was as good as his word and had found a drummer, Greg, and introduced Ian to a painfully thin young thing called Mathew Rich (who joined in on some of the songs). None of the band really knew each other which meant that they got straight down to work and two hours later a grand total of eight songs were created. Graham put music to Ian's lyrics, which were edited to fit into the new song structures.

"We should play, tonight, at The White Noise Club! What do you think"?

asked Graham, who was obviously very pleased with how well the first rehearsal had gone.

"Yeah! Let's go for it!" beamed Ian and the other two band members had no objections, so that was that.

It seemed like such a good idea to Ian at the time, a mere seven days after leaving The Hamsters he was already playing his first gig with his new band 'The Do Do's' – that would really show Bobby and Steven! He couldn't wait to tell them and took the bus to Didsbury where he knew they would be rehearsing. Ian admits there was an element of spite in his intentions.

When he arrived at the cellar of Ronnie Middlehurst's shop he was desperate to show them what they had foolishly let go as he very generously invited them to the evening's concert. His ego appears to have got the better of him as he also invited Steve Hanley to bring his bass to appear on stage.

Bobby, Steven and Martin decided to accept Ian's invitation, but turned up drunk and in a bad mood. Steven especially, as he decided to take his anger out, not on Ian, but some shop windows. This was food and drink to Ian's inflated ego as he revelled in their obvious unhappiness. Like spurned lovers, the rest of the Hamsters attempted to disrupt the show by switching off electricity

Ian, at the time of the writing of this book consulted Martin who maintained that Steven would have been really wound up by the fact that a book was being written about him, but despite all the fights and heartache, he really did love Ian.

At around midnight, the 'Do Do's' debut with Steve Hanley on bass was not the momentous occasion that Ian had been hoping for. It is not to say that this first show was a disaster, it was worse it was mediocre. The band didn't thrill or amaze and the general consensus was that they were 'Ok'. Ian tried to rationalise to himself that this concert could have been better if the band had taken the time to rehearse and really polished the songs up; but there was a nagging feeling that persisted. Quite simply the audience had been expecting something akin to the sound of The Hamsters and instead had been confronted by something much funkier; this confused and disorientated the audience whose expectations had not been met.

The band were determined to carry on and played their second set, also at 'The White Noise Club', with Tim Oliver on bass and more new songs. It could be said that the 'Do Do's' became the resident 'house band' of the club and a small band of supporters were attracted. But the die had already been cast, the band had been judged on their unimpressive debut performance and it was generally felt that Ian's best work was now behind him by those who had loved The Hamsters.

Who says a Rock Band Can't Play Funk Funkadelic

Tim was the perfect funky bass player and made for a very cohesive unit.

Ian liked the entire band and there was a pleasant, almost relaxed atmosphere in which the band enjoyed making music. On the surface it was a very creative band which was technically very proficient.

And yet, and yet... one very important ingredient was missing from Ian's creative ability – conflict. Steven was the cult of creative violence in The Hamsters, the grit in the oyster that created magic. The Hamsters lived to make music; The Do Do's made music. Music was a matter of life and death for The Hamsters, music was an enjoyable lifestyle for The Do Do's. Moet lived out Steven's lyrics but sang his own. Even the drugs were contained in The Do Do's were dealt with effectively. Life and love with Steven was one psychological drama after another, slight musical differences might surface in The Do Do's but were soon resolved. In short The Do Do's lacked fire.

However, the band was gigging on a regular basis and soon acquired a friendly, bohemian set of fans. Within a matter of weeks the group were invited to record at 'The Kitchen' studio in Hulme. The session was recorded by Adam, who was to remain a faithful and loyal supporter of the band. Ian felt that the sessions showed promise and that the group had certainly come a long way very quickly. There was still a long way to go but Ian felt confident that his band could achieve great things.

The relationship between Ian and The Hamsters improved to the extent that they were soon able to socialise again. The Hamsters had a new vocalist in Steven's wife Trisha, who was brought in not only as Ian's replacement, but as a concerted effort by Steven to rekindle their relationship. The Hamsters went into an expensive recording studio and recorded 'Pot Horse Street', 'The Chicken Song' as well as newer material such as 'Intermediate Range'. Ian believes that they were badly let down by the studio engineer, who failed to grasp what they were about, and it was a very mediocre session, they just sounded like a lot of other bands of the time.

The Hamsters played to a tiny audience at Manchester University and didn't set the place on fire. Worse was to follow at The Cyprus Tavern where they were openly heckled and when Ian was spotted in the audience, cries of;

"Bring Moet Back, bring Moet Back!"

rebounded around the hall. Ian took no pleasure in these demands and felt particular sympathy for Trisha who was doing her best. This adverse audience reaction was not to deter Steven in the least, he was like a man possessed with his desire to create. Ian describes them as 'working like moles' in a dark cellar for two further years. They worked very, very hard and despite burrowing out some good songs never recaptured the original magic. Trish retired gracefully, and Bob took over on lead vocals. They only ever played live on three more occasions.

DJ David Bowie

Despite appearances, Ian could still be subject to bouts of lack of confidence and shyness, although he had become a master at concealing this. However, the relaxed vibe of this new group made him feel appreciated and more at ease with himself.

Talking of appearances, Ian had discovered the joy of wearing suits from Charity Shops and managed to afford an expensive, yet easily affordable new look. Mr Moss of Moss Bros started arriving at venues, not only well turned out but also stone cold sober. This new smart image impressed the glitterati of Manchester Nightlife that the presence of Ian was 'good for businesses' and he not only managed to get free entry, but was also given admission to more exclusive events.

"If only they knew...."

murmured Ian, to himself, as yet another red rope was lowered for him.

One such venue, which Ian patronised, was 'The Beach Club' at 'Oozits' on Shudhill. On one level it had a floor that showed continental 'Art' films and the upper floor was reserved for live music and also featured DJ sets from members of the group A Certain Ratio. These group members played a predominantly funk set consisting of War, Parliament and Ohio Players. It so happened that the magazine 'City Fun' took over the running of the night and Ian was invited by Andy Zero to become the resident DJ. Besides playing a funk staple, Ian would also add to the sonic palette an eclectic range of styles such as Salsa, Disco, Reggae and Northern Soul which fitted in rather well. However Ian was not above flinging in the odd record by Pere Ubu or the Raincoats.

Ian enjoyed his stint as the resident DJ and his set was generally awarded with an appreciative round of applause at the end and this added to Ian's sense of well-being. Ian was very grateful for the little acts of kindness that were done for him.

Anne and The Don't Don'ts

Ian was greatly saddened by the messy split between his two good friends Anne and John. Anne in particular was very distraught and suggested a day out in Blackpool to Ian to give her a break from all her troubles; Ian is still very touched by the fact she chose him. This seemed to work and Ian even braved the rollercoaster, once, but suggested a drink rather than closing his eyes and screaming through the ride one more time.

At the pub, Ian suddenly had an idea;

"Anne, you know I told you that the band was missing something?"

"Yes...."

Anne had a sneaking feeling this idea was going to involve her somehow.

"Why don't you join?!!"

Anne was taken aback and replied

"I can't play and anyway I don't have an instrument!"

Ian was not going to have a little technicality get in the way and reasoned:

"You can play the keyboards! I've got an organ at home and you can use that. Go on, it'll be good for you!"

Anne reluctantly pointed out

"I agree I need something to keep me occupied, but I can't play a note!"

Ian was not going to be put off:

"That doesn't matter! A bit of discord is what we need!"

Anne seemed to see the possibilities and agreed;

"Ok, I'll give it a try then and see how it goes."

"Great! That's settled then!"

Beamed Ian.

Next week, Anne had a go on the keyboards at rehearsals. The good thing was that everyone liked her but she was nervous and acutely aware of her limitations. Ian didn't mind a bit as he now had a true friend in the band, someone who knew how he ticked

Anne made her debut at Rafters, in front of a sizable crowd and was very nervous. What made matters worse was;

"Moet, I can't hear myself."

Ian decided that the best thing to do was to keep 'going for it' rather than stopping to solve any technical issues and so the band ploughed through the set, but afterwards asked the band what could have gone wrong.

The rest of the band looked very sheepish and replied;

"Ummm. We knew that Anne would benefit from being on stage but we thought it would be cruel for her to be heard…"

"YOU FUCKING WHAT??"

Ian demanded, even though he already knew the answer

"We unplugged her; we thought it was for the best, sorry"

Ian could understand their rationale for doing this, to a point but it felt treacherous and their reasoning really upset Anne and this in turn upset Ian who demanded, through gritted teeth;

"Don't you ever, EVER, do anything like that again"

The band readily agreed but Ian felt that a little something in the band died on that night; trust.

Grandmaster Hamster and the Groove of The Do Do's

The proprietors of The War on Want Shop eventually discovered that their basement was being used as 'The White Noise Club'. It could have been an ideal opportunity to hitch their wagon to all this musical talent, but foolishly, they decided to close the venue down.

The Do Do's certainly appeared to be respected and liked, but there was 'something missing' and that 'something' was an unknown quantity. However Anne's swirling keyboard sound managed to capture some of the creative anarchy of The Hamsters and the songs were getting better and better so maybe it was a process of working towards 'this something'. One song, 'Superman', captures Ian's feelings at the time;

People I don't know seem to know my name
Suppose this is the price I pay for my minor fame
I'm subjected to hate all people saying 'great'
I want to run a mile, but I just put on a smile
See it for what it is or perpetuate the myth
The myth is just the lie
Flatter the people; persuade them to buy......

Another strong song was 'The Ultimate Thrill' which was a first person account of a degenerate spiral into alcohol, drugs, sex, crime and ultimately, murder. Maybe the departure of Mathew (who eventually became a heroin addict) behind this particular song?

The band moved rehearsals to a recording studio that Tim was working at and gigs became more and more regular owing to the fact that they were a good live band. Sometimes there was a real groove with Greg and Tim, serving as a vital anchor for Anne's more 'free fall' sound and Ian's improvised vocal style which was somewhat akin to 'Rap' as he spewed out a torrent of words rythmatically working against the grain of melody. Dear reader, it would be so legendary to proudly present to you that Grandmaster Flash had been present at a 'Do Do's gig and plagiarised Ian's new vocal style but no, although this is an instance of a similar vocal evolution happening in two very different places as the same time.

I'm Gonna Make You A Star by David Essex

One memorable gig was played at the interval between the support act and Squeeze at Manchester University. The audience filtered into the 'Solum Bar' to listen to 'The Do Do's' and some new found fans liked what they heard so much they decided to stay to listen to another set instead of going to hear the main act.

Another memorable gig, for the wrong reasons, also took place in the interval between The Meteors and The Cramps. This time, instead of shouting for more, the bequiffed morons (which included members of The Meteors) heckled 'The Do Do's' white boy punk funk sound. Just as the first occasion had been exhilarating this was just as depressing. The evening was saved, for Ian; by The Cramps who managed to put a smile back on his face again.

On one occasion, just after the band played a set at a venue near The Free Trade Hall, Tosh Ryan of Rabid Records (Home label to Slaughter and the Dogs, Jilted John, John Cooper Clarke) beckoned for Ian to come over;

"That was better than 'The Blue Orchids"

This observation was meant to be a compliment but left Ian non plussed and he shook his head and replied;

"We're nothing like the Blue Orchids"

Tosh responded;

"I think you are!"

Ian was rather fed up at this lazy comparison and stated

"No, just because we both have female keyboard players, doesn't mean we are like them"

End of conversation.

Greg had managed to get the band a gig in Banbury via his Oxford connections and the day started well enough with the band heading down in the van. This change of scenery was just what everyone needed, somewhere fresh to play with some good songs. Ian felt really positive on this journey and was pleased to find that the venue was packed out and everything was set for a really good gig.....but as soon as the band played, everything went flat for some unfathomable reason. Ian felt the band, himself in particular, were going through the motions. Ian bravely carried on, but felt false, pathetic and miserable.

Anyone with an ounce of perception could tell that Ian was not to be approached when he was sitting in the bar after this miserable excuse for a gig. But there's always one isn't there...???

A middle aged chap decided to sit down right next to Ian and opened up with the gambit of;

"I have influence and contacts; I was once Gary Glitter's Manager"

"Hmmmmmm?"

grunted Ian.

Undeterred, Gary Glitters ex manager continued;

"You are Great! A Natural! I can make you a star, earn a fortune!"

and then he made his real faux pas with;

"The band will have to go, of course, they're no good. We just have to find the right image for you"

Ian glared at this middle aged intruder, who was by now, looking at him like a love struck teenager and decided to put him straight (in a manner of speaking);

"Thanks for that mate, but I've no intention of leaving the band or having someone else telling me what to do."

This new fan looked absolutely aghast, but worse was to follow with;

"So if you don't mind, just leave me alone and Fuck Off!"

This would be manager, did exactly as he was told and limped away like a rejected little puppy dog.

The band travelled back to Manchester in complete silence, not a word was said and as Ian recounts;

"Respecting that old adage: If you haven't got anything nice to say, say nothing"

It costs nothing to say 'Thanks'

Ian was slipping into a form of malaise regarding the declining fortunes of 'The Do Do's', he felt that fate had dealt him a hard blow with this band. They really should have been doing much better and yet Ian did not want to be perceived as being 'weak' and unbend to anyone.

A perfect example of Ian's uncompromising attitude is when The 'Do Do's' were to play a gig with the industrial band, 'Tools You Can Trust',. It so happened that Greg was unavailable and the percussionist, Eddie, very kindly offered his services. He was a genial, bearded Geordie and very easy to get on with. However, he got nothing in the way of thanks for this favour; Ian didn't even bother to speak to him and hardly looked at Eddie on stage except to cast him the odd malevolent glare.

It says much for Eddie's amiable character that he was to work with Ian in future projects but, years later, he told Ian how unappreciative he had been on that miserable night.

Lip Up Fatty Bad Manners

In some ways, Steven was like that girl with a curl, when he was good, he was very, very good and when he was bad he was...well horrid.

When it was good boisterous fun, like the occasion when he, Bobby and Wayne gate crashed the Lord Mayors banquet, good natured mayhem ensued. But when Steve's darker side manifested itself.....

One evening Steve, Wayne and Andy Zero went to Rafters and decided to hold an impromptu Hamsters performance and were promptly ejected offstage by the promoter Alan Wise. Nothing particularly untoward appeared to have happened and the lads calmly downed a few more pints until it was time to go. On the way out, Wayne turned to Steven, espying the corpulent bulk that was Alan, and jokingly ordered;

"Let him have it!"

Something inside Steven must have snapped as he suddenly punched Alan so hard that his spectacles flew on to the floor. The inevitable happened, the police were called and Steve was arrested and charged with common assault.

In court, Steven turned around to Andy Zero and threatened;

"If you write about this, I will fucking kill you"

There really was no need, as Andy Zero was already terrified and did not want any more trouble. Steven was fined £200.

Bob was really livid, albeit in his own quiet way and wanted some form of condolence from Ian. He was to be disappointed by Ian's dismissive reply;

"How do you ever expect to get a gig in Manchester now?"

Ian may well have been thinking of his own career as he had been implicated in Steve's previous outlandish behaviour albeit by 'guilt by association'. Shit the shadow of the Hamster still loomed large in Ian's life, despite his best efforts to lock the cage and get away.

However, Ian was to be surprised, very surprised in fact.

"Ian, You're wanted on the phone mate"

Robert called out to Ian one day at work.

Ian was busy and didn't really want to take this unless it was really important and snapped back;

"Who is it? I'm busy!"

The reply resulted in Ian dropping his handbag.

"Alan Wise."

"Fuck me."

was Ian's reaction and hurried to the phone wondering what an earth Alan Wise wanted with him?

"Hello, Alan!"

greeted Ian

"Hi"

came back the friendly greeting and Alan continued;

"I'm ringing on behalf of ITV who are casting for a Manchester based project"

"Oh yeah?"

Ian was interested.

"It's about a National Front Skinhead in a band. He wants some authenticity, like someone who's really in a band and looks the part. The lads out of New Order and Eric Random are willing to shave their hair, given half the chance, but I really thought of you as the one who could do it. What do you think?"

Ian's heart had really sunk and had already thought

"No."

he replied;

"Thanks for thinking of me, Alan, but I don't want any association with the NF. I have enough problems in this town already."

Ian heard a sharp intake of breath on the other end of the line;

"I think you're passing up a great opportunity."

stated Alan, but continued;

"But, it's your choice, bye."

The receiver went dead.

"What was that phone call all about then?"

enquired Robert when Ian returned to the floor and listened open mouthed to what Ian had to say. Robert's response was swift and pained:

"You must be fucking mad!"

Ian has reflected over his instinctive decision and eventually agreed with Robert. He should have jumped at the chance offered to him by Alan Wise (who had gained new respect in Ian's eyes). It certainly wasn't that he was too scared to leap in to the unknown Possibly Ian was too foolish or even plain stubborn but now he knows that there was one crucial ingredient that was missing...... Ambition.

I think it was an ITV project Manchester-based not London which went out on Sun 11 April 1982. **Steve Mardy**

Moss in Moss Side

The summer of 1981 was a period of huge civil unrest nationwide in England's major cities. Riots took place in the ghettos of Brixton, Toxteth and Moss Side in Manchester. The hot evenings were lit by flames and the sound of continual police sirens blared throughout the night, as anger of the young of the minority communities finally spilled out over onto the streets.

Ian remembers that tensions were running high and that the police often triggered into action at the slightest disturbance. There wasn't an official curfew as such, but the police would stop young bands of men who were out on the street after dark. Very often, these innocent groups would be subjected to verbal abuse, pushed around and even beaten up by the Police. It was not unknown to be arrested, simply for being in 'the wrong place'.

Bobby, Ian, Steven and Wayne came out of the Cyprus Tavern early one morning and were ready to go home. Almost immediately, a Police Riot Van pulled up beside them and a window was pulled down. The group was beckoned over and were questioned through the open window. The van was full of Policemen in body armour all ready for action........

"BOOOOOMMMMMM!!!!!!"

The Police Force inside the van nearly shit their pants at this loud bang! Was it a bomb? Was it a Missile? No; Bobby had banged on the van and the loud sound not only reverberated around the street it had obviously terrified the Police Unit as they came charging out to see what had caused this massive disturbance. The Police Team surrounded the lads and Bobby had to confess it was him and apologised;

"Sorry."
"You little Fucker!"
Yelled one of the Policemen in Bobby's face.
"Just a Joke,"
"Do you think that's funny, you shit"
"No, it wasn't funny, I'm sorry"
apologised Bobby.

It could have been that the boys in blue were actually rather relieved the bang hadn't been more serious and just contented themselves with a bit more verbal abuse until the order:

"Fuck Off Home!"

The lads did as they were told and when they safely got round the corner, looked at each other and burst out laughing uproariously until each got a stitch from the pain of laughing so hard.

Police and Thieves The Clash

Ian was worried about his little brother Neil.

The 'Do Do's unofficial headquarters was at Graham's flat in Robert Alan Crescent and Neil and Mick Hucknall shared a flat in nearby Robert Adam Crescent, which was also located in Hulme. Ian usually popped in to take both lads out for a drink and was concerned that both lads were constantly being bullied and burgled. Mick was made of tough stuff but Neil was becoming increasingly withdrawn and paranoid. So much so, he had taken to wearing black trousers and shoes, with a white shirt in deluded attempt to pass himself off as an off duty policeman. Maybe he hoped that the criminal element would 'leave them alone' with this disguise?

The architecture of Hulme was not dissimilar to Thamesmead, in South London, where 'The Clockwork Orange' was filmed and Ian genuinely believes it was these menacing buildings that gave rise to a curious mix of artistic Bohemia and outright criminal violence – this was to be the setting for the forthcoming summer carnival, at which 'The Do Do's' were due to play.

Them a SUS them a SUS right here in The Moss
Them a SUS them a SUS don't let them pressure us

SUS Harlem Spirit

The Hulme festival was to be headlined by the reggae band 'Harlem Spirit', who's current single, SUS, was about the stop and search policy devised by the Police purely to harass young black men, Ian feels that it is this single that had its finger right on the pulse of what was going on.

Second on the bill were 'The Do Do's' who augmented their line up with

Mathew on trumpet and a trombone player. The band wanted to put on a lively show as they knew that plenty of people were coming to join in the party with them.

The stage was set up on top of the toilet block outside 'The White Horse' pub which faced the horseshoe of a crescent and created a natural form of amphitheatre. The festival kicked off around midday and had a real festival atmosphere with young families mixing together enjoying a real child friendly day, which was a refreshing break in the 'Summer of Hate'. However, the day progressed and darkness began to fall, the families began to drift away to be replaced by a more alternative kind of audience consisting of anarchist types with A's stencilled on their leather or parka jackets, Black and White Rasta's and general drop outs. The heady aroma of marijuana wafted through the air and the relaxed atmosphere continued as everyone mixed and mingled together.

The band was just getting ready to go on stage and were approached by a couple of members from Harlem Spirit who enquired;

"Do you fancy swapping places with us and closing the show?"

This was an opportunity to good to refuse, headlining the Hulme Carnival!

Harlem Spirit came on stage and played a blistering, shit hot set and went down a storm. They really captured the crowd but The Do Do's were not put off by this in the least and felt they could carry on with the great atmosphere with their funky sound and spirit.

As the band walked on to the stage, the attitude was very much 'Ok, let's show 'em what WE can do". Confidence and self-belief were high, the band were ready to play the set of their lives.

As soon as the band started playing, there were problems because the monitors had mysteriously vanished and the prevailing breeze carried the sound away and no one could hear what they were playing. The whole performance became a dreadful mess with the band playing two different songs at the same time. Ian describes the whole performance as 'humiliating and depressing' and the audience was far from impressed. The band struggled to the end of this dire set and Ian went off to find the organisers to find out;

"What the Fuck happened?"

This demand was merely met with shrugged shoulders and the reply

"That PA system belonged to Harlem Spirit and they took it away after their set along with the microphones and monitors"

and then as an afterthought, as a response to the incredulous silence, added "Sorry."

The Do Do's had well and truly been stitched up, fucked over and hung up to dry.

The evening at Rafters, after the set, was supposed to have been a celebration, but it turned out to be the post mortem and funeral of The Do Do's. The band sat in silence, nursing their drinks, not a word needed to be said; The Do Do's had become the Dodo's.

Anne returned to the education system, Greg moved down South and Tim concentrated on his studio work. Graham enjoyed taking a lot of mushrooms and speed and eventually went on to work with Andy Robinson (New Order's roadie and future manager) forming the band "Life" - recording two singles with Factory(as well as working with Ian on future projects). And as for Ian, Ian licked his wounds and brooded a lot.

Boys Keep Swinging by David Bowie

When Ian wasn't brooding he was out with Steve, Bobby and Wayne, actually he was out with them increasingly more and more as he had no band to occupy himself. One of their chosen haunts was 'Romeo's' which was a strip club next door to The Cyprus Tavern which was owned by Kosto's and Pam (managers of The Cyprus Tavern) and run by Sherry and Bertie.

Now, this wasn't what you might think, four young lads spending all their time in a strip club ogling the talent and hassling the curvaceous young ladies in their various stages of undress. No, it was, in fact quite the opposite. The girls were of a similar age to the lads and the relationship was mutually platonic, if the 'one eyed snake' had ever stirred and attempted to have gone into action that would have been a real abuse of trust. Backstage, with their friends, was an oasis of calm, respect and friendship. Sherry noticed that the young lad's presence appeared to unsettle the mainly middle aged and elderly clientele at the front of the house, so they were much better off back stage, chatting, drinking and smoking dope with the artists.

Ian spent a weekend with Craig Scanlon in London to see 'The Blue Orchids' at The Moonlight one evening, followed by John Cale at The Lyceum the next. The weekend was spent in a warm and cosy bus at Victoria Station in order to save money, Ian was becoming quite the expert in knowing how to 'rough it' and save valuable drink and drug money. During the evening, on the bus, Craig confided to Ian;

"Marc's on his way out from The Fall"

"Yeah, that was that remark about the Hamsters being Marc's 'Drug and Cider Mates' in the song 'Middlemas'...."

Mused Ian.

"Got it in one, it's an attack on him"

Later, Craig's suspicions were founded during a gig at The Lesser Free Trade Hall where Marc was openly abused, both physically and verbally by Kay Carrol in front of the audience. Marc really didn't see this one coming and was chucked out from the band he loved so much.

"You mean we could have been friends?"

Baby Jane Hudson to Blanche Hudson ("What Ever Happened to Baby Jane?") 1982

Ian, besides socialising with Bobby, Steven and Wayne, also found himself being invited to offer opinions on their new band 'The Nightwatchmen'. After a short time, Steven ventured that, maybe Ian would like to sing on certain numbers and Ian was happy to do so. As Ian wasn't actually an 'official' member it meant that a lot of the stress and strains of 'the old days' were no longer present. Although, neither party attempted a reconciliation to bring Ian back into the fold again, Ian was able to offer songs and work in a 'loose fashion'. Bobby got hold of a banjo and violin to add texture to Ian's new work. 'Electric Impulse', 'Sinking Feeling' and 'Stereotype' were created. The fourth song, 'Big Brown Eyes', was actually about Ian's experience with The Hamsters, and Ian relished the irony that he was actually singing this with his old band members.

At one rehearsal, Ian had an idea;

"Why don't we play a gig together?"

The rest of the band looked interested so Ian continued:

"Make it a real event, summat different?"

"Yes!"

Bobby, Steven and Wayne were warming up to Ian's suggestion.

"Ok, How about we play a set of these songs we've done together and then you play a Nightwatchmen set, to finish off we'll all do a few Hamsters numbers?"

"Yeah, that would work nicely!"

Agreed Bobby, Steven and Wayne nodding enthusiastically

"If you're up for it.? I'll ask Sherry and Bertie if we can play at Romeo's?"

"Fucking brilliant idea, we must do this"

Enthused Steve, who it must be said was getting on much better with Ian as a collaborator rather than vying to lead the band.

The band rehearsed eagerly, both Sherry and Bertie agreed for the band to play at the strip club and Bobby made some posters:

The Nightwatchmen V the Bears from Belle Vue
Meet
The Hamsters
Uptown

The day before the Saturday Night Gig, Ian went to check with Romeo's if everything was ready for the big night. As Ian was waiting at the bar, an official looking man entered, it turned out he was a Policeman as he warned Sherry;

"We can see that you intend to put some groups on in here. Your licence doesn't cover live music. If you go ahead tomorrow, you will be contravening these terms. You stand to lose your licence and face closure."

This was a real blow to the band as everyone had been looking forward to this gig. However, the band knew not to take this personally as 'God's Cop's' wanted the city to be cleansed of all strip joints and Ian was reminded of the lyrics by Bob Dylan;

"We just happened to be there, that's all"

Bears from Belle Vue Zoo Go to The Kitchen

The band decided to record the four songs (under the name Bears From Belle Vue Zoo)jn at The Kitchen and the session was engineered by Adam. The Bears were joined by Ann, on Keyboard and yodelling.

The demo's sound tighter than those recorded at Street Level and demonstrate greater technical competence. Fortunately, they don't sound like just 'another eighties band' as 'Electric Impulse' and 'Sinking Feeling', in particular are very strong songs. Both Ann's keyboards and Bobby's banjo playing are inspired.

The band enjoyed recording this session, and this comes across in the sound. In particular Ian is singing and stretching himself more than the 'holler of The Hamsters'. Interestingly, Steven's drumming, although by no means conventional, is not so much at the forefront of these songs but shows a clear development in expertise. Listing to the demos, it is apparent why Ian had wondered at the time, why they were not working on such good material eight or nine months earlier.

Maybe because it was agreed that this recording session was strictly to be a 'one off' the results are so good and not under or overworked? However, once the session was recorded Ian and The Nightwatchmen had an unspoken agreement to, amicably, go their own separate ways. Ian was offered gigs but preferred to recommend The Nightwatchmen instead. On one occasion, this suggestion was taken up and the band played a solid, but unspectacular gig at The Gallery on St Peter Street.

However, for reasons best known to himself, Ian finally agreed to do a solo gig at The Lamplight in Chorton Cum Hardy, despite the fact he couldn't play a note. Never mind, this had never stopped Brian Eno, so Ian purchased a drum machine and borrowed Steve Mardy's guitar. Ian's (over) confidence was such that he wrote a mass of lyrics and decided to 'go for it' on the night, he had, he figured out around 40 minutes of material for his solo set.

On the night of this memorable gig, Ian took the drum machine out of the box and plugged it in. The beats were set to up-tempo and Ian began to perform his set to the expectant audience……

Ian lurches into a manic rap in a lunatic attempt to keep up with the pitiless drum machine and tenses himself with the sheer effort. Soon his jaw is aching and he is drenched in sweat, he has turned a rather fetching shade of red and his poor temples are throbbing with the tension. Once in a while, Ian remembers the guitar that is slung around his neck and assaults the strings. In fact his arm appears to be the only part of his body that is not paralysed by the increasing tension that is quickly rendering him static. His banshee howl echoes around the silent, incredulous room.

Eventually, Ian manages to get to the end of his set, and with one last slash at the guitar strings, and booting the drum machine off stage, Ian has come to the end of his ordeal.

For twenty seconds there is no a murmur from the audience who have been stunned into silent submission. Eventually, some brave soul claps and the rest of the audience join in.

A soaking wet Ian is approached by a beaming Steve Mardy who asks;

"I thought you were going to be on stage for around three quarters of an hour?"

It certainly felt like it to Ian who wonders;

"It might have been a bit shorter"

Steve Mardy shakes his head and laughingly informs Ian that;

"You were on stage for nine minutes at the most mate! Come on, I'll drive you home."

This evening turned out to be more memorable than Ian suspected as a mere twenty seven years later, when visiting a friend in hospital, he was approached by a stranger, who asked, in tones of awe;

"Didn't I see you years ago in Chorlton?"

Ian gets asked this question all the time, but generally in association with The Hamsters, but somehow felt that this was different and sought clarification;

"You may have done?"

In a voice of hushed reverence the stranger replied;

"Yes! I'm sure it was you doing indescribable things in a club! Mad, noisy poetry!"

Ian couldn't deny it and nodded in affirmation;

"Yeah, I remember that night."

he recalled with a neutral smile.

"I have never forgotten that"

begins the stranger shaking his head and continued;

"I have never seen anything like it."

Ian felt a little uncomfortable as the stranger's eyes began to burn into him; maybe he was trying to locate some of the mystery of that night? Ian decided to make his excuses and leave;

"Nice to meet you, but I need to see my friend on a ward."

In which Jon shows touching concern for Pope John Paul

Ian was keen to enlist the services of Jon, who was playing in a Goth band called 'Cabal' along with Andy Zero. According to Ian, although 'Cabal' got several gigs through Andy's connections, they were a 'complete load of rubbish'. Maybe this realisation eventually dawned upon them as they packed away their black velvet costumes with lace edgings and called it a day.

Now this was good news, according to Ian, as he wanted to enlist Jon's services and felt confident that Jon would gladly accept. Well, it was Steven who had rudely chucked Jon out and surely Jon's high heels would come striding back?

"Jon, mate, would you be interested in forming a band with me?"

asked Ian, as a matter of formality.

"No can do!"

came the cheerful riposte

"What???"

replied Ian, who it must be said, was taken aback with this reply.

"Steven's been in touch, I'm joining them as a guitarist"

Never had Ian's flabber been so ghasted and he snapped back;

"You must need your head testing!"

"I think I turned up to two rehearsals with the Nightwatchmen and hated it. Not the music you understand, just Bob and Steve. If Moet had not been connected, I would not have bothered at all" **Jon Rowlinson**

Ian had heard that 'The Spurtz' had called it a day he decided to approach Rat, the drummer with an interesting proposition;

"Rat, mate, would you be interested in forming a band with me?"

asked Ian, feeling sure that Rat would jump at the chance.

"No, Moet, Steven's asked me to be the drummer, so he can sing"

Ian wasn't quite so bothered with this refusal as he had the feeling that this set up would not last very long. He was proved to be correct, in this instance, as Rat barely lasted one rehearsal. Rat had blown his chances with Ian and would not be asked again.

Grant Showbizz invited both Ian and The Nightwatchmen to play a couple of gigs in London. Ian was eager but initially refused as he had no backing musicians, but Steven gladly accepted and had the sense to realise that Ian was part of the package;

"Moet..."

began Steven

"What?"

snapped Ian, he had the feeling Steven wanted something.

"You can borrow Jon....if you want."

came the slightly patronising offer;

"Ok"

Ian replied as neutrally as he could. Secretly, he welcomed this olive branch and continued;

"I'll just do the Saturday evening though."

Ian's reasoning for this was that he didn't want really want to be associated with The Nightwatchmen as he viewed them as a form of competition, also, he didn't really want them to catch his act and have something to respond to on the Saturday evening at the 'Meanwhile Gardens' when both bands went 'head to head'.

The Nightwatchmen were in a tube overflowing with Nuns and Catholic Priests to travel to their concert on the Friday. It was a really hot, sweltering day and the carriage was like a sauna. This extreme heat was not lost on Jon and he chose to share the following observation, loudly, with Bobby:

"Fucking Hell! I bet The Pope's sweating like a cunt in that Pope mobile."

The carriage went silent all of a sudden as the thong of worshippers appeared to contemplate Jon's obvious concern for the Pope. But Jon wasn't finished, as a reaction to the sound of silence he wanted to know;

"Fucking Hell! Has someone died then"?"

"I expect the Pope was rather moist on that day – it was fucking warm" **Jon Rowlinson**

Bobby, Steven and Wayne genuinely didn't know whether to laugh or cry. . God must have been smiling on Jon that day, as that evening's gig went rather well.

Ian had made extensive preparations for his solo debut in London, he had read the instruction manual for the drum machine and when he arrived at Meanwhile Gardens, the following evening there was a real party atmosphere. Ian was determined to keep a clear head and refused offers of both drinks and smokes, so determined was he to remain focused.

The Nightwatchmen's set was not as good as the previous evenings had been, it was proficient but somewhat dull Ian thought as he got ready to follow them.

"Jon, you set the tempo of the drum machine and play the fuck out of the bass, and, oh yeah, use a fucking plectrum!"

The audience mostly wore the regulatory uniform of the early 'eighties, matt black, but Ian was a bit more original with his white trousers and shirt and wide homburg hat. This look ensured that he got everyone's attention when he came on stage and announced;

"I've come from Manchester to sing some songs for you" and nodded to Jon to start the rhythm section.......

"GUITARS TWANG .....TWANG, TWANG
DRUMERS BANG........AND CLANG AND CLANG
EMPORERS CLOTHES (WOLF WHISTLE)
JUST A POSE (WOLF WHISTLE)
BREAKING TOYS....SMASH THEM UP
TOO MUCH NOISE...TURN IT DOWN
LEADERS LIARS.......UNIFORMS
FREE YOUR MINDS...FREEDOM"

Ian had the black clad audience exactly where he wanted them: pinned by the throat and he kept on going, improvising in a clear stream of conscious thought with a thunderstorm of bass as a backing sound track.

"....mad as fuck, I can tell you, and not the way I like to do things .Moet is a performance artist, and this was a perfect gig for him" **Jon**

Both Ian and Jon got a huge round of applause and the first person to come and congratulate Ian was Bobby;

"Nice one, Moet!"

Bobby grinned and added:

"That was ace."

Steven also came up to Ian and enthused:

"That was really good, Moet. Miles better than we were."

"Thanks Steven"

replied Ian managing to play it cool at this genuine compliment

Later on, Grant came and told Ian;

"They were ok, nice to have them down here."

He nodded at the Nightwatchmen and continued;

"You were really good however, different to anything else."

"Thanks Mate."

responded Ian

"But where are you going to take it?"

asked Grant with furrowed brow.

Ian was too busy basking in the glory and honestly replied;
"I don't know."

Jazz, Delicious hot, disgusting cold Bonzo Dog Doo Dah Band

Ian was fast becoming very disillusioned with the musical scene and was looking for a new direction to embrace. Punk was now no more than a form of 'shorthand stupidity' which was safe and conformist. Even the current sounds from Jamaica failed to thrill Ian any more. Critically acclaimed bands, such as 'Kid Creole and The Coconuts', and Spandau Ballet, were preening and vacuous; Ian loathed them with a vengeance.

Even Ian's other love, Manchester United, had become dull, boring automatons under the new leadership of Dave Sexton. Still, Ian traipsed around the country hoping for some return to form, but beyond the odd magical moment, it was often 90 minutes of tedium.

The post punk scene, besides the influence of the mighty Fall, threw up the odd gem such as the cross dressing Virgin Prunes from Ireland and Dexy's Midnight runners. Like many disaffected youth of the early eighties the polemics and aggression of Crass also appealed to Ian.

In an effort to find 'that certain something', Ian revisited his extensive back catalogue of Captain Beefheart, Faust and Syd Barrett, which temporarily satisfied his craving but still Ian wanted to experience new sounds. In an effort to locate something that he may just have overlooked Ian tried jazz. Although the recordings were often impenetrable, Ian found live jazz a very liberating experience and often with Bobby and Steven would be dancing around an empty dance floor (admittedly somewhat inebriated and drugged up) at The Band on The Wall. The Jazz musicians often made a point of thanking the lads after such a visual display of enthusiastic dancing, this in turn had inspired them to play harder to the exuberant dance that was taking place in front of them.

It was great to have a liberating dance and interact with the musicians, but eventually morning would come and Ian was soon back in the old, boring routine.

Ain't no Soul Major Lance 1983

Most Saturday mornings would find Ian at the very same record shop where he had found 'Fun House' all those years ago. Most material, such as 'The Boomtown Rats' would be studiously avoided and Ian would make straight for the seven inch section where he would choose records by Gene Vincent and Buddy Holly. However, it was the 'Northern Soul' section that interested him the most and he sought recommendations from the shop owners, John Hillel and David Stubbs. The thing that appealed to Ian was that each record was judged by its merit rather than market forces. Ian loved the vibrant sounds of Major Lance, Lorraine Chandler and Lou Ragland and even wrote an (unpublished) article for 'City Fun' in which he stated that Northern Soul was the real underground scene which existed well away from the vulgar thirst for publicity and was fuelled by a love for the music.

Ian was taking part in 'all-nighters' and there was something thrilling and romantic about waiting on a railway station, late at night, to be taken to a club full of likeminded souls. Armed with a bottle of concealed vodka and a gramme of speed, Ian was set up for the early hours of the morning and it would be great to report that the actual events lived up to his expectations, but no this genre had gone past its heyday and was fraying around the edges. The venue that was once the Wigan Casino was now a car park and Ian realised that the best years were very likely behind him. But Ian was determined to enjoy what morsels remained and flung himself with gay abandon onto sprung dance floors, such as The Carousel Club on Plymouth Grove and held his own against the club veterans.

One memorable evening, for the wrong reasons, Ian was at the 'Superbowl' on the Morecombe coastal front. Ian set off through the freezing rain, with seven or eight friends, and arrived at the sparsely attended club. Still they decided to make the most of it and danced as much as they could in an effort to fill the empty dance floor. At around 3am, the place was suddenly flooded by a tidal wave and they had to find refuge on the high ground and spent the next few hours shivering. The next available train didn't depart until 8am.

"I'm on the right track"

The Right Track by Billy Butler

"We later formed a band called The Bears from Belle View Zoo. Not one of our greatest triumphs, but we had a few gigs out of it" **Jon**

Ian wanted to spread the word of 'Northern Soul' with an evangelical zeal and formed a new band with the name of 'Bears from Belle Vue' The band consisted of Graham Ellis; Jon was back on bass and his girlfriend, Debbie, providing occasional keyboards. The advertisement for a 'Hard Hitting Drummer' resulted in Mike Prendergast being recruited.

The message was upbeat and in positive praise of the human spirit and the first song was a stomping cover of 'The Right Track, which in many ways was intended to be the blueprint for a really rousing, inspirational sound. What transpired however was Ian's world weary lyrics, which the band was supposed to transform into dance floor smashes. In addition plodding cover versions such as Simon and Garfunkel's 'The Boxer' and Leonard Cohen's 'The Stranger' were also rehearsed.

It is quite possible Ian lost the plot with this strange mixture of aspirations. But Ian didn't care, he had a band again, and it didn't really matter that they were somewhat bemused by his eclectic manifesto. Ian genuinely believed that he had a direction, and a mission, that would come together somehow. He sought to broadcast the gospel of freedom and believed that his audience would let out the love that was truly in their hearts to pleas of;

"FREE YOURSELVES!"

Ian describes himself as being ' part missionary and part avenging angel' and the fact that people described them as a 'pretty good band' allowed himself to retreat further into his own little world.

Caucasian Walk Virgin Prunes

Ian's reading material of Aldous Huxley, Kurt Vonnegut Jnr, formed the basis of his lyrical input for the musical soundtrack for The Bears from Belle Vue. He describes this latest venture as a 'pretty cool outfit, if slightly frayed around the edges psychologically'. For example, Graham, greeted Ian when calling at his flat, all covered in paint; in fact all his belongings were covered in paint and looked rather like a Jackson Pollock art enactment. Only Michael looked a bit astonished, when the rest of the band came later and at the end of rehearsals, Graham had pretty much 'dried out' and Ian took him out for a drink.

Graham and Ian discussed that the band, whilst doing fairly well, deserved better. At the bar, Ian bumped into Rob Gretton and straight away came out with;

"Rob, we need more gigs, can you sort us out?"

Rob mused for a second and replied;

"Come and do a single with Factory Records and then I can get you some gigs!"

Ian shook his head and firmly stated:

"I don't want to record for Factory, Rob"

Rob raised his eyebrows at this and Ian continued:

"I just want some gigs!"

It wasn't the first time that this conversation had taken place, and it wouldn't be the last. Eventually, it became a standing joke between them, Rob offering a contract with Factory and Ian refusing.

At the next rehearsal Ian had a proposition for The Bears;

"We should go to places where people are queuing to see bands, let's say at The Apollo or University, and play"

The band appeared to think this a good idea and nodded; Jon especially liked the idea and replied;

"Like busking you mean?"

"No! No! No!"

Exclaimed Ian shaking his head horrified;
"If anyone throws money, throw it back"
Jon looked really puzzled and grunted
"Uh?!"
"Tell them this is our art and we can't prostitute it!"
Jon didn't seem so keen on this idea, and neither did the rest of the band. Unfortunately, owing to the less than enthusiastic response this plan was never carried out.

Ian, after enjoying the antics of the two front men from Virgin Prunes, Gavin and Guggi, agreed to go back to a party in Hulme. When he arrived he found the venue was, in fact, an empty flat with the door kicked in and the electricity filtered through an elaborate system of wires from next door.

Whist it is true to say Ian wasn't exactly in the best state at the beginning of the party, he went downhill fast and suspects that his drink had been spiked as he passed out. When he eventually came to, he found himself naked and shivering in a cupboard. Fortunately, he found his clothes and used the toilet, I say fortunately as he soon found out that he was not the only party goer who had been left somewhat dishevelled in this hovel, this poor guy had no trousers and they were nowhere to be seen.....

Ian Moss a muse

Ian met several famous people whilst working at the shop in Didsbury such as Nico (whom he used to buy her favourite chocolate for) as well as members of Magazine and Blue Orchids. Didbury was somewhat of a magnet for musicians, actors and clientele from Manchester University. One such character was Professor Ulrich Finke who besides being the Head of the Art Department was also the son of a German Contessa. Professor Finke was fascinated by what their mutual interest in creative art and really wanted to see him perform.

John Bidet came rushing into the shop and beckoned Ian to come over;
"Moet, we've got a gig at Manchester University and we desperately need another band to appear with us at 'The Toast Rack' tonight!"
"There is nothing more than I would like to support 'Bathroom Renovations" began Ian but shook his head as he explained;'
"There is no way I can get The Bears to play at such short notice"
"Oh no! I don't know what I am going to do."
John looked really worried and explained
"I was relying on you, Mo!"
Ian was always up to help another musician, especially when this involved another musician and suddenly the ideal solution came to him;

"Tell you what, John, I could get some sort of band together, not The Bears though, leave it with me and I will be there tonight"

John looked really relieved, Ian's reputation was such that he would keep his word and provide a band, besides the audience would know Ian and that was a bonus.

Ian got on the phone to Bobby and Steven and asked them if they were interested in being his backing band for that evening, both agreed enthusiastically. It just so happened that Ulrich appeared in the shop and was immediately informed;

"Well you keep on asking me when you can see me perform, well tonight's the night, so are you coming or what?"

Ulrich readily agreed and promised to attend after Ian gave him the details.

Bobby, Ian and Steven decided to be as minimal and as unsettling as possible. Armed with a single steel drum, Bobby's debut as a violin player and Ian on improvised vocals this surely would be another assault on the senses of a, largely, unsuspecting audience?

The first band that appeared that evening was dull and boring, but more exiting material was to make a debut…well…would when Steven managed to get his steel drum to a stand assisted unably by Bobby and Ian. The audience thought this was part of the act and roared with laughter. Eventually, Mark Jones was persuaded to squat on the stage, cross legged, and held the drum above his good looking head. Mark earnt his drink money that night as Steven pummelled the single drum in a merciless sonic attack which was totally unlike the calypso rhythm that usually results from the particular instrument. Bobby was doing his own 'John Cale' on the violin, coaxed shards of cutting sound leaving Ian free to let forth in a free conscious primal scream of lyrics, movement and visuals. At the end of this improvised set, the band received a very enthusiastic round of applause and cheers. Ian felt liberated by this experience, but most of all it was simply magical to be on the same stage as Bobby and Steven, his band of brothers.

The next day Ian was called to the phone and on the other end was an overly excited Ulrich;

"I came to see you last night…….."

Ian waited

"YOU ARE A GENIUS!!!!"

Ian felt chuffed and murmured his thanks, but Ulrich had plans for Ian;

"I want to make a film about you!"

"Eh?"

was Ian's instinctive reaction, was Ulrich actually taking the piss here, but no;

"Are you agreeable to this?"

Ian still wasn't sure about Ulrich but tentatively answered;
"Yeah, why not?"
Steven was present and wanted to know;
"What was that about then, Mo?"
"Oh it was Ulrich."
"What did that nutty German professor want with you?"
"He thinks I'm a GENIUS Steven!"
"Oh yeah?"
"He wants to make a film about me..."
The look on Steven's face was reward enough for Ian, as he really looked as if he was chewing on a wasp.
Both Ian and Steven looked at each other and both burst out laughing.

The other side of Ian Moss

From the beginning of the film project there were disagreements between artist and muse about how this art work was to be depicted. Ian maintained, first and foremost that he was a singer and to take his lyrics out of this context and depict them as a form of 'poetry' did not depict what his art was really about. It was this difference of artistic vision, Ian believes, that lead this project to be vague and somewhat lacking in direction, however Ulrich was keen to work with Ian and at least the film was finished.

Ian enjoyed the process of filming and liked working with the interesting and learned Ulrich. Ian really only had to stand his ground on one occasion, when Ulrich wanted him to recite his lyrics on a crowded bus;
"No I'm not going to"
"Why, it would be so interesting?"
"I have to travel on this bus every day and my name isn't Coco the fucking clown"
articulated Ian firmly. The message got home

Filming consisted of Ian rehearsing with the band at Graham's flat, interspliced with some moody shoots of prowling around the streets of Hulme and (the now derelict) Belle Vue showground. The one shot that really worked, Ian believed, was of him reciting a special composition, concerning faith, at a heavily overgrown churchyard in Cheetham Hill;

"On the day I'm deceased, don't mourn the loss
of the money wasted on funeral costs.
Don't put me through that pagan ceremony
I don't believe it's going to save me
So if you're hungry and want to
Eat me......"

Ian was not at all pleased when Ulrich added a dreary soundtrack by Pink Floyd to add 'atmosphere' to the wandering Moss. The film was entitled 'The Other Side' an allusion to the many different parts that made up the whole.

This masterpiece received its premier upstairs at 'The Victoria Pub' off Deansgate, along with other films from Ulrich's student collaborators. Ian remembers being rather impressed with the contributions from the student film makers and likewise the audience was very enthusiastic about 'The Other Side'. Ian accepted the congratulations but felt that this was another missed opportunity which could have been even better.

Steven summed the whole experience up rather succinctly when he hugged Moet;

"Great that Mo!"

He paused and emphasised:

"BUT it would have been better about ME!"

Ian didn't comment but tactfully suggested

"Let's go for a drink then, shall we?"

He ain't heavy; he's my brother The Hollies

Neil was not in a good state. His depression and drinking had worsened and he increasingly hid from the word in his flat, playing endless games of chess against himself. Mick Hucknall was slowly, but surely losing patience with Neil and confided to Ian before a gig at The Band on The Wall:

"Ian can you have a word with him, please? See if you can get through to him because he's just drinking far too much I have had to drop songs that he says he can't play 'em. It's driving me mad and affecting the band!"

Whilst Ian sympathised, he knew that there wasn't really a great deal he could do or say as the gap between the brothers had grown so far. Both brothers loved each other but could only communicate in a casual offhand manner like polite strangers. Ian now acknowledges that both he and Neil were both guilty of torturing each other with indifference, although both would have denied this.

Once the Frantics were a joyous event but on that particular evening they were a 'bummer'. Ian likens the experience of watching a condemned man in his cell and felt that the band's days were numbered.

Therefore, it really came as no surprise when Mick, upon being persuaded by the band's manager, Elliot Rushman, left to go solo and the rest is history. Neil regarded this decision as no less than betrayal from both Elliot and Mick. The self-financed single, 'Holding back the years', co-written with Neil, had barely sold two hundred copies and resulted in having to pay off a bank loan. Another single, 'Haven't got the power', although recorded, was not released until Mick went solo.

Bob, meanwhile, really surprised Ian with a major decision;

"Moet, I've left the Nightwatchmen."

"Bloody Hell! What's Steven done now then?"

replied Ian, who was rather taken aback. He'd not seen this one coming.

"It's not Steven. I'm fed up with this endless, pointless rehearsing."

"But you're a good band, you're a great guitarist mate, don't waste it."

reasoned Ian

"Thanks, but we've got absolutely nowhere and there's one more thing..."

"Yes?"

enquired Ian, interested

"I don't like Steven's material; in fact you're a much better song writer these days."

"Well, thanks Mate!"

Ian was really chuffed by Bobby's observation.

"But don't tell him I said that."

added Bobby as an afterthought and continued;

"I still want us all to be friends, not like the Frantics."

Ian agreed, well there were no musical ties and there were no real reasons why they couldn't remain friends.

Everything's Alright The Mojo's

"The Other Side", Ian decided, could benefit from being shown when The Bears played, so a gig was arranged in the upstairs of The Thompson's Arms, which also happened to be Manchester's Premier Gay Venue. John Bidet and Bathroom Renovations helped to set up this gig and Ian augmented The Bears line up with the saxophonist Chris.

On the evening of the gig Ian was gratified to see a large mixture of straight and gays in the audience. Some of the 'Blokes' were clearly discomforted by the large element of 'Poofs'; Ian derived great pleasure by this obvious unease with difference.

The Frantics opened with Neil taking over on lead vocals. To his credit, Mick Hucknall came along to demonstrate his support and despite the fact that The Frantics played a good set, Neil was an uncomfortable front man. The vocals were there, but the presence was not and this was to be the Frantics first and last gig. Next on were the poppy Bathroom Fixtures, with John Bidet clearly relishing the role of lead vocalist, a complete contrast to Neil.

Mick Hucknall looked more fraught watching from the side than Neil singing up front. Mick appeared to me to be very worried what would happen to Neil now he'd left the band. He felt for his well-being **Steve Mardy**

"The other side" was shown and was, again, well received. This mixture of media really gave the gig a 'Festival Type' atmosphere and the Bears came on straight after the film.

Ian felt that, with the added addition of saxophone, a really good set was performed and that this triumph could now be built on.

Ian had an unexpected surprise that evening.

Julie turned up with her friend who was a devout Catholic. Julie must have taken some sort of interest in what Ian was up to and decided to turn up that evening with her best friend, who just happened to be a fervent Roman Catholic.

Julie's 'escort' was very, very unhappy with Ian's Graveyard Sermon and took huge offence at Ian and screamed at him,

"May you rot in Hell!!"

Ian thought this 'curse' terribly funny and roared with laughter at the zealot.

When Ian and Julie were alone, Julie simply said;

"I miss you, Ian."

Ian kissed her by means of reply and both arranged to meet up sometime.

Steven was curious as to where Ian and Julie had snuck off to and came out with;

"Why did you two slip away, it's not what I think it is, is it?"

Ian couldn't lie and admitted;

"Yes, we're going to be back together, I just know it."

"She's married"

stated Steven.

"Yeah, I know it's not right and even now I feel guilty, nothing much happened but it will, I just can't stop myself as I still long to be with he."

Steven gave Ian some wise advice, which Ian now wishes he had taken;

"Don't get involved Mo. If you go back now, you won't know how to stop."

Boy, Can You Remember? The Bears from Belle Vue

Ian felt that he was writing his very best material for a really good band, and in particular, a great new song, 'Boy, Can You Remember?" which was inspired by Ray Charles was added to the set.

The band was to record a session at Adam's new studio, 'Out of the blue', which was situated in Ancoats. Adam had not only managed to get the band free studio time, but was also able to provide a rehearsal room at very reasonable rates. Everything was going ahead for the first studio session until the saxophonist, Chris, left the band. Chris had an offer he really couldn't refuse, to join Albertos Y Los Paranoia's and did not want to go ahead with the Bears from Belle Vue Session. This was a real body blow and the resulting session results were very disappointing. Ian didn't blame Chris, he knew the real reason; the poisonous bubble that was himself and Julie. Now that she was back in his life, he had lost his focus. There was the added complication of Julie's marriage and a familiar pattern of ending and beginning their relationship was established for the next few years.

The band lasted a few more weeks after the less than spectacular session and drifted apart, owing to Ian's reawakened obsession with Julie.

Steven had recruited Andy Zero to collaborate with him and was presented with a 'Manifesto' which Steve showed to Ian. After scanning this document Ian told Steven;

"It's preposterous and it's not you Steven."

Steven agreed with Ian at the time, but still ended up sacking loyal Wayne who was very upset. Both Bobby and Ian liked Wayne and even empathised with him, up to a point, but in the sick word of The Brotherhood of Hamsters, they both managed to see the funny side and roared with laughter upon hearing this tragic news.

Neil was cajoled by Steven into rehearsals to play guitar, as Steven had decided to become the vocalist, whilst Andy Zero filled the vacant drum seat. This arrangement ended when Neil tactfully informed Steve;

"Andy's hopeless on drums and you're a much better drummer."

This home truth resulted in Andy becoming the latest casualty; no manifesto could save him now. However, Neil was really only helping out and was not prepared to commit to joining any band; therefore Steven was the only Nightwatchman, like Ian he was without a proper band.

"Up Your Junta" Sun Newspaper Headline

Ian was now spending a lot of time with Anne and her new friends at her University hometown of Wrexham. They were a resourceful bunch too managing to cook up a delicious meal that consisted of left overs, literally left lying on the pavement, after the meat and veg market stalls had packed up for the evening. This meant more money for wine and the evening was spent debating about the current sham that was The Falklands War that was instigated by the tyrannical Margaret Thatcher. Like many young people who were on the outside, they were able to see this unjust war for what it really was, an exercise in jingoistic morality and power.

Ian recalls that a close friend of his, Dennis Downworth, dared to voice an alternative viewpoint in the company of a 'Pro' War faction and was badly beaten up for being 'unpatriotic'.

He really, really enjoyed the company of Anne and his new, likeminded friends. They debated current topics around an open fire and Ian felt stimulated and inspired by the intelligent conversation. These were good people with a deep seated conviction on the wrongs and rights of society. Ian felt that there was indeed a glimmer of hope and things could change for the better.

A Night Out With The Girls

Ian was invited along to a feminist convention which took place at Manchester University by Anne and his new friends. He found out that he was one of the few smattering of 'token' men at the event, not that this bothered him. But what did irritate him was the 'entertainment' provided by the all-female bands who merely aped the posturing and sounds of macho male acts such as 'ACDC' and 'Thin Lizzy'.

He had quite enough and was quite prepared to go home after this tiresome display of unoriginality but one of the gang asked Ian;

"Want to come to 'Trinian's' with us?"

Ian knew all about this particular club and knew that he would not be especially welcomed as it catered for a mainly lesbian clientele and was just about to politely decline when another part of the group objected;

"No he can't go with us!"

Another member insisted;

"But men can go in there, I've seen a few."

"Men are to be tolerated and not encouraged."

This last remark really set Anne and her friends off and both factors of the group really had a tussle over whether Ian should, or should not be allowed to come with them. Ian listened and kept out of this lively discussion, although in truth he felt like a pawn in a game of feminist ideology. Ian would have been quite happy to have gone home, there and then, but Anne's friends won the argument and, well, it was sort of compulsory for Ian to go now.

The whole 'Men aren't allowed in here' debate erupted on the door of 'Trinian's' with the female bouncers determined to enforce their 'Women Only' policy, but such was the ferocity of Anne's set that they reluctantly back tracked and allowed the whole group, including Ian, in to the club.

Ian really stood out, for the wrong reasons, and to make things even more miserable the music was rotten and nobody appeared to be having any sort of good time. But being a typical bloke, he decided to make the best of a bad time and headed straight for the pool table which was surrounded by a group of 'Butch' Bull Dykes.

"Hello, ladies, fancy a game of pool with me."

Ian chirped up in a friendly fashion. This offer was met by sneers and open contempt. Ian remembers thinking 'Why are they being like this to me? I bet some of them wish they were me', but wisely decided not to share this observation with his new playmates.

"Come on now."

Ian placed the marker on the on the table;

"Scared you'll lose?"

This challenge was too much to ignore and the gang guffawed that they could;

"Beat you with one hand tied behind our back!"

This boast was proven to be empty, as one by one, with no hands tied behind their back, each contender was soundly thrashed by Ian. It is true that he did take pleasure in beating his would be detractors and after the last victory;

"Adios!"

he cheerily smiled and left while he was still ahead. He made straight for 'Illuminated 666 Club', on Fenel Street, where he listened to Jonathon Richmond, which was the real highlight of the evening for him.

A Fairy-tale in Manchester

Christmas Eve '83 was a memorable occasion for Ian, for all the wrong reasons.....

It started off innocently enough with well-wishers coming into the shop and dropping off cards and presents. One couple, Mike and Judy, ushered Ian away from the counter as they had baked him a very special treat, hash cakes. In all fairness they did warn;

"Be careful with these, Mo, they're really strong...a full one is really pushing it!"

Did Ian listen? Did he, fuck.

Meeting up with Anne at the 'Old Garret', some welcome drinks were consumed and Ian decided that he couldn't go round carrying 15 hash cakes all night long and made an executive decision and gestured towards the cakes;

"We'll have to eat them"

Anne wasn't so sure but was persuaded to help Ian out, she had a few but Ian munched through the majority.

Next both went to the resident's bar of 'The Rembrandt, situated on Canal Street, to consume several cocktails between them. After this orgy of 'Brandy Alexander's', Ian was beginning to feel a bit out of it but decided to head off to 'The Hacienda' as it was Alan Wise's Birthday party and a live band, 'Life', who had just released a single on Factory records, were to play live. The band featured Graham on guitar, which was the main reason why Ian wanted to go. The bill was also to feature, rather bizarrely, the 'blue comedian' Bernard Manning and a stripper.

Ian felt queasy, decidedly ill, during a lifeless performance by 'Life' and decided to go to an area, underneath the stage, which served as the backstage and mingle. After perilously negotiating a flight of stairs down to the 'backstage' Ian found

himself in a private area crammed with 'Muso's' and assorted hangers on. They weren't his kind of people and he found the conversation even more irritating than usual in his drugged state. Oh! enough was enough and Ian opened his mouth to tell this bunch of wankers what a load of old crap they were spouting;
"......"

Ian had managed to open his mouth, but no sound came out! Ian had a few more attempts but not a single syllable of contempt escaped his vocal chords. This sensation increased his already high level of drug induced paranoia and he decided to leave and tottered up the stairs. As he managed to, somehow, reach the top of the stairs, he recognised the sound of the theme from 'The Stripper' and to get out he would have to cross the stage to where a nubile young female (fortunately not Bernard Manning) was disrobing. He decided this was too much and sat down.

A few minutes later the stripper exited to the sound of polite applause and Ian made an effort to get up, but not only had his power of speech been robbed, it transpired the power of movement had also vanished.

Ian saw a vision of wobbly pink and mauve flesh come towards him and it leaned over and asked:

"Are you alright, Love."

Ian opened his mouth, and at last something finally came out
"BAAAAAAARFFF"

A projectile of vomit hit the pubes of the fleshy stripper and ran down her thighs. The stripper didn't say a word, merely pushed past Ian and headed off down stairs.

Somehow, Ian managed to get himself off the floor and got out of the venue........

Ian can remember waking and looking out over Ashton Market and the clock chiming 9 O Clock. He was in the doorway of Marks and Spencers, festively dusted with a layer of snow. How Ian had arrived there, he couldn't remember. He'd obviously attempted to make it home but had gone badly wrong. He rose up and felt a real aching all over his body and made his way home. A much repentant Ian decided to lay low at his parent's house that day and tried his best not to spoil Christmas for his parents.

Pondering about this latest experience, Ian knew that he could have died, either from hypothermia or being violently assaulted when defenceless and vulnerable. He hadn't quite begun to ponder his mortality.......yet.

Big Moet is watching you; life after The Hamsters 1984 – 1986

"When it was time to reform the Hamsters, Bob had forgotten everything – it was like turning the clock back to before I joined the band. The rehearsal was a joke; I wanted nothing more to do with the Hamsters" **Jon**

Several years later I was in a band called the Brigade. We were playing at a gay club called Manhattans a small intimate venue which was ideal for us. Now this night my heroes The Hamsters made one of their comebacks supporting us. Our soundman was of a very nervous disposition and the Hamsters sound check, where they refused to comply to normal protocol, literally drove him to drink. We retired to the local pub to calm him down and returned 90 mins later stoned. Needless to say the gig descended into chaos once again. Mick Hucknall was there that night and made a lot of notes and never looked back **Simmo**

"Hey Moet."
"What?"
Ian was approached by Muppet, who was now in the band', Brigade". He had a proposition;
"Why not reform The Hamsters and play with us at The Manhattan Club next week!"
"You mean that club on Spring Gardens?"
Queried Ian.
"Yes! That's the one, how about it then?"
Ian's curiosity about whether The Hamsters could still hack it got the better of him and answered;
"Let me put it to the rest of the lads and I'll get back to you."
Muppet seemed happy to wait, it wasn't a downright 'No' so was prepared to give Ian a bit of leeway before he confirmed.
Bobby and Steven were well up for it and it was decided to ask Jon if he wanted to come in on this 'one off'. This would work out rather well, as none of them was actually doing anything and Ian was in the middle of an unpaid three month sabbatical from work (as a result of informing Ronnie Middlehurst that he wanted to leave).
The reformed brotherhood met at Steven's new house, which was bigger to accommodate his second son, Brendan. Jon turned up, bass guitar and amp,

eager to rehearse but the rest of the band had other ideas. The brotherhood's idea of a rehearsal was social drinking and discussing which songs to perform.

Ian managed to arrange a van, driven by Simon Taylor, from the band 'Red Alert and on the afternoon of the gig rang the band members to arrange to pick up Bobby and Jon.

"Hi Jon."

greeted Ian from the telephone box

There was a long pause on the other end of the line and then just when Ian thought there may be a fault with the connection;

".....I'm not doing it, Moet."

"What?!!"

Ian was a bit taken aback;

"its madness....We've not rehearsed."

"So what?"

reasoned Ian.

"Moet, please don't play...YOU'LL RUIN EVERYTHING THE HAMSTERS EVER STOOD FOR!"

Ian's knees suddenly went, not from shock but from laughing loudly at Jon. He was laughing so hard that tears were running down his cheeks. Eventually Ian managed to gulp back and chirp;

"Bye Jon, You really haven't got a clue have you, mate?!"

"I knew he would (go on with it). Moet is a great performance artist but lacks any kind of quality control" **Jon**

Simon, when told he was going to be the Hamsters bassist for the 'one off' was really pleased. However when Steven arrived, after travelling by bus, he visibly bristled at this proposition and snapped back, in the presence of Simon;

"I'm not having that cunt on stage with us."

Simon turned beetroot red, but wisely chose to say nothing. Ian attempted logic;

"Well, who's going to play with us?"

Steven had the solution;

"What about your brother Neil?"

Ian pondered;

"Well, I can ask....."

Neil was at the venue and he nodded his acceptance. Everybody was happy, except Simon but such is the fate of The Hamsters bassist. After a quick sound check The Hamsters were ready, it was great fun to play again and there were smiles everywhere (except.... Oh, I won't go on).

Fuelled by a few drinks, it was soon time for The Hamsters to take to the stage after an absence of over two years. At first the sound was dodgy, but Mick Hucknall decided to commandeer the mixing desk on The Hamsters behalf and was able to sort things out. Now that the band could hear what they were playing the set finally took flight and sounded fresh and vibrant. Each band member was smiling at each other as Ian chose a selection of Nightwatchmen numbers and Neil was more than holding his own, indeed he was treated as an equal.

The band finished with all the old favourites such as 'Chip Shop', 'I'm a Cunt', 'Animals' and 'Stupid Songs'. As they left the stage to appreciative applause and cheers, Ian was grabbed by a total stranger who enthused;

"You are the best band I've ever seen! Thank you! Thank you!"

The stranger embraced Ian, who modestly accepted his thanks

After getting some drinks in, the band sat down and Ian asked;

"Shall I get us another gig then?!'

"YES!!!!"

"Putting in The Match"   The Hamsters

The 'one off' gig had spread like wildfire and word got around that The Hamsters were very much a going proposition once more.

"The Battle of The Bands", took part at The Hacienda and Ian had no hesitation in accepting the invitation to play at this event. In the meantime, Steven left Trish and his children in order to move in with the statuesque Rose. Whereas Trish vigorously fought against Steven's drug use, this new ex-model girlfriend joined in enthusiastically and they soon gained a certain reputation as a 'glamorous drug couple' (Manchester's answer to Sid and Nancy?) amongst the drug users set. Indeed, to these damaged individuals, Steven gained a 'cult' status, which verged on 'Genius,' and was re-christened 'Mad Midi' as a result of his notorious behaviour.

On the evening of 'The Battle' everyone arrived for the sound check (Neil playing bass again) except Steven. The band were still able to complete the check with the aid of Alex Sidebottom ('The Distractions') and eventually Steven arrived with his junkie entourage in tow and.......a troupe of fire eaters. None of the band had been consulted over this addition. Oh dear, this was a case of history repeating itself, much to Ian's dismay. Still Ian kept quiet and didn't argue the case when Steven informed 'his' band to play as loudly as they could when they took to the stage.

Steven's idea having fire eaters blowing out fire and smoke on the dance floor below the stage certainly sounds like a great visual display....in theory. But in practice, the fumes from the fire sticks frequently overpowered Ian, who spent the vast majority of the time in between verses, spluttering and chocking. One also wonders how much of the band were seen through the smoke as security had to intervene to keep the performers away from the video screens for fear of the whole venue going up.

Ian believed this display of bombastic 'Rawk and Roll' imagery wasn't suited to the band and felt the whole performance was underwhelming from his perspective. However, the audience certainly appeared to enjoy this theatrical spectacle and this added to Ian's serious feelings of misgiving about the future of The Hamsters. Rather than basking in the post glory of this outrageous carnival of decadence, Ian preferred to slip away quietly.

The 'Inbetweenies' By Ian Dury

Ian really had no intention of pushing The Hamsters any further after the brush with fire but, to his surprise, he got a phone call from The Hacienda, inviting them to play on the 'final' of the Battle of The Bands.

In some way, this show was almost a precursor of the 'unplugged' sets as Neil had the novel idea of performing with the amplification turned down low. This meant that audience members would need to come in closer to listen to what was being performed and Ian felt a certain intimacy was established on that particular evening; and rates this as, very probably, the finest Hamsters show.

Karl Burns (ex-Fall and PIL) who was one of the 'celebrity' Judges that evening. Ian knew him well enough to have invited him to join the Bears from Belle to drum. Ian was absolutely elated immediately after this brilliant set and joked to Karl;

"What's the prize and when do we get it?!!"

Karl grinned and gestured to a group of lads who were standing close by;

"That group won it before anyone played"

Ian wasn't that concerned and asked;

"Who are they?"

"They're Factory records latest signing; The Happy Mondays."

Ian shrugged;

"Oh well, best of luck to 'em."

He watched them perform later that evening and didn't think there was anything that special about them, but now acknowledges that they later turned out to be a refreshing alternative to the musical genre to be known as 'Madchester' and 'Britpop'.

It was time to go and The Hamsters were in the process of loading their gear into the van and as a car pulled by; a youth leaned out of the open window and shouted;

"Time to pack it in!"

and as an afterthought:

"You're too old!!"

The car suddenly sped off in case of retaliation.

Ian was only 26 at the time and remembers shaking his head at the absurdity of that insult. But with hindsight, he now realises that the rude observation was actually more astute than he realised at the time. The music industry is obsessed with extreme youth and looks and as good as the band had been that same evening they were already 'Yesterdays Men'.

D.I.V.O.R.C.E Tammy Wynette

Brian Turner, once a member of 'The Frantic Elevators' now held the frantically elevated position of Social Secretary at Manchester Polytechnic. He could book who he liked and chose the Hamsters for the massive fee of £150. This was twice as much as the band had been paid and when they arrived to play; a food and drink rider was waiting for them. This appeared to auger well for the evening and in addition, one of Ian's favourite reggae musicians – Lee Scratch Perry was performing in an adjoining room.

Ian was really looking forward to finally seeing one of his all-time reggae heroes and when he came on stage Ian was expecting great things. But, Lee Scratch Perry appeared to have totally lost the plot and was content to coast along with a dreadful, insipid set. It was embarrassing to watch him play the cheery buffoon to the young audience.

As soon as Steven got on the stage –his whole demeanour suddenly changed for the worst. He sat behind his kit and glowered malevolently and created not only confusion but bewilderment as he drummed along with totally inappropriate rhymes and beats to what was actually being played. Bob, Ian and Neil exchanged glances as if to ask;

"What the fuck is going on?"

The answer was soon to come on stage in the form of Rose and assorted hangers on, who proceeded to plug in their instruments and play along as the band attempted their fourth number. Rose took her position at the microphone and began to wail, and, at last Steve was smiling. Bob, Ian and Neil decided to leave them to this avant garde mess. Steve had obviously planned this all along, maybe he believed he was creating a new free form, or perhaps he was just showing the lads who really was 'boss' in the band, anyway Ian just didn't care anymore.

Brian paid up in full (pretty amazing when you consider what he actually paid for) and when the cacophony had eventually run out of steam, Ian went to give Steve his share of the fee.

Steve grinned at Ian and by way of a greeting, explained;

"Thought we'd try something new, Mo!"

"Yeah, that was great Steven."
Ian deadpanned and added;
"I think it's the future."

At that moment, Ian knew that no matter what happened between them as friends, artistically they were divorced and Ian wouldn't even argue over who got to keep The Hamster.

Bumble Bee and the Nut Rockers

Ian had an idea that he wanted to try out and invited Jon. The concept was to have four or five acoustic guitars playing at once to create a' drone', not dissimilar to a swarm of wasps. This was to be a hive of activity for the Queen Bee (aka Ian) to sing songs of disease, corruption and Human Failings. In other words, an acute and perceptive observation of Thatcherite Britain.

The band, known as 'The Plague Rats' rehearsed in Jon's bedroom, which had turned into a kind of wildlife rescue centre for Fuzzypeg Hedgehog. Whilst this was truly lovely of Jon, the dear little thing had fleas which scared away two of the would Bee Swarm. Apparently, Jon had to later burn the bed and have his room fumigated, so severe was the infestation.

Ian managed to get a debut for 'The Plague Rat's' at The Young Communist League's Garden Party. This was to be held on a Sunday afternoon on the lawns behind 'The Toast rack'.

Robert picked Ian up and they buzzed to pick up Jon en route to Fallowfield. Ian spotted the familiar, lanky (but lovely) figure outside the venue, but didn't espy a guitar case.

The car stopped and Jon bent down and gestured for Ian to open the window;
"We can't do it, Moet."
Ian just glared at Jon for want of a reply.
"We're not ready, we need more rehearsal!"
insisted Jon, by means of an explanation
Ian snapped, rather waspishly it must be said;
"Buzz off then Jon!"
and added, for good measure;
"You're a Fucking Coward!"

After ordering Robert to drive on, as was Ian contemplating this disappointing experience with Jon pulling out, again, Robert piped up;
"Why don't you ask Neil to play?"
Ian was broken out of his sulky reverie and agreed;
"That's not a bad idea, Rob, let's go and invite him to play."

Neil agreed, both brothers didn't want to let people down and a great acoustic set was played in place of 'The Plague Rat' material. A mixture of Hamster and Frantic Elevators material along with an eclectic range of covers including 'Tonight's the night', by Neil Young, 'I got you, I feel good' by James Brown, The Sex Pistols 'Anarchy in The UK'. The set was finished with a rousing version of 'The Red Flag' and the audience were delighted. So much so, another gig was offered, but Neil politely declined this offer and as he had stepped into the breach, Ian didn't persist.

The perfect end to a perfect day was spent with Dennis Downworth, who had a studio apartment which was close by and both he and Ian drank fine malt whisky in a warm glow.

Ian was getting more and more fed up with his job, but a change in his employment occurred when an indulgent Ron bought Robert his very own shop in Stockport. This shop didn't fair at all well and Ian was invited to move there and turn the situation around. Despite his very best efforts the shop finally closed on Christmas Eve. Ron offered to give Ian his old job back in Didsbury, but Ian decided that he couldn't stomach another day of the hum drum monotony and chose to go on the dole.

Keeping the elements at bay", A Comedy Review in aid of Denton's Peoples Centre. (Poster advertising THE review of 1985)

Bob was going to be married but a week before the wedding the whirlwind romance had blown its course and he was now living with a new love – Karen Knott. Karen was part of a circle that was involved in working at Denton's Peoples centre, which was now under threat of closure owing to the usual lack of funding. Ever the optimist, Bob wanted to help out by staging some sort of fundraising event, but he wasn't sure so asked Ian for suggestions.

Ian and Bobby wondered if they could put on a play, maybe something by Joe Orton or Shaun O Casey? But they weren't too sure if they would need to pay some sort of copyright charge and abandoned this idea as counterproductive to a fund raising benefit. Ian seriously considered staging a version of 'A Clockwork Orange' and even adapted the book for the event, going to the extent of learning huge chunks of dialogue just in case this transpired. But, was Denton's Peoples Centre ready for this?

Another alternative was that Bobby and Ian could write and direct a comedy review. This sounded more like it, something that the audience would be certain to enjoy and relate to? Constance Smith was a much respected Grande Dame of the Theatre and graciously gave her time, as well as several strong cups of Earl Grey and strongly advised;

"Dear boys, do not even attempt to write, let alone stage a review!"

Both lads were humbled in her presence and sipped their tea in fine bone china cups and as if to exemplify her point, she continued;

"It's far too difficult, notoriously prone to abject failure, even for the most seasoned directors!"

Ian and Bobby nodded and thanked her for her time and guidance.

After bidding their gracious hostess a very polite 'Good Evening Ma'am' both looked at each other on the doorstep and Ian asked;

"Are we doing the right thing?"

"Dead Right."

This was the response Ian knew he would get and that decided that.

The 'Cast Members Wanted' Poster at The Peoples centre resulted in four fourteen year old girls who were going to perform alongside Bobby and Ian. Lawrence Rafter and his girlfriend, Kathy, were also recruited and Robert volunteered his services as writer and performer. Besides performing, Bobby and Ian also doubled as writers and drama teachers. This was a serious venture and committed rehearsals and meetings were frequently held.

Robert turned up to one such rehearsal and proudly handed over his composition, 'The Seven Ages of Women', to Ian for inclusion in the review. Ian read it and passed the work over to Bobby to read....Robert couldn't bear the silence any longer and asked, as modestly as he could;

"What do you think of it then?"

"I don't think it's suitable."

was Ian's candid answer

"I don't either."

backed Bobby.

"Well, Fuck the pair of you then!"

cursed the frustrated author and slammed out of the centre, not before a few more choice artistic differences were hurled at the burgeoning directors. Ian never really understood Robert's over-dramatic reaction to this refusal. The work was not only misogynistic pseudo-intellectual clap trap, but even worse it just wasn't remotely funny. Never mind, just like Judy Garland and Mickey Rooney they got on with the show and re-cast Robert's parts between them.

There's No Business Like Grant Show Business

The evening finally arrived and the audience was not only diverse in age range but conventionality. Everyone from 8 to 80 was there. Bohemian types and traditional Uncles with Aunties rubbed shoulders together. There were a few 'back stage nerves' amongst the younger cast members, a quick peak behind the curtain revealed a packed hall, but the seasoned old pro's, well Bobby and Ian actually, were able to reassure that all would be well 'on the night'.

The evening kicked off with an ambitious dance routine, choreographed by no less than Busby Berkley Bobby. The cast were clad in fetching green tights and cherry red boots and the audience roared their approval of this outrageous site. The cast knew that they had won the audience over and that they were on their side, any nerves and concerns had quickly vanished.

What the show may have lacked in slickness, it more than made up for in terms of being 'Quick fire' and the evening went full steam ahead. There were three Ivor Cutler pieces adapted for the evening as well as skits worked out by Bobby and Ian. These sketches mostly lampooned sexist 'Macho' Male homophobic behaviour. To give further texture to their material, both Ian and Bobby performed songs such as 'Big Bad John' and an ironic comment on the Miner's strikes 'Working down a coal mine'(not for very much longer if Thatcher got her way).

An exotic belly dance was performed by Ian....no, if only, was performed by Kath that certainly steamed the hall windows up.

The evening progressed with Ian dressed in a white Doctor's coat sitting at a desk giving the punch lines to various 'Doctor, Doctor ' jokes. Unfortunately, Ian managed to get his cards mixed up and gave the wrong punch lines not that this really mattered, the audience laughed even more.

The evening was finished off with a rousing version of 'The Red Flag' and the audience went home very happy.

The only thought that prevailed when the cast were packing away was; "What Next?"

Across The Lines Billy Bragg

The Miners' strike 1984 -85 was constantly on the news and despite a valiant fight against the Thatcher Government; it was the end of the beginning for the Unions. The Police were now involved in violently breaking up picket lines and you were either 'for' or 'against' the strike. The largely Tory tabloid press depicted the strikers as 'trouble makers' at best or some sort of extreme Communists who were holding 'the Iron lady' and her country of decent citizens to ransom.

Ian, of course, was on the side of the Miners, and threw what little he could into the Charity buckets. It was at this time the 'Red Wedge' collective formed, consisting of musicians such as Jimmy Somerville, Billy Bragg and Paul Weller. The Red Wedge, along with a whole host of famous and lesser known bands played benefit gigs to raise funds for the families of miners. Ian really applauded the sentiment behind these support events, but was painfully aware that he had no band of his own to join and fight for the cause.

Whilst Ian's parents would have gladly looked after him, he felt that he couldn't take advantage of their kindness and, anyway, it was time for him to stand on his own two feet. Anne was in the process of relocating to Fort William, in Scotland, and needed a tenant to live in her cottage at Glossop. A mutually beneficially deal was stuck and Ian moved in, with what few possessions he had, in the dead of winter to the snow covered countryside. A picturesque scene, but one that was fucking freezing.

Voyage, voyage Desireless

Ian was able to catch up on reading, sometimes consuming three books a day from Anne's considerable library. His favourite authors of that period were Faulkner, Joseph Conrad, Iris Murdoch and Ernest Hemmingway. The early winter days of that year were spent wrapped in hats, scarves, coats and gloves in an effort to keep warm that freezing winter, quite simply he couldn't afford the coal for a cosy fire. Fortunately, he didn't need to spend a huge amount of money on food as he existed on a vegetarian diet. To keep expenditure down, he walked everywhere he possibly could, for example it was a twenty mile round trip to his parents, but he walked it.

Barry Corthorn lived in nearby Hadfield (later to become 'Royston Vasey' in 'The League of Gentlemen Television series), who knew Ian via his football circle, used to come over and buy rounds at the pub when he could afford it. He shared his flat with Paul and their main form of entertainment was listening to 'The Wall' by Pink Floyd (a record which Ian hates to this very day), whilst consuming magic mushrooms, painting and talking. Sometimes they were able to entice a pretty young girl they both shared back to their flat. Ian had the choice to play gooseberry or walk home.

Local employment was not available, but a suggestion was put to Ian by a friend;

"Listen mate, as you're not from these parts you will not get a job here."

"Don't I know it?"

agreed Ian.

"Why don't you do what Bobby did then?"

"You mean work abroad?!!"

"That's it; there are always vacancies for deckhands."

At first, Ian dismissed this idea, but the more he thought about it the more it made sense and to be truthful, working abroad did sound rather glamorous and exiting. True, Bobby had made a good living out of this, as had John, Anne's exhusband. If they could do it, why shouldn't he?

A momentous decision was reached, Ian withdrew what finances he had (£250) and gave Anne notice on her cottage and in March of 1985, prepared to travel and hoped never to come back.

Ferry Nice Man

Ian reflected on just what he had left behind as he saw the white cliffs of Dover becoming smaller and smaller on the horizon. He had just heard the miners' strike had been smashed by the Thatcher Government and saw the proud community marching, with full brass band, back to work on the television. It was, indeed, the passing of an era and Ian felt quite emotional.

On the Ferry destined for Calais he met an elder gentleman who had a really interesting history. This chap had fought in the Second World War and had been taken prisoner by the German Army whilst fighting in France. When the war ended, he chose to stay behind and became a farm owner with wife and family. He had managed to forge a new life just outside Paris and this was very inspirational to Ian. They chatted over wine and the pair boarded the Paris bound train. During this journey, Ian was invited to work on the farm, but Ian declined as his heart was set on working on an exotic yacht on the Mediterranean. As the train approached the gentleman's station, he wished Ian well and after giving him a hug, slipped a crisp £20 note into Ian's grateful hand.

After managing to negotiate the Parisian Metro System, Ian not only found the Cannes bound train, but also his berth. However, Ian had a very heavy cold and rather than keep the rest of his cabin awake, chose to remain outside in the corridor and spent the journey watching France by night. John Cale's 'Half past France' kept playing inside his mind's jukebox and Ian was filled with hope.

At 8.00 the train pulled into a bright sunny Cannes railway station and Ian felt this was a good omen.

There's a new Cabin Boy in Town

"This is the life!"

Ian thought to himself as he stretched back in his seat outside a quayside Café. He felt just like a character in a Truffaut movie as he sipped his café au lait and munched upon a delicious croissant, musing that he was experiencing the real thing and was congratulating himself on his escape from the cold, grey drudgery of Northern England.

After basking in the sunshine (I don't think there were Basques in the café, but I digress...) Ian decided to follow the advice given;

"Just get down to the harbour, offer your services in helping to prepare the yachts for the season."

Ian mused it would be so easy to be able to put on a lick of paint and soon gain a heady reputation so that when the summer deck hand vacancies came up the owners would very likely be fighting amongst themselves to secure his services. He would soon be able to rent a little apartment, maybe a few records and books on philosophy, who knows maybe he may become the British voice of existentialism?

With these daydreams unfolding themselves in this glorious weather, Ian decided to put these ambitions into practice and commenced his walk along the harbour with his rucksack on his back.

Ian walked, and walked….and walked. There wasn't a soul to be seen and every boat appeared to be covered in tarpaulin. He went as far as Antibes and all the way to Juan Le Pins. The rucksack became heavier and heavier and Ian became more and more despondent. Eventually, there was a boat with a person on, who appeared to be tending to the craft. At last! Ian began in his best French;

"Parlez vous….."

"You are English?"

replied the figure, in perfect English.

"Yes, that's right. I was wondering if you needed any help with your boat?"

"Oh no, not for a good two weeks yet."

came the polite, yet firm reply.

"I see, do you know of anyone else who might need help then?"

"Not really, you've come at the wrong time of year, a few weeks' time maybe. Excuse me for being so rude but I do need to finish this job."

Ian thanked the owner and just as he made his way around, just in case, it began to rain.

He wandered, rather aimlessly, wondering what he could do next, when he was aware that a minibus had not only passed him once, but appeared to be circling around the harbour, Ian got the distinct impression that he was being stalked. Eventually, the bus pulled up alongside him and the door was flung open and the question;

"Anglaise??"

came from within the van.

"Yes, how did you know?"

asked Ian.

"Ah! Somehow we guessed, come on in out of the rain Monsieur!"

As it was bucketing down by now, Ian didn't heed the advice of his Mother but chose to get in a van with several strange, foreign men. As it turned out, this was the right decision as after introducing themselves, they revealed that they were from Belgium and;

"Would you like to come for a drink with us?"

"I'd love to but I have no money, I hoped to find work but haven't"

"Ah! No problem! You will be our guest!"

Well, it would be rude to refuse such generous hospitality wouldn't it?

Ian's glass was overflowing during the next four hours as these kind Belgians ensured that he had a really good time during the next four hours at a local bar. One Belgian, in particular seemed rather taken with Ian and kept smiling and winking rather a lot for Ian's comfort. However, this new friend rather blew his chances with Ian as he kept raising his glass and insisted that everyone toast;

"Margaret Thatcher! Europe's Strongest Leader!"

Ian went along, well they were paying for the drink but eventually this became too much for him and he made his apologies to leave. His new found friends, especially one in particular, insisted that they stay with him but Ian managed to extricate himself, eventually, and made his way out into the cold night air.

After wandering around, Ian managed to find some sort of cover outside a Café that was boarded up for the season. After unrolling his sleeping bag, Ian tried to sleep but it was freezing cold. Ian wandered, teeth chattering, about what to do next as he only had limited funds…….

After a sleepless night, Ian decided to not only pack up his sleeping bag but pack in this new way of life. He was bitterly disappointed but resigned himself to defeat. He then took a train to Paris and stopped at a cheap hotel, near the Gare Du Nord, and basically wandered the streets. After a great deal of thought he finally made the phone call;

"Anne, its Ian here."

"Hello, Moet, how's it going I bet…"

Ian had to be a bit rude as he didn't have much time to spend on the international phone call and had to butt in with;

"Anne, it's turned out to be a disaster. Can I come back to Glossop?"

Anne was a good friend, she sympathised and agreed immediately. At least Ian had a house to return to.

It was as if Ian had never left. Life continued very much along in Glossop as it had before the dream of life on The French Riviera turned out to be a reality nightmare.

Life was turning out quite differently for little brother though. Neil had signed away his royalty rights to the songs he co-wrote with Mick Hucknall for a song, as he was in desperate straits. But even so Neil was receiving substantial cheques for the performing rights of 'Holding back the years' which Mick Hucknall had re-recorded with Simply Red. This gave him a tidy income and financial security.

Both brothers were now able to sit in the same room and make a real effort to get on with each other. They would have a coffee and listen to music at Neil's flat in Stalybridge. Ian acknowledges that neither brother was the easiest company, but instead of getting irritated and tetchy with each other, each was able to accept the other, quite simply, for what he was.

Ian's financial circumstances were still pretty dire and he was, despite trying, unable to secure employment. The weekends were spent playing football at Denton for The White Inn Gates. Ian would try to get over whenever he could, because this would be the only form of camaraderie he would experience during a week.

Bobby and Karen had purchased a house in Denton which needed extensive refurbishment. Ian would pitch in and help out as much as he could but after an accident with the wiring, Eddie stepped in and managed to solve this potentially fatal issue, Eddie earned the name, with some justification, of 'Steady Eddie' from Bobby and was grateful for continued help.

One night Bobby turned up unexpectedly on Ian's Glossop doorstep. Ian knew it had to be something pretty serious for Bobby to just turn up and his suspicions were confirmed when Bobby blurted out:

"Karen and I are splitting up"

This was a genuine surprise to Ian, he hadn't seen that one coming and sympathised with Bobby.

"Can I stay here for a bit, mate; things aren't too good between us?"

asked Bobby hopefully.

This was absolutely no problem with Ian, he was glad of the company and Bobby stayed the weekend.

Before Bobby left he asked Ian;

"Why don't you come in and move in with me?"

Ian saw the advantage immediately, the house was in a better location, he wouldn't be alone and had always got on with Bobby but said;

"I'll think about it then."

Two weeks later, Ian moved into Bobby's house on Ashton Road, Denton.

Feed The World Band Aid 13 July 1985

It would be no exaggeration to say that life at Bob's was somewhat complicated. Not only was Karen still living in the house, but Slavita, Bob's current squeeze (and still is) had moved in also. Wisely, Ian decided to keep himself to himself and not take anyone's side. In order to keep out of everyone's way, Ian took to painting his room in a kaleidoscopic psychedelic design and continued to read avidly.

The move had worked out rather well, besides being much better located, he was also able to claim more money as a lodger than he had as Anne's tenant and was able to get the occasional 'Cash in hand' job to supplement his benefit.

When Karen finally moved out, Bobby and Slav regularly invited a small crowd of five or six friends around, much drink and drugs were consumed. But Ian did not relate to this little crowd and much preferred to listen to his records, alone, in the back room. Anyway, Ian had found a new diversion as Neil took him to a contact Karate session one Thursday evening. Something about the self-discipline and physical well-being appealed to Ian about this somewhat violent strand of martial art. Abstinence from alcohol was one major factor and Ian was hardly drinking anyway.

But Ian was aware that before he began the strict regime on the following Tuesday, there was the small matter of getting through the 'Live Aid' weekend. Whilst Ian believed that the motivation behind the event was commendable, he doubted the intentions behind some of the bands commercial visibility and knew that the vast majority of music would be rock of the blandest kind. Both he and Bobby decided to go out and pretend nothing unpleasant was happening and avoid the whole shebang.

They both started the day, the way they meant to continue, at 'The Pitt and Nelson' in Ashton under Lyne. As soon as the television was switched on, both managed to miss Adam Ant's performance which he hoped would resurrect his faded career (it didn't) and escaped to another pub. Each time the television was switched on (if it was already on, this meant a 'no go' area) each downed his pint to ensure minimal exposure to the toxic rays of Queen or U2.

Needless to say, both were very, very pissed when they staggered into 'The Kings Head' at around ten o'clock that evening. Both are well known and Ian decides to demonstrate his newly learnt prowess at contact karate. He playfully throws punches and kicks at people, stopping millimetres short of actually hitting them. Each time he aimed a blow, he cheerfully exclaims;

"Trained to miss!"

He then gets bolder and bolder, throwing kicks at punches at total strangers

"Trained to miss!"

The front door opens and a familiar face comes in, Steve Lowe is a bouncer at a local nightclub, together with a pretty young girl (who later, it transpires, is his fiancé) and a rather ferocious looking man.

Ian decides to welcome the newly engaged couple with his now familiar war cry of;

"Trained to miss!"

Only he didn't.....

He whacks Steve Lowe right in the eye, which immediately gushes out blood. All he can do is look at Ian in shock and his fiancé bursts into tears. It transpires that their furious looking companion is none other than a champion bare knuckle prize-fighter and he decides to make a lunge for Ian, roaring like a lion with sheer malevolent intent etched across his face. However, unbeknown to him, Denis Downworth has collapsed with laughter and the gypsy champion falls over the prone antiques dealer who is still convulsed with merriment. He bashes into an innocent bystander and soon all hell breaks loose with a huge crowd of around twenty people pushing, shoving and yelling at each other.

Ian surveys the scene of utter havoc that has been created by his drunken behaviour and decides to make a quick exit.

Several weeks later he sees Steve Lowe and apologises for ruining his engagement drink. Steve and his new fiancé can now see the humour in the situation and even Jackie manages to quip;

"I'll never forget my engagement!"

As for the gypsy prize fighter, Ian never saw him again.

Little Brother

Ian was taking his karate lessons seriously and was not only abstaining from alcohol, he was also working out. There was something about the prevalent 'Loadsa Money' ethos of the day that Ian detested. Ian felt very much apart from the 'I'm alright Jack' attitude (later to be covered in a song with his brother Neil) that appeared to condone the capitalist actions of the Thatcher Government. Ian describes this period as 'the middle class attitude of fondue parties and the dismantlement of state services'. When Ian went training, he was able to unleash all his anger

Occasionally, he went too far.

Another lad called 'Ian Moss', was a pleasant enough guy and both agreed to have a fight at the end of the session, this resulted in a broken leg for 'Ian' and the real Ian was very much upset at this unintentional injury he had inflicted.

Little brother, Neil, showed great aptitude and besides being a teacher in this sport, also progressed to become a fourth Dan and black belt. The inevitable finally happened, Ian was put into spar with his younger brother.

With hindsight, Ian reflects if Neil had been waiting for this opportunity to beat the crap out of his supposedly omnipotent older brother. Indeed, all the sibling rivalry appeared to become unleashed in this 'friendly'. Ian couldn't lay a gloved hand on him and took a horrible punishment as he desperately attempted to remain on his feet. Eventually, Ian hit the mat with a sickening 'thud' and 'Stars' (not of the Simply Red variety) appeared before his very eyes.

"Are you OK?"

asked a concerned Neil as he stood over the semi-conscious form of Ian

After each Karate session, Ian arrived back at Ashton road, usually with his shirt covered in blood. He would merely greet Bobby, Slavita and any of their friends who happened to be in the front room with a grunt, perhaps a nod and make straight for his back room sanctuary. Once ensconced, he would proceed to play 'The Stooges', or perhaps 'Suicide' at full blast whilst working out. Occasionally, a brave social soul would venture into his territory and attempt to engage him in polite conversation. If they were lucky they would receive a monosyllabic reply to convey that they weren't welcome.

*"Hot Dog! Jumpin' Frog!
Alberque !"*

The King of Rock and Roll of 1986

Simon Taylor was persistent; Ian can say that for him. Not only had he had his services as a bass player rudely refused by Steve a couple of years back, but his attempts to get to know Ian better were coldly shunned. Eventually Simon resorted to begging;

"Please give me a chance"

"Uh?"

"I want to learn from you"

"Um"

"Just give me a break!"

"What?"

"Let me go out for a night with you!"

Ian, essentially likes to be listened to, and he concedes that he is somewhat of a sucker for flattery. He missed the social interaction of being in a band and maybe, just maybe, he wanted some attention.

"Alright then, we'll go out for a night."

"That's great!"

"Mind you, this is a one off."

"Ok then."

agreed Simon.

Little did Simon know just what he was letting himself in for. There was blackness in Ian's heart and he describes his soul as having 'an open wound'. Simon was going to experience Ian at his very worst.

Ian's alcohol resistance was lowered, owing to the fact he had not drunk for some time and soon the tap of obnoxious egotism spouted out. The more Ian drank the louder and more obnoxious, the more outrageous his proclamations became. Simon just nodded as Ian ranted on about things that he knew Simon had no comprehension of. Ian was in full flow and confided in Simon that;

"I am THE KING OF ROCK AND ROLL!!!"

Simon nodded in agreement, and almost to test Simon's gullibility, Ian continued;

"I am the spiritual descendant of Little Richard, in a line that has only been interrupted by John Lennon and Iggy Pop!"

"You are."

agreed Simon, perfectly seriously.

As Simon wasn't going to argue with him, he decided to start a few arguments off with total strangers for good measure. Ian was a complete embarrassment and upset people everywhere they went. Eventually, they ended up at The Hacienda, where Ian thought it would be a good idea to set off the fire alarm. Nobody heard this as Prince Charles and The City Beat were playing so loudly that the alarm blended in with the sound.

Ian woke up the following morning with the hangover from hell, he had been downing cocktails down his throat like there was no tomorrow, but there was and it was today.

Slowly, but surely, recollections of his outrageous behaviour came flooding back and he winced, not only in pain, but from embarrassment.

Simon called around later and asked
"Can we go out again?"
"Yeah of course."

In which Ian gets his Mojo working – temporarily

I wonder if Simon was hoping to 'get in' with Ian, in order to form a band with him. Certainly, Bobby was keen to play on stage and Simon managed to recruit no less than the current British Judo Champion, Nick Kokotaylo, as a drummer.

"Moet, how about being the singer in this band?"
"No."
was the firm reply.
"Aw, come on! Why not"
Ian felt this needed some explanation and insisted;
"I don't want to do it because it's just been too long since I last performed, I've lost my mojo."
Simon didn't give up so easily
"It's something you were born with, Moet, you can't lose it!"
"Well, I haven't got the will to find it then!"
However, Simon persisted and didn't give up. Over a period of time Ian eventually weakened and the excuses became more and more half-hearted;
"I can't come to rehearsals on Sunday as I play football."
"No problem, we can pick you up from the pub and take you to rehearse at Nicks."

If Ian could have got them to rehearse on the ground floor, as he 'didn't do stairs' he would have done.

So the big day arrived and the reluctant Diva was picked up from the pub to rehearse. The band had worked up some tunes and Ian was able to put lyrics to them. Slowly, but surely, Ian warmed to the band, although it never got 'hot' owing to the general musical direction. It was too much 'Rock and Roll', like The Clash in their 'USA Stadium' period for Ian's own personal liking. However, one good song, 'Body Building' was composed and Bobby suggested an interesting direction, 'Country and Western'. It just so happened that Karen had written a C&W style number called 'The Horses Tale', with her friends Sue and Rhonda.

"This is more like it!

Exclaimed the excited Diva.

'Horses Tale' was fun, quirky and, more to the point, totally unlike anything any other band was doing. Ian admits to 'becoming almost enthusiastic' and even suggested a gig to showcase this number in particular. In fact, so animated was Ian, he managed to get two gigs on consecutive Sundays at 'The Wellington Inn' in Hyde.

But the band now needed a name and instead of Ian christening the band, the name 'Oochykomis' (a Judo move) which meant 'repetition of movement' came into being, Ian hated this name but went along with the democratic process.

The first gig was described as 'safe, but fun' by Ian so it looked as if the repetitive ones would have a future. However, the next week, by the second song, Ian was forcing himself to continue. It wasn't even fun and Ian hated having to get through the set, this feeling built up until he made an announcement, just before the last number;

"We would like to thank you for attending our last show, this is not only the last show of the residency but the last time this band will ever play. Thank you."

I wish I could tell you that there were gasps from the audience and not unlike when David Bowie killed Ziggy Stardust off at the Hammersmith Odeon there were pleas of;

"No! Moet! No! Moet! Don't do it"

But the audience didn't, however they were genuinely surprised and disappointed

This impromptu decision came as an instant relief to Ian and he felt he had made peace with himself as soon as he had made his dramatic announcement.

I was at one of those Wellington Inn gigs – met Karen for the first time. I even bought a copy of The Horses Tail. I loved it **Steve Mardy**

The Fruit and Veg Man

Dave Holmes was a well-known figure on the Manchester Music Scene having played in 'Dr Filth' and 'The Things'. He enrolled into Manchester Polytechnic, studied Criminal Psychology and eventually became a real life 'Cracker'. Now I am not suggesting that Dave was using Ian as some sort of case study, but was acutely aware that Ian was wasting his potential and suggested that Ian, too, would benefit from becoming a mature student. Ian wasn't sure, but Dave offered him help and support and the more Ian thought about this, the more it made sense. At last, Ian had a new direction that was obtainable and one that would open a sea of possibility.

This direction was to be thwarted when Ian was offered temporary work in a franchised green grocery outlet with in a busy supermarket. This unit was owned by Mike Ratchford (a potato merchant) and he was keen to have someone he knew and trusted to manage this for him;

"Come on Moet, you're the only one who can do this!"

"No, thanks all the same, ask someone else"

"But you have managed staff."

"Yeah, but I really want to go in to Full Time Education"

Mike looked visibly crushed by Ian's refusal and admitted;

"Moet, I was relying on you to do this for me. Without your all your experience and expertise this won't stand a chance, I'll just have to turn this down.'

Ian didn't want to let him down and suggested;

"OK, why don't I set the place up for you, term won't start for another six or so weeks and I could do with the cash?"

This sounded like an ideal solution to Mike, who readily agreed.

Ian rose to the challenge, worked hard and was well paid. But six weeks became eight weeks and weeks became months and months became two years. Ian stayed put owing to having a safety net and betrayed himself with a lack of ambition and confidence. Ian was to pay dearly for this weakness as Mike Rachford eventually betrayed his trust and a bitter falling out ensued.

The Horses Tail

"I liked it, but it was a detraction from anything he had done before. What I found poignant about the track, was the fact he was working with his brother, Neil" **Jon**

Ian purchased a very run down house, which had previously been owned by Colin and Susan Swan, who had split up. As he was now earning good money he was readily accepted for a mortgage. However this, virtually derelict dwelling needed considerable work doing to it and very soon became somewhat of a ball and chain to Ian.

In the meantime, Ian's room at Aston Street was taken over by a young lad called Billy Petrie. Ian liked Billy's roguish cheek and laughed when he heard that, despite several layers of paint, enough of Ian's original psychedelic design still remained to give Billy migraines. Ian was terribly saddened, a few years later, when he learnt that Billy had been murdered in Greece, very likely over a drug deal that had gone horribly wrong. Ian still misses Billy's big smile, and even bigger heart to this very day.

Simon had become very friendly with Karen, Sue and Rhonda often spending considerable time with them. He suggested that 'The Horses Tail' be recorded, as a demo, with them as vocalists. The girls really liked the sound of this and wondered if Ian could be persuaded to join them in the studio. Ian was approached by Simon to join in with Nick on the drums;

"No, those days are behind me and anyway, you used to detest this number!"

"The girls really, really want you to do this."

"Ok."

Simon may well have planned for Ian to join in on this project, but he didn't ask Bobby, who had helped promote a song that he, Simon, had a strong, initial aversion to. Bobby, upon learning of this venture, felt upset and betrayed by Simon, who he had considered a friend.

The band was named 'Whipcrackaway' by the girls and the song was recorded in a studio at Denton. Ian's role was fairly minimal; he provided a vocal guide for the girls to follow, a couple of interjections and generally encouraged everyone to have a good time as he left to go to the pub.

Simon played Ian the track the next day and asked;

"What do you think of it?"

"It's nice."

demurred Ian.

Simon was much more enthusiastic and stated;

"I think someone will release this!"

"Really?"

asked Ian.

"No, but I was hoping you might...."

Simon had something that Ian always lacked, ambition, hence Ian's involvement. Simon wanted to trade on the goodwill that Ian's name still carries.

"Well there's always Marc Riley's record label. Tell you what I'll send him a copy, no promises mind. I haven't seen him for about a year or so"

"That would be great!"

exclaimed Simon.

"Mind you, if he doesn't like it, he may know someone who can help."

mused Ian, who was beginning to get caught up in Simon's enthusiasm. So much so, he rang Marc the very same day and Simon drove them both around to Sale, where Marc and his wife, Tracy lived the next day. It was a pleasant afternoon, spent at the pub and a tape of 'A Horses Tail' is left for Marc to listen to.

No one was more surprised than Ian was, when the phone rang the next day;

"Hi Moet, its Marc."

"Oh yeah, how are you doing?"

asked Ian.

"Yeah, I really like your record. We'll release it for you."

You could have knocked Ian down with a feather.

It was decided to re-record 'A Horses Tail' for official release, plus other material at a studio in Hekmanwike (Yorkshire) with Bill Clarke who was somewhat of a cult Country and Western hero as he had played with no less than the George Hamilton IV band. Owing to his considerable experience, Neil was also lassoed in to play bass and some guitar parts. Neil's prior studio knowledge would also help the band communicate what they wanted as regarding engineering and mixing.

The girls had now become 'Coyote Karen', 'Stetson Sue' and 'Rhinestone Rhonda' and had written a number called 'Gingham Dress'. The premise of this particular number portrayed Country and Western genius, Hank Williams, as a cross dresser. Whilst Ian could see the funny side, he pointed out its gross inaccuracy and potential for offence and changed a few words which altered the whole emphasis of the piece.

The third number, 'Betrayed', was an old Bears from Belle Vue song, written about Steve, and was polished up for use by Simon.

Now, Bill was a nice enough guy, very friendly and talented but it soon transpired that he was totally unsuitable for the 'Whipcrackaway' ethos of fun. What should have sounded like 'a messy party' turned out to be a 'canteen lunch'. The band wanted dirty, Bill provided clean and straight.

The Girls felt that what had started out as a bit of fun, turned into a hijack as a means to Simon's own ends, he was taking things much too seriously. As a result, these ebullient and cheerful characters became sullen and even rather withdrawn. The session became so bad; that Rhinestone Rita could only be bribed out of the toilets to sing with a promise of raw sausage meat (she was very partial to this delicacy).

Nick also got the hump, when drum machines were used on 'Gingham Dress', and according to Ian, spent the rest of the session with his lower lip jutting out like that of a petulant child.

The only bright spot was when Neil played a lovely one note guitar solo, on 'Betrayed', as a form of homage to the Buzzcock's 'Boredom. But unfortunately, this tribute was not enough to salvage the mood of the group as they travelled back, 'a group of depressed people pulling in different directions'.

Marc and Jim listened to the new version of 'A Horses Tail' and both exclaimed;

"It's awful."

This version ended up on a compilation LP and the demo recording was released as the official version.

Fame of a kind....

"The Horses Tail' is a jolly romp, although I think 'Gingham Dress' would have worked much better in its original (en Transvestite) format; it is a tongue in cheek 'homage to Hank'. 'Betrayed' is a darker song altogether, although the strongest number, for me it does not sit easily with its camper counterparts.

The front cover is a hoot as it features the band members posing around a Cadillac against a cartoon 'Desert'. It was obviously shot in a car park, cut out and pasted over the tacky 'Deadwood trail'. The funniest part of the cover is Ian. He is sitting on a cart horse, cracking his cartoon whip. The legend goes that he is sitting on the horse naked, as a piss take of a current Prince cover. Personally, I think he is actually wearing pants, which have been 'doctored' to imply that the Moss Jewels have been airbrushed out. On the credits on the back, it is interesting to note that Simon has top billing above Ian.

The record was released to universally dreadful reviews, which Simon really took to heart, but worse was to follow........

London's Capital Radio got in contact and they informed the band that the record was getting a lot of airplay and would very likely enter their charts that same week. There was no reason to disbelieve them, Simon was ecstatic, whereas Ian and the girls felt slightly embarrassed, with good reason as it turned out

An interview was set up and here is some of the transcript that was broadcast to the London audience over a breakfast show....

EXCERPT FROM 'HORSES TAIIL

DJ
"One of the great things about working at Capital is that you get to mix with the right people. You know, people of influence in the music business? So when I hit upon this smash single by Whipcrackaway and realised that it was hot stuff, I felt I could use my quite considerable influence at the station to get it played on the air....."

DJ
"Mr Dean, Mr Dean would you please play this record on your Show?"

Graham Dean
"What record is that?"

DJ
"Whipcrackaway"

Graham Dean
"Oh! Whipcrackaway!"

DJ
"The same!"

Graham Dean
"I've already played it"

DJ
"So you're going play it again?!"
Graham Dean
"Oh, no"
DJ (simpering)
"Oh, but they're my PROTOGES! And they're SO keen and I really would like them to be stars!"
Graham Dean
"I don't care if they're part of my family I still wouldn't play them again"
EXCERPT FROM 'Horses Tail'

Etc., etc., more comedic disc jockey mayhem ensues

Clearly, the band were set up as a big joke to be gently mocked for a cheap laugh. Surprise, surprise the single didn't chart and sold a grand total of 450 copies. With the exception of Simon, the whole band hoped the embarrassment would be forgotten.

But no, two weeks later, Ian is in the International Club, run by the late, great Roger Eagle who refuses to speak to Ian for releasing a travesty of a record that he feels takes the piss out of his beloved Country Music. Ian tells him to get a fucking life which left Roger shaking in his winkle pickers, furious at Ian's lack of contrition.

This Charming Man by The Smiths

"One of Moet's best songs (in my opinion) was a song called Digging in the dirt. I forget what band it was, but I think we covered it with the Sheep Dog Trials but never recorded it or played it live. Great pity about that .Perhaps Ian will read this and want to revitalise it with Sicknurse" **Jon**

The song, 'Digging in the dirt', divulged by Simon during the Capital Radio Interview as the follow up single, was in fact no more than a title given to him by the sisterhood of Karen, Sue and Rhonda. Ian liked the title and composed a set of lyrics during a lunch break at 'The Lowes Arms' in Stockport. He had been inspired by the recent war graves exhumed in Russia and what had been envisaged as a 'light' Whipcrackaway' number became something much darker and macabre.

Simon provided the music and Ian was very proud of this particular number and wanted to record this. He was thinking of who to enlist and bumped into none other than Mike Joyce one drunken Friday night at The Hacienda. Mike Joyce was riding high on the current mega success as the drummer of The Smiths. Both got chatting and Mike referred, rather irreverently, to Morrissey as;

"That Stretford Nobhead."

Mike asked Ian what he was up to and Ian told him of his plans to record 'Digging in the dirt' and, all of a sudden – off the top of his head, a cover of Marc Bolan's 'Baby Strange'. Ian had an idea;

"Mike, would you like to join me in the studio?"

"I'd be up for it, mate, just need to check it out with Morrissey and Marr." nodded Mike.

Both Morrissey and Marr gave the 'thumbs up' to the loan of their drummer. In addition came Marc Riley on guitar, Neil on bass and Mike Gallagher (Frank Side Bottoms 'Cor Blimey Band') on sax. An old mate, Ged Berry was to provide 'Micky Finn' bongos and also Dawn, who had worked with Ian on the Peoples Centre Review, was also drawn in as she had quite a monumental voice.

The studio, just around the corner from where Ian lived, was booked. Things were looking up.

All the Madmen – David Bowie

The band, was named 'The Thin Men' rather ironically (Ian, like myself, is a 'before' rather than 'after' for a slimming advertisement) and as a tribute to the above Bowie number.

So, Ian found himself, again, one pleasant Sunday morning at the very same studio where 'Horses Tale' was recorded. The studio positively buzzed with excitement owing to the presence of a member of The Smiths in their midst. But the mood was too relaxed and owing to this, Ian managed to get totally pissed out of his head. According to Ian, he slurred his way through 'Baby Strange', although listening to the recording this isn't at all apparent. Dawn sings splendidly, not unlike the vocals of Alison Moyet, on 'Digging in the dirt' as Ian was in no fit state to sing on this number.

The recordings are regarded by Ian as a 'wasted opportunity' but he hoped to salvage something from this disappointing session by playing Mick Joyce 'Slow Death' by 'The Flaming Groovies'. After hearing this Mike had an idea and said;

"I can really hear Johnny Marr playing guitar on this number"

"Do you think he'd consider joining us on this one?"

asked Ian casually, secretly beaming with delight that Mike was running with the ball that had been thrown to him.

"I don't know, I'll ask him when we go back in the studio tomorrow then to finish off Strangeways."

The potential for further recording was dashed as Mike rang up a few days later and confided to Ian;

"It's all going wrong here....Johnny's left the band."

Ian received daily updates on the disintegration of The Smiths until Mike made the decision to leave the band as well.

Miseries, mithering and Moet 1987 - 1992

The Miseries 1987

".....I don't remember working with Moet in The Miseries? Or is it just me?" **Peter Hook**

Simon's attempts to ingratiate himself in Marc Riley's circle of friends were to come to a rude awakening when he decided to pay Craig Scanlon a quick social call when Ian was in the car with him
"Wait in here."
"What for?"
asked Ian, who was a bit perplexed by this order.
"I need to check if it is ok for you to come in as well."
explained Simon seriously.

Ian didn't respond to this outrage, as he wondered if he had committed some awful social faux pas? He hadn't actually seen Craig for a couple of years, but Ian had been drinking very heavily and couldn't remember if 'something' had happened.

Craig answered the door:
"Is it ok if Moet comes in as well?"
Simon asked, gesturing towards the car
"Moet's welcome in my house anytime."
Craig shot Simon a withering look and continued tersely:
"It's you who needs to ask."

In all fairness, Ian didn't really blame anyone for giving him a wide berth at that particular period in his life as he describes himself as acting like 'an obnoxious prat'. He recalls that when going to The Boardwalk (Manchester's premier live music venue) that if he didn't enjoy a particular performance he would transform into a rude and boorish devil. Music writer and future 'Lad's Mag' James Brown, was a frequent target of Moet's drunken diatribe. Ian got into a punch up with Eric Faulkner (ex-Bay City Rollers) as a result of alcohol fuelled goading. Once Ian was on the guest list for a big showcase gig at the Free trade Hall and was to be found backstage dismissing The Chameleons, whilst happily helping himself to their drink.

Simon and Ian attended a Factory Records Quiz Night at the Boardwalk. This was a very prestigious occasion for Simon as he was amongst the 'movers and shakers' of the Manchester Music Industry, whilst Ian was non plussed – they were just people after all.

Alan Wise, the acting quiz master, asked the question:
"Who were Guy Burgess, Kim Philby and Anthony Mclean?"
Simon leaned across to Ian and whispered conspiratorially behind his hand;
"Pink Floyd."
This emission of sheer stupidity resulted in Ian spurting out a mouth full of beer as he couldn't control his merriment.

"I walk through life in dead men's shoes"

The Miserys

When Andy Warhol died in 1987, a moving tribute was paid to him by former band members, Lou Reed and John Cale, 'Songs for Drella'. So it was entirely appropriate (as well as lucrative) for Nico to pay her own tribute, at Manchester's Town Hall, later that year. Ian describes the gothic 'Frozen Warnings' number as 'particularly moving and magnificent'.

Ian bumped into Peter Hook that same evening and decided to ask;
"I'm going to do some recording, will you play bass?"
Peter Hook appeared to be pleased to be asked and offered;
"If you like, we can use the recording studio I own?"
"You mean, 'Sweet Sixteen', in Rochdale? Yes Please!"
agreed Ian very readily.
"Yeah."
"I'll drop a cassette to you with the songs to be recorded."
Simon had to be pinched, to ensure he wasn't dreaming, when Ian told him that no less than the bass player for New Order would be playing with them. In addition, Marc Riley was to play on guitar and initially Mike Joyce was going to be on drums. However, Mike was now jobless and needed a flat fee of £40 for the session. Hiring and paying session musicians was against Ian's ethos and pointed out that this was a golden opportunity as Hooky was now playing in the band, this could lead to bigger things. However, Mike needed the money and Ian understood. Paul Hanley had recently left The Fall on a matter of principal, and was more than happy to fill the vacant drummer's seat.

The band was christened 'The Miserys', - *'a playful lampooning of perceived Mancunianness'.*

Word of this 'Supergroup', consisting of members from The Fall and New Order had reached the London based music press and during an interview for 'The Creepers', Marc Riley's current band, he was repeatedly pushed about 'The Miserys' until Marc acknowledged to the disbelieving hack;
"We're just helping our old friend, Moet, out"

Why Don't You Smile Now? Lou Reed

The Miserys had a very productive day in Sweet Sixteen Studio recording covers of 'Why don't you smile now?', 'Would you believe' (Screamin' Lord Sutch), and 'I can only give you everything (Van Morrison). Ian was still very much kitted out in Charity Shop attire and this inspired 'Dead Man's shoes' to become the fourth, self-penned, track.

The session was tight and Hooky kept everyone in stitches with his indiscreet tales of what it was to be a member of New Order. He also imparted a stomach churning anecdote about rising Factory stars- 'The Happy Mondays' which cannot be imparted in this book. However, one such anecdote, regarding Mark E Smith uprooting a bush to beat his errant band mates with is the material of legends and had Ian rolling in mirth.

The sound of this demo session, in particular Hooky's bass, is very impressive. The production was purposefully minimal, as a reaction to the general over lush sound of the 'eighties. John Langford, of Mekons/Three Johns was the engineer on this session and nearly everyone was reasonably happy with the end result. However, Ian felt that his vocals were restrained. He had not sung live for some time and he feels this contributed to a lacklustre performance. Compared with the roar of 'Street Level Sessions'; what turned out to be rather good could have been brilliant.

Marc appeared to be keen to release The Miserys session as an In Tape EP. But fate, yet again intervened, in the form of Jim Khambata, who was the co-owner of the record label. Marc was increasingly concentrating on The Creepers and recruited Simon as a member. Ian believes, Jim, in order to emphasise his independence from Marc, did not take up The Miserys.

What's New Pussycat? Tom Jones

Pussycats? What was I thinking?? I don't even like Cats!! **Mick Hucknall**

After spending a traditional Christmas Day with his family, Ian decided to pop over for a quick pint at 'The Jolly Hatters' (opposite Denton Police Station) where he met up with Sue and Rhonda. It was set to be a quiet evening, when who should suddenly walk in the pub, but no less that Mick Hucknall complete with sycophantic entourage in tow!

Mick espies Ian's little group and decides to join them. He has just come back from a trip to Latin America and informs them that;

"You have to command respect. I hired a massive Mercedes Car and demanded the best rooms in the hotels that I stayed at. They understand and respect power"

This lesson is somewhat wasted on Ian but he grunts affirmation, accompanied by the odd giggle from Sue and Rhonda. Mick then decides to reward Ian with his opinion of the Moss Brothers;

"You're both pussycats."

Ian decided to take this statement as a compliment and accepts an invite to a party.

After some more drink the group arrive, somewhat worse for wear, but are welcomed by the host ("any friend of Mick's' etc.) who provides more alcohol. Mick is seated in an expansive armchair and holds court, but he fails to impress either Sue or Rhonda, in whom he displays a keen interest. More drink is drunk and Ian is pulled up to dance with the two girls. Now the fun began, in an effort to wind up Mick Hucknall, and despite being platonic friends with Ian, the girls start to paw at Ian. This pawing results in Ian having his shirt undone and having his chest tongued, in between having the inside of his thighs caressed.

The music was loud, but it was clear that the rest of the party were becoming quite dismayed by this display of blatant pornography. They snogged and groped each other and if they had not been with Mick Hucknall, they would certainly have been asked to leave. Mick Hucknall did not get the joke and sat stony faced on his throne.

Eventually the sex show came to an end and the girls fell into a drunken sleep on the sofa (to face the accusing eyes of their hosts, complete with killer hangovers), Ian was given a taxi lift from Mick.

Two weeks later, Ian was back in 'The Old Garrett' and who should pop into the pub for a quick drink but Mick Hucknall who demanded;

"Were those two girls Lesbians?"

The Brotherhood of Moss - 1988

Ian managed to purchase a four track recorder, and called his boffin of a younger brother, guitar in hand to decipher the instruction manual. By means of testing the equipment a cover of Syd Barrett's 'Chapter 23' was recorded. Both brothers had a great deal of fun recording this track, This lead to Ian and Neil meeting up each Tuesday afternoon to record self-penned numbers as well as recording a version of 'South end incident' (Beacon St Union).

Ian realised that some of the tracks were worthy of playing live, although Neil was not so keen. Simon wanted to get Ian back on stage, with him on guitar, and was able to arrange a gig at a cellar beneath 'The Birch' at Ashton under Lyne. Eddie Fenn, drums, and Pete Keogh, bass, from The Creepers were recruited and were called 'Brickbats' (after a Captain Beefheart song). Art rockers - 13, topped the bill. Ian was not at all bothered about being support, some of the pressure would be taken off and he just knew that he would be a very, very tough act to follow. His old conceit, arrogance and confidence (that was lacking from The Miserys recording) had returned; his monster horns were back with a vengeance.

The set consisted of some of the Moss Bros material, 'The Horses Tale', oddments from The Hamsters, The Do do's, The Bears and a thunderous cover of The Standells 'Sometimes the good guys don't wear white'. Ian had some real fun as he hollered, whispered and jumped around the stage. It was if the old Moet had never been away to those audience members who had seen him before in his various incarnations and a huge surprise for those of his newer friends who were experiencing the phenomenon known as Ian Moss for the first time. Ian was hugely satisfied at the enthusiastic reception he received and it felt really good to be back where he belonged.

As Ian predicted, 13, died a death. Ian knew the duo, Phil and Graham, and liked them. They argued that 'Brickbats' had gone down well was because they were 'Popularist.'

Ian snapped back;

"Oh! I thought it was just because we were BETTER."

Holidays in The Sun By The Sex Pistols

Ian was earning good money from the fruit 'n' veg business. So much so, that he was able to afford holidays abroad with Robert Middlehurst. Amongst the countries they visited were France, Portugal, Croatia (when it was part of Yugoslavia) and Italy. Robert proved to be a rather good travel companion as he was also interested in immersing himself in each country's culture and so both were able to enjoy a visit to an art gallery as much as a revel in a local bar.

One night in St Nazir Robert insisted on ordering the meal in the native tongue, despite the fact the waiter could speak excellent English. In all fairness, two meals and wine arrived and were consumed with much relish, but on requesting the bill a confused look came over the waiters face as he explained;

"But Pardon, Monsieur, there are two more meals to come."

Sure enough two more plates arrived at the table and Ian instantly realised what Robert had done;

"You fucking dunce!"

chided Ian, in fits of laughter.

"You've ordered us TWO meals each!"

One year **(1992)** both Ian and Robert were in Dubrovnik in the months leading up to the Bosnian Conflict, where the worst atrocities since the Second world war would leave a beautiful country drenched in blood. The atmosphere could sometimes be very disturbing as the lads often settled down for a simple meal at a café; Ian could feel the mistrust radiating from the darkened enclaves where the local men sat scrutinising them in absolute silence.

Ian and Robert made a trip of around 100 miles to the historic Muslim town of Mostar, one baking hot day by bus. Upon waiting for the bus they were joined by a group of boys, who couldn't have been more than seven or eight years in age, in a group of football on a gravel pitch. When it was time to go the boys started to chase the bus, banging on the side to attract the driver's attention to stop. When the door was opened, the boys got on and gave Ian back his bag (which contained not only his camera, but money) which he must have left behind in his hurry to get on the bus. He tried to push some currency into their little palms and even then they had to be told to keep this reward with Ian's sincere thanks. Ian believes that, six months later, there was every chance that maybe, one or all of these innocent children, with nothing but good in their hearts, was killed when Mostar was enveloped in hatred. Ian still wells up every time he thinks of this simple act of honesty.

The Hamsters on Thirty Three Revolutions Per Minute (1988)

Ian and Mark E Smith continued to get on well on the rare occasions they bumped in to each other. Ok, they didn't always see eye to eye on certain subjects. For instance Ian adored The Flaming Groovies, whereas Mark E Smith thought;

"....they were ok, before they wore those fucking suits."

After one heated difference of opinion at a reggae gig at the International Club Mark E told Ian;

"I've always liked your voice."

Ian knew Mark E Smith wasn't just being 'nice', this meant a lot;

"I've been working on a kind of rap intro thing for the band to come on to live, yer know?"

"Oh yeah."

replied Ian.

"Would you agree to appear with us and, yer know, start the gig off with that?"

Ian was thrilled to be asked, but gave a measured response so as not too seem too impressed.

"Yeah, that could work."

"Ok, we'll get something together then and have you still got them Hamster tapes?"

"I think I could lay my hands on them."

replied Ian, casually.

"I'm thinking of starting a label up and I would like to put out four, perhaps five Hamster tracks as the first release, waddya think?"

Ian knew he had to act quickly, if Steve was consulted there could be the potential for sabotage and replied, still in a matter of fact way;

"Grant Showbiz has the tapes"

and had the nerve to add

"You still work with him, right?"

Mark E Smith nodded and a shake of the hands sealed the deal.

Ian was in regular contact with Mark E Smith by letter and phone, but the live rap opening is never discussed. Whether this is because Mark E Smith changed his mind, or wanted Ian to bring this up, is uncertain but five tracks are chosen for The Hamsters EP. Art work is selected and Ian bumped into John the Postman (who worked for Mark E Smith's record label) who had a wide grin on his face:

"What the fuck are the photos about?"

laughed John the Postman.

"What photos?"

teased Ian.

"The photos of the band mate, they're all in pubs with fucking long hair."

Ian laughed and replied;

"We never had 'proper band' photos because we wouldn't dream of it! What are we supposed to look like?? Funny haircuts and leather jackets, you mean!"

John the Postman chuckled;

"Anyway, they get up Mark E's nose!"

However, Mark didn't mention this to Ian when he next rang up and appeared to be more interested in Ian's opinion of sweet sixteen studios as he was considering this as a possible venue for recording. Obviously, news of The Miserys had reached Mark E Smiths ears;

"I'll send you a recording, Mark, to let you know what the studio can do."

Whilst Ian heard no more about The Miserys tape, he did get another phone call from Mark E Smith,

"There isn't enough money to release the ep."

Ian felt that fate had knocked him down again but ....:

"I'd like to use two tracks on a compilation album I'm doing."

Contracts are signed and a few weeks later, 'The Disparate Cogncienti' compilation is released, complete with photos of The Long Haired Hamsters. The band have been paid £80, between them, and Ian pops around, with complimentary copies to give to Steven and Bobby. Both are pleased, even though Steven attempted to hide this and Jon is called to join them at the newly opened Dry Bar (owned by Factory), were the money is spent on downing fancy Danish lager in huge tins.

"Locked in towers of false promise"

The Moss Bros

Ian describes the eighties as 'the decade, dominated by Thatcher, was dribbling away down blind alley after blind alley'. But whereas Ian was having to work conventionally for a living Steve was enjoying a high public profile, appearing regularly at 'The Night and Day Café,' as a form of 'Performance Poet. In his reviews he was compared to Charles Bukowski, emoting over a freeform music backdrop to his work. In addition, Steve had also become something of a successful artist and there is no doubt that he was a talented painter. Ian however, thought Steve was in danger of becoming a 'cheap sensationalist' as his paintings depicted religious imagery and syringes, there was something of the 'shock value' that reared its ugly head too often for Ian's liking.

During this period, Ian recorded, with Bobby on his home studio, a fantastic version of 'Positively 4th Street' by Bob Dylan, complete with mad, off the wall backup vocals. This is my very favourite vocal performance by him too. In addition, 'Every Dog Has His Day' (Skip James Blues) was reworked and although the songs pleased Ian, he describes them as *Flashes in the archives of oblivion (after Roy Harper)*'.

Eric Mansell, an intelligent and intense sort of chap, collaborated with Ian on a synthesiser/vocals project. The idea of a 'marriage' between 'Man and Machine' fascinated and enthused Ian's creative process. But when a cover of Led Zeppelin's 'Rock and Roll' was mooted it became clear that a divorce was on the cards. Ian wanted to strip this song of the bombast and machismo and replace it with something much more sinister and added a lyric concerning the use of pornographic magazines and masturbation. Eric wanted a more sombre approach. At the end of the day, Ian concedes that the last thing the world wanted was another Orchestral Manoeuvres in the Dark and thus the project was abandoned.

AIDS

Despite the continuing element of competition in Steve and Ian's relationship, it should be mentioned that there was no real falling out as such. Occasionally, as Ian puts it; 'if stars were correctly aligned, we would tumble into each other's orbit and have fun'. But Bobby, Ian and Steven became somewhat estranged over a period of time owing to the fact each moved in very different social circles.

Brian Leah's house in Denton was a magnet for junkies who travelled as far away as Birmingham to experience the dubious delights of shooting up and other forms of excessive drug consumption. Ian viewed the partakers of these 'shooting parties' with pity more than anything. He was aware that they mostly came from desolate council estates and dead end jobs to get away from the misery of their everyday lives. But, the fact that many had turned to crime to fund their ever consuming drug habit lead Ian to shun these 'party goers', many of whom Bobby befriended.

Steven was also well known by the junkie community but his behaviour scared even the most ardent needle user. He had a reputation for being a loud and dangerous maniac who would fly off the handle when no provocation was intended. Ian, in the Sicknurse myspace introduction, names Steven as 'Rasputin'. Ian believed that he had some of the 'mad monk's' charisma and intelligence, but still preferred to avoid him if at all possible.

"Moet its Robert here."

Ian picked up the phone to Robert, who sounded distinctly distraught.

"What's up then mate?"

asked Ian calmly

"It's Steven, he's got AIDS."

This awful news grabbed at Ian's heart, this was when AIDS was a death sentence. Ian couldn't ignore this, he loved Steven despite everything.

The best way to help Steven, Ian decided, was to be practical. Instead to offering to listen, he thought it best to call on Steven on a regular basis and help out financially. This was hard and Ian would leave Steven, and have a little cry on the way back home.

And yet.......and yet.....Steven seemed to be bucking the trend for AIDS patients and Ian decided to confront him;

"Steve, AIDS patients lose weight, you put it on, have you got AIDS?"

For just a nano second, Steven almost looked contrite and then boldly stated;

"No, but I'm bound to get it."

Ian was apoplectic with rage and fury.

"You've told your fucking family you've got that fucking disease! Put them through Hell! To get some money out of them?!!"

Steven shook his head and replied, rather matter of factly;

"They should thank me; I'm preparing them for the inevitable."

This resulted in a real slanging match which resulted in a bitter falling out and Ian did not want to see Steven for a very, very long time.

About, maybe six months later, Ian heard a knock at his door: it was Steven. No way was Ian going to answer, he was still mad. But he became of a wailing voice, interspersed with loud sobbing....

"Bloody come on in then and stop making a show in front of the neighbours."

ordered Ian, as he shut the door behind this wretched creature. Steven was in a bad emotional state and rambled on about how Ian was really Dylan Thomas and had haunted him.

The only way to pacify him, Ian found out, was to comply with his repeated requests to play Jim Carroll's 'People who Died, over and over again. As Steven calmed down, Ian managed to find out what had upset him. It transpired that Steve had turned up at 'The Kings Head' to meet up with his druggy mates and Bobby. But they all went off and left him alone. In short, it was self-pity, which had Steven crying and banging at Ian's door.

Ian was not impressed by this childish behaviour but offered to include him on a visit to Anne and her new partner, Richard. Steven perked up but soon blotted his copy book by being aggressive to Simon, who was the driver, making him stop at an off licence where he stole a bottle of vodka.

Steven's behaviour went from bad to worse. Richard was a sweet gentle man, who had met Steven for the first time. However, almost instantly, Steven set about intimidating him and threatening him with violence. Ian couldn't take any more and shouted at Steven;

"LEAVE HIM ALONE! IF YOU WANT A FUCKIN' FIGHT I'LL GIVE YOU ONE!!!"

Steve backtracked and the horrible experience ended. Ian finished off the awful day by consuming a whole bottle of whisky listening to Was Not Was 'Out come the freaks'.

*"I'm so bored
with the USA"*
The Clash

Marc was partly financing The Creepers with a weekly live review in 'Sounds' music paper. One has to admire Simon's tenacity, as he managed to blag a spot as photographer for this magazine. Simon suggested that Ian and he go and holiday in New York as Simon hoped to combine this with work.' It had long been a dream of Ian's to go to New York and he found he was able to afford the flight.

Dennis and Lois were legendry figures on the New York Music Scene via their association with The Ramones during their early CBGB's era. This Brooklyn based duo had crossed 'the big pond' and made friends with The Human League and had formed a friendly reputation with bands from Manchester. It just so happened that Ian and Wayne, decided to pay Marc and Tracey a visit after a drunken night out and both Dennis and Lois were staying at their house. Although neither had actually heard The Hamsters, they were certainly aware of their reputation. Therefore they were perfectly willing to have Ian stay (and Simon by association) at their apartment in Bensonhurst. There was an unsaid, reciprocal agreement that the hosts would show their guests all the sites, but that the lads would pay for the food and drink. This seemed like a really good deal and helped to finance Ian's dream to become a reality.

New York, New York Frank Sinatra

"How much money do you have with you?"
asked Simon in the flight departure lounge.
"About £500, and you?"
Ian replied, suddenly wondering if he had brought enough cash;
"£50"
answered Simon.
Ian was absolutely flabbergasted and enquired;
"Do you think that's going to be enough?"
Simon had obviously decided to put the wit and wisdom of Quentin Crisp to the test and coyly replied;
"I'm an Englishman in New York."
Now what is mildly amusing in a Sting song simply didn't cut the mustard with Ian. Simon was going to ponce off as many people as he possibly could. However, Ian kept quiet as he resolved to have as good a time as possible but he couldn't quite bring himself to socialise with Simon on the flight beyond a one word answer or two.

A long delay in customs did not improve Ian's mood as they were due at Tramps in Manhattan, to meet their hosts and to watch The Mekons. They were on the guest list and Ian had to fork out $60 to get a taxi to the venue. He also paid for a round of drinks at the club, $15 and another. But The Mekons were well worth Ian's expense, they were great and Ian considered them, at that time, to be the best band in the world.

Jon Langford recognised Ian and beckoned them backstage for some welcome drinks. It was very hot and Ian was attired in a heavy Crombie overcoat and lugging a suitcase to boot as well. So as a result Ian's T-shirt was drenched by the time he got into the dressing room and he was greeted by an executive from A&M (The Mekons record label) who emoted to Ian, looking him right in the eye to express his sincerity;

"Great gig Jon!"
Ian shook his head and replied;
"Wrong fella mate"
and turned around to the real Jon and asked;
"Pass us a beer will you Jon?"
This tickled Jon who saw the humour in the mistaken identity.

Lois drove Ian and Simon back to an apartment crammed with toys, records, books and all manner of souvenirs. Ian paid for a meal on the way back, well it was the least he could do for his hostess.

You get the picture? A sizable chunk of Ian's £500 had gone; Simon's £50 remained untouched.

A Mancunian in New York

As soon as Ian saw New York, he wanted it.

He compares his first visit to being on a funfair of delight as he got to sing 'Where were you', onstage with the Mekons, playing football in Central Park with the writers from 'Village Voice'. Even being mugged was a different sort of experience in New York. It so happened that he had his pocket picked after beating two guys at pool and falling asleep in the bar. He realised what had happened and made his way out of the bar, only to collapse in a heap. Fortunately, help was at hand in the form of two girls, Suzi and Hebe, who scooped him up and took him home to sleep in their spare bed. Ian was woken by the sound of swishing curtains to a grand view of The Empire State Building and heard giggles;

"I've seen your bum!"

exclaimed Suzi.

This was a small price to pay for the girls who had taken a total stranger into their home, undressed him and put him to bed.

Ian's wallet had taken a large knock, but he still continued to pay for everyone's meals and drinks.

Fortunately, Jon Langford, who didn't really know Ian all that well, lent him £200. With this large injection of funds Ian could afford to misbehave, very badly as it turned out. He met up with Lu Edmonds (a musician who had played with The Damned and Public Image) at a restaurant in the Little Odessa district, and both drank a bottle of vodka, each. Lu decided enough was enough and wisely decided to go to bed. Ian being Ian, decided to let the whole of Little Italy know that;

"The Mafia are just a bunch of wankers in Puffy Suits!"

Not surprisingly, the streets soon cleared around him.

Ian managed to get the address of Gary Lucas, who had played guitar in Captain Beefheart, when he was in Tramps. It seemed like a really good idea to pay him a visit in the early hours of the morning. Somehow he got to the apartment, hollered and a very amenable Gary let him in. Ian was treated to songs and several potent bongs before daylight shone brightly and it was time for him to visit some more bars.

When he woke up, he was so ill; all he could do was lie motionless. For the last two days of his holiday he was bedridden in Lois's apartment. Lois had to check up on him every hour or so and dab his lips with water. Ian was aware that Simon wanted to go and see Iggy Pop at a club in Manhattan, but hadn't the funds to do so (his £50 had been spent on a nice jacket) and Ian had none left. Ian went through hangover hell and would have loved to have gone to see Iggy

Pop. But at least he derived a certain, perverse form of satisfaction in that Simon couldn't go either.

The Meek Ones support The Mekons

Ian paid back Jon Langford the money he had borrowed in New York, in the letter he suggested that, maybe, he could be the support act for their up and coming gig at The Manchester Club? Jon had written about The Mekons in NYC, for a Sounds article, in which Ian was mentioned as a member of 'The Legendary Hamsters', so it was no real surprise when his offer of support was accepted.

Even though Ian's opinion of Simon was at an all-time low, he still recruited him to play guitar. It was a tasty line up; Marc Riley was on keyboards, Eddie Fenn on drums, Pete Keogh on bass and Mike Gallagher on saxophone.

On the big day, another significant event was playing – Derby Day in which Manchester United were playing against their old rivals – Manchester City, at Main Road. This event always involved copious amounts of alcoholic consumption and that day was to prove to be no exception. Ian recounts 'the drinking went as planned, the game didn't', Manchester United were diabolical and lost five goals to one. Ian was drowning his sorrows, when he bumped into City's Goalkeeper and abused him to such an extent, a minor skirmish ensued.

Ian eventually arrived at The International Club and replenished his drink level. He wondered where Neil was and rang him to find out where he was. The fact that Neil's girlfriend was ill didn't wash with Ian and he abused his younger brother over the phone. He admits he was disappointed, but this rudeness was inexcusable.

"What name do we introduce you as?"
asked Jon Langford,
"The Meek One's"
dead panned Ian
"You're a very cheeky chappie!"
chided Jon, eyes twinkling.

Ian thought it would be a good idea to have some cheaper drinks at 'The Rampant Lion' pub whilst he composed a set list.

Finally, it was time to go on stage and Ian was as drunk as a skunk but this made great theatre. 'Digging in the dirt', 'Dead Man's Shoes', 'I can only give you everything' were attacked with much gusto and bravado by Ian. The band also played 'Going Rate', which was a Marc Riley song as well as 'Big Brown Eyes' and 'Electric Impulses'. The band were extremely well received and Ian made a moving speech about football in which Faith played a key component. He had to be dragged offstage whilst performing an impromptu version of The Manchester United Calypso.

"It was an honour being on stage with you tonight!"
beamed Marc Riley.
"Cheers."
mumbled Ian, in-between glugging down some more cider.
"You are every inch the equal of Marc E Smith."
added Marc.

Tom Greenhaugh, also from The Mekons, came over and shook Ian's hand, enthusiastically informing him;

"It's really refreshing to be served up with something real!"

Ian drank in his success and realised that maybe he had imbibed a bit too much. He went out for some fresh night air and promptly collapsed on the pavement outside. He tried to get up but he was bent double as he vomited, and vomited, and vomited.

"Isn't that the singer from the first band?"

He heard someone ask as he raised his watery eyes up to a crowd of people who were just coming out of the club.

Oh Dear! It would be thirteen years before Ian felt he was able to perform again.

DJ David Bowie

Ian was doing rather well at the beginning of 1990. He had a job with good pay, a house, a car (after finally passing on his ninth driving test attempt in 1986) and he was popular and well respected. But yet something was eating away at him, he couldn't find any contentment and his notorious excesses didn't prevent the familiar spiral into depression.

Ian, owing to his New York experience, kept Simon at arm's length but still gave him lyrics to put music to. When Simon insisted that Ian's lyrics were 'too political', Ian's response was swift;

"Fuck off then; don't tell me what to write!"

Simon skulked off, but not without taking the name 'Miserys' (which included Nigel Blinston and Damien of whom you will hear more). Simon even managed to get gigs and cultivated record contracts, but the material was dire. Ian describes one demo of the bands 'big' number, 'Deborah Anne' as *laughably inept, with all the spirit of a dishcloth*.

Bobby, who was now living on a barge, blagged Ian and himself the job as DJ's at 'The Kings Head' on Thursday evenings. The duo named themselves 'The Suicide Sisters' and wore silly hats and played even sillier jingles. The main aim was to have as much fun as possible, Ian selected all the records and Bobby manned the microphone.

The regulars, at the debut of 'The Suicide Sisters' could not help but notice the alarming change in what sort of music was now being played. Whereas previous Thursday evenings consisted of the bland, yet inevitable diet of 'George Michael' or 'Whitney Houston' this had transformed into 'The Stone Roses', 'Happy Mondays' and 'The World Of Twist'. And yet, both Bobby and Ian were very much forerunners, in that around a year later, these new bands would also become much more familiar on a DJ Set. They played 'Public Enemy', 'The Butthole Surfers' and the piece de la resistance, a twenty minute scratch rendition of 'Boy named Sue'.

One brave soul wandered up to the DJ booth and requested a record by "The Bee Gees, please"

What he got was 'Electricity'; by Captain Beefheart (well it had a 'B' in it....)

Both "Suicide Sisters' were in danger of living up to their name as a rock was hurled through Ian's window, when both Sisters were relaxing after a hard nights work. They heard the smash and a car speeding away.

Somehow 'Suicide Sisters' managed a decent run, but they were subjected to the laws of diminishing returns, the pub attendance got smaller and smaller but they always pocketed their fee of £100 each Thursday Night.

However on the sixth week, when Alan Vega was wailing to an empty dance floor, with only the bar staff present. Alan, the landlord, came over and informed the duo;

"I really like what you're doing lads"

and looking embarrassed continued;

"But.... I think from next week, I'll have to try someone new."

Ian had to acknowledge that this was the most polite sacking under the circumstances, but it had been a good run for the money and mission completed.

Last Night an Angel saved my life

I believe Moet may be slightly Bi-polar. He has great, bellowing highs and deep worthless lows. This is a common trait of depression, bi-polar, call it what you like. It's sometimes called 'Life'. **Craig Scanlon**

Ian fell into a deep, deep state of hopeless and awful depression. He had learnt, most of his life, how to hide this and he believed no one who knew him would have the remotest suspicion of how miserable he really was. To say he felt 'lonely' would be an understatement, his internal world was hell.

One Friday evening, Ian went to see 'Gun Club' at The International Club. This band was fronted by ex-cramps guitarist Kid Congo, who Ian managed to chat to and describes him as 'charm personified'. It should have been a really good evening, as Ian enjoyed the band and was with a group of close friends whose company he enjoyed. And yet, and yet when he was dancing to T- Rex, with Marc's wife Tracey, he recalls feeling really empty and covering this with a plastic smile. Then and there he decided that he couldn't keep going on with this façade much longer. He managed his 'goodbyes' and embraced everyone and to all intents and purposes, everyone would 'see him soon'.

After Ian took the taxi home, he composed himself;

"Is this really it?"

He already knew the answer.

Ian went upstairs to run a hot bath and placed a pristine razor blade by the side. When the water was running, he wondered if there was something missing......

"A letter."

Yes, his family and friends were owed that much and he went downstairs to locate paper and pen, when......

"Knock, knock"

Ian ignored it, very likely kids pissing about anyway. Who was going to come and pay him a visit at 2.00 am?

"KNOCK, KNOCK!!"

Whoever it was, they were persistent but still Ian ignored it.

He went upstairs to turn the taps off.

"KNOCK, KNOCK, KNOCK!!!!"

The caller was clearly not going to take 'no' for an answer. Ian couldn't help but reflect on the irony of the situation. Here he was, about to take his own life, and he had callers. Oh dear, whoever it was clearly wasn't going to go away until he answered the door. Never mind, it would only take a minute to get rid of them.

When Ian finally opened the door he saw Steve Wright (no, not THAT one) and his wife. Ian knew Steve very slightly; he was more of an acquaintance than anything.

"We've been to the 'Upstairs Downstairs' and saw your light on so we thought we'd call. Can we come in?"

Ian could hardly answer that they couldn't come in, because he was just about to kill himself. Dearie me, this was MOST inconvenient so instead;

"Yes, in you come, would you like a drink of summat?"

Ian made his unexpected guests comfortable and made small talk. Steve became most insistent that Ian come back with them to their home; in order that he would know where they lived. This was a slightly odd request, but Ian agreed and accompanied them, through the damp and dank night to their home. Upon arriving on their doorstep, Steve insisted;

"You must stay here with us."

"No.."

Ian weakly replied;

"I have to go."

"No, no. You're staying here tonight."

Ian meekly agreed and Steve sat him down to make some tea and his wife went to bed. After the tea was made, Steve sat down with Ian and talked quietly, asking questions. Steve didn't appear to be getting tired and Ian felt in a curious limbo between life and death. Steve continued talking all through the early hours of the morning; he had a kind and empathetic presence about him, previously unnoticed by Ian.

Eventually, it was day light and Steve went upstairs to change into his work clothes. A knock came at the door and Steve told Ian;

"Right, I've got to go to work now. You can stay here if you like?"

"No, I'll go home now, Thanks Steve."

"Ok, you take care?"

On the walk home, Ian tried to unravel exactly what had taken place. What had prompted Steve to knock on the door at 2.00 am? Why was he so insistent that Ian wasn't left alone? Maybe Steve was 'an Angel' sent to save Ian? Whatever Steve's intentions the darkness had passed and Ian no longer wished to end it all. He was drained, unhappy but alive and the crisis had passed.

A decade later, Ian found himself with Steve Wright, outside a bar in Athens in a crowd of others. Ian pulled his chair close to Steve and said in a quiet voice;

"Steve, I've never had a chance to thank you. I owe you so much, you saved my life."

Steve admitted he had a vague recollection of that fateful evening but claimed not to have known about the significance of his actions, but he had an enigmatic smile playing around his lips which conveyed otherwise

At Home With Mo

Moet's place was a non-descript mid-terraced house, facing a desolate looking car park with its herd of abandoned shopping trolleys. The front door led directly to a cluttered, musky-smelling living room. It was like Dennis Neilson had eased off the spring cleaning. The room seemed to ache for company. Like most people who grew up in the seventies, Moet had an eclectic mass of books and records. Tastes then were not so one-dimensional. This was true of all aficionados of 'punk' – a term abhorred by the cognoscenti, only embraced by geriatric, last chance, former pub-rockers like Charlie Harper and his UK Subs and similar London based chancers. The night was spent pleasantly - drinking, talking and arguing about music. Moet and I were both passionate about music and, in different ways, quite opinionated about it. Moet was prone to sulking when I frequently beat him in a discussion

Craig Scanlon

Ian missed being in a band, However, whilst other people had a huge amount of fun, and satisfaction, that comes from being in a band, Ian's fleeting moments of genuine pleasure were limited by his refusal to compromise. On one hand, he has always held onto his integrity and credibility, yet the repeated 'near misses' taunted him and he decided he was 'better off without it'. In an attempt to compensate for his decision to 'retire' from creative endeavour, Ian not only worked hard; he played hard.

After a night avoiding linking arms and singing during the sea shanties at the Stalybridge train station bar, myself and Wayne would stock up on the Leifmann cherry and raspberry beers, fully prepared for a night at Moet's house, fully aware of his dire lack of alcoholic beverages **Craig Scanlon**

Ian's house may have been damp and cold but there was always a warm welcome for friends such as Craig, Marc and Wayne. Everyone was kept entertained by the large amount of drink that flowed and Ian's vast record collection numbering around 8,000 albums and 5,000 singles. The sound track to these 'all-nighter's' was often provided by Lou Reed's 'Berlin' and 'Street Hassle'. On occasions, Ian would meet his friends to play games of pool in 'The Crown' in Deansgate and to put the world to right.

When the drink and conversation had dried up, me and Wayne would toss a coin to see who got the bedroom and who slept on the couch. As the bedroom was an ice-box housing a mysteriously stained bed with clammy sheets, the winner got to sleep on the couch, the two-bar gas fire blazing away. Moet did finally leave the house and moved to a pristine, laminate floored 'apartment' in A-hole-under-Lyne. After a few months he had successfully transformed it into his previous Denton pit. As the sergeant said, you can't beat sitting in your own mess **Craig Scanlon**

Craig got married to a lovely German girl called Silke and invited Ian to be the DJ for the evening. Understandably, Ian believed that the wedding guests at the reception would very likely be band members, people from the music industry and artists. Oh dear, Ian had got it very, very wrong the Wedding guests were elderly aunts and uncles, young nephews and nieces and worse. He couldn't back out of it and had to go ahead with his set list.

Personally, I would love to have 'Virgin Prunes', 'Can', 'Stooges' played at any Wedding reception, unfortunately the guests at Craig's reception were not of the same opinion. Ian was confronted by an elderly lady, complete with nice twin set and pearls, who marched to the DJ booth, rapped loudly on the window and glowered at Ian.

"What's up love?"

enquired Ian, strongly suspecting what the answer was going to be. He was right;

"I've come all the way from bloody Blackpool and you've ruined my bloody night!"

was the reply, in a tone of barely controlled fury

"Sorry..."

murmured Ian as the elderly guest stormed off.

But Ian had no alternative but to continue playing The Velvet Underground, The Birthday Party....... Both Craig and Silke seemed unperturbed by the soundtrack to their wedding reception but it was a bloody long night for Ian.

More and more 'Social Drinking'

It had to be said, Ian could hold his drink. A lethal combination of Champagne, Single Malt Whiskey, Metaxa Brandy and Tequila Cocktails were gleefully thrown down, and that was before Ian went out for a night on the town.

Travelling to Football matches was the perfect excuse to hit the bottle especially if the game was in London. The soundtrack of many a journey to a match was accompanied by the 'ACCEEED' house music that swept the country. When Manchester United beat Barcelona for the Cup Winners cup, at Rotterdam, in 1991 there was almost a psychedelic tinge to the proceedings. When in 1992, when Manchester United won their first League Title for 24 years, a stranger recognised Ian underneath K Stand at half time and came rushing towards him;

"Moet! The Hamsters! You don't know how much you meant to me."

cried the stranger as he clasped Ian in a warm embrace:

"and how special it is seeing you tonight of all nights makes it even more special"

Ian maintains that 'Manchester's collective hangover was palpable but merely a prelude to more regular Euro away days as the quest to win another European Cup began'.

Honved were Manchester United's first opposition in Budapest, this necessitated a five day trip, including 3 nights in Prague. As is his want, Ian experienced the rich culture of this ancient city but acknowledges that a large amount of time was spent seeking 'sins of the flesh'. Ian visited some of the dingiest bars he could find in Budapest. On the night of the game, he purchased no less than 12 bottles of Russian Champagne (from the black market) and consumed the vast majority whilst being watched by a group of Hungarian Youths, who were fascinated by the wild bunch of Mancunians carousing on the grass verges near the rickety stadium. Indeed, this wild excess formed much of a trip to a game abroad.

Ian remembers the most excessive trip very likely took place in Vienna, where he thought it would be a good idea to liberate a Christmas tree to take back to the hotel where he was staying. On the second night he was befriended by a group of Mercedes Salesmen, who managed to persuade him to come to a fetish club with them. Ian remembers that a man was being whip lashed on a cartwheel by whoever felt like it. In the famous Prater Wheel, Ian emptied the contents of his stomach to the horror and disgust of a party of school children and their teachers. Whilst on this trip he frequented a bar called 'Einstein's, which was covered wall to wall in related memorabilia. Even the staff wore T shirts and braces all sporting his image. The catchy tune, 'Einstein a Go-Go', by Landscape, was the most played record in that particular bar. Once when in this bar, a mate called Peter Catlow, pointed at the image on a waiter's T Shirt and rather naively asked;

"Is that Sigmund Freud?"

As a result Ian fell off his chair in fits of laughter.

'Fyffe's Bananas' sponsored a corporate day out at Manchester City's Maine Road; this was owing to the fans waving huge yellow banana's each match, how zany. Ian and a group of twenty others were treated to a free slap up meal, and..... yes you've guessed it, a free bar. Ex-United Legend, Norman Whiteside joined the group's ferocious drinking session and the City Team came along, just to unwind. This proved to be a stupid mistake as Ian became embroiled in an argument with the City Captain and Liverpool FC supporter, Steve Redmond. Punches were thrown and as Steve Redmond's father attempted to separate Ian from his son, Norman Whiteside yelled out an encouraging;

"Hit the scouse bastard!"

As Ian eventually made his way out, in disgrace, he wondered why on earth he kept acting like an arsehole all the time? However, he very much valued the opinions of his peers and liked being a 'real character' and thus continued on his mission of self-destruction.

Party in Paris UK Subs

As well as football trips Ian continued to go on holiday with Robert, or Wayne, which usually included an annual trip to New York.

On one holiday, in Bordeaux (1992), Robert had become especially boorish and unpleasant. After having to suffer Robert's sullen rudeness, through what should have been a pleasant evening wining and dining, Ian simply had had enough. Already sloshed, owing to Robert's behaviour, Ian picked up a one litre bottle of Ricard, took a slug and laid in to Robert;

"I'm fucking sick of being your fucking nursemaid and psychiatrist! You need to take a good long hard look at yourself and your behaviour."

Another slug;

"I don't fucking think you'll like what you see?"

Robert could only bow his head in reply, he knew Ian was right. Ian continued to liberally disperse some more home truths to Robert, in between swigs. The only time Robert spoke was;

"Can I have a drink?"

Ian's response to this request was explosive;

"Give YOU a fucking DRINK? Are you fucking MAD?"

Ian held the bottle away from Robert, covering the mouth and continued;

"You can't DRINK you fucking idiot, CAN YOU???!!"

Robert didn't argue and this silence provoked Ian with more vitriol;

"Every time you drink it ends in fucking tears"

Ian ranted on and on in this vein, not really appreciating the irony in the situation, he of all people was telling Robert HE had a drink problem. The words 'Kettle' and 'pot' spring to mind. Eventually Ian finished his diatribe, along with the bottle of Ricard and it was time for lights out.

When Ian woke up, it was pitch black and he felt very, very ill. He managed to stagger from his bed to get to the bathroom, but somehow managed to wander into the adjoining corridor where he was violently sick and couldn't get up. Robert must have heard him retching and found Ian covered in vomit and excrement, barely conscious. To Robert's credit, he not only managed to carry Ian into the shower, he cleaned up the stomach churning mess in the corridor after putting Ian to bed. When he came back into the hotel bedroom, he saw that Ian had not only vomited, he had soiled himself and the bed sheets as well. Robert was really worried as Ian's eyes were rolling unfocused. Robert managed to get him out of bed and stripped the bedding and cleaned up the best he could.

Ian was completely oblivious to everything that was going on and Robert realised there was no money to pay for the damage that Ian had caused. So rather than face the music, Robert bundled Ian out of the hotel window and literally carried him to the train station. It was standing room only on the bullet train to Paris and anxious travellers inched away from the vile smelling, wrenching and sweaty Mancunian, in fact Ian can vaguely recall anxious mothers pulling their children away from him.

Robert checked them into a hotel, just around the corner from The Gare Du Nord, carrying Ian up several flights of stairs to their room. Ian collapsed into bed, virtually unconscious where he remained for the best part of 36 hours. He felt weak, but gradually recovered, although he was to feel the after effects for the best part of a fortnight to come. He had pushed his limits but still had to learn his lesson.

The Clitheroe Kid

Every once, in a while Ian would totally abstain from either drug use or alcohol consumption. During these periodic periods Ian found that whilst his energy levels rose he quickly became bored and frustrated. There were a few 'one night stands' and minor relationships which fizzled into a form of friendship as Ian appeared to be incapable of forging a deep and meaningful relationship with a woman. This inability puzzled his female friends;

"You have so MUCH to give"

Ian didn't disagree.

One night Ian decided to have some clean, sober fun and go out in his 'geek' disguise to a pub called 'The Silver Springs'. This consisted of an outfit of sensible shoes and trousers, an old anorak, a brimmed Austrian hat and a pair of thick rimmed spectacles, with clear lenses, to complete this oddball 'look'. Ian had gone out as 'the geek' before and managed to remain in character as he continually got 'followed' by store detectives who were convinced they were on 'a right one' as he picked up products and put them down. The Geek created disruption where ever he went, delaying a bus load of passengers as this imbecile fumbled around for loose change. Ian could positively feel the agitated frustration that was emitting from his fellow passengers, who daren't confront him to 'hurry up'. This was when Ian discovered that people are frightened of 'strangeness' and that this odd behaviour could be worn like a shield.

At the Bar, Ian saw that the local 'glamour couple', Ashley and Stacey, were in deep meaningful conversation. Both were immaculately dressed and groomed – a perfect match. Stacey owned a successful hairdressing salon and Ashley was a 'dashing young thing'.

"Can I have lemonade, please, Miss?"

asked Ian in a high pitched voice, not dissimilar to the radio character 'The Clitheroe Kid'

Both Ashley and Stacey stopped mid-sentence when they heard this sound and vision of strangeness enter their midst but immediately started up their conversation in vain hope of keeping this creature at bay. Both were initially taken aback but decided to patronise 'the geek' for their amusement but found that this one answered back and Ashley was very quickly becoming heated. When Ian thought that events could take a turn for the worse, he removed his hat and glasses;

"Ian Moss! You complete bastard! You had me fooled!"

Ashley's anger had turned into laughter and Stacey, also laughing, had to admit

"Me too! I didn't recognise you Moet!"

Both insisted that Ian join them and they all sat down together. Ian remained with his lemonade but both Ashley and Stacey were knocking their alcoholic drinks back and getting very drunk. So much so, Ashley had to keep paying a visit to the Gents rather a lot. During these numerous trips to the lavatory, Stacey would lean over to Ian and grope Ian, whispering;

"I've always WANTED you, you know Ian?"

It was getting a bit embarrassing and Ian continually made excuses to leave but was over ruled each time. The threesome (?) made their way back to Stacey's flat Ian wondered if Ashley was turned on by another man having sex with his girlfriend? This suspicion was becoming stronger and stronger as Ashley snuggled into a cushion on the floor and appeared to fall asleep; how convenient. Ian, as has been remarked, has a lot to give and he happily obliged Stacey on the plush leather Chesterfield......when, during mid-act, Ashley woke up and walked out of the room.

"Get dressed and act like nothing's happened."

suggested Stacey, somewhat implausibly.

Ian did as he was bid and heard that Ashley was in the toilet

"Fancy a cup of tea, Ash."

asked Stacey, cheerily, as she struggled to get her knickers back on

"FUCK OFF"

roared Ashley, who clearly wasn't fooled, nor into voyeurism and sharing. Ian had got that one wrong, rather badly.

Ashley stormed back into the room. He was a big, powerfully built lad and he turned on Ian;

"You are fucking vermin, you traitor."

snarled Ashley raising his fist.

Ian knew what was going to come to him and already decided he would take this punishment as he thoroughly deserved what was going to happen. But he was wrong.

Ashley's fist struck alright but it struck Stacey in the eye with fearful force. He then ran out, slammed the door and was gone.

Stacey was in dreadful physical and emotional pain; Ian comforted her the best he could and held her. Eventually she drifted off to sleep and Ian crept away like a thief in the night. . There was only one thing for it, when Ian arrived home, he reached for a bottle of whiskey and proceeded to consume it whilst hating the man he had become.

Better in Hoboken by Franz Ferdinand

Ian loves staying at the 'city that never sleeps' and so good they named it twice, New York, New York. He usually travelled with Wayne, although Craig and Silke joined them on one occasion.

By a strange quirk of fate, on one holiday trip to New York, The Mekons were appearing at 'Maxwells" in Hoboken and were joined by Gibby Haines from 'The Butthole Surfers' on vocals. It was a great evening, much alcohol was consumed and part of this up on a park bench with a lovely looking girl called Susan in sexual congress. However, it so transpired that Susan had mistaken Ian for Jon Langford (yet again) …

Jon only understood what had taken place on a park bench in Hoboken, when he started to receive letters from Susan who thanked him for an 'unforgettable' night and suggested that she would come over and live with him. Ian, whilst being rather ashamed at the situation, could not help be amused to and likened this experience to 'a Whitehall Farce' (where more than his trousers came down).

A few months later, Ian went to see Gary Lucas play at Hebden Bridge Trades and Labour Club. And who should walk through the door, identically dressed in the same black over coat and jeans as Ian? Jon Langford, that's who! As both faced each other, like a scene from 'The OK Corall', Jon struggled to look serious and ordered;

"I want a fucking word with you!"

and then cracked up into laughter.

Jon and Ian had a good drink together and later joined Gary on stage to sing 'Planet Attack'.

As Ian sang he realised he was up on stage with the guitar player from Captain Beefheart and if Scotty could have beamed him up there and then…..

The Stepbrothers 1992 – 2001

Ian had decided 'to pack his dreams away' after the humiliating spectacle he made of himself after The International appearance. Although he had given up performing, he believed that the music of the early nineties had taken a turn for the better with groups such as Massive Attack, Bjork and The Pixies.

Marc Riley disbanded The Creepers and was working in a Public Relations company and eventually became a Disc Jockey for Radio One. Whilst working for the company Marc was able to bring Ian along as a guest for complimentary gigs and local radio sessions (Peter Perret and John Cale being the most memorable).

Eddie Fenn had installed a recording studio in his cellar at Rhodes, Middleton, and, in the summer of 1992, invited Ian along to try out the facility. Ian was intrigued enough, and also because Eddie was a good friend, to record a self-penned composition that was rather derivative of 'Sympathy for the Devil' in one afternoon. The process was very enjoyable and the end result was very encouraging considering this was the first recording in three years. After the 'whoo whoo's' were completed, Eddie played a collage of sounds put together by John Gill This soundtrack was unique as it sampled political speeches and had been donated to the Socialist Workers Party. This organisation had set up a huge rig outside the Manchester branch of HMV and had blasted the shoppers with this 'blitzkrieg'.

It had been an enjoyable diversion with Eddie, or so Ian thought. John Gill heard the recordings and wanted to know if Ian was interested in maybe doing some more recording with him. Ian was aware of John's reputation as a 'Studio Wizard' and readily agreed.

Demolition Derby by The Get

Ian admits that it was an act of sheer stupidity to drive a friend home, after a session of heavy drinking. He managed to drop his friend off at Ashton at around 3am and then drove home in his brand new car, but unfortunately he fell asleep at the wheel and was only woken up as his car hit the pavement. He pulled on the steering wheel and hit a wall sideways instead of crashing into it full on.

As Ian sat in his car, shocked and stunned, the full horror of his irresponsible actions hit home. He could have had someone in the passenger seat, which was a lump of crushed metal and glass. This stupidity could have involved another car, it was luck that it didn't and that he was able to walk away from the wreckage unscathed.

A police car with siren and lights blazing arrived just as Ian was inspecting the massive damage. It was a fair cop, Ian knew he was solely responsible and as he approached the Policeman to explain what had happened, the officer held up a hand and asked;

"Have you been drinking, Sir?"

Ian decided to take the consequences and admitted;

"Yes and I'm damn lucky to be alive."

A breathalyser was produced and Ian was asked to blow into this. The policeman looked at the reading and smiled;

"It hasn't even registered; this MUST be your lucky night!"

The officer gave Ian the bag; he was off the hook;

"Keep this as a souvenir."

Ian's car was less than two weeks old and it had cost him £11,000. When it was examined for repair he was informed that the bill would come to £9,000. Ian still considers this the luckiest night of his life.

John Gill

Ian had been happy enough recording the fun demo with Eddie, but the thought of working alongside him on this studio project was quite another matter. This multitalented musician had worked with The Creepers, Crawling Chaos, Tools You Can Trust, Bargepole and many other artists of considerable merit. In addition to this was John's considerable reputation to contend with. John had introduced The Mekons to Country Music and had previously worked with hugely diverse genres from Reggae to Jazz. Although Ian had met John several times previously, it was only during the studio project that he really got to know and respect him as a person.

Ian started the recording sessions full of self-doubt and a severe lack of confidence in his vocal abilities and the more he dwelt on John's musical pedigree the more of an impostor he felt. But John instinctively realised an innate, raw talent in Ian and encouraged him to stretch himself vocally. John impressed Ian with his fine taste in music and his considerable knowledge. Ian never felt lectured to but felt he had been educated by this quiet and gentle man.

"Sorry John."

Sighed Ian after recording an embarrassingly tentative vocal

"What for?"

Came John's reply via the studio earphones

"I don't think I can do it, you had better find another vocalist"

was Ian's sad reply.

"Oh really? I thought it was rather good for a first attempt, and this can be built on."

reassured John positively.

John further added, after a few more takes, that Ian had a wide vocal range and was fortunate in that he displayed a gift for rhythm and timing, not unlike 'Ragga' Artists. Ian was pleased by this comparison and in order to emphasise this point John played Ian some tracks by Shabba Ranks to demonstrate the paced, vocal similarities. Although Ian didn't quite believe John's affirmation that Ian's vocals were often better than this 'Ghetto Superstar', he felt that his confidence was just starting to return.

A Lovetractor gives birth

Recording the studio sessions was a relaxing and non-pressurised experience for Ian, thanks to John's gentle guidance. He became a more confident vocalist who was able to stretch his range.

After Ed and John had spent a week constructing a particular track Ian would call at John's flat on a Sunday. Ian was always eager to listen to John's inspirational discourse on political theory Reggae or Brian Wilson would usually be playing in the background. Every once in a while Ian would bring along a record of his own choosing and introduced John to the music of Mary Margaret O'Hara, which John enjoyed tremendously.

Afterwards, they would go to Ed's basement studio, and after further cups of tea and conversation, it would be time for Ian to listen to the week's work and give feedback. Whilst Ed and John were tweaking the track, often as a result of Ian's suggestions, it was time to write some accompanying lyrics. Ian usually went upstairs and fuelled by another cup of tea, made by Ed's wife Helen, he would compose the lyrics. Usually, these lyrics were inspired by that day's conversation with John, or maybe resulted from an earlier set of ideas which needed to be polished up. Some ideas were 'inspired' by his continued unhappy relationship with Julie; 'Acetone' in particular has a strong masochistic streak running through the vein of the song. Every once in a while a subject from current affairs (often as a result of talking with John) would be worked on, 'Ararat' was about Kim Philby's photograph of this particular mountain range....taken from the Eastern Block side.

When Ian was ready, he went down into the cramped basement to sing his parts, freely and without any form of inhibiting embarrassment; he received nothing but encouragement and validation from Ed and John. Upon listening to this body of work, my opinion is that the vocals for these sessions are amongst the best Ian has ever recorded.

Once Ian was satisfied with the recorded vocal further embellishments, such as horns and backup vocals, would be added later on that week. These session musicians were happy to contribute to this high quality work. Interest in the early stages of this work was displayed by Waarp Records a Sheffield based company who signed up mainly electronic bands. However, as the finished product became more organic, Waarp felt that this unique sound no longer fitted their profile and lost interest.

At the end of each five or six hour studio session the day was wound up in a local pub. During one session the discussion of a name for the work came up;
"Lovetractor?"
suggested John keenly.
"Stepbrothers."
countermanded Ian firmly, and that was that.

Camera Stepbrothers

The recording sessions were going well and Ian's mood lifted considerably as a result. So much so, that he began to call on Steven, whom he had not seen for some time. As far as Ian was concerned, he just wanted to enjoy Steven's company, but got the distinct impression he was barely tolerated. Admittedly, Steven was painting and sculpturing, but any attempts at music were mostly rehash of old material along with John West and Bendy. Eventually, Ian stopped calling as it was not only depressing, but frustrating. After the last meeting with Steven, Ian wrote 'Funny, Frightened and Sad', it would be the last time he and Steven would meet for some time. This song attempts to convey Ian's mixed emotions regarding his complex relationship with Steven.

Ian took a break during the Stepbrother recordings, to go to New York with Wayne, Craig and Silke. An apartment in Greenwich Village was rented in time to enjoy the Fourth of July Celebrations to see Sonic Youth and Sun Ra in Central Park. Ian and Silke went out swimming and left Craig to compose on a piano in the apartment. Inspiration for a Stepbrothers song, 'Coney Island' was to be found after visiting a 'Freak Show', in addition Bernie Worrall, from Funkadelic, was seen performing a show at a small intimate club.

After blagging their way into the 'Limelight Club' as members of The Fall Ian was impressed by the fact that this venue was set in an old church, complete with stained glass windows and pulpits. He was in a bit of a mischievous mood that night and decided to pay a visit to the crypt. He heard loud voices and decided to investigate further and appeared at a doorway where he saw two men, at a desk, counting 'a VERY LARGE amount of money'. One of the men looked at Ian and pulled a gun up from the desk, Ian managed to stammer

"SSSSorrryy..."

before he ran out of the club. He was so shocked by this incident that he couldn't get to sleep later that evening. It was no use, he had to get up and went to one of his favourite hangouts, which was "A Bistro on the Corner". He got into a conversation with an Irish Man, which started off innocently enough, but soon became a full blown row about the funding of the IRA. Indeed the discussion became so loud and heated; it was only brought to an abrupt end by the barman crashing a baseball bat loudly on the area of the bar between them. The subject was changed into a more civilised discussion about the merits of 'De Profundis' by Oscar Wilde. Eventually, at around 7.30 Ian came out blinking in to the sunshine as he did with his new best friend who offered him a job as a construction worker with his company. Ian politely declined, but still wonders about the ramifications of this offer had he accepted.

Just a quick look for a bootleg copy of 'Smile', by The Beach Boys, as a welcome present for John Gill and the break was soon over.

Iggy Pop Culture

Further material from The Stepbrothers and an album worth of material was sent to select record companies who were receptive to this new genre. Although some companies offered encouragement, 'Switched at Birth' was not taken up for release.

Ian's disappointment regarding the non-release of The Stepbrothers album was put into perspective by his father's heart attack in August. This was a huge shock to the family as Eddie was a non-smoker, barely touched alcohol and had remained fit and active. Eddie was rushed to hospital where he remained for over a week and it was a very upsetting time for the whole family. Ian was determined to support his mother and when he received a phone call from Marc, who was enquiring after his father, he got an offer:

"Come and see Iggy Pop, I'm interviewing him after the show at The Academy."

"No, thanks"

"Ring me if you change your mind."

Ian's Mum overheard the telephone conversation and persuaded Ian that it would be perfectly OK for him to go; it might even be just the little break he needed.

Ian enjoyed the show and yes, his mother was perfectly right, it was a real tonic to be out with Marc. After the show, Ian sat in on Marc's interview on the tour bus. Iggy turned out to be friendly and funny, and yet Ian had the distinct impression that Iggy was merely 'taking care of businesses'. Ian had regarded Iggy as the greatest Rock and Roller ever, and to a certain extent still does, but Iggy's hackneyed spiel reminded him of a well versed politician.

Ian was hugely disappointed after meeting his idol and; 'the old adage about never meeting your heroes rang true that night'

Eddie Moss (1925- 1992)

The effects of the heart attack had left Ian's father severely debilitated. Eddie tried hard to appear optimistic and cheerful, but he was not well and the concern for her husband bought Ian's mother close to tears on several occasions. It was hard for the whole family to see someone who had been so strong and solid become so helpless and vulnerable.

Ian went ahead to record further material for 'The Stepbrothers' but acknowledges that his efforts were somewhat half hearted as he was distracted by his father's condition. However, Lu Edmonds and Tom Greenhalgh (Mekons) came all the way from London to offer their considerable services and this spurred Ian on to write new material rather than rehash old lyrics. Two new songs were recorded and Ian was particularly pleased with the autobiographical 'Vegetable Man', inspired by a Syd Barrett title.

Unfortunately, this new found inspiration and effervescence was curtailed by Ian's father being rushed into hospital with severe swelling of the stomach. The Surgical Team decided to operate on an infection for fear that this inflammation may bring about a cardiac arrest.

Eddie was a fighter and managed to pull through the operation, although the toll of this emergency procedure was clear to Ian and his mother when he returned to a side room on a ward. Ian went home to sleep, but returned in the evening to sit with his parents;

"I've not seen you hold your Dad's hand since you were a little boy."

smiled his Mother. Ian had held his father's hand all night.

"I don't think he's wanted me to……until now."

replied Ian and upon hearing this, Eddie smiled at both his wife and his eldest son with love in his eyes.

"You go home Mum, you need some sleep."

insisted Ian. Although his mother didn't want to leave Eddie's bedside she saw the logic in this and, after protesting, went back home.

Eddie was wretched with pain and slept fitfully. His main concern was for Ian;

"Try to sleep, Ian.'"

he whispered as day turned to night and Sunday arrived.

Ian did his best and managed to dab his father's forehead and lips with water. His father's pain increased and Ian called a nurse as the pain had become intolerable. The syringe drive that contained the morphine, to ease the pain had broken down and this was replaced and the pain appeared to ease. But less than an hour had occurred and this syringe driver too malfunctioned. The nursing team were great and it looked as if the worst was over when Ian's mother returned.

Ian was exhausted and agreed to go back home and tried to sleep. At around six thirty he returned and found that Neil and his Aunty Jean had been around earlier on that day. The mood appeared to be a bit more upbeat, much to Ian's relief; his mother smiled and informed Ian;

"He was singing Waltzing Matilda earlier on!"

Eddie whispered to his wife, who turned to Ian and asked;

"Can you help me lift your father a little further up the bed to get him a bit more comfy?"

Both mother and son gently took an arm each and began to help; Eddie shifted and gasped, his colour changed dramatically;

"What have we done?"

cried Ian's mother as she staggered backwards

Ian ran for assistance and the crash team urgently ushered the family out of the cubical as the curtains were drawn tightly. Ian's mother was inconsolable, believing that they had contributed to this sudden attack.

Ian already knew but attempted to reassure his mother:

"We've done nothing, Mother. Don't feel any guilt; please don't make this any harder for yourself"

A doctor appeared and Ian could tell what was going to happen;

"I'm very sorry, but despite our best efforts your husband has died. He was incredibly brave but his heart could not stand up after the trauma of the last two days."

Ian went to sit with his father and promised that he would look after his mother. After Neil and his wife, Gaynor, Aunty Jean and Uncle Frank, and Ian's mother had said their 'goodbyes' Ian drove his mother to her home and she went to bed.

Ian stayed on the sofa in the living room and cried and cried and cried.

The Flowers of Manchester The Spinners

Ian's emotions were very, very raw after the death of his father. He felt shell-shocked and retreated into himself as a result of the severe grief that he experienced. One of the potential emotions following the death of a loved one is anger and this was to manifest itself in a terrifying way.

Around two weeks after his father's funeral Ian decided to distract himself with a footy trip to Newcastle. The day began well enough in a pub in the suburbs of Dunster and there was some good natured drinking with the local folk. On the way to the Stadium Ian's group was approached by a jeering mob of Newcastle supporters who were clearly hostile. No problem, this was to be expected and a deaf ear was turned to the taunts until;

"Munich! Munich!"

This was more than Ian could stand as this was a mocking reference to the Munich Air Disaster of 1958, where 8 young Manchester United Football Players were amongst those killed in the tragic crash.

Ian saw red and went for the idiot who had shouted this sick taunt. Punching him around the head Ian screamed hysterically;

"You think people dying is funny? Death's a bit of a laugh.....Well, I'll fucking kill you!!!"

The Newcastle supporters backed off at the sight of this maniac and the police stepped in. This incident was not taken further and Ian retreated back into himself, remaining silent and as he describes was 'a stepping razor blade, very dangerous'.

The family's first Christmas without Eddie was awful. Ian, Neil and Gaynor attempted to try to cheer Ian's mother up (who was in an even worse state of grief than Ian, but without the anger), but nobody was fooled by this display of 'jollity' and a thick cloud of depression had descended on the Moss household by mid-afternoon.

There was a faint knocking on the door and Ian got up to answer it and found it was none other than a very sick looking Steven Middlehurst on the doorstep who, upon seeing Ian said;

"Help me, Mo."

"God, you look dreadful come on in"

Ian got Steven to sit down and asked what on earth had happened;

"I took too much heroin last night and got taken to hospital"

"Did they discharge you, on Christmas Day?"

asked Ian incredulously.

"No, mate, I discharged myself."

answered Steven, taking a folder of medical notes out of his overcoat to show the family.

It was clear to Ian that Steven had come over to Ian's mother's house, as he knew that he could get help.

Steven continued;

"It was really bad this time. My heart stopped in the hospital and the Doctors managed to resuscitate me."

Putting their own grief to one side the family looked after Steven and sent him home in a taxi, not before Ian pressed a twenty pound note into his palm.

Over the following weeks, Ian received several phone calls from Steven who expressed his gratitude to both him and his mother. Despite Ian hoping, yet again, that this near death experience would wake Steven up to his hopeless predicament, it was not to be.

When Ian called around to find out how Steven was fairing, he found that Steven had reverted back to his old belligerent and obnoxious behaviour. It transpired that Steven had somewhat revealed the contents of his medical notes to his father, just to torment and upset him. Ian and Steven 'had words', this was to be the last occasion that Ian saw Steven for some considerable time.

Ian Swears 'He Was There' and Punches Lofty the Lion

The early to mid-nineties were a period in which Ian settled into a pattern of what he describes as 'working hard and drinking harder'. His relationship with Julie had become the most stable it ever had been in that there was virtually no drama on either side. He saw a lot of Debbie, an old work friend, and her husband Shaun who ran a pub and spent many weekends in their company.

Whilst Ian was not involved with any musical projects at this time, it should be mentioned that his services as an eye witness to the famous Sex Pistols Free Trade Hall gig, were very much in demand. He not only contributed to a Granada TV Documentary in 1996 but was to feature five years later in a more in depth programme; 'I Swear I was There' and was in the accompanying book by David Nolan.

Ian had become a spectator, courtesy of Marc Riley, at gigs around two to three times a week. He had lost none of his enthusiasm for music and remembers watching Neil Young, from the side of the stage, at the Reading Festival as being particularly memorable. Craig Scanlon regularly invited him to Fall gigs, usually with Wayne and Bobby and managed to consistently wind Mark E Smith up, who took his wrath out on Craig for the following week. As enjoyable as it was going to gigs, Ian felt not the slightest temptation to return to the stage.

Ian is a die-hard Manchester United Supporter, but the offer of a VIP box, complete with free food and drink, to watch Bolton Wanderers, courtesy of a fruit supplier from Bolton by the name of Tony Longworthy, was too tempting to refuse. In addition, Ian was entitled to post match access into the players' lounge and enjoyed meeting football legends such as Matt 'The Lion of Vienna' Lofthouse and Roy Hartle. However, he was not so keen on the latter-day counterparts and found himself in an argument with Scott Sellars (who had been signed up from Newcastle United) about who would win that season's League Title. Scott's companion was a city slicker in a cashmere overcoat and designer suit who appeared to be very keen to hear Ian's opinions, which he then promptly disagreed with; all of a sudden the penny dropped;

"Are you a player's agent?"

asked Ian and received a nod in reply; Ian later learned that this was Paul Stretford and then he really lost it;

"WELL DON'T YOU TRY AND TELL ME ANYTHING ABOUT FOOTBALL, YOU FUCKING LEACH!! PEOPLE LIKE ME, WORKING

CLASS PEOPLE, PUT OUR MONEY AND PASSION INTO THE GAME, UPPER CLASS CUNTS LIKE YOU JUST TAKE"

Ian really let rip into Paul Stretford, and not even Scott pulling his sleeve, insisting that he too was working class, didn't help. Indeed it had quite the opposite effect as Ian smacked Scott with a back hander, well he wouldn't let go and shut up, and there was a stunned silence. Security moved in and Ian was forcefully ejected from the ground and told never to return.

Two weeks later, Ian receives an invitation from Tony Longworthy, assuring him that everything was smoothed over and would he like to come to watch Bolton versus Chelsea in a League Cup Tie? This sounded like too good an offer to refuse and Ian arrived at the stadium with torrential rain pouring down and high winds (Ian later learnt that a helicopter chartered by Chelsea Director and Financial Backer, Mathew Harding, had crashed to the ground killing all passengers).

Half time had arrived and Ian had polished off the best part of a bottle of vodka. A message arrived for him to make the imminent lottery draw on the pitch. Tony catches Ian's puzzled expression and reassures him that;

"It's a conciliatory gesture."

So on goes Ian to the pitch accompanied by the announcement:

"Let's have a BIG hand for our guest making the half time draw.....from MANCHESTER UNITED.....Ian Moss!!!"

There are boos and catcalls from every spectator in the stadium and Ian pulls out the winning ticket to the deafening cacophony of abuse. But worse is to happen, 'Lofty the Lion (who wasn't really a lion but was a man dressed up in a giant Lion outfit)' decides to wrestle with Ian, in a vain attempt to throw Ian onto the soaking turf. But Ian is too strong for him and ends up punching him. Ian concedes that the scene must have looking like 'Gladiator meets Laurel and Hardy' and it certainly amused the audience. Ian actually walked back with a few cheers and handclaps ringing in his ears as he made for the relative sanctuary of the bar.

"I think Bolton Wanderers FC Versus Ian Moss ended in an honourable draw."

The Stepbrothers

"Better a dreamer than a cynical schemer'

The rest of the nineties are somewhat of a 'lost decade' for Ian as he did the same things from day to day; working, drinking, watching football and attending gigs. One sad, memorable event was the death of Dennis Downworth, who at least got to realise his dream of travelling the world before dying of AIDS related causes. Ian still misses his infectious smile, although there was a cloak of sadness surrounding him before his early death. There were numerous other funerals to attend, notably Brian Leah, ravaged by drug addiction; he simply collapsed on the street and died.

Ian was overseeing eight fruit and a vegetable outlets, the turnover was around a quarter of a million pounds each year. He earned good wages, but worked very hard for them. He felt liked, respected and appreciated, but the main aim for him was that he believed that one day the business would become his, or failing that a large amount of money had been set aside for him just in case of some mishap. That mishap happened in early 1998 when the relationship between Mike Ratchford and the landlord had become untenable and Mike handed in his notice. Ian had an offer from the franchise to overtake the existing business, but this felt really disloyal to Mike and, anyway, there was a large nest egg to come his way. He resigned and when the supposed large bonus was to come his way, he only received half the amount he had been promised. He believed Mike's tearful pleas that this was all the money that was available. Much later, he found out that Mike had ripped him off.

Upon reflection Ian believed that whilst he was rather naive and gullible to place so much trust in Mike's word, he knew he had behaved honourably and that his credibility remained intact:

...I held my head high, I didn't recoil from the mirror in shame every morning, I'd move on."

Mr Ed's of Hazel Grove

Before Ian found out the truth about Mike Ratchford he had a proposition;
"Mike, I've found this prime site for a greengrocer on the busy shopping parade in Droylesden."
Mike didn't look all that interested but Ian continued;
"I've done the pricings for fixtures and fittings with a van too and it's a bit more than I can afford."
"That's a pity then."
Mike was not responding in the way that Ian hoped, but still he pressed on;
"I was wondering if you wanted to come in with me, like a silent party?"
Mike's reply was firm;
"No thank you, I am never, ever getting back into that game ever again."
Ian was disappointed in Mike's reaction but was determined to set himself up as a greengrocer. However, as Mike was not going to help out, Ian had to aim his sights a little lower on a less prestigious site in Stockport. After some more costing, and negotiation with the landlord, Ian found that he could just about afford this if he sold his house. His mother was only too happy to take him back in during the interim time when he was setting up; it would be nice for her to

have someone around the house again. Ian's friends strongly advised him against risking so much on this venture but nothing was going to deter him.

Ian moved into his mother's house in March 1997, after selling his house very quickly – owing to a low price and was busy preparing for his own business. One Sunday, his mother called to Ian;

"I don't feel at all well, can you get me to a doctor!"

Ian instinctively knew something must be very wrong as his mother had never asked for this before. Fortunately, he was able to get her into an emergency clinic, where she was transferred to hospital immediately. She was diagnosed as having Erysipelas, which is an airborne virus, which resulted in painful, erupting blisters which wouldn't heal. At the worst stage, half her body was an exposed painful sore. She remained in a great deal of pain for the next three months in her hospital bed and as her joints became so infected down one side of her body she was virtually immobilised. It was dreadful for Ian to see his poor mother in so much pain and he was very concerned that she simply didn't have the strength to fight the mounting infection. He visited her every day; both of them agreed that he had to get the shop ready for opening.

One day, by her bedside, Ian had some news for his mother;

"Mum, I've decided to name the shop after my Dad."

He could see his mother's interest visibly perk up and informed her;

"I'm calling the shop Mr Ed's."

For the first time in months, his mother smiled and Ian knew that she now had something to cling to. She wanted to get better and see her son's simple tribute to his dad, her husband.

Somehow, it didn't really matter that Ian's career as an entrepreneur came to a disastrous end in which he became homeless and in debt, her fight back to recovery was, and is, reward enough.

'I'm going to Mr Ed's fruit shop in Hazel Grove to buy some quality produce off the friendly shop keeper Moet"

"Oh! That sounds great! Think I'll join you"

On Ian's 41st birthday, 25 June 1998, Mr Ed's was opened and with casual remarks, like the above exchange between Mike Radcliff and Marc Riley on BBC Radio, a steady supply of students bought produce had their suspicions that this was indeed the Grocers mentioned on the radio happily confirmed by the friendly shop keeper. Business was becoming so brisk that Mike Ratchford, who was taking a 'friendly' interest confirmed;

"I'm getting back in to the job........in Droyelsden"

Of course he immediately bought up the premises which he had been invited to become a partner in, and fitted the shop with state of the art fittings (whereas Ian could only afford cheap second hand shelves). To add insult to injury Mike then attempted to poach Ian's staff away via a series of unsuccessful clandestine phone calls. Finally, Mike's true nature became apparent to Ian and he asked himself the rhetorical question;

"When is a friend not a friend? When he's no longer useful."

Ian felt betrayed and knew that he had been treated very shabbily by his former employer and 'friend'.

Traditionally the fruit and veg business takes a bit of a down turn as the winter months approach, but instead of drawing his horns in; Ian became more impulsive and invested in three more shops which quadrupled his initial outlay. Only 'Mr Ed's' turned in any form of profit, which was soon swallowed by the other outlets. Ian found himself working a 70 hour week with no wages. The only form of compensation to be found was by successfully obtaining a site in Droylsden market and going into direct competition with Mike, but even then he acknowledges that he was 'merely cutting my nose to spite my face'. But this had the desired result, Mike was seething with anger to such a degree that he attempted to demand that local suppliers should not work with Ian; otherwise they would lose their business with him. Fortunately, the suppliers ignored his threats and Ian continued to get on Mike's pips.

Larry Gott (Ian's old school and bedroom band mate) was currently enjoying mega success with the pop group 'James'. Very often, a drink or two with Larry was the only enjoyment Ian experienced during this hectic work schedule, and he was always made welcome at Larry, and his partner Jane's home.

Ian could barely afford the odd pint as he successfully struggled to pay the bills and buying CD's and records became a thing of the past. He even had to sell his car to finance the ever growing mountain of debts.

So it was something of a treat for him to be out at a birthday party at Audenshaw, with his friends Debbie and Shaun. But unfortunately both of his friends somehow became embroiled in an argument with another couple (who were part of a larger group) and it was decided to make an early exit and as they were about to go Ian was attacked and had a bottle smashed into his face. The irony of it was he wasn't even involved in the argument, but being 'the big one' he was targeted. Ian was pushed to the floor and was repeatedly kicked until he lost consciousness. When he came to, he was more concerned about the amount of blood over his leopard print shirt and remembers thinking 'it's ruined'. He felt a twinge of sadness, which soon turned into fear and sheer panic as people were tending to his face and informing him that

"There's glass smashed in your eye!"

He was taken to hospital where he caught site of his swollen, completely closed right eye and by the fact that his 'Roman Nose' looked like Henry Cooper after the notorious bout with Mohamed Ali. He also noted that his left eye didn't look too pretty either before he writhed in pain to the injuries sustained by the rest of his body, particularly his skull, inflicted by his attackers' kicks.

Ian was terrified and felt vulnerable and fragile. He had never welcomed violence but had never been frightened and was always in calm control and had felt invincible. That feeling had gone for ever. The good news was that the glass hadn't penetrated into his eye ball and that his sight was not going to be affected. He was stitched up and even discharged that same evening, but a very different, quieter one who had 'stepped out loud and proud a few hours earlier'.

Ian was in a shocking state, totally disfigured and, owing to his injuries, he couldn't work. This was the last thing he needed as it was his expertise that kept the businesses above water. His staff rallied round and did their best but by the time he was able to return to work, his business was around £3,000 in debt.

The Police were confident that they would secure a conviction against the lad who had glassed him, but Ian had an uneasy feeling at the back of his mind. Unfortunately, this worry was well founded as, after several court cancellations, Ian was advised to accept that the perpetrator of the attack be 'bound over' owing to 'lack of evidence. The main delay had been that a married couple, who had been witness to the attack, lived in Cornwall and the Police evidently decided it was too far to go to obtain statements from them and they thought they had enough evidence. Ian knew that they had been complacent and negligent and his attacker had got off, it was a bitter pill for him to swallow.

The Lasagne Incident

"Hello, Ian, its Reg, how are you?"

This was a pleasant surprise on a spring day a phone call from Mick Hucknall's father.

After an initial exchange of pleasantries, Reg got through to the core of the reason for ringing;

"You know that Mick's band is playing that big concert at Haydock Race Track?"

"Yeah."

Replied Ian, who knew but hadn't got the slightest intention to go and see Simply Red.

"Mick would love for you to attend and bring a couple of old friends along as Mick wants to get back in touch"

"Mmmm..."

Murmured Ian politely.

"There's going to be a party afterwards and you'll get the chance to have a chat with Alex Ferguson."

Now, this was more like it, the chance to meet the actual manager of Manchester United!

Ian happily agreed and invited Derek Howarth (THE mega United Fan) to come along.

It started off as a very pleasant day, both Ian and Derek were treated well and United thrashed Arsenal. It was nice to meet up with Reg, but in truth the experience was rather bland. Things picked up a bit when Alex Ferguson arrived with his family, along with David May. Simply Red take to the stage, a bit too smooth and slick for Ian's tastes, but the crowd appeared to enjoy their performance. After the show everyone congregates into a VIP lounge and an excited Mick comes over to Ian and asks

"What did you think of the show?"

Ian, as demonstrated before, is very honest and his previous candour usually managed to upset Mick. It's an old game, and Ian decided to focus on what he considered to be one of the positive aspects of the show;

"That Homer Banks song, 'A whole lotta love' was an interesting cover. I can't say I liked it as much as the original but it moved a bit."

"It's a Sam and Dave song! Who the fuck's Homer Banks?!"

Barked back Mick,

Mick then takes both Ian and Derek to meet Alex Ferguson and introduces them as;

"Two old friends of mine who used to take me to the match when I was younger."

This was a bare-faced lie, maybe spurred on by the fact Mick wanted to appear to be a 'Man of the people'. However, Ian bit his lip but realised, he had been invited'. Still, there was Alex and Ian had a great time listening to this legend, who regaled the party with unprintable indiscretions about Manchester United.

Mick pulled the same stunt again when he introduced Ian and Derek to Alex Ferguson's wife, again Ian didn't want to rock the boat and kept a blank face, but felt increasingly uncomfortable going along with this charade.

The party is transported by coach to 'Barca' which is a rather uptown bar owned by Mick. By this time, the whole party is very merry with drink and there is more to flow. Everyone is escorted into a private section where they are greeted by several 'Showbiz' personalities, including much of the cast of 'Coronation Street'. Mick comes over to chat and Ian feels on easier ground as the animated conversation focuses on music. They are chatting like old friends, agreeing to disagree on their favourite groups, when all of a sudden a glamorous young starlet comes over to speak to Mick, who immediately turns his back on Ian mid-sentence to give her his full attention. The sight of a nice, orderly celebrity packed queue for a buffet captures Ian's eye. The devil in Ian comes out and he goes straight to the front of the queue and begins to start shovelling the lasagne straight into his mouth. The vision of Ian with lasagne dripping down his nice shirt causes the celebrity queue to recoil in disgust and horror. Ian chuckles at the gasps and decides to flick the lasagne all over their designer outfits.

Ian is promptly ejected by security but he is happy in the fact that he hasn't sold out.

One of the doormen shook his head and informed Ian that
"You've burned your bridges there mate"
"Yeah....and I don't give a fuck!"
Replied Ian.

Coming out of hibernation 2001 – 2005

In all these years, this may shock Ian, Bob and Robert that I never actually went along to see the Hamsters **Colin Swan**

"Would you fancy doing some Hamsters stuff again?"
was the, largely, rhetorical question posed by Ian to the (less) cute Bobby and added
"..........Without Steven."
Steve had suffered a stroke which had left him incapable of drumming, and if truth be told, Ian knew that Steve's very presence would cause him concern over his own sanity.
"I'd love to..."
ruminated Bobby and gave his stipulation of:
"As long as Steven gave it his blessing."
Ian knew that this was an empty proposition (which did the rounds every now and then) and that it was very unlikely to come to any form of fruition.
That very same weekend he bumped into Steven in Market Street, on the way to Piccadilly.
"Hey Mo! Can you buy me a bottle of Collis Brown from Boots?"
Ian happily complied with his request and both headed to Mother Macs.
"I'm thinking about playing as the Hamsters again......without you. But maybe you could be represented, if you like, by creating some stage art or pre-recorded sounds."
Steven happily agrees, but both know that this venture is very unlikely to take place; it was one of Moet's pipe dreams. A very pleasant afternoon was spent discussing this idea and both part on good terms.
"I saw Steven last week and he was OK with us doing the Hamsters without him."
"That's because we'll never do it."
Both Ian and Bobby smiled, realising the probable truth of this situation.

Sex is between the legs, Gender is in the head

"I hear the Hamsters are reforming?"
asks a local promoter called Pod (Prince of Darkness)
This was news to Ian and he looks at Pod, rather perplexed.
"That's the rumour"
persisted Pod
"Well, it's no more than a rumour, but we have talked about playing again"
acknowledged Ian

"If you decide to do it, I'd love to promote you"
And that was that.

Bobby was up for the Hamsters reunion but it had been the best part of two decades since he had played guitar and he expressed concern over this lack of confidence.

"How about if you get your mate, Nigel Blinston, to play second guitar then?" suggested Ian.

"That could work, but we will need a drummer"

"Get Nigel to bring his mate, Damien"

"I think you'd better tell Steven about this."

"Ah, yes....I'm sure he'll be fine."

Bob didn't look convinced.

Next was the matter of approaching Jon to resume his role of bassist. A lot had happened since Ian had last met Jon and instead of the gawky teenager came a bald headed, bulky 'Out' Tranny wearing a skirt

---

Well, it took 2 years of treatment to realise that it was not gender dysphoric. This is what the real life test is all about to be honest, .I had pretty much completed 2 years of cross living and then got made redundant. After failing to get a job because of my attire, I decided to revert back to male to keep up with the mortgage payments. I have never been happier to get out of a dress in my life. I was still transgendered, but had exorcised my demons. After a few months of being in drab, skirts became an issue again, but this time I was going to tackle it head on! Instead of piling on shit loads of makeup, false tits and a wig and only having contact with other loons doing the same thing, I decided to be true to myself and just wear whatever I want.

Tranny shops and tranny clubs are nothing more than big closets and do nothing for the transgender movement. They go out in the dead of night, dressed to an extent their own mother does not recognise them and talk about hemlines with a 6 ft. 5" wrestler named Crystal. What a complete waste of time!!

It's better to wear what you want in the company of friends who accept you for what you are. **Jon Rowlinson**

"I went into work at the engineering plant and told everyone that I was transitioning into a woman and would be known as Joanne"

Informed Jon perfectly amiably and continued;

"My bosses and workmates weren't best pleased but they had to agree with my wishes. They didn't want to use the same toilet as me, so they had to build me my own toilet block. They sacked me a few months later, I took them to a tribunal and won substantial damage and then......I decided to be a bloke again"

"Brilliant, brilliant"

enthused Ian and hugged Jon, who was perfectly happy to be part of the reunion.

The Triptych Completed

From the early 1980's until 2008 I never clapped eyes on Steve Midi again. It was quite a shock when we eventually met again. I was driving a bus through Chorlton in Manchester when Steve got on my bus, he looked very dishevelled and it took me a while to recognize him. Steve told me of his not too optimistic future; it took another two meetings before I finally believed him. Being a bus driver around Manchester let me see people I once knew from the safety of being behind a Perspex screen. Neil Moss, Ian's brother kept me informed of his brother's progress from being a passenger **Colin Swan**

Ian decided to 'break the bad news' to Steven gently after a couple of pints in the pub. Steve senses something is up and asks;

"So what is it?"

Ian takes a big breath and launches into the reason why Steven is being treated;

"We now have a date for the Hamsters show and as you said that you'd be happy for us to play without you, we have got another drummer."

Steven was dumbstruck and looked really hurt and retaliated with;

"I didn't think you'd actually go ahead and do it though."

"It's settled mate, we are going to play without you."

replied Ian firmly but calmly

"You can't do this to me Mo!"

protested Steven.

Ian explained to Steven that not only was he now incapable of playing the drums but that also the 'old problems' were bound to resurface but;

"You could design the stage set for the band."

Steven believed he saw a tiny crack of compromise and decided to build on this by;

"Can I support you? I could get a band together."

"Yeah, of course."

demurred Ian. Oddly enough this ambivalent reply appeared to antagonise Steve even more. When Steven had calmed down he attempted to coax his way back into the band, but was met by the same polite refusal and Steve would get all annoyed again.

Steven and Ian walked back to Steven's house in silence. Steven looked devastated and Ian felt really awful. After leaving Steven's house, Ian's anguish was just too much for him to bear, he couldn't go ahead with this coldly logical plan

and had to give in to his heart, so he turned back ....
"How did it go?"
asked Bobby.
"It was awful; he looked like a condemned man..."
replied Ian, and Bobby looked sad and nodded;
"He's playing keyboards."
Bobby's face lit up and said;
"Good!"

You Belong in Rock and Roll David Bowie

The newly reformed Hamsters had the luxury of three months rehearsal, in a practice room, before their reunion gig at the Witchwood.

Ian decided that the easiest approach would be to perform all the songs that Steven had written in order to keep tension down to a minimum. There were also a few additions and revisions, 'Ordinary' which dated from the very first gig was updated with new lyrics and was renamed 'Cute Bobby'. Steven had a little lyric 'the bee stung me' and this was turned into a rather catchy sing-along number. 'Animals' gained an additional chorus hook and the band considered cover versions of Grandmaster Flash's 'The Message' (Jon's face was an absolute picture of bewilderment apparently) 'and 'Worst Band in the World' by 10cc; but it was Syd Barrett's 'Bike' and 'Open up', by Mungo Jerry which made it to performance.

Bobby had virtually forgotten how to play the guitar, let alone remember the songs. This lead to a lot of numbers having to be 'reinvented'. Another challenge was that, despite a great deal of initial enthusiasm, Steven hadn't learnt his part on the keyboards that Ian had lent him to practice on. In fact, the keyboards were very likely sold. Rather than go over old ground, it was decided that Steven could share vocal duties with Ian, which seemed like a reasonable compromise. But Steven preferred to 'wind' the new boys up with contradictory demands and 'borrow' money from his oldest mates to go down the pub during rehearsal time.

The band relied very heavily on Jon's musical expertise, which in turn lead to his increasing empathy with Nigel and Damien. This disturbed Ian somewhat, as the band was in danger of sounding like a traditional band, which was not the sound of the Hamsters. Fortunately, Ian in his usual dictatorial stance took control;

"This isn't fucking Guns and Roses!!!"

The band felt that they had a considerable body of work, but it was the re-emerging bond between Steven, Bobby and Ian that really mattered. Steve would often spend the weekend with Bobby and Slavita during the rehearsal period and Ian would drive him home on the Monday morning. Steven was usually animated and informed Ian that;

"I took a bath for the first time in two years around Bob's."

Ian had already heard, apparently the house-proud Slavita was mortified and rushed up to scrub the bath straight away. But Ian merely nodded, well everything was going well and the love of the brotherhood was re-established.

Moet in the Middle

Steve, at his last performance on stage described Ian as a "fascist cunt!" I would call him, an emotionally charged Mastodon; a complex intellectual who thinks with his penis. But I love him **Jon**

Ian had become reacquainted with Rose, Steven's ex-partner, who was leading a life of sobriety with their daughter Eve (who was now in her mid-teens). Eve had a job in a hairdressing salon at the weekend and was being 'stalked' by Steven who had not seen her since she was five. She had very painful memories of her father and asked her mother to stop him from hanging around the salon.

Rose asked Ian if he could have a quiet word with Steven in order to keep him away from Eve at the present time;

"When her exams are over, I'll speak to her again and try and get her to see Steven. I think it would be really good for them both."

This was a really hard dilemma for Ian, he knew that Steven genuinely loved his daughter and wanted nothing more than to re-establish contact with her, but he knew that he was the only person that Steven would listen to and maybe comply.

Ian had the onerous task of explaining the situation to Steven, who was understandably hurt and frustrated. Steven had a strong sense of 'Family' despite his maverick streak and this request wounded him to the core. Although he agreed to stop peering at his daughter from a distance he sort of took it out on the messenger.

Ian recounts '*if Steven had a gun he would have shot me through the heart where I stood with my head hung low after performing this task that had hurt my dear friend so badly*'.

"What do wanky old punk bands do when they're bored? They play their wanky old songs in wanky venues." **The Manchester Evening News**

"WANKY!"

Screamed Steven to Ian and Bobby (who were more amused than annoyed) and ranted;

"I'm going to daub the building with the word WANKY and when that reviewer wonders why I am hitting him....I'll just scream "WANKY" in his face!!!"

Fortunately, Steven never carried out this threat.......

"Ok, Steve it's time to go now."

Steven was wearing a rather fetching Chinese mandarin outfit and continued being the diva not only during the journey to the venue but during the journey;

"You're not going to wear THAT are you?"

Ian and Bobby were somewhat more casually attired for the gig, and Ian was wearing a short sleeved shirt;

"Honestly, that shirt shows your greengrocer arms."

scolded Steven.

Little did they realise that this comically demanding behaviour was a symptom of Steve's building nervous agitation.

This boorish behaviour continued during the sound check as he bossed everyone around attempting to exercise some form of control.

""He'll be choreographing dance moves next."

whispered Ian to Bobby, whilst Steven was ensuring that a key light was being pointed at him.

"Yeah, shall we bugger off down the pub then?"

So they did.

The venue, upon return, was filling up with fans and well-wishers. It felt good and Ian believed that this set the atmosphere for a glorious celebration of friendship and music. Ian was psyching himself up for his first gig in thirteen years when;

"Shall I wear this hat, Mo?"

Steven had interrupted Ian's preparation and persisted

"What do you think?

"It's not important, Steven, wear it if you like."

said Ian rather bluntly, resulting in Steven becoming even wilder in intensity;

"Craig Scanlon said I should wear it because it looks good. NOT IMPORTANT what do you fucking mean? Why don't you want me to wear my hat??"

Ian shook his head in dismay and replied;

"Calm down will you? It's not fucking important; it's just a fucking hat!"

For the past few months everything had been relative sweetness and light, and now, five minutes before the Hamsters were to go on, the old destructive monster had returned. In a way it was good that Steven's drug buddies came into the dressing room and had overheard the 'argument';

"Oh Midi, wear it, wear it!"

they both cooed and this response appeared to mollify Steven, who jammed the much discussed hat on his head, with a defiant glare at Ian. Furthermore, Steven's attention was distracted by the huge lines of cocaine that were being chopped up by his druggy entourage. In all fairness, Ian was offered a line but politely declined. Steven overheard this offer and jeered;

"Don't waste any on that cunt!"

Ian glares at Steven to let him know that he is not to be intimidated, but at the same time wonders whether it was a wise thing to rise to his jibes. The rest of the band come into the dressing room and within minutes' walk on stage.

Moet, The Man Who Killed The Hamsters

Title of a painting by Steven Middlehurst.

It was only in 2001 that we reformed for the Witchwood gig as the Hamsters that I decided to give it a last chance. We sounded pretty good as we had a second guitarist in Nigel who could fucking play. Bob had forgotten how to play guitar at this point; I put it down to copious amounts of cannabis. We also had Damien on drums. Steve was as useless as Bob at this point not to mention, he was physically ill as well. The Hamsters sounded like a proper band once more – clearly down to Nigel and Damien. **Jon Rowlinson**

I was at the Hamsters reunion gig – watched from the very back of the venue in case Steve Middi saw me. This was the last time I saw him alive. **Steve Mardy**

The audience was a respectable 120 people and there exists a video documentation of this gig (which, unfortunately is on the side resulting in the viewer having to crane his head to see this).

Ian begins the concert by reading from a book, 'How to look after your hamster' to giggles from the audience. He describes the performance as perfunctory rather than inspired, but although there are one or two false beginnings I believe it is actually incredibly powerful. Steven still looks like a very young, attractive man; but when the camera closes up on him it is clear that his drug abuse has ravaged his face, he looks like a scary, gnarled old junkie. Jon is wearing jeans and is very much on the outskirts (no pun intended) but looks as if he is enjoying himself and even manages to make the animal sounds,. What is apparent is that, despite the tension with Steven, Ian is relating to Bobby, who attempts valiantly to play the guitar. Both Nigel and Damien really work hard and, in my opinion hold the thing together.

Ian has a goatee beard and commands the stage. He exudes confidence and charisma. However, Ian's memory of this event differs from the visual representation, owing mainly to the tension between him and Steven;

"It's ok, Steven, just calm it a little."

mouthed Ian after Steven was a bit too fast in his vocal delivery

"Fuck You! Don't tell me what to do."

came back the venomous reply

Ian would have walked off there and then but kept going until the band came to 'Cute Bobby'

"This one is by Moet….which is why no one will know it"

Sneered Steven.

Ian momentarily considered punching Steven, but decided it wasn't worth the bother and chose not to react to this jibe.

Back in the dressing room the band were having a break before the final four numbers and Steven and Ian exchanged hard glares. When the band came back on stage Steve announces/

"This cunt has been telling me to calm down… I don't want to calm down… Who likes Moet better than me? Let's have a poll! This cunt has the nerve to tell ME I can't see my own daughter"

Some of the audience laughs and, like me, believes this to be part of the act, but others look visibly uncomfortable and Ian replies

"Let's get on with it."

The later part of the show has people dancing, but unfortunately there is a young skinhead prat who is doing Nazi salutes and this image jars.

Ian wanted to leave the building but he needed to collect the band's fee. As he left the concert room he was aware that a fracas had broken out between Steven's friends, who had continued chopping up lines of cocaine, and the doormen. Things became very heated, knives brandished, more doormen were summoned from other premises. So when Ian asked for the fee from the proprietor he received not only the fee, but a torrent of abuse which resulted in the Hamsters being banned from the venue. The fee was considerably less than agreed, but Ian wanted to go and divided it up with the band.

As he gave Steven his share, he received a joyous beam and;

"That was great Mo! Thanks for everything that was the proudest day of my life."

Ian was dumbfounded but managed to blurt out;

"Ok, bye."

Ian had no intention of ever speaking to Steven again.

The Sheepdog Trials

Ian was smarting over Steven and talked this through with Bobby and Slav. Whilst it should be pointed out that both were sympathetic they clearly were not going to take sides;

"I was just glad to be on the opposite side of the stage to Steven with you in the middle"

empathised Bobby and laughed;

"Ha! Ha" I felt quite safe."

On one occasion, he had narrowly missed Steve when calling round to see Bobby;

"He was going on about how great the gig was and I told him how he mightily pissed you off"

explained Bobby and continued;

"He wanted me to tell him that he was right and you were wrong and when I didn't....he stormed off. He had a right tantrum and I thought it was funny... ..I've never seen Steve like that before"

It was true, neither Bobby nor Steven had an axe to grind with each other, but neither made the effort to stay in contact.

The brotherly love of Rock Musicianship between Jon, Nigel and Damien, continued to flourish and they were keen to progress as a band, but they wanted one thing;

"Moet, will you join us then?"

"No, no! Please No!"

"Please, please, please! Moet, we need you!"

"Oh fucking hell, go on then! But I warn you, I want my own way!"

"OK! No problem."

"We are to be called Sheepdog Trials."

"Fantastic!"

So this preposterous name bluff backfired against Moet and

"Oh fuck, here we go again......"

Moet Trials

Ian liked the lads in The Sheepdog Trials, but felt rather reluctant. However he managed to get the band a gig at the Witchwood (the owners hadn't clocked on that this band basically was the Hamsters minus Steven) as part of an all-day Punk Event headlined by 'Vice Squad'.

The band set to rehearse for two weeks beforehand and Ian made the conscious decision to remove Steven's lyrics from the newer songs and replace them with his own. He now acknowledges that this was rather petulant behaviour, but at the time he half hoped that Steven would get to hear about this.

However, Ian gained more satisfaction from the newer numbers, 'Crash and Burn' and 'Lawnmower' which, whilst deliberately dumbed down, were fresh and pleasing and showed that the band could work together. There would be more personal songs to follow, but these would do just fine for now.

The Grind The Do Do's

The Sheepdog Trials were a welcome distraction from Ian's business life which was in tatters. Only 'Mr Ed's' kept on going, but at a cost. Owing to moving into other premises, Ian had to spend one hell of a lot of money on an expensive refurbishment, not to mention a considerable increase in rent. To add insult to injury, an aircraft hangar of a supermarket had opened about 200 yards away from the premises.

Ian tried his best, sometimes only taking home around £50 in wages, but he was fighting a losing battle. His poor mother often took the brunt of Ian's moods but still remained incredibly supportive of her son. In addition, Julie was getting fed up with Ian and his moods and didn't really want to listen to him. Ian drank heavily and often woke up with the mother of all hangovers around Debbie and Shaun's. What little money he had was squandered on football matches around Europe.

On 25 June 2003, Ian's 45th Birthday, 'Mr Ed's' finally finished trading. What initially felt like a huge relief soon turned into yet another struggle, Ian was in debt to the tune of £18,000 to the Inland Revenue.

I'm Coming Out Diana Ross

Although Ian got on well with the rest of The Sheepdog Trails, he felt somewhat on the outside and then it occurred to him what was missing;

"Bobby, do you fancy becoming a member?"

The rest of the band were not exactly pleased when they were introduced to their new 'addition' but as it was Moet's band they had to do as they were told. Bobby's presence added an extra frisson of tension into the proceedings, as there was a 'history' between him and Jon in particular. But Bobby was able to compose great quirky melodies such as 'Not waving but drowning' and 'Buried Alive". Another great number, composed by Jon and Nigel was 'Porpoise' with very personal lyrics, full of pain and confusion, from Ian.

Derek Howarth was a true friend in Ian's hour of need, paying for every Manchester United fixture and sorting out the food and drink into the bargain. Ian was even taken on a four day trip to Athens for a Champions League Fixture against Panathanykos. Derek was a life raft of kindness as Ian struggled to pay his mounting debt off and applying, unsuccessfully, for jobs.

Ian finally took control of his relationship with Julie and managed to break this by having a one night stand with another woman. Although it was perfectly ok for Julie to be unfaithful to her husband, she would not tolerate Ian's infidelity. It should be noted that Ian was deliberately unfaithful to get away from Julie as he had a much more powerful and confusing urge to contend with and he wanted her out of the way in order to explore this more fully.

For years Ian found he had the occasional homosexual urge, but believed that the greater part of his sexual orientation was heterosexual and didn't really feel the need to explore this aspect of his sexuality. But this aspect of Ian's sexual orientation was becoming stronger and stronger and he needed to do something about it.

Kevin Ayres

Whilst the band was doing fine, the underlying tensions between group members meant that the experience wasn't always a barrelful of laughs at times. Still, Sheepdog Trials managed some pretty prestigious support slots such as 'Men They Couldn't Hang' and Theatre of Hate. Apparently, Kirk Brandon's face was an absolute picture as he viewed a pencil skirted Jon trying to mount the stage in his stiletto heels to the sound of much merriment from the audience. However, his expression turned into that of fury after the Sheepdog set, as it transpired that this support band had stolen some of his thunder.

Ian managed to get an acoustic set to support his schoolboy hero, Kevin Ayres. The band had to 'cough up' to buy new instruments but it was worth it. Ian decided to become an ersatz 'Noel Coward', complete with bow tie and tuxedo. However the effect was more akin to 'Jake La Motta'(as portrayed by Robert De Niro in 'Raging Bull') as Ian swore, and swore some more.

Kevin Ayres watched from the wings and proffered his opinion;

"I rather liked your performance......It was most eccentric................................. for Northerners"

Ian's reaction was to grin from ear to ear at this compliment.

Sheepdog were invited to play at the Witchwood Charity Jamboree over two nights during the Christmas period by POD, who informed Ian:

"The first night is all speed metal bands and on the second night, when you appear, it is more alternative types of bands"

"No problem."

agreed Ian, well, it sounded fun.

The Trial of Sheepdog

"What are you lot doing here? You're on tomorrow; it's the metal bands on tonight!"

Informed a rather bemused POD when Sheepdog turned up to do their set.

"Moet! You got the wrong night!"

Explained Bobby, along with collective groans from the rest of the band.

"Oh Dear."

said Ian and looked at POD who appeared to be considering something and replied

"Mmmmmmm, just so happens that the last band on tonight have pulled out....."

the sentence trails off as he appears to reconsider, but Ian jumps in

"No problem, We'll do it!"

It should be said that not all the band were happy with this snap decision made by their vocalist, but it would save having coming back the following evening again.

The band head off to "The Friendship" down the road for the next five hours. Ian entertains the band with a 'Mogodon' paced version of 'Silent Night' which is intended for set inclusion that same evening.

It would be no exaggeration to say that Sheepdog Trails were 'well refreshed' upon their return and it would, again, not be a form of artistic licence to state that the band stuck out like a sore thumb with the hordes of hairy bikers. Bobby in particular was a sticking figure in his crash helmet and high visibility jacket. You could cut the animosity radiating from the biker boys (what is it with Ian and bikers?) but Ian didn't care.

"Hey mate, is it ok if I use your amp?"

asked a cheery Nigel

"No it fuckin' ain't"!

snapped back the previous band's guitarist.

Nigel is a nice chap but this pushes him too far and an argument ensues to the sound of catcalls and boo's from the audience. Eventually, a compromise is reluctantly reached and the band begins to play.

Within fifteen seconds, two lads at the front of the stage start pushing Bobby around aggressively. Ian leaps to his defence and pours a glass of cider over one of the assailants. This doesn't exactly dampen down the fracas and Bobby is leapt upon and his attacker is trying to wrestle him to the floor, the crash helmet turned out to be a really smart move on Bobby's part and he can be viewed laughing through the visor. Ian was not so lucky, a punch is thrown at him by a gangling six footer and Ian reacts to this by hitting him around the head with the microphone. A grapple ensues and both tumble off the stage onto the audience floor. Ian takes a kick in the eye from a well-aimed motorbike boot but is rescued by security. His eyebrow is now a gaping wound and is spurting blood everywhere...

"You'll never play here again! You're banned!"

Screeches the harridan landlady of the Witchwood, just before the ambulance doors are closed. Quite frankly, my dear, Ian didn't give a damn.

Take Me Out by Franz Ferdinand

Ian looked absolutely dreadful and felt just as bad over the Christmas of 2003.

He spent the vast majority of time at home, alone (lack of finance justified this isolation) and describes himself as 'wallowing in misery'.

Fortunately, things took a turn for the better when he was invited for an interview for the position of Salesman on Manchester's Wholesale Fruit and Vegetable Market. Ian looked at himself in the mirror on the day of the interview and as he regarded his swollen and bruised face he thought;

"They'll never take me on looking like this"

But he was wrong, his reputation preceded him and he was able to start work on Monday February 02 2004. Later on in January (31st to be precise), he went to see Manchester United beat Southampton FC 3:2 with Louis Saha scoring twice on his debut. Ian had around five hours to kill before meeting Marc and Tracey Riley to watch Franz Ferdinand and The Rapture at The Academy.....so Ian took a deep breath and went into a Gay Bar to see what would happen.

Mathew was 24 but looked a great deal younger and was initially scared by Ian's appearance;

"You looked like a Gangster"

Mathew admitted later on.

Despite Mathew's reservations he listened to Ian;

"I'm sure I'm straight, but I need to try and have sex with another man. I've got to get it out of my system."

"Alright Ian, shall we go to a hotel then?"

They went to The Gardens Hotel in Piccadilly and went to bed together in a tiny room.

Ian was anxious and nervous, but this wasn't Mathews first time and he was kind and understanding:

"....he thrilled me, I was blown away by him, and it was a revelation."

Mathew gave Ian a lift to the Academy, kissed him and said

"Have a good night."

Ian went to seek out Marc and Tracey and wondered if they'd see the difference in him and 'smell the sex of another man about me'. He wanted to shout out:

"I've had sex with a man......and it was great."

But he didn't and although he watched the band, his mind was elsewhere and he felt more alive than he had done for a long, long time.

Ian went back to the hotel, but upon returning to the room it became cold and forbidding without Mathew. He sat on the bed and scribbled down some lyrics;

"I've seen out the old year and rung in the new

I'm hoisting a pink flag in tribute to you"

This became the chorus for a new song that became 'Salute'

"......every time I've ever sung it, I see Mathew's sweet smile and I thank him for showing me the secret that was locked up inside me"

Come out; come out, where ever you are The Wizard of Oz

I was surprised, more the fact of the age he was. To this day, I don't know how you can get to the age of 47 and not realise your prefer sausage to taco **Jon Rowlinson**

Ian's job, in which he is currently employed at the time of writing, has the most unsocial hours starting at 2am and often lasting until midday on occasion. During the winter it is bitterly cold and means that Ian's social life is usually confined until Saturday Evening.

However, the job pays reasonably well and Ian was able to start to pay his debts off and was able to find a place to rent. Mathew was able to share the benefits of his experience with Ian and introduced mild S&M role play into their relationship. Ian was increasingly becoming open to new experiences with Mathew, that would have been taboo a month or so before.

A few weeks after Ian met Mathew, the band played a gig and Ian came out to Bobby and Slav. Bobby wondered if it was a 'phase' that Ian was going through and commented;

"You sexually experimenting rascal!"

A week later, Ian went to The Bridgewater Hall to see a spoken word evening featuring John Cooper Clarke, Howard Devoto, Peter Shelly and Marc E Smith. Fuelled by champagne and ecstasy, Ian came out to Nigel and Damien and then informed around half the audience present at Bridgewater Hall. Everyone reacted positively, and much kissing and hugging was involved (I did ask Ian if he kissed Marc E Smith, but sadly the answer was 'no'). Ian hit Manchester's Gay Village with a few friends and they drank and danced to dawn.

"...the monkey was off my back, I was free"

The Boys in the Band

The only problem I and indeed the band had with it was that he tried to change the name of the band to some awful name that had obviously gay references. I forget what the name was now, but his second attempt was to rename the band "Pink Flamingo"

You see, the rest of the band was in it for the music, and Moet was trying to turn it into a platform for his own private agenda.
Nobody gives a flying fuck who anybody sleeps with, because what happens behind closed doors is about as private and personal as it gets, so when Ian wanted the rest

of the band to join his gay parade without even asking us to, he was met with opposition. Jon Rowlinson

"We're not a Gay band, you're misrepresenting us."
protested the heterosexual majority.

Ian could see their point, to a degree, but his long buried homosexuality had finally been given a voice and he was going to sing it loud and proud. Not to have expressed this new found part of his sexual identity would have been cowardly as he needed to explore his newly found sexual orientation in public.

POD rang up to express his sympathy at Ian being beaten up and added
"I've got you a good support with Wilco Johnson."
"That's great, whereabouts mate?!"
enthused Ian
"....at the Witchwood"
Ian burst out laughing and chuckled
"Wow! Cheers that's great....there's just the small matter of being banned."
"Don't worry about that."
reassured POD;
"She thinks that you're still the Hamsters, Sheepdog Trial aren't banned."

In the run up to the gig, Ian heard that his attacker fully intended to cause further trouble, the fact that Ian was 'now' Gay added further vitriol to his hateful cause. Whilst Ian wasn't frightened of this threat, he was concerned that, yet again, trouble had found him. It was all very destructive and draining, but Ian was determined not to bow out and concede defeat to bullies.

Wilco and Norman Watt Ray (bassist from Ian Dury's Blockheads) turned out to be very pleasant, and being non-drinkers gave Sheepdog their 'rider' after sound check. Ian was psyching himself up for the imminent confrontation. Pacing the floor in his calf length boots, resplendent in tight pink shorts and Minnie Mouse T Shirt he looked ready for battle.

The band caught the attention of the audience from the very second they came on stage and played hard. Ian flew himself around the stage in gay abandon and roared his new life out. Most of the crowd loved it, apart from a very small pocket at the back of the audience who kept hurling abuse in between songs, but even then they were shouted down by the audience majority. Finally, one of them threw a really witty, clearly audible;
"You're a big Fucking Puff!"
"By George, I think you've got it"
smirked back Ian with perfect comedic timing.

The crowd clapped and voiced their approval. Ian's would be 'tormentors' were quickly manhandled out of the venue and the band continued on towards a minor triumph.

Hangin' on the telephone Blondie

Mathew had very much become part of Ian's life, but Ian accepted that Mathew had his own life to lead and valued what time they spent together. Ian gave Mathew a birthday present of a book of Robert Mapplethorpe's photographs and Mathew was genuinely delighted.

During a meeting in July, Mathew was more emotionally needy than Ian had experienced before. He appeared to be somewhat subdued and Ian asked him what had happened. It transpired that Mathew had been raped by two 'friends' and despite his tough talk, Ian could tell that he was deeply wounded. Ian was angry and horrified, and although he offered support he knew that there was very little he could do. That evening Ian was driven by Mathew to see Television and Patti Smith;

"I've got a new phone number."

informed Mathew and Ian put this into his phone's memory; at least Ian could now contact Mathew and see if he was ok.

Whereas Television were cathartic and uplifting, Patti Smith rambled and Ian's thoughts turned to Mathew. Eventually, Patti became too much and Ian left before the end, his mind was full of Mathew's plight and this reduced him to tears on the walk home.

The next day, Ian decided to bite the bullet and give Mathew a call, but a digit was missing and there was no other way of contacting him (Ian believes that this was a mistake on his part entering the number).

Ships in the Night by Be Bop Deluxe

Ian was really very worried about Mathew and, although he conceded that they had been little more than 'Ships in the night', their relationship had been one of mutual trust and respect. It was clear that they were not going to become a couple, but Ian felt that he could at least counsel and provide a listening ear from time to time. The thought that he may never see Mathew again was very painful and despite the fact that Ian kept adding random digits to the incomplete mobile number he was unable to reach him. The concern and affection that Ian felt for Mathew, even drove him to drive around Preston, where he knew Mathew lived, on the faint off-chance he would spot him.

By October, Ian became more or less resolved to his loss and decided it was time to enter the fray of The Gay Scene. He needed to go outside the previous comfort zone of occasional, private meetings. It so happened that Ian had travelled to France, with his 'Guardian Angel' – Steve Wright, to watch Manchester

United in Lyon. After a festival of drunken misbehaviour with bouts of violent confrontational behaviour Ian realised that he needed to sort himself out in two respects. Firstly, he needed to stop drinking for two months and secondly, and more importantly during his post-match solo sojourn in Nice, he would need to find a nice man to have sex with in order to move on and learn some lessons in life.

'My life is full of sex, sex, sex'   XXX Sicknurse

Ian drove into Nice by himself, fully armed with information on the local Gay scene (kindly downloaded by Steve Wright) and ready to hit the town to 'explore both the lay of the land and mind and body'.

It was a sober and very self-conscious Ian that went to the Gay bars and he felt too shy to initiate contact (and of course there was the language barrier to contend with). So he decided to experiment with universal body language and went to a local 'Cruising' Spot (which, for the very innocent amongst you, generally tends to be an open air area, where men initiate contact in a variety of ways in order to have sex). As Ian was a virgin, in this respect, he wasn't sure of the etiquette and this proved a dismal end to a dismal first night.

The next afternoon, he plucked up enough courage to go to the local Gay Sex Club, Club 51. When Ian paid this club a visit there was somewhat of a slack period; three men, including himself, were the total clientele. But what was lacking in numbers was soon made up for in action as these kind gentlemen allowed Ian to join in as one. Ian describes the experience as 'charged with electricity, and unlocking secrets locked in my subconsciouses. He found this experience highly liberating and went out to have some lunch, and then came back to Club 21 in order to make up for lost time and to catch up on wasted years. One has to marvel at his stamina, dear reader.......

John Gill

This stamina carried on when he arrived home, or should that be homo? He thoroughly enjoyed his new found promiscuity and owing to finally earning some good money was able to start paying his debts off. Sheepdog Trials were becoming a tight band, but subtle ageism was working against them as they found it very hard to get gigs at the right places.

One day in November, Ian was toying around with his phone and a dial tone suddenly came in to play;

"Hiya, Mathew here."

Ian was overjoyed to hear his voice again, but this joy soon turned into concern for his young friend. His fears had been well founded and owing to the rape trauma Mathew had become so depressed and paranoid that he had had to be sectioned under the Mental Health Act They were able to meet up again and although it transpired that the sexual element of their relationship fizzled out, the mutual trust and respect blossomed into a true and close platonic friendship.

"Ian, its Eddie Fenn."

"Oh, aye, what's up mate?"

"Bad news, John Gill is seriously ill in hospital."

It had been some time since Ian had seen Eddie and John, but they still remained very dear to him and Ian rang John at the hospital;

"Is there any books, or anything I can bring for you?"

"No."

John's tired voice came over the receiver;

"Thanks but I'm too tired for books or visitors."

That reply really bought the gravitas of the situation home to Ian, John had always thirsted for knowledge and somehow Ian had a feeling that things were very, very serious.

His feeling was proved to be correct, when Eddie rang him within 48 hours to let him know that John had died.

Ian attended John's humanistic funeral in Derby. The funeral was like John, very dignified and sincere. John's family were touched by the huge attendance and took pains to ensure that everyone was welcomed. Ian was moved by the numerous tributes that were paid to this kind, gentle and unassuming man. In death, as in life, Ian was terribly impressed by everything about John and remembers him as a wonderful man.

Computer Dating; Not So Frustrating

In March 2005 Ian finally managed to move out of his mother's house into a one bedroom one in Ashton Under Lyne: at last a place he could call his own.

Zac Blinston (son of Nigel) was a drama student at the Royal Scottish Academy. Although he was only 19 became fast friends with Ian. They shared a common empathy and supported each other's artistic endeavours. However it was difficult to tell who was leading who astray as they had the same wild, hedonistic streak. Side by side they were loud, brash and outlandish. With the benefit of hindsight Ian compares this friendship to 'a car crash waiting to happen' with weekend bouts of excessive alcohol and drug consumption around Ian's base.

Mathew visited Ian's new flat and gave him a computer. After a brief tutorial, he fixed Ian up with a profile on 'Gaydar', which is a networking site for men seeking sex with others.

"Have fun."

winked Mathew before he headed off.

Ian's sex life was revolutionised by on-line dating and it is true to say that all manners of men paid this 'Flying Nun' a flying visit.

The Band on the Wall Memorial Concert for John Gill

In a lot of respects Ian's life was going really well but working with the band was becoming somewhat of a battleground;

"Bobby's got to go."

Ian would be the first to admit that Bobby was nowhere as proficient as he had been as a guitarist around two decades ago

"He's hopeless Moet."

But Bobby's place within the band was non-negotiable: not only was he Ian's closest friend, but his cack-handedness kept the 'Rockist' element at bay and also he still had something of a gift for melody for writing a great song, so;

"I wouldn't betray Bobby by sacking him. It's quite simple, if he goes, I go."

A memorial concert was being planned for John Gill by Eddie Fenn at the legendary Band on the wall in May 2005. John's memory was synonymous with this venue and various artists were approached who had worked with this great man. One such band was The Mekons and they were prepared to travel from the USA to perform at this tribute concert. A Stepbrothers set, with Eddie Fenn had been mooted, but in the end, it was decided that Sheepdog Trials perform there instead.

Jon's Trials in Sheepdog

"Moet tonight will be the last time I play with Sheepdog."

announced Jon just before the sound check at the Band on the Wall;

"Why?"

asked Ian, although he had strong suspicions

"I can't play with Bob anymore."

replied Jon

"Ok then, we'll make it a good one tonight then."

decided Ian who wasn't really too bothered, Jon was a grown tranny who could make his own decisions after all. Besides there were several people who Ian hadn't seen for ages and it would be good to catch up with them. Everyone had offered their services willingly as they were thankful for the help John had given them

John was present, in a pretty macabre way, as an urn containing his ashes was placed on an onstage piano throughout this tribute.

Ian introduced John's nephew who made his stage debut and spent much of his time laughing and joking with his old mates, The Mekons.

Sheepdog went down really, really well and played to an enthusiastic audience. Ian raised a glass in tribute to John and played a horrific tin whistle solo during 'Drowning'. All too soon it was over and Jon was given a hug and was wished well by Ian.

"You look such an odd bunch."
smiled Sarah the bass player from The Mekons
"Eh?"
Ian wasn't sure what she meant.
"In a good way I mean! You grabbed the audience's attention the very second you went on stage."
clarified Sarah and Jon Langford upon overhearing this observation butted in;
"Go to America!"
he raved;
"They'll never get you over here. In the States they'd lap you up!"
"Yeah, well we're not in a position to put it to the test just yet!"
laughed Ian, who secretly agreed with what Jon Langford had just said.

Ian got roaring drunk and 'danced like a maniac' to The Mekons. He remembers waking up at home, not knowing how he had got there but when he next met Nigel he was brought up to date on what had happened between Bobby and Jon;

"It wasn't pretty. It was a right bloodletting with Bobby really savaging Jon to the extent that I could see the tears in Jon's eyes. It was nasty, he went too far."

Ian was genuinely sorry to hear this but he had no intention of getting involved, it was time to move on.

Sheepdog turn into Sicknurse

"Moet, Damien and I are going to rehearse with Jon just to see what happens."
informed Nigel.
"OK, Yeah Good."
replied Ian ambivalently.
Next week, at the rehearsal, Ian made small talk by enquiring how they had faired with Jon;
"It wasn't any good.....it didn't have that edge that you bring to it."
admitted Nigel.

A new bass player, Chris Dutton, had been recruited after he had listened to a cd by Sheepdog Trials. Now, on first glance Chris appears quite normal, but like the rest of the band, he is a 'man living on the edges of lunacy'. Whenever Chris passes a historic monument he literally likes to leave his own mark on this in the form of ejaculated sperm. This Ian could live with, but was rather dubious about Chris's taste in music. He was lucky to remain with the band when he owned up to liking The Libertines and New Order, which is basically 'classic rock' according to the gospel of Moet. When Chris joined, the band re-named themselves 'Sicknurse' after a contemporary of Damien's (a name which Ian has never liked)

Bobby came up with a great riff during rehearsals and Ian provided the lyrics to the song that became known as 'Jon Joanne', which lamented Jon's passing but also alludes to the fact that he can take himself a mite too seriously and should liven up every now and then. Jon hated it when Ian first sang this to him, but it remains part of the Sicknurse set to this very day.

Another new song was about 'The Wickedest Man in the World' all about the Satanist Alistair Crowley. Ian was especially pleased as he managed to insert his two favourite comedy lines in

"Infamy, infamy...they've all got it in for me."

"He's not the Messiah; he's a very naughty boy!"

The band recorded a studio session in Eddie Fenwick's shed and although Ian claims it is chock full of mistakes, it sounds very powerful and contains a terrific version of 'Drowning'. My favourite bit is when Ian can be heard offering grapes.....

Jon left Sheepdog and joined Sicknurse

"I'm re-joining the band."

informed Jon, rather firmly, on the phone to Ian.

"Hmm.."

demurred Ian;

"I've no objections to you coming back but I'll have to ask the others and, of course, we have a bass player so you can't do that....."

"I'm not asking, I'm TELLING you I'm coming back!"

interrupted an uncharacteristically forceful Jon.

If it had been anyone else, Ian would have told them where to go, but he had been considering adding keyboard to the band for some time and here was the perfect opportunity. However, at the evening rehearsal, oddly enough, only Bobby agreed with this addition, but Ian knew that he would get his way in the end and, anyway, it wouldn't do any harm to let Jon sweat for a while.

In order to show Jon there were no hard feelings; Ian joined him in an evening out at the Manchester Goth Club, Satan's Hollow, to go and see Jayne County and finally heard why Jon had left the band.

"We are all sick of Bobby, so if I left first and was followed by Nigel and Damien, we thought you would join us.

"Trouble with that is that you all should have known that I wasn't going to desert Bobby""

"Yeah they decided to remain with you as you are much more fun, but this plan backfired and I found myself out of the group."

Ian found this 'Machiavellian' plot rather amusing and told Jon to buy some keyboards. Of course news of this failed 'uprising' got back to Bobby who, unlike Ian, was upset and angry.

The Football Thoughts of Chairman Mo

"Anyone who thinks football is anything to do with football, knows nothing about football" **Under The Broad Walk (Football Fanzine)**

Ian has always taken his football dead seriously. He understood that it was the camaraderie and passion that mattered more than any results or trophies attained by Manchester United. But football was slowly but surely taking a turn for the worse and was becoming owned by business and commercialism. What was once a common shared experience was becoming hype and brand names. Football supporters were being told what to experience and become part of the conglomerate; all this was against Ian's socialist principals. Kick off times were held later and later, to meet the demands of fee paying satellite viewers and it became more and more apparent that the clubs were in it 'for the money'.

Ian was disgusted by what 'the beautiful game' was degenerating into and felt strongly enough to write protest letters to the system that was blatantly cheating the fans (read 'Customers'), there was truly no point in asking, he got no reply. What was worse was that Manchester United had attracted an unsavoury faction of racist, homophobic bigots who were revelling in the glory of 'their' club. They frequently chanted vile abuse in the hope of gaining notoriety. All Ian received was lip service to his demands that his club do something about these 'Fan's'

The last straw for Ian occurred when the likes of Roman Abromovitch came along and created an even wider schism between football clubs and their fans, creating a commercial industry that was more concerned with using football players as a form of share on their 'stock market'. More salt was rubbed into Ian's wound when Manchester United's very own drug cheat, Rio Ferdinand, demanded that his wage of £80,000 per week be increased to stay with the club - that was obscene.

But the event that finally broke Ian was when an American businessman purchased Manchester United and immediately inflated ticket prices. What had been build up by a loyal working class backbone had now deteriorated into a Capitalist industry. As far as Ian was concerned, his club had now been taken away from him and divorce was on the cards. Ian is one of those rare people who does exactly what he says and time was up and the whistle was blown on his love affair with Manchester United.

Punk Football

Over the years I used to see Moet on the Red Issue/United We Stand unofficial coaches to Manchester United aways matches (as I was a home & away fan of the mighty reds like Moet) & used to think wow there's the singer of the Hamsters &

occasionally plucked up the courage to speak to him depending on how many Stella I had supped! **Stephen Doyle**

Now, Ian was through with Manchester United but he was far from through with football. He preferred to go and watch the non-league Hyde United or go to see the fan owned Barcelona every once in a while. Attending these matches allowed him to at least watch non-commercial football, but when he heard that there was a move to form a breakaway 'Team F C United of Manchester', one that was not under the control of Glazer, he immediately came up with a cheque to donate to find a football ground, with players and management, that would be home to this 'unofficial team'. Against all the odds, enough disenchanted supporters were able to raise enough funds in a mere six weeks to make this dream a reality.

Ian and thousands of fellow supporters were at the debut match in the Lancashire Town of Leigh. This really was invigorating and the T Shirts and Badges proudly stated;

"Our Club, our rules."

A form of 'Punk Football' had been created and Ian loved the spirit of anarchy and freedom but there was a price to pay for this. When Ian identified as Gay, his fellow Manchester United Supporters accepted him for the person he is, but when he became a part of 'FC United of Manchester', he was shunned by all with the exception of Derek Howarth.

Not that this really mattered, as he soon found new friends amongst his fellow 'FC' supporters. Tony Buckly and Paul Aspin became fast friends as did one former acquaintance, Rod Armstrong. Another person from Ian's distant past (Graham Parker and the Rumour gig, 1974), Vinnie Thompson recognised him and soon Ian was a guest at Vinnie's house with good food and heated debate.

The club's chairman, Andy Walsh, had the honourable distinction of being the first person to be jailed for refusing to pay his poll tax, was now somewhat more of a 'conventional' character who was always friendly and approachable.

Ian was approached by another fellow supporter, Stephen Doyle, and was greeted with a big bear hug and exclaimed;

"Moet! From the Hamsters! I loved that band!"

Ian's enthusiasm and excitement was revived and he describes himself as '.... Falling back in love with the working class ballet'.

Do your best and fuck the rest

John Pennington was a highly respected soundman who was a pupil of the legendary Martin Hannet. He worked with such luminaries as Moby and was also the drummer in 'Dark Matter' which just happened to be a band Nigel had played in. Through this connection it was agreed for Sicknurse to go into a studio to do some serious recording with John in the spring of 2006.

It was a long hard session and Damien, although he worked really hard, got fed up with repeating his parts time and time again. John was not too happy with Bobby, who managed to spill red wine over the cream studio furnishings.... The only person who escaped having to constantly re-record their parts was Ian, owing to a nasty case of laryngitis. Ian ended up singing 'Helsinki', 'Sheepnesting', 'Flip Your Wig', 'Salute' and 'Club Kids' each in one take. Ian was pleasantly surprised by his strong vocal performance.

Ian remains ambivalent about the mixing process to this very day and believes that 'too many cooks spoil the broth' and didn't sit in on the engineering session. However, when he finally heard the finished results he was amazed at the power and cohesion of the tracks, which was a direct contrast to any previous, rather ramshackle work. Copies of the session were pressed as cd's and sent out to record companies.

It seemed like the same old story; no reply was forthcoming from any label until Ian got an excited phone call from Andrew Perry who was a musical writer from Mojo;

"I really love your cd and am knocked out by the sheer quality and energy of your songs!"

This was nice, but Ian had a feeling about what was going to follow;

"It is such a shame you weren't discovered decades ago as, unfortunately, the world of music is for the young"

Ian mused on this call and decided;

"Fuck it the most important thing is to write and perform to a standard I can be proud of. I will continue to do my best and fuck the rest."

One Cock or Two?

Ian wanted the band to break outside the conventional rock venues, which he considered were all very soulless and rather dull. His chance finally came in the form of 'Simmi' (an old Hamsters fan from the Mayflower days) who was a keen supporter and staunch champion of Sicknurse. Simmi was a great friend of the band, even to the extent of putting in some money to help out with the cost of T-Shirts and recording costs.

With the help of Simmi, who had booked a city cellar bar called 'Joshua Brooks' and hired a DJ, the band played a reasonable set but 'lacked oomph'. On a night out, in Manchester's Gay quarters, Canal Street, Ian was hit by an idea of genius proportions. - the Gay Community needed was something a little different, a little more outside the box....Sicknurse!! Ian spoke to Simmi who managed to book a room above Thompson's Arms (where the Bears from Belle Vue had played twenty years earlier), which still earnt the reputation of being one of the busiest Gay Bars in the North.

Another change Ian wanted to make was the band's name, which irritated him. Sat in a pub before an FC United Game, Ian noticed a fantastic, exotic bird in a cage....immediately the name came to him and he exclaimed out loud;

"COCKATOO!!!"

The rest of his would-be feathered band mates were not so keen on this change of name but 'allowed' Ian to use this name to christen the forthcoming evening as taking place at 'The Cockatoo Club'. Bobby took some rather fetching photos of a naked, axe wielding Moet for publicity purposes. Jon Joanne looked at them with disapproval and turned to Ian and asked;

"What if children see them?"

"I couldn't give a fuck."

was the defiant reply.

But at the end of the day a rather bland guitar motif was used to advertise the coming of Sicknurse.

Back in a closet

The first night at the Cockatoo Sicknurse played a rather perfunctory set to around an audience of 50. Even the addition of a DJ set from Steve Toon (another face from the distant past) and Ian failed to make any impact; it was a lot of hard work for very little return. To rub salt into the wounds, the club downstairs was overflowing. Ian mused on what could have resulted in such a disappointing turn out and wondered if the choice of venue had kept the straight followers away?

The second night, which followed the next month, wasn't much better. Sicknurse were unable to play as Damien was on holiday and a replacement drummer had not been found. Ian listed the services of a band he really liked called Dr Mandrake and he provided the DJ set. Again there was a sparse turn out, which had Ian wondering if they should continue booking this venue as they had yet to even break even.

The third (and final) evening was a complete contrast. Ian went out for a quiet drink and when he returned he found that the upstairs dancehall was heaving with people who were having a really good time.

"What's gone right?"

exclaimed an astonished Ian as the place was not only full of friends but there was a large Gay contingent also present.

The band took to the stage to an eager and responsive crowd and buzzed off the enthusiasm of the audience. The only exception was Jon, who resented being 'relegated' to keyboards when he would have much preferred to play bass. Also, despite being an open minded kinda tranny, he resented the Gay direction that Ian appeared to be taking the band.

Ian couldn't have cared less about Jon, he was having a ball and suddenly announced;

"We are now going to play 'I can't get no Satisfaction'!"

Now, the bands had never played this song before but were perfectly prepared to give it ago, but Jon hissed;

"Can't we fucking play songs we fucking know??"

Ian wheeled around and felt his hand form the shape of a fist and history was in danger of repeating itself, but Ian merely snapped back;

"Just fucking play it you cunt!"

Although the set had gone down really well and the audience were appreciative, Ian was now in a foul mood. As he got a drink from the bar he was approached by John Pennington who offered his congratulations and proposed some live recording;

"We've got to try and capture that magic."

"It will be without that cunt on the keyboards."

hissy fitted Ian in reply. It was to take quite some considerable time before he was able to look on Jon's presence with anything other than anger but for now there was another distraction.

"You did really well mate."

congratulated an attractive dark haired boy who stroked Ian's chest as he said so.

Ian is not slow in coming forward and, smiling, took the lad by the hand upstairs to a tiny room (used to store cleaning equipment) and a mutual bout of sexual release followed.

The band packed up their gear but Ian stayed to the end to burn off his negative energy. When he woke up, late the next day, he not only had a massive hanger but also a nasty case of gonorrhoea too.

"Pull Down Your Pants" Sicknurse

Sicknurse gained a reputation as a fun band leaving a trail of destruction and chaos behind them. What an earth the organiser of an 'art event' thought they were up to by inviting the band to this rather pretentious 'Beardy Happening'.

Sicknurse managed to single handedly demolish the gentle folk vibe with their loud and raucous noise. They went over time and had to be ejected by Julia, a rather buxom actress friend, and Ian pretended to throw a real strop by destroying a child's plastic guitar to loud applause from the audience.

In Bolton, Sicknurse played with a young, Swiss Ska band who were on a 'World Tour' and much mutual appreciation was swapped between both groups. However, Ian and the bass player got into a rather passionate embrace which unfortunately ended when Stephan expressed his admiration for Pink Floyd and.....Dire Straits. He promptly pulled the young offenders trousers down, pulled him across his knees and delivered a good spanking in full view of the astonished Saturday Night Crowd. Ian was immediately ejected from the premises.

John Pennington reiterated his wish to capture the live power of Sicknurse and the band rehearsed in a Cotton Mill in Mossley, the rehearsal space was owned by one Jim McGuire, an energetic drummer, of whom you will hear of later on. Ian had mixed feelings about this venture and would have preferred to have gone into a studio but bowed to the majority's wishes. The plan was to record the session in the Cotton Mill, complete with mobile rig and invited audience.

A Sicknurse Induced Birth Technique....

John Pennington had spent most of the previous evening setting up the recording and curled up to get some sleep, on a sofa, in the small hours. The band arrived around mid-morning to set their equipment up and sound check recording levels. Everyone had arrived with best intentions but technical problems and being a very hot July day meant that everyone was sagging under the effort.

Ian decided to have a drink, as he wasn't really needed, and had another drink and another. The band were sweltering in the hot sweaty environment and felt as if they were imprisoned, Eventually, at around 09.30 the tired, deflated and drunken band hit the stage in front of the invited audience and it transpired that Jon and Bobby's parts could not be recorded owing to further technical glitches. Ian describes their performance as 'awful' and decided to covert around the stage attired only in the briefest of red briefs. The very sight of seeing Ian jumping up and down gave cause to a heavily pregnant lady to break her waters and give birth later that same day. The band was joined on stage by Zak, pissed out of his head, who hollered gibberish into the microphones. By then no one really cared to stop him.

After the travesty was over, there was talk about the tracks as forming some sort of basis, but Ian knew that the day had been a huge, expensive and wasteful folly. Drunk as a skunk, he headed into Manchester to 'fuck the pain away'.

Too Much, Too Soon The Debut LP from The New York Dolls

Some of Ian's circle thought that he was a genuinely entertaining spectacle whose life was dominated by a prodigious lust for sex, drugs and alcohol. He was hanging out with a much younger crowd. However, Ian's older friends were openly and genuinely concerned for his mental and physical well-being, so much so they took him home before he had 'too much of a good thing'.

Jon and Chris were now in the position of getting gigs for Sicknurse, and some of these outings took place in desperate places with abysmal bands to play alongside. One gig that Ian had no hesitation in accepting was a Fortieth Birthday Bash for Dave, who had been a fan since the days of the Hamsters. Dave had developed into a chronic alcoholic with cirrhosis of the liver, if ever Ian needed a wakeup call.....

Sicknurse performed for Dave at Hyde Golf Club and regular patrons mixed with the party going revellers. Instead of a swift half after the eighteenth, they were treated to a display of overtly lewd homosexuality from Ian and an aural assault upon their hearing aids by the band. Ian loved this gig and was really, really pleased that Dave did too. When the gig ended Ian got a massive hug from Dave and Ian thought he caught a glimpse of the teenager who he knew all those years ago; six months later Dave was dead.

As the night drew to a close a drunk and sweaty Ian spied a membership form at the bar and a mischievous notion entered his head;

"Can I have a membership form?"

he enquired after beckoning to the bar steward;

"Fuck Off.""

was the emphatic retort.

(The best part of breaking up is when we're) Making Up – Ronni Griffith

"What shall I go and do now?"

Thought Ian as he found himself driving through Didsbury without a plan;

"I could go and see Robert Middlehurst, he's around here somewhere....Na, I know I could go for some heavy action at Heat Sauna in Chorlton....."

and then, a thought came from nowhere;

"I'll go and see Steven...it's been long enough."

Soon Ian was parked outside Steven's house in Chorlton and the heavy army surplus camouflage draping at the windows gave no indication whether Steve was even in. Ian knew better and rapped at the door:

Silence

Ian rapped again, a bit louder

"Who is it?"
enquired Steven's voice with a characteristic twinge of defiance;
"It's me.....open up!"
replied Ian, not really needing to say who 'me' was.
The door flew open and Steven grinned;
"Mo!"
and held him in a warm embrace.
They went inside and sat down; Ian had something to tell Steve;
"Well, I suppose the big news you've missed is....."
Ian paused for drama queen effect;
"I've stumbled across my true sexuality....I'm Gay Steve!"
"You Bastard!!!"
Steven beamed and continued;
"I always wanted to be the GAY one"
He shook his head and considered aloud;
"Always wanted to be Black.....and Gay!

After laughing at this last remark, Steven hugged Ian again and both set to chatting.

It was blissful to be in each other's company after so long and as happy as Steven was, Ian could tell that he looked visibly unwell and wanted to know why;

"My liver's fucked, Mo. I'm going to die pretty soon."

This was said without self-pity or histrionics and Ian knew that Steve was really telling the truth this time. It hurt Ian to hear this but it was no shock and Ian asked about what type of treatment Steven was receiving. Steven replied with honesty but was more interested to show Ian his most recent paintings.

Whereas Steven's previous artwork was all syringes and crucifixes, there was a certain playfulness to his current work depicted in nature, leaves and sunshine, this revealing a much less tortured soul.

Steven spoke with pride at his daughter, Chira's, achievements at Sheffield University and revealed that Ruth, his partner, had managed to sort herself out and had a responsible job at the Imperial War Museum at Trafford Park.

Ian gave him a copy of the Sicknurse cd and received a 'Here Come the Warm Jet's' poster from Steven in return. Steve walked Ian to his car and as they were about to part, he hugged him and kissed him full on the lips and insisted;

"Take good care Mo. Make sure I see you soon, love you."

Each time, Ian and Steven parted in future occasions; Steven repeated the hug, kiss and sincere farewell every time.

Ian was saddened by the suicide of Tony Ogden (lead singer in World of Twist), who had been blighted by the curse of depression. Ian called on Steven, unaware that it was the day of Tony's funeral and agreed to come to Tony's funeral, even though he didn't know Tony that well and felt slightly awkward. However, on the way to the funeral Steven changed his mind about going and asked;

"I'd love to see your flat, can we go there instead?"

"Yeah, I've been meaning to invite you round, yes, why not?"

Steve's agitation lifted like a cloud when Ian agreed to his change of plans and immediately started to enthuse about the Sicknurse cd;

"I'm really proud of you, Mo! I'm glad that one of us is still going on."

Ian smiled in reply, as he concentrated on the road;

"You'll have to do it for both of us now"

and with a conspiratorial grin added;

"I've told that jumped up playwright, John West that I drummed on the Sicknurse cd!"

Ian laughed and replied

"Ah the one who wrote 48 hours about John Cooper Clark?"

"Yeah, it was a big success at the Edinburgh Festival you know?"

"'Course I know! Ok I won't blow your cover if I bump into him!"

"Well, he's got such a lot going on; I wanted him to think that I had a few cards up my sleeve…"

Ian was secretly pleased at this fabrication and rather flattered that Steven deemed Sicknurse worthy of his 'participation'.

But there was one thing that Steven didn't like about the band.

"I must say Sicknurse is an awful name…..ugggg SICKNURSE!"

spat Steven with contempt.

"I don't like it myself, Steve."

admitted Ian.

"Well, as a present I'll give you this name…..Demons in Bed???"

offered Steven, scanning Ian's face for approval

"I fuckin' love it!"

was Ian's reaction.

Ian did try to get the band to change their name, but the band dug their high heels in. However, Ian did manage to get Steve's suggestion on the Sicknurse Myspace site in some guise and often introduced the band as 'Demons in Bed'.

When they got back to the flat both got roaring drunk (little did they know it but this would be their last drinking session together), played music and danced around the room. Ian thought it would be a good addition to put some Gay Porn on whilst they danced around the room and can still remember the look on Steven's face, as he kept turning round, in amazement whilst still dancing. The atmosphere was like a child's birthday party as they feasted on ice cream and cakes. It was as if Steven and Ian had gone back thirty years to the day when Steven demanded that Ian be HIS friend, they talked as they had done when their friendship was first forged.

As an apt tribute to Tony Ogden, Ian played 'Sons of The Stage' by The World of Twist, and they saluted Tony. This was a bit too much for Steven who suddenly wanted to go home but as he was getting his coat on he chirped;

"This Gay Thing has given you a lease of life."

"No, you're not wrong there, mate."

agreed Ian;

"You're.....Young again and I'm getting old."

Steven was to repeat this phrase time and time again, he knew that his oldest friend's life had changed for the better and understood the thirst for adventure and experience. Steven was genuinely delighted for Ian and Ian was grateful for his understanding and approval. There was a lot of love between them again.

There's a New Guitar in Town

"Moet, I've had enough of all this humping around with speakers and amplifiers."

"Yeah, know what you mean."

"No, I don't think you do, I'm leaving the band."

clarified Bobby.

So Bobby quietly left the band in early 2007 and whilst Ian was genuinely sorry to see him go there was the consideration that he felt that the band needed 'freshening up and that change was nothing to fear'.

Ian took it upon himself to recruit Simon Benson, a young friend of Chris's on second guitar. Although he had a penchant for hard rock music; he also loved Captain Beefheart and Frank Zappa which meant he passed Ian's litmus test.

The rest of the band weren't exactly thrilled when young Simon turned up for rehearsal as they hadn't been consulted and the sight of this young chap with his flowing golden locks was a bit of a shock for them. There were murmurs....

"Listen up lads. I've bought Simon in to add some sonic enhancement and I am not going back on this."

"Well, you could have asked us."

pouted Jon

"You wanted Bobby to go and you got what you wanted."

"Yes, but I've got nothing against this lad but you can't just go ahead without asking us"

replied Nigel.

"Well that's a good start, Simon is an ace guitarist and I am not going back on this decision."

The band decided to 'audition' Simon, although Ian made it clear that he was already in the band. It transpired that Ian was absolutely correct to install Simon in on guitar as the rest of the band readily agreed that whilst it would have been nice to have been consulted, he certainly was a top notch musician and added to the sound considerably.

Simon's confident guitar playing filled in what had been embarrassing gaps in the live sound of Sicknurse and Ian liked to see jaws dropping in the audience at the transformation that had taken place in the band.

Upon hearing Simon play live for the first time, Bobby came over and offered;
"You've not quite got it..."
he deadpanned;
"Shall I show you how to play it?"

Most of the Sicknurse fan base felt that Simon was a step forward, although one or two mithered that the sound was teetering on over-indulgence. What mattered was that Ian liked it and as he puts it;
"Fuck the rest".

The Cover Band from Hell – Simon, Moet, Chris and Nigel

Now Ian should have been quite content, he had a band again that was gaining recognition and notoriety. But, no dear reader, you should know Ian well enough by now....

Ian describes himself as isolating himself from the rest of his band mates and getting rather 'intense and strange'. Maybe he was pouring too much of himself into his performance, which certainly gave great entertainment value, but with hindsight he wonders if he should have held back. Certainly, every song was given greater and greater intensity as he immersed himself emotionally to give his truth to the world. He now admits that every performance was draining and he was spiritually and physically exhausted for several days afterwards.

Ian and Zac had become mutually very close during this period and they were able to help each other out. Ian was a form of mentor to Zac as he offered encouragement, cinema trips and books to help him in his studies. Zac in return was able to offer a listening ear and this 'odd couple' needed each other's friendship.

It was taking Ian a long time to enjoy himself on stage again but the fates conspired against him in order to help him from taking himself too seriously as an artist and performer.

Only six people turned up for a gig in Bolton and there was a 'no show' from Chris and Damian, but no matter the band were determined to give the audience a good time. So much so that a buxom girl decided to leap up on stage and join the band in a lewd dance. The 'Lad's' didn't take much encouragement to join in with her and acts of sexual intercourse were simulated. Eventually, this became more than a joke for her partner who, red faced, dragged her offstage and out of the venue. The band was rewarded by loud cheers and applause from the remaining four members of the diminished audience.

Sicknurse were invited to be part of the entertainment to at FC United's final game of season in which they stood to gain promotion to the Unibond League. The jubilant crowd was excited to find Sicknurse on a flat bedded truck playing their version of 'Anarchy in the UK' (which with the amended lyrics was the FC United anthem):

"I am an FC Fan.
I am Mancunian.
I know what I want and know how to get it
I want to destroy Glazer and Sky
'Cos I want to be at FC"

It was sheer magic to play to such an exhilarated crowd of thousands and this lifted Ian's spirits.

The band were to play at Nigel's daughter's eighteenth birthday, just before the set Ian announced from the stage;

"We are going to be playing a set of cover versions, some of which we have never played before!"

The lads merely shook their heads and decided to get on with:

20th Century Boy by T-Rex
I fought the law by Bobby Fuller
You can't do that by The Beatles
I heard it through the grapevine by Marvin Gaye
Tracks of my tears by Smokey Robinson
1977 by The Clash
and of course;
I can't get no satisfaction by The Rolling Stones.

This fun resulted in Ian wearing a smile on the way home that night.

But all was not well within the ranks of Sicknurse and Ian made the conscious decision not to attend rehearsals as he regarded them as a waste of time. Any new material was written around Ian's flat. As a result, although the band was still fiery on stage the creative process had more or less ground to a halt and there was collective disgruntlement.

When do I get to sing 'my way' Sparks

Ian was becoming quite a regular visitor to Steve's abode and they normally went out for a couple of drinks, being all that Steven's liver could take, but usually they would have a coffee in Chorlton.

"So this Policeman comes in, I pinch his bottom and asked him if he was the stripper gram!"

Steven doubled up with laughter at Ian's latest revelation and, spluttering begged;

"Ha! Stop....Ha! Ha! You're trying to kill me..... with ha, laugher Mo!"

Sparks were in the process of having a rather successful tour and together with Bobby and Chiara, Ian and Steven went to see these legends at The Lowery Ian remembers that Steve danced the limbo to 'Amateur Hour'.

Ian was invited to go to see Devo at The Hammersmith Apollo by Steve, but as he was otherwise engaged, Chiara went with him instead and had a great time. Steven bought a Devo T Shirt as a consolation and presented this to a delighted Ian.

Ian took Zac along to meet Steven and was struck by the similarities in character traits.

"Typical Actor!"

remarked Steven of Zac;

"Talks too much!"

Ian knew this was a sign that Steven approved of Zac.

Ian persuaded Bobby and Slav to accompany him to the Supersonic Festival, headlined by Psychic TV, at Birmingham's Custard Factory. Ian overdid the intake of recreational drugs and couldn't work out why the music had suddenly stopped;

"What's going on?"

asked a confused Ian

"There is a terrorist alert; we need to get out quick."

ordered Bobby as he took control and managed to get the party out of the building.

The situation seemed surreal to Ian as they made their way out of the Police cordon towards the safety of their hotel. Surrealism turned to amusement in Ian's drugged state and he giggled at the 'absurdity' of what was taking place. But when he started 'coming down', this amusement soon turned to terror.

Life Begins at 50 June 2007

Ian believed that travel certainly broadened his horizons and went to Gambia where he had befriended the Jammeh Family. Although they were not rich people they took Ian into their own home where they prepared delicious meals for him. These friendly people, with their simple existence gave him more than Chicken Yassa for thought. Their serious dignity in living with poverty lead him to feel guilt about the disposable, wasteful Western Society and although he literally gave what he had to the country, he is acutely aware that it is the infrastructure of the country that needs to be overhauled rather than existing on hand-out's. Ian carried this guilt around for months after his visit.

The Peter Pan of Punk was not looking forward to being half a century old and decided to have a 'quiet drink' with a few friends at 'The Peveril of The Peak'. Where Ian ever got the notion that it would be quiet is a mystery as eventually around 80 friends turned up to wish him a Happy Birthday. It was a strange mix of people, yet miraculously every one appeared to get on and even Steven not only behaved, but enjoyed himself. This could be due to the low intake of alcohol (he just couldn't drink like he used to) and the fact that he was 'holding court'.

"It was great to be there, Mo!"

Beamed Steven, when Ian made sure he was able to hail a cab home safely.

Ian decided to pay Mark Reeder (ex-Frantic Elevator) a visit in Berlin, as an extended part of his Fiftieth Birthday celebrations. Mark specialises in Techno music and is a much respected figure of this particular genre. Ian's visit managed to coincide with a Gay Pride Festival and was greeted by Mark with a bag of hash cookies and a bike to explore the sites. It was a grand day which culminated in a laser display at Club Trezor, which was housed in an old power station. Ian enjoyed the non-threatening liberal atmosphere of Berlin and he felt safe to explore the joys of The Berlin Gay Scene.

A more sombre visit was paid to the concentration camp at Sachenhousen; this experience moved Ian to tears as he read the testimonials of the survivors. Furthermore, this reinforced his hatred for any extreme right movement.

Upon his return to Manchester, Ian describes himself as having a 'magical day' in which he met Jonny from St Helens; after an afternoon of bliss at Ian's flat they went out for a drink at a Gay Bar down Canal Street. This was Jonny's first time in a Gay Bar and he exclaimed;

"I understand the term 'Gay Liberation' now."

Ian liked Jonny very much but it was time to put him on a train and go to meet Craig Scanlon, Wayne Edwards and Julia Nelson for drinks before a performance at The Apollo of 'Berlin' by Lou Reed (which Ian had purchased at the sweet and tender age of Sixteen). Besides having his ticket paid for by Marc and Tracey Riley, Wayne also paid for a slap up post gig meal explaining;

"Your Birthday treat, Mo."

There is a saying that never mind the age you feel, feel the age of the body next to you and by the end of the week it was true that Ian had become a teenager again, his fears of becoming 50 were unfounded.

Ian decided to embark on an artistic endeavour that commemorated the following year and his new found sexual freedom. To celebrate the fact that 'life begins at 50' He embarked on a series of collages that consisted of the detritus of each sexual encounter.

Before he put condom to paper he consulted Steve who gave the following sage advice
"Make sure EVERY piece means something to you"

(I am) The Naughty Lola by Marlene Dietrich

Any doubts about not being able to carry on partying at 50 very soon disappeared and Ian embraced his new found lust for life. He acknowledges that his weekends were spent in an orgy of sex and drugs and reckons that he must have had fun (of varying degrees) with around a thousand men (not at the same time) ranging from teenage years to mature gentlemen in their seventies. As Ian says;
"...rather than my libido slowing down it now went into over drive"
Ian was able to draw on his heightened sexual experiences for some new songs. One particular number 'Joey Steffano' was about a Gay porn icon who was dead at the age of 25 from AIDS as a result of a hedonistic lifestyle (the number also name checks Eddie Sedgewick, a Warhol Star, who also died an early death from lethal excess). When I heard another song 'X' I genuinely thought this was an autobiographical number but it was actually inspired by a young man called Andrew, who Ian had met at Manchester's Gay Pride. Andrew was aware of his mistakes and was a warm hearted and good natured individual but he just couldn't help himself. Ian sought to capture Andrew's confusion with an end exhortation to hit the dance floor to dance our troubles away (as Ian often had done in the past).

The weird and wonderful world of the Hamsters had not come to an end though:
"Hi, is Moet there?"
drawled an American voice at the end of the line.
"Yes, do I know you?"
enquired a mystified Ian, wondering if this was a prank
"No, but I know the music of the Hamster's"
"Yes."
"My name is Chuck Warner and I own my own label, Messthetics, and I would like to release some Hamsters material on Cd"
"Ok, I'll send you some stuff over"
Ian thought no more of this and if anything did look like taking off, he could let Bobby and Steve know.

Moet and Nigel Tribute Bands

If truth be known Ian felt unfulfilled and rather detached from the rest of Sicknurse. He only joined the band on live gigs and had not rehearsed with them. Ian didn't blame the lads for having other musical projects, a proposed

'Joy Division' Tribute Band with Nigel and Chris never actually transpired (if this had come to pass this would have been the end). Jon was in around a dozen bands and Damien, a frustrated guitar player rehearsed with a hard rock band called 'Blind Beggar'.

Ian started to look for projects in order to satisfy his creative drive and end Sicknurse. But despite discussions with Eddie Fenn, nothing actually came to fruition. Ian vented his frustrations to Craig Scanlon, after watching an art house movie at the Cornerhouse, and mid moan and idea suddenly came to him;

"I think I could put together a stripped down Hamsters."

"How?"

Craig suddenly looked interested

"Steve could play on a child's drum kit; Bobby could go through a practise amp."

"Bass player?"

"No we've done without those. Come to think of it...this would bring the words more to the fore and make it even more theatrical...a bit Noel Coward even."

replied Ian who was visibly bubbling with excitement.

"Good Idea, Mo! Go for it!"

encouraged Craig, pleased to see Ian liven up all of a sudden.

A couple of days later, Ian called on Steve with the notion to air this idea. But as Steve was in such visible pain Ian decided not to bring this idea into play just yet. It would have been cruel to bring this idea up as Steve clearly wasn't well enough to play. No, best wait for now.

Ian's only option was to give Sicknurse a new lease of life;

"Lads, I want us to record an album."

Ian informed Chris on the phone;

"Who with?"

enquired Chris

"Jon Pennington's too expensive....I know...let's try Dingo worked with The Fall"

Chris agreed with Ian and this suggestion was mooted to the rest of the band who took this idea up with enthusiasm. The only trouble was that they wanted to adopt a really meticulous approach and spend months recording the songs a little at a time but Ian had an answer;

"Fuck that for a game of soldiers! It's a single weekend job, bash the fucking songs, get 'em mixed and see what happens."

"We'll have to rehearse."

the band chorused as one.

"Oh Fuck!"

Ian realised and then wearily agreed;
"I suppose we will...Ok. Let's rehearse"
New life was to be breathed into the tired band.

January 2008

Ian was not at all well as the album recording session loomed nearer and nearer. Every winter got progressively worse as he suffered repeated chest and throat infections. His breathing became more and more difficult and on top of severe headaches came crippling pain from ear ache.

One morning, he awoke to find he could barely walk owing to swollen legs covered by a nasty rash. Ian feared the worst and went to the STD Clinic, where he was quite a well-known character, and was reassured that this was very unlikely to be symptomatic of HIV. Whilst this was somewhat of a relief, it transpired that the Tameside General Hospital were unable to diagnose what was causing this problem and Ian's mood quickly reverted back to one of anxiety. He was convinced that his symptoms very serious and genuinely believed that he would die. One night, in dreadful pain, he repeatedly listened to Nina Simone's 'Wild is the wind' and he morbidly imagined his friends and family sobbing at his funeral.

This was a frightening time for Ian, but fortunately the swelling and rash was attributed to side effects of some tablets he had been taking. As soon as he ceased this medication he began to recover and was even able to laugh at himself for his paranoia.

In early January he received a phone call from John Smethurst;
"I was visiting Manchester Royal Hospital today and I bumped into Steven Middlehurst"
"How was he?"
Ian just knew the answer somehow;
"He's in a bad way I'm afraid and if I hadn't have seen him at your Birthday do, I don't think I would have even recognised him"
"He looked that bad did he?"
"He made me promise not to tell anyone he was in hospital because he doesn't want people to see him like this"
"I see."
Ian wondered if he should 'disobey' this request but;
"As I was leaving he said...You can tell Mo though will you?"
"Thank you for letting me know."
Ian knew that he owed John a lot for all his kindness over the years.
Steven's failing health certainly gave Ian a sense of perspective and wondered if he should go and see him that evening. He looked at the clock and knew it

would be too late for visiting hours and resolved to go and visit him the following day which was a Saturday.

Visiting Hours

Ian was relieved to be greeted by Steven's broad grin and was shown sketches that he had done of the nursing staff.

"My bollocks are the size of an elephant's."

"Do I really want to know that Steven!"

"Here's the cord I have to pull if I need to move 'em."

It was obvious that Steven was in great pain, but he wasn't going to show his concern and decided to turn his predicament into a form of comedy sitcom. There was no way he wanted pity and sought to put Ian at ease.

"Bobby bumped into Arron!"

"How is my oldest?"

"He's fine and what's more he was asking after you and wants to see you."

Steven positively radiated happiness upon hearing this, it was clear that he loved Arron. But as soon as the beam lit up it was clouded over with concern;

"I can't let him see me like this, Mo. But please tell him how much I want to see him when I'm better. Make sure he knows?"

"Of course I will and I know how you feel. I'm sure Arron will understand."

"Thanks, Mo. I know you will."

Conversation turned to the imminent release of the Messthetics Manchester Compilation CD which would include material from the Hamsters Street Level session recorded all those years ago.

Upon hearing this, Steven's eyes narrowed momentarily and then he smiled;

"I suppose I'll have to put my trust in you to handle this one for us."

"Did you know that there is a William Blake exhibition at the Whitworth Art Gallery?"

"That's just across the road. Will you take me over as I'd love to see it?"

Ian agreed and after fastening his overcoat up high and settling his sailors cap at a jaunty angle Steven was ready for his outing and was led out, clasping the cord to hold his scrotum up.

After enjoying the exhibition Ian treated Steven to a coffee and cake in the café in the gallery. Ian ruminated that it was an entirely appropriate place to be as both shared an appreciation of this particular artist's work and Ian had once given him a beautifully decorated book of Blake's work.

Steven did well, but it was clear that this unexpected outing was tiring him out and before they left, Steve asked;

"Can you buy me a cheese sandwich for later?

and he grimaced for dramatic effect

".. the hospital food is awful!"

When they reached the hospital, Ian received his customary hug kiss and ;

"Great to see you Mo! Make sure you come back and see me soon, Love you."

When Steve was released from hospital, a few days later, his mind was full of the meeting with Arron;

"I just want to get myself well enough Mo."

Ian knew he wanted to look better for his son, to create a good impression.

Chiara reiterated his wishes the next day and Ian replied;

"I know, don't worry, nothing's going to stop this happening!"

People who Died by Jim Carroll

Dingo worked on the Sicknurse session, recorded in late January, with the minimum of fuss and the fact that Ian had actually rehearsed with the band on the previous week certainly helped things along. During the rehearsal Ian managed to make a few changes to each song, for example a drum break during 'Funhouse' was added and the lyrics scanned much better.

A total of eleven songs were recorded during the two days session and the tracks were mixed by the following weekend and Ian was very pleased with the results, Jon and Simon had excelled in colouring the tracks. Nigel's rhythm guitar provided an excellent spring board for Simon's more florid approach, but he felt over-shadowed and Ian had to reassure him about the validity of his contribution, taking into account the somewhat 'hot house' nature of creative personalities within the band.

Bobby designed the artwork for the cd, but logistical problems kept compounding themselves and in the end Ian had to make an executive decision and instructed the printer;

"Do whatever the fuck you like for the sleeve!"

The reason behind this lack of patience was that Ian was very eager for Steve to hear the latest recordings and the sleeve sort of took second place. It wasn't to be.

Ian received a phone call from Ruth;

"Ian, Steven has been readmitted to Hospital. I'm afraid to tell you that this time it is very serious and that we should all be prepared for the worst."

Ruth was trying to be calm, but the tremor in her voice revealed her distress.

Ian felt like he had been hit with a sledgehammer and learnt that Steve had to be in an unconscious state in order for the doctors to attempt to save him. He had to really force himself not to go and be with Steven but instead concentrated his efforts on supporting Ruth and Chiara.

Sex became an essential distraction during this period; he met Jonny again and was able to confide his fears about Steven's predicament to him. On another occasion he went to an orgy consisting of eight men, but his heart wasn't in it and he left to everyone's chagrin. He met a man called Steve, whose partner, Ian, died the year before and they were able to offer each other mutual comfort and at last Ian was able to weep.

In the early hours of Wednesday 26th March, Ian received a phone call from Robert at work. He knew what Robert would say;

"He's gone Mo."

Ian immediately went behind a stack of pallets and wept bitter tears and then pulled himself together, continued to work '....better than going home alone with nothing but sadness in my heart'.

Verdi's Requiem Mass (Played at Steve's Funeral)

Ian was able to offer Chiara and Ruth practical and emotional support and also spent time with Robert and Ronnie. Bobby and Slav, in turn were able to help Ian and Steve's immediate family.

Steven once requested:

"I would like you to speak at my funeral, Mo, because I know you won't embarrass me."

Karen Knott accompanied Ian to the humanist service of Steven's life, which was extremely well attended. Although Karen's calming presence helped Ian it was time to speak about Steven's life. Ian acknowledges this as the hardest thing he has ever had to do as he was on the edge of breaking down from start to finish, but he did his old love proud and, with hindsight, believes this painful process was cathartic.

Rather than socialise, Ian went home with Karen and began to live with this painful loss.

Someone to watch over me

Ian was really subdued and didn't really want to go anywhere for weeks after Stevne's funeral. Fortunately, he welcomed Bobby, Slav, Ann and Richard into the comfort zone of his flat, and it was good to talk and listen to music.

Pete Zest, a more recent friend, was to do a spot of DJ at 'Out of the Range' in Didsbury, on 10 May, and as the music was aimed at an older crowd Ian was persuaded to give this a go and was rather pleased he did as the music was good and so was the atmosphere. However, after an evening of pleasant drinking and a shed load of drugs, it seemed like a good idea to go and have some sex;

"Ok, I'm off now."

waved Ian

"You're in no fit state to go anywhere.

Said Penny, Pete's partner, sternly.

"Yes, she's right. Your judgement has gone out of the window and you are putting yourself at risk!"

agreed Pete.

Ian was touched by their concern, despite his inebriated state, and agreed to come back with some fellow revellers to continue partying through the night. Ian felt it was good to return to the land of the living and the human warmth he experienced was balm to his soul. Indeed so much so, Ian was to be found the next morning springing through the leafy streets of Didsbury.

When Ian arrived home, he checked his computers for messages and thought he would have a cruise through some Gay Chat Rooms, when something caught his eye;

"R.I.P Andrew Tong."

This took Ian by surprise and he checked the thread to see if this was the same Andrew that he had met around six or so months ago; it was. Andrew's openness and honest, as well as his startling good looks, had stayed with Ian. Andrew was self-aware and had wanted to move on from the mistakes he had made in his life and the last time Ian and Andrew met everything was looking good for Andrew as he had cut down on drug use and had a regular boyfriend. Ian had expressed concern at Andrew's excessive use of Ketamine and GHB (the drugs of choice on the Gay Scene); but Andrew had died two weeks after his twenty first birthday.

Ian was devastated and managed to get hold of the details of Andrew's funeral and travelled to Enfield to pay his last respects and to say goodbye. The tragic death of Andrew, so close after Steve, sent Ian in to a pit of despair.

Messthetics # 106 the Manchester Musicians Collective 1977 - 1982

The above compilation cd release was to have featured 'Telivisionitus' as the representative track from the Street Level Sessions, but Ian was adamant that 'Clouds of Flies' should be the main track as he thought it was a 'meatier track'. A compromise was arrived in that 'Telivisionitus' was available as a download track and 'Clouds of Flies' was on the CD.

The CD was released in the summer of 2009 and was marketed as 'The Manchester Musicians Collective' which was rather ironic as Ian never considered the Hamsters as part of this, but this was a minor quibble and he was amazed to find a photograph taken from the very first gig of Steve chastising the audience (covering Moet's face with his hand) that he had never seen; He had to hand it to Chuck.

A launch party was held at the home of Louise Alderman of 'The Passage' and Ian, Bobby and Slav attended. Although they were made welcome 'The

Collective' began to reminisce and history repeated itself in that Ian felt that they were on the outside.

Harder, louder, faster

It seemed appropriate to reintroduce three numbers with lyrics from Steve in the Hamster days, 'Couldn't stand the house', 'Maggots' and 'Low gears'. Ian announced them as a tribute to Steve and also 'I'm a cunt' was exhumed on these live performances. In addition, 'Joey Steffano' and 'X' were dedicated to Andrew. It was like taking the maverick spirits of Steve and Andrew onstage and this took its toll on Ian both emotionally and physically. This energy galvanised the band to play these particular numbers all out and great power was added to the emotional intensity.

On one occasion, Ruth and Chiara came back stage, no words needed to be spoken as everyone was in tears. Ruth understood why Ian needed to bring Steve back onstage and hugged him.

In between gigs Ian just had to say 'Yes' to another excess of every conceivable nature and this lead to problems. During one 'spaced out' conversation, Ian said too much in the presence of Zac and his pregnant girlfriend. Ian was very sorry for the hurt he had caused and knew that things could never be quite the same again between him and his younger friend.

The Second Dingo Session February 2009

I am then a guest on my mate Tony Thornboroughs radio show on Salford City Radio in 2009 & the Chip Shop Song get its very first airing on the radio to great acclaim. **Stephen Doyle**

Sicknurse never failed to play well live but rehearsals were virtually non-existent apart from a couple of 'quiet' sessions at Ian's flat with Simon providing music to lyrics. Jon maintained that:

"Sicknurse doesn't exist anymore."

and joined other bands, citing Ian's inertia as a major reason for doing so. Nigel and Damien's quietness betrayed the fact that enthusiasm was slowly but surely draining away from them and Chris, realising that the band was beginning the eventual path of disintegration, urged Ian to step back into the breach. But such was Ian's lack of commitment that he purposefully 'booked leave' when Jon had organised a gig at Jacksons Pit, in Oldham and Zac took over on vocal duties.

At another gig organised by Jon, against Ian's wishes the petulant singer railed against the world it can be mentioned that at the adjoining bar, a grand total of nine out of the twelve drinkers registered a complaint against the filth they were being subjected to.

On an occasion that Ian did sing at the support band were very lavish in their praise of Sicknurse only to be rewarded by a candid critique from Mr Moss:

"...Compared to how shit you are, we must have seemed fucking great!"

The lesson being; never flannel Mister Moss otherwise you might just get the truth in return. Karen was dismayed by this dismissive comment and groaned;

"One night you'll get yourself killed!"

Ian respected Karen's opinion but chose to act nonchalantly and had another drink.

Ian booked another session with Dingo in Salford; gracing one rehearsal in which he worked changes to three songs. 'Maggots' was originally recorded on the Street Level sessions and, owing to Ian's revision, is virtually unrecognisable in this new incarnation. 'Imaginary Dog', a lively number also benefited from Ian's reimagination. The lyrics to 'Jon Joanne' were also changed and Ian forbade the use of any percussion such as cymbal accompaniment on the studio session. In fact Ian had a very clear idea of how he wanted the songs to sound in the studio and took on a much more 'hands on approach' on conveying what he heard in his head. For instance, he wanted a cleaner, 'Chuck Berry' no frills approach from Simon on guitar.

Ian was delighted with the results of this session, which also includes 'Couldn't Stand The House' and 'Brudder Mouse' which sound much more playful then previous recordings. Indeed this session reminded Karen of;

"....The spirit of the Hamsters."

Ian knew this was a compliment and felt re enthused to the degree of booking more gigs. Damien, quite simply had had enough, and left the band informing them that he needed to do his own thing. There were no hard feelings between either side and indeed Damien, at the time of writing, sat behind the Sicknurse drum kit again.

Sicknurse Live in 2009

"Having travelled all the way from Manchester for this gig, Sicknurse are indeed an interesting prospect – they've decked the stage out with blow up dolls, a hobby horse and stag do decorations, their (male) keyboardist is looking resplendent in high heeled boots and the vocalist has a Buster Bloodvessel quality to him. I must admit I didn't know what I was in for as the band took to the stage but they actually delivered a fantastic set of solid, anthemic punk tunes with a twist thanks to the keyboard touches. Track such as 'You don't belong here' and 'X' had most of the room singing along. A teddy bear is used as a prop for another song and a mass stage invasion towards the end of the set sees everyone having a good time" **Noisy Fanzine issue 9**

Damien's drum seat was taken by Jim McGuire. He stepped off a plane from Australia (where he had spent twelve months) and that same evening he was drumming for Sicknurse at the Dry Bar, after being instructed to listen and learn from a Sicknurse CD by Jon.

Damien's drumming had been dependable, steady and solid, whereas Jim was somewhat more erratic but added an exciting edge to the sound.

"You're noticeably punkier."

remarked Craig Scanlon after a wild performance in Salford.

During another performance Jim's jeans split to reveal that he wasn't wearing any underpants, so the audience got treated to seeing a little more of Jim at The Thatched House. He was not the only member of the band to treat the lucky audience to a flash of their genitalia as Ian was sweating inside his inflatable Sumo Wrestlers suit and had to strip down to a pair of red underpants. Jon was most unladylike as he decided to rip the red undies off Ian to reveal the birthday suit. Ian pretended nothing had happened and continued in his naked glory.

The band were invited to play at The Ship, 18 June 2009, for the Southend on Sea Fringe Festivals as part of The Old Guard (along with The Get) versus the Young Guns (Syd and the Small Kids, Stolen Jackets). Both old bands got on very well together and Jim even borrowed a dress from The Get to wear during his set and demonstrated to all and sundry how to drink whisky through his eye.

Jim was not feeling well the next day and vomited in Nigel's van on the return journey, but this was merely setting the stage for what he would do next. In the middle of the night he chose to go for a dip and ended up in a mud pit. Upon his return, the awful stench woke Jon (who had the misfortune to share a tent with him) who fled retching and vowing to keep well, well away from the smelly monster from the deep lagoon.

Simon had decided not to come down to Southend and had been getting rather moody of late; the band was unsure how much longer he would remain with them. It should be noted that Sicknurse were such a success that they were invited to play in Southend for the following June.

Oh, the Demon Alcohol The Kinks

Ian has always had a huge capacity for alcohol and whilst he could easily leave others in his wake there was usually a price to pay for his excessive consumption. It was not uncommon for Ian to actually pass out and when he eventually came round he found he was coated in his own vomit and urine. Some friends expressed concern over his excessive drinking, but others thought he was a great character.

The only occasions that Ian found himself virtually sober were when he was with Mathew. It was not a good idea for Mathew to drink alcohol owing to his mental health problems and Ian needed to be at his sharpest in Mathew's Company so tended not to drink beyond the odd pint. Not that Ian needed alcohol to enjoy Mathew's company as he often managed to lift Ian's mood and they laughed a lot together. Ian learnt an important lesson;

".....doing nothing at all could be fun, as long as you were doing nothing along with someone you liked and doing nothing sober was fine"

However, there was the rare instance when Ian lapsed. One such occasion was when Ian and Mathew made a weekend trip to Amsterdam and their travel and hotel arrangements became hopelessly entangled and as a result found themselves in a sleepy town called Liedesrstadt which was about forty miles outside Amsterdam. One night was more than enough and they got to Amsterdam the next day and managed to find accommodation; but frustration eventually got the better of Ian and he downed a cocktail of Mathew's anti-psychotic drugs, space cakes and Mexican hallucinogenic mushrooms. Their roles reversed and Mathew became the carer and was fascinated by Ian's totally wired status.

Stone Pony

He (Ian) doesn't seem to have changed that much. Ian seems more at peace these days, perhaps more comfortable in his own skin x **Mick Hucknall**

Despite a couple of really good live gigs, inertia ruled the band and this lack of rehearsal resulted in more ragged performances, which in Ian's book was no bad thing but Simon in particular, was increasingly becoming upset by the lack of 'professionalism'.

It was apparent that Sicknurse were on 'the critical list' and would surely fade away, but as Ian says, 'fate plays cruel tricks sometimes.

Chris had confided in Ian regarding the increasingly shaky state of his marriage, and whilst Ian sympathised there wasn't really a great deal he could do besides listen. Things were to come to a head one evening in the autumn of 2009;

"Moet, it's Nigel here. Chris is in Trafford Hospital, he's tried to take his own life"

"We've got to go and see him."

Within the hour they arrived at the Hospital and they asked at the Nurse's station if they could see their friend.

"Who shall I say it is?"

"Kinky and Blackrock have come to see Stone Pony."

replied Ian, using their stage names.

Chris was very ill but clearly pleased to see his mates and have them for the rest of the afternoon. Ian instinctively knew that Chris needed human warmth and held his hand, making him laugh from his huge collection of dirty stories. With the laughter came tears as it became apparent that Chris lived for Sicknurse and Ian talked about ideas for songs and promised to make a new start when Chris was better. This lifted Chris's spirits and Sicknurse began the slow road to recovery.

Ian visited Chris several times during his stay in hospital and read to him from 'The Wind in the Willows'. The chapter, 'Piper at the Gates of Dawn' was one that never failed to move Ian and Chris was captivated. He later told Ian that it was a moment that he cherishes and comforted him.

Ian's resolve to carry on was too little too late for Simon who suspected that this particular piper was heralding yet another false dawn. Whilst it is true that Ian wanted to revive Sicknurse for Chris, he also realised that he wanted to do it for himself too and I think that I really should leave Ian to finish his story in his own words but not before thanking him and giving him a quick kiss X

"..I decided to pick up the pieces and start again. I wanted to feel the satisfaction of creating something worthwhile again. I wanted to feel that enjoyment and that kinship with people I realised I loved far more than I'd thought. To do this there would have to be a change. From the outside it looked like I'd made a difficult decision and people expected me to fail, that remains to be seen. But I'd stopped drinking once and for all and decided to get on with living my life. I can't undo the mistakes I've made in the past or the damage I've brought upon myself and others. But I'm not condemning myself to endlessly repeat those mistakes. I am my own man and I've decided to change, 'It's never too late' I'm told."

Post Script 29 December 2011

And there the book was supposed to finish. I went up to see Sicknurse in December 2010 only to find out that the band had split but was assured that 'the band would perform in some format or other'.

We lived in the same town then and occasionally drank in the same pub, but never really became close friends until 2011, when I was privileged to see the final performance of "Sicknurse" in Salford.

I was with Ken from The Blimp and we were both amazed at the courage, charisma and incredible set that Ian and Chris performed, together with a certain Mr. Toska Wilde on nail varnish!!! The rest of the band had quit that day, so Ian and Chris did the whole set as a duo.

Ken and I both felt that what we had witnessed was true art and were very sorry that it was the end of such a great band. **Michael John Leigh**

The Hamsters reformed in 2011, with Chris, his son Josh, Bobby and Moet and performed one memorable session for Salford City Radio as well as a couple of local gigs.

A few weeks later, I was invited to see The Hamsters at Ian's birthday party and the day before, he asked me to bring some drum sticks and sit in with them. I had a great time with The Hamsters that night **Michael John Leigh**

As you are perfectly aware the history of The Hamsters remains a turbulent one and this line up only lasted a few months. However, Moet had a side project 'Kill Pretty' with Chris and very soon one young Josh on bass and one 'young at heart' former 'Cabaret Circuit drummer from decades ago...

I knew Chris from his replacing my good friend Steve Hanley in Factory Star and in a subsequent chat; he asked if I would be interested in collaborating with his and Ian's new project, "Kill Pretty," to which I readily agreed. **Michael John Leigh**

This definitive line up performed locally and (as The Hamsters) in London in November 2011. They have just finished their debut studio session and I am just about to listen to the results.

I look on Ian and all the guys in Kill Pretty as good friends and we have formed a special bond in the 5 months that we've been in the band together.
Ian is one of the warmest people I have met and his musical knowledge is incredible. He's introduced me to bands that I had not heard of and he knows I like similar music to him.
He and Chris seem to rate me as a drummer much more highly than I rate myself and we've had a fantastic few months with Kill Pretty together. Long may it continue. **Michael John Leigh**

When I get my own show The Hamsters/Sicknurse/Kill Pretty become almost the house band. Great gigs & great times follow & the bonus is that Mr Moss is a REALLY nice bloke! **Stephen Doyle Salford City Radio**

Lightning Source UK Ltd.
Milton Keynes UK
UKOW05f1957081113

220726UK00009B/674/P